# JSP™, Servlets, and MySQL™

# JSP™, Servlets, and MySQL™

David Harms

## M&T Books

An imprint of Hungry Minds, Inc.

New York, NY • Cleveland, OH • Indianapolis, IN

JSP™, Servlets, and MySQL™

Published by
**M&T Books**
An imprint of Hungry Minds, Inc.
909 Third Avenue
New York, NY 10022
www.hungryminds.com

Library of Congress Control Number: 2001016954

ISBN: 0-7645-4787-9

Printed in the United States of America

10 9 8 7 6 5 4 3 2 1

10/QV/QU/QR/IN

Distributed in the United States by Hungry Minds, Inc.

Distributed by CDG Books Canada Inc. for Canada; by Transworld Publishers Limited in the United Kingdom; by IDG Norge Books for Norway; by IDG Sweden Books for Sweden; by IDG Books Australia Publishing Corporation Pty. Ltd. for Australia and New Zealand; by TransQuest Publishers Pte Ltd. for Singapore, Malaysia, Thailand, Indonesia, and Hong Kong; by Gotop Information Inc. for Taiwan; by ICG Muse, Inc. for Japan; by Intersoft for South Africa; by Eyrolles for France; by International Thomson Publishing for Germany, Austria, and Switzerland; by Distribuidora Cuspide for Argentina; by LR International for Brazil; by Galileo Libros for Chile; by Ediciones ZETA S.C.R. Ltda. for Peru; by WS Computer Publishing Corporation, Inc., for the Philippines; by Contemporanea de Ediciones for Venezuela; by Express Computer Distributors for the Caribbean and West Indies; by Micronesia Media Distributor, Inc. for Micronesia; by Chips Computadoras S.A. de C.V. for Mexico; by Editorial Norma de Panama S.A. for Panama; by American Bookshops for Finland.

For general information on Hungry Minds' products and services please contact our Customer Care department within the U.S. at 800-762-2974, outside the U.S. at 317-572-3993 or fax 317-572-4002.

For sales inquiries and reseller information, including discounts, premium and bulk quantity sales, and foreign-language translations, please contact our Customer Care department at 800-434-3422, fax 317-572-4002 or write to Hungry Minds, Inc., Attn: Customer Care Department, 10475 Crosspoint Boulevard, Indianapolis, IN 46256.

For information on licensing foreign or domestic rights, please contact our Sub-Rights Customer Care department at 212-884-5000.

For information on using Hungry Minds' products and services or for ordering examination copies, please contact our Educational Sales department at 800-434-2086 or fax 317-572-4005.

For press review copies, author interviews, or other publicity information, please contact our Public Relations department at 650-653-7000 or fax 650-653-7500.

For authorization to photocopy items for corporate, personal, or educational use, please contact Copyright Clearance Center, 222 Rosewood Drive, Danvers, MA 01923, or fax 978-750-4470.

Hungry Minds· is a trademark of Hungry Minds, Inc.

is a trademark of Hungry Minds, Inc.

# About the Author

**David Harms** is an author and consultant with more than ten years' experience developing applications for the broadcast industry and the educational sector. His work as a software developer, conference speaker, and course instructor has taken him around the world. Harms is the founder and president of CoveComm, Inc., which specializes in electronic publishing using Java technology.

# Credits

**ACQUISITIONS EDITOR**
Debra Williams Cauley

**PROJECT EDITOR**
Terrence O'Donnell

**TECHNICAL EDITOR**
Al Williams

**COPY EDITOR**
Lisa Blake

**PROJECT COORDINATOR**
Nancee Reeves

**GRAPHICS AND PRODUCTION SPECIALISTS**
Amy Adrian, Gabriele McCann,
Jackie Nicholas, Kendra Span

**QUALITY CONTROL TECHNICIANS**
Andy Hollandbeck, Susan Moritz,
Carl Pierce, Nancy Price

**BOOK DESIGNER**
Jim Donohue

**PROOFREADING AND INDEXING**
York Production Services, Inc.

**COVER IMAGE**
© Noma/Images.com

*This book is dedicated to my wife, Bonny*

# Preface

Some years ago I sat down to create my first Web site. I converted a few documents into HTML, added some (fairly ugly) graphics in an attempt to spruce up the HTML pages, and threw a few hyperlinks into the mix. And, as long as my Web site stayed small, there really wasn't a whole lot more I needed to know about the mechanics of my Web site.

But Web sites grow and become more complex. After a while that site became an online magazine, with subscriber-only areas and a large number of documents. Eventually, I had to rethink my approach to Web-site management. I realized that a lot of the information on that site belonged not in static pages but in a database.

The process I went through in moving from a static site to a dynamic, database-driven site is one that a lot of Web developers face. Web sites are becoming more complex: users expect greater functionality and a higher level of interactivity.

Server-side Java and databases are a perfect combination for dynamic Web site development. With a Java Server Page and Servlet engine such as the Apache Jakarta project's Tomcat, and a database like MySQL, both of which are freely available and open source, you can both manage a growing Web site and create some very slick interactive features.

When I mention Java, I find that a lot of people who aren't Java developers wonder if this language is a good choice for Web development. Most of the time they're thinking of applets, those snippets of code that we were once promised would transform the wired (and wireless) world.

The focus in those early years was Java on the client side. We were all going to be using our Web browsers to run applets that were safe, modestly efficient blocks of code downloaded across the Internet, WANs, or LANs. Applets (like all Java code) ran in Java Virtual Machines, or JVMs, and different browsers implemented different JVMs. And not everyone had the bandwidth to download cool little applets— not that there were that many really useful cool little applets anyway, or if they existed, they didn't run on all browsers because of JVM incompatibilities. And so there was what the industry lovingly calls FUD (Fear, Uncertainty, and Doubt).

In the midst of all this, some in the Java developer community began to use Java on the other—that is, server—side of the network connection. Server-side Web development is ancient stuff, in terms of the Web's history. For years, developers have used tools such as CGI (Common Gateway Interface) to add custom logic to a Web server. Rather than simply serve up static pages, CGI and its many derivatives and competitors let you plug in your own code to manufacture customized pages in real time.

Traditional server-side technologies certainly fill a need, but because they are not, for the most part, tightly integrated into the server, they usually eat memory and processor cycles and can be difficult to debug. This loose integration also limits the effectiveness of these server-side technologies.

Server-side Java fits the model of extending Web server capabilities, but in a highly efficient and tightly integrated way. You can get complete control over the delivery of Web content through the use of Java servlets and JavaServer Pages. In fact, when you're using a Java Servlet/JSP engine like Tomcat, you can even replace parts of the server itself, if that suits your needs.

# How This Book Is Organized

This book presents information on developing database-driven Web sites in four parts. The first part starts you off with introductions to server-side Java, servlets, JavaServer Pages, and configuring Tomcat and then progresses through delivery of dynamic content in MySQL databases and strategies for developing database-driven Web sites. Notes, Tips, and sidebar material support the discussion, and two appendixes provide a tag library reference and development resources.

## Part 1: Getting Started

The first part of the book covers the basics of installing, writing, and using servlets and JSPs. By the time you reach Part II, you should have a good grasp of the role that server-side Java can play in Web development.

## Part II: Web Sites and Databases

Part II introduces the MySQL database server, a popular choice among Web developers, and covers its installation and basic use. Along the way, you'll look at some database design issues as applied to a Web site and cover MySQL's approach to securing access to the database.

## Part III: Delivering Content

Driving a Web site with database storage does raise some interesting challenges and opportunities. Part III looks more closely at the programmatic issues, such as threading. Java is designed to use as few resources as possible in a Web environment, and that means managing access to shared resources. You learn how to keep your servlets and JSPs light on their feet, how to extract data from a database to the Web page, and how to put data back in. This part of the book also covers the Model-View-Controller, or Model 2, approach to Web-application design in some detail.

## Part IV: Database-Driven Site Strategies

The possibilities for using Web databases go well beyond delivering rows and columns of data, and that's the focus of Part IV, which discusses authenticating users, creating and handling HTML forms, surveying user opinions and graphing results, and logging user access to a database. This part also provides an overview of the Jakarta Struts project, one of the up-and-coming Web application frameworks.

## Appendixes

Appendix A contains further information on the Struts tag libraries, and Appendix B provides a list of development resources.

# Conventions Used in This Book

Each chapter in this book begins with a heads-up of the topics covered in the chapter and ends with a summary of what you should have learned by reading the chapter.

Throughout this book, you will find icons in the margins that highlight special or important information. Keep an eye out for the following icons:

 This icon means that the text that follows is an aside to the main point. The information is not long enough for a sidebar.

 This icon indicates tidbits that I picked up along the way and want to share with you.

 This icon indicates where in the book you can find more information on the topic at hand.

In addition to the preceding icons, the following formatting and typographical conventions appear throughout the book:

- Code examples appear in a `fixed width font`.
- When a line of code is too long to fit on a single line, the character ↵ indicates that the line continues.
- Other code elements, such as data structures and variable names, appear in `fixed width`.
- File, function, and macro names as well as World Wide Web addresses (URLs) appear in `fixed width`.

> ## What Is a Sidebar?
>
> Topics in sidebars provide some extra information that relates to the topic at hand but is separate enough to warrant its own special place. In some cases, sidebars address questions that I found myself asking when I was writing the particular topic. In other cases, the information covered in the sidebar is important enough to highlight to make sure the reader does not miss it.

# Getting the Source Code

There is no CD-ROM with this book, since anyone interested in reading it and creating any of the examples almost certainly has Internet access. You can find the code examples at:

```
http://www.covecomm.com/java
```

You can also contact me through this Web page. I will post corrections to the code and to the book text as necessary.

# Acknowledgments

I owe a debt of thanks to many people who in one way or another contributed to this book's becoming a reality. My agent Lisa Swayne started me down the Java path years ago, and it was her suggestion that I write this book. Debra Williams Cauley at Hungry Minds helped shape my initial proposal into a meaningful book. My editors, Terrence O'Donnell and Lisa Blake, improved the text greatly with their questions, comments, corrections, and excisions. Al Williams, my technical editor, kept me on the straight and narrow as much as anyone could.

The members of the Jakarta Tomcat team have created a first-class open source Servlet and JSP engine in Tomcat, and I'm grateful for their many contributions to Web development. I've also learned a lot from the participants in the tomcat-dev, tomcat-user, struts-dev, and struts-user mailing lists, particularly Craig McClanahan, the creator of Struts.

Most of all, I want to thank my wife, Bonny, for supporting me in so many ways while I wrote the book, and for putting up with my too-frequent absences from our life together.

# Contents at a Glance

# Contents

# Part I

## Getting Started

# Chapter 1

# Introducing Server-Side Java

## IN THIS CHAPTER

♦ Understanding Java's current status as a programming language and run-time environment

♦ Understanding Java's benefits for server-side development

♦ Understanding the importance of databases

♦ Understanding the role of JavaServer Pages (JSPs) and the division of presentation and business logic

♦ Integrating servlets, JSPs, and databases

♦ Choosing a Web server

♦ Understanding the future of databases in Web site development

♦ Designing database-using Web sites

♦ Understanding database-centric Web sites

AS A DEVELOPER, you have the full range of options for developing dynamic, database-enabled Web sites. You can use the Common Gateway Interface (CGI) or one of its many derivatives to integrate separate database applications into a Web server's operations; you can write custom code that calls the Web server's own API; you can employ server- and client-side scripting languages such as PHP, VBScript, and JavaScript; and you can use various combinations of the preceding technologies. Of course, you can also use Java, and save yourself a lot of trouble.

This chapter will get you started by introducing server-side Java code to build Web sites around databases and the role of JavaServer Pages (JSPs) in making Web sites dynamic. The chapter will also take a brief look at database categories and why SQL is well suited to work with servlets through the Java database connectivity (JDBC) application programming interface (API).

# Why Java?

If Java isn't alone in its ability to extend Web server capabilities, then why is it gaining such popularity for server-side development? I think there are four main reasons:

♦ *Java is a productive language.* Although it owes much to C++, it is by comparison a simpler, more forgiving language. The lack of pointers (and attendant pointer math) helps make code more readable. Automatic garbage collection frees the developer from (most) memory de-allocation worries.

♦ *Java has application programming interfaces (APIs) that make it very useful for Web development.* Not the least of these are the Servlet and JavaServer Pages APIs, but other aspects of the language make developing a complete Web application that much easier. For instance, you can use Java Database Connectivity (JDBC) to connect to a back-end database, or use the graphics library to create on-the-fly images (that is, charts and graphs) for your Web site.

♦ *Java has wide industry support.* Yes, much has been made about bickering over the future of Java standards. And the lack of standards on the client side has clearly hurt the acceptance of Java applets. At the same time, there has been massive industry investment in Java technology. Large corporations like IBM and Oracle have invested in and supported numerous Java projects, many of them server related. IBM's VisualAge for Java is consistently one of the top-rated Java development environments. Java is also popular in the financial industry, which was initially attracted by the possibilities of applets.

♦ *Java is lightweight and scalable.* You probably want your Web site to be massively successful, and that means a lot of traffic. Can whatever solution you choose be expanded as necessary to handle that traffic? You can always throw more hardware at a problem, but what happens when you start dealing with a distributed solution? Can your solution be deployed across multiple systems and platforms for purposes of speed or reliability? Will your software scale as well as your hardware? Although Java does carry a slight (but diminishing) performance and resource penalty compared to languages like C++, it is also designed to tread as lightly as possible, mainly because Java does not have to load new code to execute each request. The server simply starts another thread, which makes use of code that is already loaded.

## Getting started is easy

You don't need to be a fantastically experienced software developer to write servlets and JavaServer Pages. To be sure, a basic knowledge of Java programming is recommended. If you don't have any Java experience, then servlets and JSP are probably two of the easier places to start, provided you have some other resources on hand to help you over the language learning curve.

Servlets (and JSPs are at heart another kind of servlet with some special features) have the great advantage over other kinds of Java software of not having to deal, in real time, with user input. Much of the complexity in application development is in managing the user interface.

## Reducing user interface complexity

In Web development, the user interface is typically quite limited in its capabilities. Web pages made up of hypertext markup language (HTML) code (and possibly other client-side scripting code) are delivered to the user. If the user is to take any action, such as submit a form, the result of that action is sent back to the Web server. That's a pretty simple situation to deal with. Unlike a desktop application, where the app "knows" what's going on, in a Web application there's no constant connection between the page the user sees and the server. This kind of connection is called *stateless*, and, although there are a few tricks you can use to maintain some information at the server about what an individual user has already done at the Web site, once a page is delivered it's out of the server's control.

 It is possible to create a Web page that interacts with the user in real time, using a scripting language like Javascript. In this case, the browser interprets the script code and acts accordingly, performing tasks such as validating field values. You can also create a Java applet that acts as a form, but then you're dealing with the same problems that have limited Java client-side acceptance. Even more limiting are ActiveX controls that are similar to Java applets, but only work on Internet Explorer. These topics are outside the scope of this book.

Because of these interface constraints, servlet programming is both simpler and less flexible than other kinds of application development. Although some object-oriented programming (OOP) knowledge makes your servlet development life a lot easier, it's quite possible to write simple servlets and JSPs knowing very little about OOP. The default servlet framework provides all the basic tools for responding to Web server requests, and JSPs make use of scripting and special tags, both of which are relatively easy to learn.

Simple servlets and JSPs will take you only so far. You'll soon want to know how to use custom tag libraries, which are a way of creating your own JSP script tags. You use custom tag libraries to make JSPs much more powerful, without introducing Java code directly into the JSP itself. And you'll also discover that it's to your advantage to move some of your Java code into reusable JavaBean components.

As your servlets and JSPs grow in complexity, you'll want to give more thought to overall design issues. In recent years many of the common ways of building software out of various objects have been codified into what are called design patterns.

## Managing complexity with design patterns

Spend any amount of time around serious servlet developers and you'll hear terms like "Model-View-Controller" (usually abbreviated as MVC) and "adapter" and "façade." These people aren't talking about radio-controlled airplanes, or power supplies, or fake fronts. They're talking about standard ways that objects can be created and used together.

Code re-use is a cornerstone of software development. There's no point in writing code when you can get a fully tested and reliable equivalent from another source for less money and/or effort. The same principle applies to design concepts. You can reinvent the wheel, trying to deduce the best way to design classes from first principles, or you can save yourself a lot of work and use established, published designs.

Design patterns are a little bit like architectural plans for a house. If you decide to have a house built to your specifications, you probably won't draw all of the plans yourself. You'll look through catalogs of established house plans, and pick features that appeal to you. In doing so you're much less likely to violate certain architectural design principles. For example, you won't make the mistake of locating a bathroom on the other side of a living room wall. Most floor plans for houses use the established design pattern that best relegates a bathroom's plumbing sounds to a part of the house not adjacent to rooms used for social gatherings.

When you're developing object-oriented software, you may use a design pattern that says you can solve a particular kind of problem by using an object that contains a collection of other objects, or by creating an object that creates certain additional objects as needed. As with house-design patterns, you use software design patterns to benefit from the knowledge of many software development professionals. Although I don't explain the concept of design patterns in any great detail, I do cover some of the patterns in common use for servlet and JSP development, particularly the aforementioned MVC.

## Multithreading, a Java Web-development requirement

Servlets and JSPs can be easy to learn, but there are a few key areas that you need to watch out for. Perhaps the most important is the whole area of multithreading. Web servers often have to serve a large number of requests at the same time, and to do so efficiently they often need to share resources among those requests whenever possible. Java servlets and JSPs are designed to work this way. If two users request the same servlet (or JSP) at the same time, by default most Web servers use only one servlet, and allow it to be called by different threads of execution.

The problem is not the existence of multiple processes, but that these processes often share access to the same data or resource. Depending on the nature of the data or the resource, this access may need mediation or information may become corrupted. How access is mediated is also critical; a good implementation can make a server fly, and a bad one can bring a server to its little silicon knees.

To fully optimize servlets and to guard against runtime errors, you should have a good grasp of multithreading, which is how the server processes multiple requests at the same time. I'll explain multithreading issues as they come up in the sample code.

# Writing Server-Side Java Code

You don't need a lot of tools or a lot of money to start writing server-side Java code. At a minimum, all you really need is a Web server that knows how to load and execute servlets/JSPs, an editor, and a couple of free downloads from Sun Microsystems. To get the most out of this book, however, you should download the Jakarta Tomcat servlet container.

See Chapter 3 for instructions on downloading and installing the Jakarta Tomcat servlet container.

## The Tomcat reference implementation

The Apache Project's Tomcat is the reference implementation of Java Servlet 2.2 and JSP 1.1 technologies. Tomcat is available free from jakarta.apache.org, and you have to like that pricing structure. It's also open source under the Apache Software License version 1.1.

As a reference implementation, the focus on Tomcat is features rather than performance. Nonetheless, by the time you read this there's a good chance that Tomcat will have reached a level of speed, usability, and reliability comparable to commercial products. If you choose a different servlet/JSP implementation, you should still be able to use almost all of the code examples in this book, as they have been designed to be as server agnostic as possible.

## Choosing an IDE

Most of the Java code in this book is written using IBM's VisualAge for Java development environment. VAJava is available for numerous platforms including OS/2,

Windows, and Linux. The Entry Edition is available for download free of charge (are you noticing a trend?), and isn't limited in anyway except that you can have only up to 750 classes in the repository. This repository limitation is not an impediment for most servlet/JSP development.

You can, of course, use any IDE or text editor you like. The purpose of an IDE is to help streamline the coding process, particularly when creating visual components. With servlets and JSPs, the visual component is a Web page of some sort, and so an HTML editor is also very useful.

# Why Databases?

This book isn't just about Java and Web sites; it's about how Java makes it possible, and relatively easy, to build your Web site around a database.

A database is an ordered collection of data, stored as a single file or as a set of files (but with more than one piece of data per file). Web sites, on the other hand, have traditionally served up static Web pages, each stored as a single file or a set of files (the additional files usually being images).

Databases are also optimized for quick retrieval of data. In a well-designed database I would be able to quickly locate all product orders for unshelled peanuts placed by Rocket J. Squirrel, for instance, and probably by first name, last name, or other pertinent criteria.

When Web sites do use databases, it's usually to store information for presentation to the user. This could be something like a product catalog, order status, or package tracking. In these cases the Web site is tying in to existing corporate data.

While important, this use of databases is only a small part of the picture. As Web sites become increasingly complex, and the data they present more dynamic, the role of the database can (and should) shift from providing some key data to tracking the use and operation of the Web site and managing site content.

## An example of logging server access

Let's consider server logging. Almost all Web servers are capable of logging page access in one of several standard formats. A typical entry looks something like this, though it usually appears on a single line:

```
191.140.134.225 - - [30/Jun/2000:17:26:40 -0500]
   "GET /index.shtml HTTP/1.1" 200 17513
```

This log entry shows the IP address of the user's machine, a user ID (if using authentication, which this page isn't); the date and time; the type of request; the page; the protocol, the result code; and the number of bytes transmitted.

The log is a single file, and on a busy system logs grow rapidly. You may be purging your logs every day just to save the disk space, but probably not until you've run a utility of some sort to accumulate the statistics into, well, a database.

You may want to refer to the log in the event of a problem, such as someone repeatedly and unsuccessfully attempting to access a protected page, either because they've forgotten their password, or they're trying to guess a password. If you're monitoring the logs, you may notice a number of 401 error codes from the same IP address. Or perhaps someone who should have access reports a problem, and to establish the pages where they've had the problem you need to search a very large log file. In either case you have to look through a large amount of irrelevant data.

The solution to this kind of data access is to use a tool designed for the job. If you've used servlets to log data to a database that implements Structured Query Language (SQL), you could use a statement such as this:

```
SELECT IP, Date, Time, ResultCode FROM ServerLog
WHERE User='joebfstplk' AND ResultCode=401;
```

to retrieve just the failed accesses for the user 'joebfstplk'.

## A world of possibilities

Databases have many other uses. You can expand on the access logging concept to offer a list of unviewed pages to your users. You can dynamically create index pages based on page attributes stored in the database and even serve entire pages and/or images out of the database (although in many cases you're better off storing the file name in the database and reading the file itself directly from the file system).

If you're running a user survey, the traditional approach is to store the results of a submitted form in a text file or e-mail the results to a specified user for later collation. If your Web site has a database available, you can store user survey results directly, and even build graphs of the results for instant reader feedback.

The possibilities for database integration are as endless as the uses of databases in desktop applications. And just as databases are at the heart of most business applications, so too are databases taking their places at the heart of Web business applications.

# JavaServer Pages

Servlets are a great way to add dynamic content to a Web page, but they aren't the total answer. Consider the following code fragment that adds some HTML to a page:

```
out.println("</B><P>Ah, the old "
+ LatestKaosTrick + "trick. That's "
+ "the oldest trick in the book, Chief.</B></P>");
```

Most of the HTML generated by this fragment is hard coded, except for the contents of the `LatestKaosTrick` variable. While you can automate the creation of HTML at runtime, the problem is that any HTML available only in servlet code isn't available at page design time. Page creation then becomes a cycle of writing Java code, running the servlet, looking at the page, reacting in shock and dismay, and writing more Java code. Worse yet, any changes to the HTML, no matter how minor, require the servlet to be recompiled.

## A division of labor

Rather than generate the HTML from inside a servlet, it's much better if you create (or can at least view) the HTML visually in an HTML editor, and you create the Java code in a suitable coding environment. This code is usually in the form of JavaBeans, which are really little more than ordinary Java classes that follow a few specific rules.

In this scheme the HTML page is a template with placeholders for the dynamic content. The page designer can focus on the visual aspects without needing to know about the underlying logic, and the programmer can get the code right without needing to know the details of the presentation. In practice, some communication between both sides is still needed, but the division of labor is much easier to achieve.

JavaServer Pages are one such scheme, and Sun Microsystem's officially endorsed Java platform approach to the problem. In JSP, the server compiles a Web page (with the JSP extension) into a servlet, converting the mix of HTML and special embedded tags into print statements. When the user requests a page, the server runs the JSP servlet, which generates the HTML page. In addition to the tags that are part of the JSP specification, developers can also create their own custom tags. This capability increases the power and flexibility of JSPs considerably.

You can also embed Java code in a JSP, and this is appropriate at times, but there's a danger here as well. JSPs are easier to create and maintain if you don't load them up with Java code. This is where custom tags really shine: you can place complex Java code, and make that code available to the JSP using a simple tag statement.

## Other solutions

The separation of presentation and implementation is a thorny problem, and not all developers are happy with JSP. If it's possible to create a JSP that's completely loaded down with Java code, you can rest assured that it will happen. Just because you can do something doesn't mean it's worth doing.

One common approach to application development is codified in a design pattern called Model-View-Controller, or MVC. In this pattern, the view is that part that displays information to the user. The model is the underlying logic, and the important idea is that this logic is conceptually separate from the view. You should be able to make changes to the view without having to make any changes to the model. Views receive information from the model about the model's state. The third part of the pattern, the controller, handles user input, and passes information to the model, which may then cause the view to be updated.

You can build an MVC-compliant system that uses servlets, JavaBeans, and JSPs. You can use a controller servlet, or, if you wish, a class derived from the `RequestInterceptor` class, to channel user input (in the form of page requests) to a model made up of servlets and beans. The controller then forwards the requests to a JSP, which presents a view to the user. This concept forms the basis for many of the examples you'll see in later parts of this book. In a scheme like this, there is little scriptlet code in JSPs because the logic is largely contained in beans and custom tag-handling classes.

Because JSPs don't enforce a MVC approach, however, some developers have created their own JSP-like templating systems, which do enforce some of these requirements. There are a number of projects underway including, but not limited to, WebMacro, Cocoon, Turbine, and FreeMarker.

Whether you go with JSP or another templating system, or you roll your own, you'll definitely want to use something other than pure servlets for large sites, or where a number of people are involved in design and programming.

# Putting It All Together

Perhaps you've established that servlets, JSPs (or some other templating system), and databases will play a central role in your Web site development efforts. That's great, but how do you get from that vague concept to a working system?

The core of any Web-content delivery effort is the Web server itself, so you need a Web server that understands server-side Java. You have, broadly speaking, two options: a standalone servlet *container* that handles servlet requests, or a Web server with this capability built in.

## The servlet container

The first and probably more common solution is to find a Web server that has been extended to support servlets and JSPs. This is done through the user of a servlet/JSP container. (In past versions of the Servlet specification, these containers were called servlet engines.)

In a typical Web server environment, all requests for Web pages and servlets are first received by the Web server, which then decides, usually based on the file name or directory of the request, whether to serve up a static page or to pass control over to a servlet via the servlet container. The servlet container responds to an HTTP request for a servlet, creates/invokes that servlet as necessary, and handles any error conditions. Figure 1-1 shows the flow of information between the client (browser), the Web server, and the servlet container.

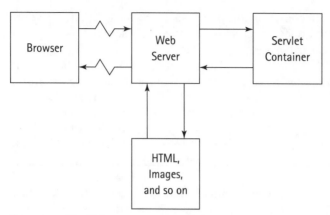

Figure 1–1: The Web server passes servlet requests to the servlet container.

# The Tomcat servlet container/Web server

It's also possible for a servlet container to function in standalone mode, and be both Web server and servlet manager. Tomcat, the reference implementation for the Servlet and JSP specifications, can be used in conjunction with an existing Web server, or in a standalone mode. Although the code discussed in this book can be used with any servlet container, the focus is on Tomcat.

Going with a completely servlet-based Web server does give you total control over site traffic. You can use servlets to log accesses and implement security features, as well as deliver data. The downside is that you'll be working with a technology that isn't as mature as many standalone Web servers, and may not stand up as well under pressure (although Tomcat is acceptably fast, and is in use in some production environments with reportedly good results).

In situations where you have an existing Web site and you mainly want to add some new functionality without disturbing existing page delivery, an add-on servlet container is a good choice.

Tomcat is available for the Web servers shown in Table 1-1 (and probably more by the time this book reaches you).

TABLE 1–1  WEB SERVERS FOR WHICH TOMCAT IS AVAILABLE

| Server | Platforms | Notes |
| --- | --- | --- |
| Standalone | Any platform with a Java 1.1.x or later JVM | Acceptable performance as a Web server in low- to medium-load situations. May work well in high-load environments. |

| Server | Platforms | Notes |
| --- | --- | --- |
| Microsoft Internet Information Server (IIS) | Windows | Requires the isapi_redirect.dll server plug-in. |
| Netscape | Windows NT, Unix | Requires the nsapi_redirect.dll server plug-in. |
| Apache | Windows, Unix, Linux | Requires a special version of mod_jserv. |

The IIS and Netscape HowTos can be found at `http://jakarta.apache.org/tomcat/`. You can find more information on configuring Tomcat for Apache in Appendix B.

# Which Web Server?

If you intend to use a Web server other than Tomcat (fronting Tomcat with another Web server is still the more common approach, although standalone Tomcat is becoming more and more popular), the choice of Web server is to some extent dependent on what hardware your company typically uses. Shops that run only Windows will probably look at IIS before Apache. Overall, however, Apache still has the biggest market share, as shown by the Netcraft Web Server Survey at `http://www.netcraft.com/survey/`.

Most of those Apache servers are running on Unix or Linux boxes; Linux in particular has become popular for Web sites with low to medium loads. Linux shares Unix's high reliability and configuration flexibility.

I began running Apache on Red Hat Linux several years ago, and I'm delighted with the uptime and the performance, but I think it's safe to say that any intensive use of Linux usually ends up involving an occasional recompile of some software available only as source, and perhaps the rare kernel build as well. Fortunately these aren't usually difficult tasks, but you will find yourself a bit closer to the metal in a Linux environment than you would with a shrink-wrapped OS from Redmond.

If you're completely platform and server agnostic (and perhaps if you're not), then Apache on Linux (or another Unix variant) deserves a thorough evaluation.

# Which Database?

As with Web servers, database choices are often limited by the standards your shop has adopted. Certainly not all databases are created equal. Broadly, databases can be placed in three categories: flat file, SQL, and object databases.

# Flat file databases

Flat file databases are the simplest and oldest kind of database. Btrieve and dBase files on Windows, and db and dbm files on Unix and Linux are all examples of flat files. Any application using a flat file database needs to know the exact structure of the data file to use it reliably. In addition, flat file databases from different vendors are generally incompatible. The closest thing to a standard is probably the dBase format and its variants.

In a nutshell, flat files are an old technology. While useful in very small installations, they're generally not a very good idea. Consider moving forward to SQL.

# SQL databases

SQL isn't technically a database type; it's the abbreviation for an IBM creation called Structured Query Language (originally Structured *English* Query Language, to be precise). The purpose behind SQL (which can be pronounced "sequel" or S-Q-L, as you prefer, but be wary of starting a religious war) was to make it possible to extract and update data in a standardized, humanly readable way. No messing with pointers, file structures, or sorting algorithms – just give me that data and let me do something with it.

SQL has become so commonplace that a database that supports SQL *is* a SQL database. The means by which the database itself is stored on disk, or the indexing approach, or even the feature set may vary widely from one vendor to the next, but all SQL databases support common core operations. Most SQL statements can be used unchanged on a variety of SQL database products.

SQL is an excellent choice for database work in Web sites because of the power of SQL, and because servlets can easily talk to SQL databases through the Java database connectivity (JDBC) API. The majority of Java database work is done in SQL and JDBC.

# Object databases

Object database technology has been around for a long time, but it's had relatively slow acceptance. In a flat file or SQL database, you store raw data. An object database can store not just the data, but the code used to manipulate the data. Java by design is well suited for object database work, and if you're an advanced developer you may want to give some consideration to serializing servlets, beans, and other objects into persistent database storage where appropriate.

For much of the work that Web site developers do, however, I feel that object databases haven't yet arrived. The evolution of Web development is similar to that of desktop development, but in many ways not as advanced. The Web interface is simpler than the desktop interface, and the Web application's use of databases is typically less complex than in desktop applications. A great deal still needs to be done with databases on the Web. Perhaps after that revolution is well under way we'll see a greater use of and need for object databases.

## Why MySQL?

Throughout this book I use the MySQL database server, freely available from www. mysql.com. MySQL is an open source product, released in 2000 under the GNU General Public License (GPL). As a result of that move, it should begin showing up on the standard Linux distributions.

 For more information on the GNU project, see www.gnu.org. Enigmatically, GNU stands for GNU's Not Unix. Oh, GNU is pronounced "guh-new" not "new." It's a good thing the G in GNU is pronounced, or else there'd be no way to differentiate the phrase "new software" from the phrase "GNU software."

I like MySQL for the same reasons a lot of other developers do; it's blazingly fast at retrieving data and very reliable. It also has a highly configurable system of user, host, table, and column access privileges. That means that I can give the world access to my database (not a bright idea) or I can say that only such and such an IP address or host name can get read-only access to one field in one table in one database, and nothing else — and anything in between.

MySQL reportedly has around one million installations worldwide, with, of course, many more users. Many ISPs offer MySQL at little or no extra charge.

MySQL isn't the perfect database for all situations. For a long time it lacked transactions and replication, and lacks other features common to high-end systems that make it difficult or impossible (at the time of this writing) to build a self-contained MySQL database that enforces referential integrity. Still, a little care in the database design and MySQL serves most purposes admirably. Should you have other needs, the SQL examples in this book are for the most part generic, and should port easily to most other SQL servers.

# Designing a Database-Using Web Site

It's not that difficult to use database access to enhance an existing Web site. Perhaps you need to display some existing data, or maybe you'd like to collect some survey data in a database. Or maybe you just want to reduce the duplication of data in your Web pages. Isn't there some way to let the content providers focus on content, and the designers on design?

All of these things can be done with servlets, JSPs and other available Java technologies, and databases. The key is to leverage the database's ability to organize information.

Driving a Web site with database storage does raise some interesting challenges and opportunities. You need to create code that uses as few resources as possible, since you will (hopefully) have many users. You must find a way of extracting data from the server for presentation to users, and often you'll need a way of letting users put data into the database. You can also use the database to store configuration data that determines the content and appearance of the HTML pages you deliver to your users.

# Database-Centric Web Sites

In a static Web site, the experience the user has is determined entirely by the individual pages designed by the webmaster. In a *database-centric* Web site, however, small changes to the data can be used to radically alter the creation of Web pages.

Web sites are really just collections of data. As the Web evolves, so have standards for how that data is presented. For example, it's common to reserve the center of the page for content, often an article or other block of text at least several paragraphs long. Sometimes this area is taken up with short blocks of text linked to other pages. On the left and right sides of this central area you may have advertisements, sidebar menus, or more links. A navigation bar usually appears at the top of the page, and another may be at the bottom.

If all of this information is coming out of the database, that's well and good. For full flexibility, however, the actual information that comes out of the database should be determined by the database, not by the servlet, JSP, or JavaBean. By that I mean that the connections between the various pieces of information that make up the Web site should be stored in the database.

If you have a bean that retrieves a sidebar menu, you can tie that menu to the article by creating linking records in the database. Change the link in the database, and the next time that article is retrieved a different sidebar menu is retrieved. Or you can create the sidebar menu on the fly from linked article records in the database. In this scheme, the database provides a coherent view of the data in your Web site, and allows you to manage that data in a more efficient way.

In Part IV of this book I cover these techniques, along with examples of user tracking, authentication, e-mail integration, and various approaches to delivering Web pages using servlets, beans, JavaServer Pages, and other JSP-like templating systems.

# Summary

This chapter provides an overview of the current state of Java server-side technologies, and discusses the Tomcat reference implementation of the servlet and JSP specifications. Key points to remember include:

◆ Java is a good choice for server-side Web development because of its high productivity and strong APIs. Java server-side code also has a light footprint and is designed to be scalable – two important qualities for larger sites.

◆ The Tomcat reference implementation provides all of JSP and servlet features mandated by the Sun specification, and provides good performance and reliability.

◆ Databases are an important part of Web development, particularly as Web sites become more complex. Web sites can reap the same benefits from database technology as do desktop business applications.

◆ JavaServer Pages provide an all-important means of separating the presentation logic from the business logic, and make it easy to visually design Web pages that can use Java server-side technology in the form of servlets, JavaBeans, and custom tag libraries.

◆ Servlet containers (like Tomcat) provide all the functionality a Web server needs to run JSPs and servlets.

◆ By blending Java Web technology and SQL databases you greatly extend the ability of your Web site to collect, manage, and present data.

◆ You can drive the organization of your Web site from a database, using stored data to manage links between pages, track user activity, customize the user's experience, and more.

# Chapter 2

# Introducing Servlets

## IN THIS CHAPTER

♦ Understanding the purpose of server-side Java

♦ Making the best of the design constraints the Web imposes

♦ Using Server-side technologies, including server-side includes, CGI, server APIs, ASP, and scripting

♦ Understanding the benefits of Java technologies on the server

♦ Knowing where to get more information

SERVLETS ARE (OR SHOULD BE) small units of Java code that execute quickly on the server in response to a browser's request for a Web page. This is in contrast to applets, which are (or should be) small units of Java code that execute quickly on the browser, usually after a painfully long wait while the server downloads the applet. The fact is, it doesn't matter how quickly code runs when it gets to you if it takes too long to get to you. And that was the problem with applets, which, as you've probably noticed, aren't around in great abundance anymore; or if they are used, function in noncritical roles, such as drawing pretty graphics or making images look as through they're reflected on waves.

So if you're a Java developer wanting to put your skills to use on a Web project, applets are, for cause of bandwidth and Java incompatibilities among browsers, still an invitation to frustration. Server-side Java technologies, however, are an opportunity for productivity. This chapter will discuss the benefits and use of server-side Java technologies as well as offer recommended references for current servlet and JSP development specifications.

## Server-Side Java

The server-side Java concept is quite simple. Any application, whether Web or desktop, needs a little intelligence and a place to keep its data. Any application may exist on a client only, or on a server only, or on both. In the case of a Web application, by definition, the application exists (that is, code executes) on both the client (the user's browser) and the Web server, and any other needed servers such as database or Enterprise JavaBeans servers.

The Web application could be an HTML page on the client side, or it could be an applet communicating with the server, or it could be some other custom code. In general, delivering HTML guarantees the highest level of access to your Web site, as even Java applets suffer from some portability issues.

## Where's that code running?

If an application has code running on both the client and the server, then to have optimal execution you need to balance the load among all the clients and the server. These are some of the questions you must consider: How fast is your connection? How much data do you have to move? How much processing power is required? How many users will access the system concurrently, and where are the bottlenecks?

Although they are improving, Internet connection speeds are still a problem and, as I mentioned, detract from the success of applets. Some or many of your users may be connecting at dial-up speeds. If the rest of your system is underused, and the pipeline is choked with data, then you want to move as much of that data back onto the server as possible, where it can flow at bus speeds.

Also consider how computationally expensive your application is. Most database programs are, like word processors, often cheap in terms of CPU cycles. In a data entry application, your users will be adding only a few records per minute. On the other hand, a complex reporting job may load the database server heavily.

In most cases, it's easier to address bottlenecks on the server than it is to solve problems with Internet connection speeds or CPU and memory limitations on the remote client's computer. Delivering a user interface as HTML pages generally places less of a demand on the network than delivering a graphically rich user interface (using remote control software such as PCAnywhere), which means that at this point in the history of computing, server-side code is often an optimum way to deliver maximum functionality.

## Design constraints

In addition to load balancing, you need to look at design constraints. To run Java code on a client you have to first deliver it. Having delivered it, you would like to have some confidence that this code finds a suitable, compatible JVM on the client and runs in the manner you expect. No such guarantee is presently available (although Sun's Java Web Start technology shows some promise). Choose a language other than Java for the client side and you have even more compatibility worries, not to mention some serious security concerns.

In short, developing on the server for an unknown variety of clients, while much easier than in the pre-Java era, is still a bit of a mess. At present, the approach most likely to win is to reduce the client-side requirement to the minimum, both in bandwidth and in capability. This means picking a target (or several) on the HTML release line and writing server-side code to generate HTML to that specification.

# Server-Side Technologies

Server-side Web development is by no means unique to Java. A number of techniques have been and are still used to extend the simple page-serving capabilities of stock Web servers. These techniques include server-side includes, the common gateway interface (CGI) and its variants (mainly WinCGI), server-side scripting languages, server application programming interfaces (APIs), the very popular PHP scripting language, and Microsoft's Active Server Pages (ASP).

## Server-side includes

Server-side includes (SSI) is one of the simplest ways to add some dynamically generated content to a Web page. SSI instructs the Web server to parse an HTML document looking for SSI tags and then takes action based on the tag contents. Since this parsing takes some time, the Web server is usually told that only files with a particular extension, often SHT, SHTM, or SHTML, contain SSI tags.

A common use of SSI is to execute a script that outputs HTML. For example, this tag

```
<!--#exec cgi="/cgi-bin/test.cgi" -->
```

tells the server to execute the test.cgi Perl script in the Web's cgi-bin directory. Such a script uses the Perl print statement to write HTML to standard output, which the browser can capture and insert into the Web page. Tags like exec enable you to include the contents of another file, read the size or attributes of a file, conditionally process data, manipulate variables, send e-mail, and even read and write ODBC data sources. Server-side includes are relatively easy to use, but they aren't particularly efficient because of the parsing requirement.

## Common Gateway Interface

The Common Gateway Interface (CGI) specification defines how programs that exist separately from the Web server can be made to produce output that is then directed back to the browser by the Web server. CGI is slow, expensive (in terms of CPU time, memory, and resources), and still in extraordinarily wide use. What you can do with CGI and with SSI overlaps somewhat, but CGI's possibilities are far greater because you can use just about any programming language you like to create a CGI program.

In traditional CGI, the Web server receives a request for a CGI program, just as it would for a regular Web page. The Web server calls the CGI program, but before it does this it sets a number of environment variables with information related to the page request, such as the Web site document root, what MIME types the browser accepts, the user's browser and language, the server name and port, and more.

For Redmondophiles, there's a variant of CGI called WinCGI. WinCGI is a lot like CGI except that it uses temporary files rather than environment variables to pass data from the server to the CGI program.

The most popular tool for creating CGI scripts is Perl, an interpreted language available for most popular platforms. The main repository for Perl code on the net is CPAN, the Comprehensive Perl Archive Network, at http://www.cpan.org/. Perl excels at the sorts of things many Web developers need to do, including string handling, regular expressions, and reading/writing data using standard input/output. Listing 2-1 shows a portion of a Perl script used to generate some HTML. The code is looping through an array of data elements to create image links.

**Listing 2-1: Perl Script Generating HTML**

```
print "Content-type: text/html\n\n";
while ($count <= $x){
        $pos++;
        if ($pos > $x){
                $pos = 0;
        }
        print "<p><a href=\"$url[$pos]\">
            <IMG SRC=\"$img[$pos]\" border=\"0\"
            WIDTH=\"$width[$pos] HEIGHT=\"$height[$pos]\">
            </a></p>\n";
        $count++;
}
```

No matter which language you use to write CGI programs, however, you're faced with some serious problems as site usage increases. Every single CGI request results in an application being loaded into memory, which takes time as well as RAM. Also, a CGI program can't interact with the Web server — all it can do is output data that is returned to the client browser. CGI programs consume a lot of resources, and if not written in Perl, typically lack portability.

## Server APIs

Some Web server vendors have published APIs that allow developers a high level of access to the server's internal workings. For a module to be linked into a server it usually has to be written in C or C++. One notable exception is Apache's mod_perl, which places a Perl interpreter inside Apache and allows Perl scripts to execute without requiring a separate process for each. Server APIs are a great way to get fast, native code running inside a Web server. The downside is a lack of portability across Web servers and across platforms.

## Server-side scripting languages

No doubt you've come across Web pages that use JavaScript or VBScript. Of course, you usually only discover this when a script breaks and you're informed which scripting language caused the error. No matter: these scripting languages have been a godsend for many developers.

Scripting languages are popular for client-side solutions because they address the inherent nonprogrammability of HTML. It's not surprising, then, that scripting languages should make their way to the server side.

Yes, I know I just mentioned Perl scripts on the server. Perl is a server-side scripting language, but when I talk about JavaScript or VBScript I'm talking about a scripting language that's tightly integrated with the server, not running as a CGI or server-side include. This means a separate process doesn't need to be spawned for each request, and the script code has access to the server itself. Server-side scripting addresses CGI performance and communication concerns, and enables you to add considerable functionality without resorting to a full-fledged programming language.

## Active Server Pages

Developers who use Microsoft's Internet Information Services (IIS) often rely on ASP technology. ASP can be grouped under server-side scripting, but its close integration with Component Object Model (COM) technologies makes it a more complex and robust environment. ASP comes from the Windows platform, but is now available on various Unix platforms courtesy of Chili!Soft (http://www.chilisoft.com/), Halcyon Software (http://www.halcyonsoft.com/), and the Active Scripting Organization (http://www.activescripting.org/).

# Servlets and JavaServer Pages

With all of these options available, why are so many developers looking to server-side Java? In large part, it's because of Java's unique combination of capability, power, portability, and productivity. Java is heavily supported by Sun Microsystems, and by numerous other vendors; as a result, you have your pick of development tools and APIs. You can write industrial strength applications, and run them on multiple platforms. And you can gain significant productivity over similar development using traditional languages like C++.

## Productivity

No one would argue that the C and C++ languages, long the mainstay of commercial software development, are powerful tools. Yet many Web developers don't use languages like these, preferring instead to work with scripting languages such as VBScript and JavaScript. Although such scripting languages have become quite powerful in recent years, the whole point of scripting is to work at a higher, more conceptual level than you typically do when using a programming language like C++. That higher level usually means greater productivity, but less capability. If the capability is there, it often comes at the expense of usability.

Java is a full-fledged programming language, but it offers many of the high-productivity benefits of scripting languages. And when you're doing Web development with Java, you can create custom tag libraries that wrap up your custom Java code in script-like custom tags that you design. In effect, you can use Java to create your own scripting language, and it's not very difficult to do.

## Power

Closely related to the language's capability (the available constructs and the extent to which it supports object-oriented methodologies) is the language's power. What APIs are available? How fast will the code run? What can you actually *do* with the code?

The amount of Java development that has taken place in the past few years is staggering. Between the standard APIs, third party products, freeware, and the various open source projects, there's hardly an area of application development that hasn't been touched by Java. On the Web-development side, Java servlets provide a bridge between Web servers and the world of Java resources. Furthermore, JSPs and a number of other templating products help separate page design from server-side coding.

Critics of Java have long pointed to a performance gap between interpreted Java code and compiled C++ code. That gap has narrowed significantly. Java now boasts performance very close to comparable C++ code, thanks to just-in-time (JIT) compiler technology and better interpreters. Certainly the tradeoff between power and productivity is now reasonable for all but the most processor-intensive tasks.

## Portability

Java's portability has always been a two-edged sword, particularly for desktop applications. For an application to run on multiple platforms it inevitably has to resort to some lowest common denominator. If you code all your important functions to be triggered by a right mouse click, your Mac users with just one mouse button will not be amused.

On the server side, however, all of the user interface issues have been pushed out to the browser. And that levels the playing field, because no matter what language you're using to write your server-side code, you still have to deal with the unfortunate situation that not all browsers support all (or even most) of the possible HTML and script language statements. Platform-related inconsistencies can still arise, but, in general, it's quite easy to develop and test servlets on, say, a Windows machine, and deploy on a Linux box.

# Recommended Reading

Anyone interested in servlet and JSP development should have a look at the current specifications from Sun Microsystems. Start at the following home pages for servlets and JSP:

◆ http://java.sun.com/products/servlet/

◆ http://java.sun.com/products/jsp/

Here you can find current specifications as well as draft specifications for future releases. The servlet specification is the shorter of the two (at about 75 pages for the 2.2 version), and covers some basics (What is a Servlet?), definitions of terms, the servlet interface and context, the request and response objects, sessions, dispatching requests, and much more. It's particularly important for Tomcat users to read this document, as this specification is exactly the one Tomcat implements.

The JSP specification is about twice the size of the servlet specification. It also provides an overview technology, and is as important to Tomcat users as the servlet specification. As indicated by the relative size of the specification, JSPs comprise a more complex concept than servlets, and in fact build on the servlet specification, since every JSP is compiled into a servlet before it can be used.

The JSP specification includes a technology overview; a discussion of Web-application models (2 1/2 tier, n-tier, using XML, and so on); syntax and semantics; the JSP container; custom tags; scripting; and an XML document format for JSPs (which is not particularly important to most JSP developers – at least not yet – but is relevant to vendors creating tools to manipulate JSPs at design time). Several appendices give examples of JSPs, cover packaging into WAR files, and deal with other implementation issues.

In addition to the servlet and JSP specifications, Sun also offers a number of documentation and training resources at http://developer.java.sun.com/developer/infodocs/index.shtml. Here you can find papers on coding conventions, Java programming essentials, technical papers and much more.

Servlet/JSP developers may be particularly interested in Designing Enterprise Applications with the Java2 Platform, Enterprise Edition, which is available at the Developers Connection Bookshelf page at http://developer.java.sun.com/developer/Books/. This book deals specifically with enterprise-wide development scenarios, but even if your installation is fairly small scale you can probably find some useful information.

Servlets and JavaServer Pages open up many new possibilities for Web developers. And fortunately, they aren't difficult to create or use. In Chapter 3 I explain how to install a servlet/JSP container and run a few servlets.

# Summary

In this chapter I discuss the constraints Web development imposes and give an overview of the common server-side Web development technologies, their strengths, and their weaknesses. Key points to remember include:

◆ Web developers have to make choices about where their code will run: on the client, on the server, or on both.

◆ Web applications can be simpler than desktop applications because the user interface options presented by HTML are a lot simpler than those available in most desktop APIs.

◆ Server-side includes (SSI) are commonly used to place boilerplate text in HTML pages, but the parsing required of each page with includes can impose a serious performance penalty.

◆ CGI and its offspring are more capable than SSI and are commonly written in Perl, but are often lacking in performance and are not always portable.

◆ Server APIs provide the tightest integration with a Web server and can be very fast, but are not that easily extended or maintained because of this tight integration, and may not be portable.

◆ ASP technology has proved popular in the Windows environment, but despite cross-platform support from vendors like Chili!Soft, ASP hasn't seen wide use outside the Windows world.

◆ Scripting languages such as VBScript and JavaScript are increasingly used on the server side, and have been a boon to many developers because of their ease of use.

◆ Despite the many options available, many developers are taking up servlets and JSP because of Java's unique combination of capability, power, portability, and productivity.

◆ The JSP and servlet specifications are the definition of Tomcat's capabilities, and are recommended reading for anyone using servlets and JSPs with any container.

# Chapter 3

# Installing and Configuring Tomcat

## IN THIS CHAPTER

◆ Understanding how the servlets function inside a servlet container

◆ Choosing between the different kinds of servlet containers

◆ Installing the Java SDK and verifying its installation

◆ Installing Tomcat and choosing between binary and source distributions

◆ Starting Tomcat and running the Tomcat example servlets and JSPs

◆ Configuring Tomcat through `server.xml` and Tomcat Web applications using `web.xml`

IN THIS CHAPTER I explain how to set up a servlet and JSP development and testing environment. Many Web servers and server add-ons support servlets and JSPs, so rather than deal with all of these, I focus on Jakarta Tomcat, the reference implementation for the Java Servlet 2.2 and JavaServer Pages 1.1 technologies. Whichever vendor's implementation of the Servlet and JSP specifications you choose, the underlying technologies function similarly. The core concept in making a Web server Java-aware is the servlet container.

## The Servlet Container

If you've worked with earlier servlet implementations, you may be familiar with the term *servlet engine*, which is used to describe the software that creates, loads, and executes servlets as needed. As of Java2, the correct terminology is *servlet container*. A container still performs the same kinds of functions servlet engines do, including providing an environment in which the servlet code executes.

Figure 3-1 shows the message flow from the HTTP request for a servlet, which is initiated by the user accessing the Web site.

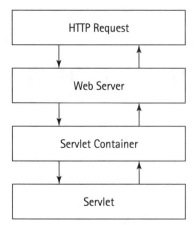

Figure 3-1: Message flow in a Web server with a servlet container

There are three ways a servlet container can be integrated into a Web environment: as an in-process container, as an out-of-process container, or as a standalone container.

## In-process containers

In an in-process implementation, the servlet container is bound to the Web server by a plug-in that mediates communication between the server and the container. The plug-in and the container run in the server's memory space, as does the JVM that executes the servlet and its container. Figure 3-2 shows the arrangement of the components.

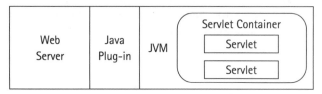

Figure 3-2: An in-process servlet container

In-process containers offer the maximum performance because the server, the plug-in, and the container can communicate using the server's memory space. However, having everything in one memory space means everything has to be on one machine as well, which limits scalability. More importantly, in an in-process container any thread can crash another thread, or the entire server. Linking Java and native code also compromises Java's security features.

## Out-of-process containers

Out-of-process containers are similar to in-process containers except that two memory spaces are involved. One is the server and a Java plug-in, which provides a Java interface to the server. The other memory space is the JVM and the servlet container. Figure 3-3 shows the separation between these components.

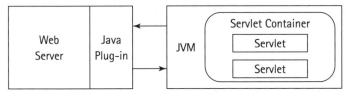

Figure 3-3: An out-of-process servlet container

Performance isn't quite as good with an out-of-process container because the two servlets and the servlet container have to use an external protocol to communicate, but by separating the Web server you get better scalability and reliability. Communication between the plug-in and the container is usually via TCP/IP, and the plug-in can be written in whatever language in which the server is written. Web servers such as Apache and IIS, which support loadable modules, make it relatively easy to develop a container plug-in.

## Standalone containers

When a servlet container is standalone, it acts as a Web server, responding directly to requests for Web pages and/or servlets. This setup is a variation on the message flow shown in Figure 3-1, since it bypasses the Web server entirely. Figure 3-4 shows the container as a self-contained unit.

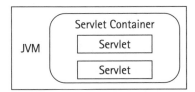

Figure 3-4: A standalone servlet container

 Tomcat functions surprisingly well as a standalone container, but when integrated with Apache or IIS it is by default an out-of-process servlet container.

Some standalone containers (like Allaire's JRun, for example) have special software that causes your usual Web server to redirect servlet and JSP requests to the standalone container. In these cases, the normal Web server typically listens on port 80 and forwards special requests to another port (for example, 8080).

# The SDK

Tomcat is Java code, and to run Java code on any computer you need a Java Virtual Machine. To develop Java code, you also need a Java compiler, and you'll probably want a few more tools, such as a debugger, class browser, and so forth.

You can get the compiler and the JVM two ways: download a suitable Java Platform from Sun's Web site (java.sun.com), or use a development tool from another vendor that includes all of the necessary tools and a JVM.

It's possible to do Java, and particularly servlet, development using nothing more than a text editor, a Java compiler, and the appropriate class libraries, but you'll probably want to investigate some of the available Integrated Development Environments (IDEs) for Java. You can find a listing at http://www.javaworld.com/javaworld/tools/jw-tools-ide.html. With approximately one hundred to choose from, you're bound to find something to your liking.

> I do most of my servlet and JSP development using IBM's VisualAge For Java, one of the most popular IDEs. VAJava, as it's called, provides a complete development environment, including the Java compiler and runtime. Just add Tomcat and you're off. Actually, as of this writing, using Tomcat with VAJava isn't completely straightforward, but, fortunately, IBM's Sheldon Bradley Wosnick has provided a step-by-step guide at http://sheldonwosnick.tripod.com/Tomcat/Tomcat31Release.html. This technique also works with Tomcat 3.2.

## Downloading and installing

Assuming you either plan to go the bare-bones editor-and-compiler route, or your IDE doesn't come with a Java runtime, you need to download some Java goodies from Sun Microsystems' Java Web site at java.sun.com.

Product version numbering in Java can be a bit confusing. Initially, Sun offered the Java Development Kit (JDK) and the Java Runtime Environment (JRE), each in several editions, depending on the capabilities included. Both were released in 1.0, 1.1, and 1.2 versions. In December of 1998 Sun announced the 1.2 releases would be renamed as Java2.

Java2 is available in three product groups. Java2 Micro Edition (J2ME) is designed for embedded systems, such as those found in consumer devices, and isn't the subject of this book. Java2 Standard Edition (J2SE) has all the essential tools, runtimes, and APIs for Java development. Java2 Enterprise Edition (J2EE) adds Enterprise Java Beans (EJBs), transactions, CORBA, JDBC, eXtensible Markup Language (XML), JavaServer Pages, and servlets.

You might think that since J2EE has JSP and servlet support, it's the logical choice for servlet development. That may not be the case, depending on where Tomcat's integration with J2EE stands at the time you read this.

One of the requirements of any J2EE implementation is a servlet container. If you're using Tomcat for servlet development and deployment, it conflicts with the J2EE servlet container. Reportedly, an adapter is under development for Tomcat 3.2 that addresses this problem, at least in Sun's J2EE SDK. You should verify Tomcat compatibility with your J2EE vendor. Unless you have a specific requirement for J2EE, start with J2SE. You'll probably find it easier to upgrade to J2EE than to downgrade from J2EE to J2SE.

 **TIP** Tomcat supports both Java 1.*x* and Java2, but unless you have a compelling reason to stick with the earlier releases, I recommend you go with Java2. The newest releases of Tomcat (such as the 4.0 betas) do not support Java 1.*x*.

# Installing Java2 Standard Edition

To install Java2 Standard Edition, go to the Java products page at `http://java.sun.com/products/`. Either select a link on the page, or use the product drop list, if present, to choose Java2 Platform, Standard Edition. The J2SE releases include the SDK, the runtime environment, and the documentation. You will also see links to earlier releases of the JDK. Follow the links to download the J2SE SDK.

### INSTALLING THE SDK UNDER WINDOWS

For Windows machines, the SDK archive is an executable install program. After you've run it, you may need to update your `PATH` to include the SDK bin directory, which contains the executable programs. This update isn't required, but if you don't, you have to specify the full path any time you want to run a program such as the compiler or debugger.

To set the path on Windows 2000 or Windows NT, bring up the Control Panel. Click on the System icon, and then click on the Environment tab. In the System Variables list, select the Path variable. You can then update the Path in the Value field at the bottom of the window. Click OK to continue.

On Windows 95/98/ME, update the C:\AUTOEXEC.BAT file. If it has a `PATH` statement, append a semicolon, followed by the path to the SDK's bin directory. If no `PATH` statement exists, add one as follows (substituting the appropriate directory name for your computer):

```
PATH=C:\JDK1.3\BIN
```

What about `CLASSPATH`? This environment variable is used to locate classes (singly, or in JAR files) that are not part of the JDK. If you already have this variable set, you want to make sure the classes it points to are compatible with this version of the SDK.

The alternative to CLASSPATH is to specify the directories and JAR files with the command line -classpath option when you run your IDE or, in this case, Tomcat. In Java2, the default CLASSPATH is "." which is shorthand for the current directory.

### INSTALLING THE SDK UNDER LINUX

To install the SDK under Linux you need to make the downloaded file executable. For Red Hat Linux users, the SDK is available in RPM format, which you install with a command such as the following:

```
rpm -i j2sdk-version_name-linux.rpm
```

You need root access to install the RPM.

The SDK is also available in a gzipped tar file (also known as a tarball). Change to the directory where you want to install the SDK and type something similar to:

```
gunzip j2sdk-version_name -linux.tar.gz
```

to unzip the file, and:

```
tar xvf j2sdk-version_name -linux.tar.gz
```

to unpack the tarball. Or you can cut right to the chase and do it all in one step, as follows:

```
tar zxvf j2sdk-version_name -linux.tar.gz
```

### INSTALLING THE SDK UNDER SOLARIS

On Solaris systems you need to make the downloaded binary executable:

```
chmod +x j2sdkversion_name-platform.bin
```

Then change to the directory where you'd like the JDK installed and run the self-extracting binary.

On Solaris systems you need to be sure that you have installed any required patches to the operating system before proceeding to install the JDK. See the installation instructions at java.sun.com for details.

# Verifying the installation

After you've installed the SDK, you should verify that everything is as it should be. To begin, check the version of the Java Runtime Environment by running:

```
java -version
```

Don't specify a path, and don't execute this command from the directory where the java program resides. You should see output similar to this:

```
java version "1.1.8"
```

## A test class

Make certain that the compiler is working. All you need is five lines of code, as follows.

```
class TestMe {
public static void main(java.lang.String[] args) {
        System.out.println("I work!");
    }
}
```

Save this code as TestMe.java (the name of the Java file must exactly match the class name), and compile it:

```
javac TestMe.java
```

If you get a bad compile, check your code against the listing. If your javac compiler is missing in action, verify that the JDK's bin directory is on the executable path.

Assuming a successful compile, run the program with:

```
java TestMe
```

The application should respond with the phrase "I work!"

Java's installed and working. You're just about ready to start writing servlets, but you still need a Web server (unless you want to use Tomcat standalone, which I discuss a little later).

# Installing Tomcat

Tomcat is available as a free download from the Jakarta Web site at http://jakarta.apache.org/tomcat/index.html. Although you don't have to worry about getting a version of Tomcat for your specific operating system and hardware platform (Tomcat is Java code, after all), several archive formats are available, including ZIP (Windows), and zipped and gzipped tarballs (Unix).

## Source or binary distributions

The first choice you have to make when downloading Tomcat is whether to choose a source or a binary distribution. If you're interested in participating in the Tomcat project, you'll want to download a source distribution. If you're not interested in making changes to the Tomcat server itself, just skip to the next subhead. Even if you think you might want to play with the Tomcat source, get the binaries first so you can get up and running. Once you know what a working Tomcat installation is supposed to be like, you'll find it easier to know when your source distribution is working properly.

You can find instructions on building Tomcat from source in the Developer's Guide in the doc/appdev subdirectory. If you don't have that subdirectory, install the binary release. It should be there.

## Binary installation

If you've decided to begin with the binary Tomcat installation, your next step is to decide which build to download. A "last stable version" release is always available and, if you want the fewest gray hairs, this is almost always the wisest choice. Often a milestone beta build is available also. This build can be a good choice if it fixes bugs in the last stable release that you can't live with, but you may find some new problems that aren't to your liking. You may even find a milestone build you want to use in a production environment.

You can also get nightly builds, if you want to live a bit more dangerously, or are interested in contributing. Open source projects like Tomcat depend on input and code from the developer community. Installation is fairly straightforward. Download the binary build and unzip/untar it into a suitable directory.

## Setting Tomcat environment variables

You need to set the TOMCAT_HOME environment variable to point to this directory. On Windows machines use the SET command, or if you're running Windows NT or 2000, set this environment variable using the Control Panel. Assuming a directory of C:\TOMCAT:

```
SET TOMCAT_HOME=C:\TOMCAT
```

On Unix/Linux systems, the command depends on which shell you're running. For sh and bash (assuming /usr/local/tomcat):

```
TOMCAT_HOME=/usr/local/tomcat; export TOMCAT_HOME
```

If you're using tcsh, the command is:

```
setenv TOMCAT_HOME /usr/local/tomcat
```

## About Jakarta

Jakarta is a collaboration between Apache developers, major corporations, smaller companies, and individual private developers. These include members of the Apache JServ project, which provided initial servlet capabilities to the Apache Web server, and software engineers from Sun and IBM. The Jakarta home page is at `jakarta.apache.org`.

Jakarta, like Apache, is an open source project. In general, open source means that the source code is always freely available. Software licensed under an open source agreement is often, though not always, managed by a core group of developers who determine when a particular version of the product, containing changes by any number of developers, is ready for release.

Anyone can participate in the Jakarta project, developers and users alike. User feedback, bug reports, and feature requests are all vital to the development process.

Contributions to the source base are also encouraged. As a Tomcat user, you're writing code with the same language in which Tomcat itself is written. If you fix a bug, or make an enhancement that others may find useful, please contribute. You don't have to have any special qualifications to do this; your code will be judged on its own merits.

Developers who make frequent, useful contributions to the project may request promotion to the status of committer. While developers can only make their contributions known by e-mail or posting on mailing lists, Committers have write access to the source repository and can vote on issues affecting the direction of the project.

Particularly active and effective committers may one day breathe the rarified air of the Project Management Committee (PMC), which is the official managing body of the Jakarta project.

For more information on participating in the Jakarta project, please go to `http://jakarta.apache.org/guidelines/index.html`.

That's it. You're now ready to run Tomcat as a standalone servlet container/Web server.

# Running Tomcat

Tomcat's control scripts are kept in the bin directory. There are two sets, one for Windows, and another for Unix. The Windows scripts are all batch files with the extension BAT, and the Unix scripts end in sh.

## Starting and stopping Tomcat

To start Tomcat under Windows, type `startup` and press Enter. This batch file sets `TOMCAT_HOME` if it doesn't already have a value, and calls `tomcat.bat` with a start parameter. The `tomcat.bat` file then adds the Tomcat JAR files to the `CLASSPATH` and runs the `org.apache.tomcat.startup.Tomcat` class. When Tomcat terminates, the `tomcat.bat` file takes over again, restoring `CLASSPATH` to its original setting.

To start Tomcat under Unix, run the `startup.sh` script. This script performs the same functions as the `startup.bat` file.

To stop Tomcat, run `shutdown.bat` or `shutdown.sh`, as appropriate. This script does some housekeeping similar to `startup.bat/startup.sh` and calls `tomcat.bat/tomcat.sh` with a `stop` parameter, which ultimately runs the `org.apache.tomcat.startup.Tomcat` class with a `-stop` parameter.

## Serving HTML

Now that you know how to start and stop Tomcat, it's time to load some pages. When you run Tomcat standalone like this, it functions as a regular Web server as well as a servlet container. Bring up your Web browser and go to:

```
http://localhost:8080
```

You should see the Tomcat home page shown in Figure 3-5.

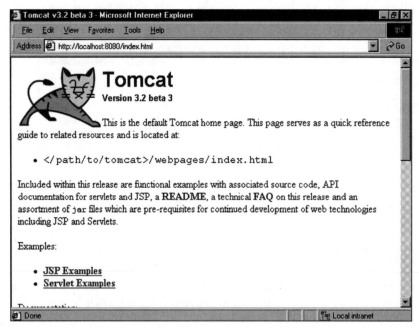

Figure 3-5: The Tomcat home page

The `localhost` portion of the URL points to the computer you're running the browser on, and the 8080 indicates which port to use for the connection. All HTTP requests, which are what a browser makes when you go to a Web site, go to port 80 unless otherwise specified. By convention, port 8080 is used for test servers, and since Tomcat doesn't want to step all over any existing Web server on your system, 8080 is a logical choice. You can change the port in `server.xml`, which is in the `conf` directory. I cover `server.xml` in just a bit.

From the Tomcat home page click on Servlet Examples. You should see a page describing the servlet examples, with links to the class and java files, as shown in Figure 3-6.

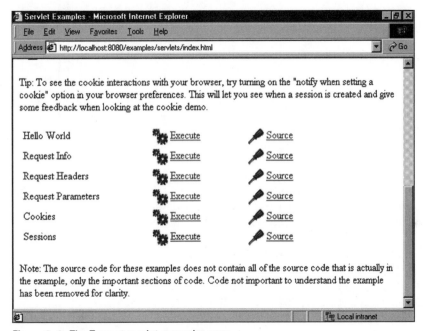

Figure 3-6: The Tomcat servlet examples page

## Executing the HelloWorldExample servlet

From the Tomcat servlet examples page, click on the Hello World execute link. The `HelloWorldExample` servlet should execute, returning the page shown in Figure 3-7.

Figure 3-7: The HelloWorldExample servlet in action

The icons on the right side of the page let you return to the previous page (swoopy arrow) or view the source (screwdriver). Click on the source icon to see the code for the HelloWorldExample servlet, as shown in Listing 3-1.

**Listing 3-1: Source Code for the HelloWorldExample Servlet**

```
import java.io.*;
import javax.servlet.*;
import javax.servlet.http.*;

public class HelloWorld extends HttpServlet {

public void doGet(HttpServletRequest request,
  HttpServletResponse response)
    throws IOException, ServletException
    {
        response.setContentType("text/html");
        PrintWriter out = response.getWriter();
        out.println("<html>");
        out.println("<body>");
        out.println("<head>");
        out.println("<title>Hello World!</title>");
        out.println("</head>");
```

```
        out.println("<body>");
        out.println("<h1>Hello World!</h1>");
        out.println("</body>");
        out.println("</html>");
    }
}
```

As Listing 3-1 shows, there isn't a whole lot of code required to write a simple servlet, and almost all of it is just writing the standard HTML tags needed for a minimal Web page. Think about how difficult it would be to do large, meaningful pages that way, and you'll know why JSPs were created.

## Handling a servlet request

You'll recall that when a servlet container gets a request for a servlet, it calls that servlet's `service` method. Since `HelloWorldExample` is derived from `HTTPServlet`, `HelloWorldExample` really contains all of that class's code and its `HTTPServlet's` `service` method that actually calls the `doGet` method you see in Listing 3-1.

The `doGet` method performs two functions. First, it sets the response's content type to `text/html`. This setting results in the page created from the response having the correct type header. All the code after this point just writes text out to the response and, therefore, ultimately the resulting page. The response's `getWriter` method returns a `PrintWriter` called `out`, and you use `out.println` to create the HTML. Few results in the world of programming are simpler. You don't have to clean up the `PrintWriter` or flush any buffers. All that is taken care of automatically after the `doGet` method completes. The Web server takes the response object and translates it into an HTTP transmission back to the client.

# The Tomcat Configuration Files

Tomcat's configuration options are stored in XML documents. XML is a relatively new text file format that bears a lot of resemblance to HTML. XML documents contain tags like HTML documents, but whereas HTML is an industry standard language, XML is an industry standard *definition* for a language. While you can't create your own HTML tags, you can create your own XML tags, although these XML tags still have to conform to certain rules of syntax. In the case of the `server.xml` and `web.xml` files, XML tags defined by Sun Microsystems and by the Tomcat developers serve to organize the configuration options for Tomcat.

## Understanding server.xml

Tomcat's main configuration options are all stored in `server.xml`, which Tomcat reads whenever the Tomcat servlet container is started. If you're working with

Tomcat as a standalone Web server, Tomcat reads `server.xml` whenever you execute `startup.sh` or `startup.  bat`. Listing 3-2 shows one example (your `server.xml` may vary).

**Listing 3-2: The server.xml Tomcat Configuration File**

```xml
<?xml version="1.0" encoding="ISO-8859-1"?>

<Server>
    <!-- Debug low-level events in XmlMapper startup -->
    <xmlmapper:debug level="0" />

    <!-- if you don't want messages on screen, add the attribute
            path="logs/tomcat.log"
      to the Logger element below
    -->
    <Logger name="tc_log"
            verbosityLevel = "INFORMATION"
    />

    <Logger name="servlet_log"
            path="logs/servlet.log"
    />

    <Logger name="JASPER_LOG"
          path="logs/jasper.log"
            verbosityLevel = "INFORMATION" />

<ContextManager debug="0" workDir="work" >
        <!--
         ContextInterceptor
className="org.apache.tomcat.context.LogEvents"↵
        -->

        <ContextInterceptor className="org.apache.tomcat. ↵
context.AutoSetup" />

        <ContextInterceptor
            className="org.apache.tomcat.context.WebXmlReader" />

        <!-- Uncomment out if you have JDK1.2 and want to use policy
        <ContextInterceptor
            className="org.apache.tomcat.context.PolicyInterceptor" />
        -->

        <ContextInterceptor
```

```
                        className="org.apache.tomcat.context.LoaderInterceptor" />
                <ContextInterceptor
                        className="org.apache.tomcat.context.DefaultCMSetter" />
                <ContextInterceptor
                        className="org.apache.tomcat.context.WorkDirInterceptor" />
                <ContextInterceptor

className="org.apache.tomcat.context.LoadOnStartupInterceptor" />

                <!-- Request processing -->
                <!-- Session interceptor will extract the session id from ↵
cookies and
                        deal with URL rewriting ( by fixing the URL )
                   -->
                <RequestInterceptor
                        className="org.apache.tomcat.request.SessionInterceptor" />

                <!-- Find the container ( context and prefix/extension map )
                        for a request.
                   -->
                <RequestInterceptor
                        className="org.apache.tomcat.request.SimpleMapper1"
                        debug="0" />

                <!-- Non-standard invoker, for backward compat. ( /servlet/*
)
                   -->
                <RequestInterceptor
                        className="org.apache.tomcat.request.InvokerInterceptor"
                        debug="0" />

                <!-- "default" handler - static files and dirs
                   -->.
                <RequestInterceptor
                        className="org.apache.tomcat.request.StaticInterceptor"
                        debug="0" />

                <!-- Plug a session manager. You can plug in more advanced ↵
session
                        modules.
                   -->
                <RequestInterceptor

className="org.apache.tomcat.session.StandardSessionInterceptor" />
```

*Continued*

Listing 3-2 *(Continued)*

```
<!-- Check if the request requires an authenticated role.
  -->
<RequestInterceptor
    className="org.apache.tomcat.request.AccessInterceptor"
    debug="0" />

<!-- Check permissions using the simple xml file. You can
     plug more advanced authentication modules.
  -->
<RequestInterceptor
    className="org.apache.tomcat.request.SimpleRealm"
    debug="0" />

<RequestInterceptor
    className="org.apache.tomcat.request.InterceptorTest"/>

<!-- UnComment the following and comment out the
     above to get a JDBC realm.
     Other options for driverName:
       driverName="oracle.jdbc.driver.OracleDriver"
       connectionURL="jdbc:oracle:thin:@ntserver:1521:ORCL"
       connectionName="scott"
       connectionPassword="tiger"

       driverName="org.gjt.mm.mysql.Driver"
       connectionURL="jdbc:mysql://localhost/authority"
       connectionName="test"
       connectionPassword="test"

     "connectionName" and "connectionPassword" are optional.
  -->
<!--
 <RequestInterceptor
     className="org.apache.tomcat.request.JDBCRealmB"
     debug="99"
   driverName="sun.jdbc.odbc.JdbcOdbcDriver"
   connectionURL="jdbc:odbc:TOMCAT"
   userTable="users"
     userNameCol="user_name"
     userCredCol="user_pass"
   userRoleTable="user_roles"
     roleNameCol="role_name" />
  -->
```

```
<!-- ==================== Connectors ==================== -->

    <!-- Normal HTTP -->
    <Connector className="org.apache.tomcat.service.⏎
PoolTcpConnector">
        <Parameter name="handler"
            value="org.apache.tomcat.service.⏎
http.HttpConnectionHandler"/>
        <Parameter name="port"
            value="8080"/>
    </Connector>

    <!--
        Uncomment this for SSL support.
        You _need_ to set up a server certificate if you want this
        to work, and you need JSSE.
        1. Add JSSE jars to CLASSPATH
        2. Edit java.home/jre/lib/security/java.security
           Add:
           security.provider.2=com.sun.net.ssl. ⏎
internal.ssl.Provider
        3. Do: keytool -genkey -alias tomcat -keyalg RSA
           RSA is essential to work with Netscape and IIS.
           Use "changeit" as password. ( or add keypass attribute )
           You don't need to sign the certificate.

        You can set parameter keystore and keypass if you want
        to change the default ( user.home/.keystore with changeit )
    -->
    <!--
        <Connector className="org.apache.tomcat.service. ⏎
PoolTcpConnector">
            <Parameter name="handler"
                value="org.apache.tomcat.service.http.⏎
HttpConnectionHandler"/>
            <Parameter name="port"
                value="8443"/>
            <Parameter name="socketFactory"
                value="org.apache.tomcat.net.SSLSocketFactory" />
        </Connector>
    -->

    <!-- Apache AJP12 support. This is also used to shut down ⏎
tomcat.
        -->
```

*Continued*

**Listing 3-2** *(Continued)*

```
        <Connector className="org.apache.tomcat.service.↵
PoolTcpConnector">
            <Parameter name="handler"

value="org.apache.tomcat.service.connector.Ajp12ConnectionHandler"/>
            <Parameter name="port" value="8007"/>
        </Connector>

        <!-- ==================== Special webapps ==================== -->
        <!-- You don't need this if you place your app in webapps/
             and use defaults.
             For security you'll also need to edit tomcat.policy

             Defaults are: debug=0, reloadable=true, trusted=false
             (trusted allows you to access tomcat internal objects
              with FacadeManager )

             If security manager is enabled, you'll have read perms.
             in the webapps dir and read/write in the workdir.
          -->

        <Context path="/examples"
                 docBase="webapps/examples"
                 debug="0"
                 reloadable="true" >
        </Context>

        <!-- Admin context will use tomcat.core to add/remove/get ↵
info about
             the webapplications and tomcat internals.
             By default it is not trusted - i.e. it is not allowed ↵
access to
             tomcat internals, only informations that are ↵
available to all
             servlets are visible.

             If you change this to true, make sure you set a password.
          -->
    <!--
        <Context path="/admin"
                 docBase="webapps/admin"
                 debug="0"
                 reloadable="true"
                 trusted="false" >
```

```
        </Context>
-->

        <!-- Virtual host example -
            In "127.0.0.1" virtual host we'll reverse "/" and
            "/examples"
            (XXX need a better example )
            (use  "http://127.0.0.1/examples" )
        <Host name="127.0.0.1" >
           <Context path=""
                    docBase="webapps/examples" />
           <Context path="/examples"
                    docBase="webapps/ROOT" />
        </Host>
         -->


    </ContextManager>
</Server>
```

I omitted some of the longer comments from the server.xml listing. In any case, you should refer to your own copy, as it will probably have changed in some respect since this writing.

Two tags in server.xml bracket all of the other information: <Server> and </Server>. Inside are other tags and tag pairs that define the various parameters Tomcat is to use on startup. There are also a number of comments – these always begin with <!-- and end with -->, and can be split across lines, much like the /* and */ comment delimiters in Java.

You shouldn't need to make any changes to server.xml to get things running, but there are a couple of points you should know. You'll see a number of declarations of context interceptors in server.xml. These interceptors are classes that implement the ContextInterceptor interface, and if you define a context interceptor in server.xml, the servlet container calls that context interceptor's methods at certain points in a context's life cycle, such as when the servlet context is created or destroyed and when servlets are created and destroyed.

More useful to most developers are the request interceptors. These classes implement the RequestInterceptor interface, and are called whenever the container receives an HTTP request, and at predefined times in a servlet's life cycle. You can use request interceptors for purposes such as logging requests to a database and authenticating users. The authentication examples that come with Tomcat are implemented as request interceptors.

Following the interceptors are the connectors that implement communication protocols. About the only thing you can expect to change here is the HTTP port (to 80, if you want to run Tomcat as your sole HTTP server), or the SSL settings that you may wish to uncomment. The rest of server.xml is devoted to Web application and hosting settings.

# Web applications

If you look at the URL for the Hello World servlet, you see that it's http://localhost:8080/examples/servlet/HelloWorldExample. There is, however, no servlet directory under the examples directory. You may see a servlets (note the "s" at the end) directory, but that's just there to confuse you. This directory contains HTML files with the source code formatted for viewing by a browser. It has nothing to do with the executable servlets.

In Tomcat, all servlets and JSPs are organized by directory into Web applications, as defined in the Servlet 2.2 API Specification. You don't actually have to list Web applications in server.xml if you don't want to, although there are several already defined. Tomcat automatically finds any WAR files and/or directories under webapps and sets them up as Web applications. If you don't want this to happen automatically, comment out the following line in server.xml:

```
<ContextInterceptor className="org.apache.tomcat.context.AutoSetup" />
```

# Web applications and web.xml

A Web application is a collection of servlets, JSPs, HTML, images, utility classes, and any other files needed by a logical grouping of Web pages that are bundled as a WAR file, which is really just a JAR file with the WAR extension. Inside the WAR file is a special purpose WEB-INF directory containing a web.xml file (shown in Listing 3-3) that defines servlet and JSP mappings, as well as any JSP tag libraries.

**Listing 3-3: The web.xml File from the examples/WEB-INF Directory**

```
<?xml version="1.0" encoding="ISO-8859-1"?>

<!DOCTYPE web-app
    PUBLIC "-//Sun Microsystems, Inc.//DTD Web Application 2.2//EN"
    "http://java.sun.com/j2ee/dtds/web-app_2.2.dtd">

<web-app>
    <servlet>
        <servlet-name>
            snoop
        </servlet-name>
        <servlet-class>
            SnoopServlet
        </servlet-class>
<!--
        <init-param>
            <param-name>foo</param-name>
            <param-value>bar</param-value>
        </init-param>
```

```
-->
    </servlet>
    <servlet>
      <servlet-name>
          servletToJsp
      </servlet-name>
      <servlet-class>
          servletToJsp
      </servlet-class>
    </servlet>
    <servlet-mapping>
        <servlet-name>
            snoop
        </servlet-name>
        <url-pattern>
            /snoop
        </url-pattern>
    </servlet-mapping>
    <servlet-mapping>
        <servlet-name>
            snoop
        </servlet-name>
        <url-pattern>
            *.snp
        </url-pattern>
    </servlet-mapping>
    <servlet-mapping>
        <servlet-name>
            servletToJsp
        </servlet-name>
        <url-pattern>
            /servletToJsp
        </url-pattern>
    </servlet-mapping>

    <taglib>
        <taglib-uri>
        http://java.apache.org/tomcat/examples-taglib
        </taglib-uri>
        <taglib-location>
            /WEB-INF/jsp/example-taglib.tld
        </taglib-location>
    </taglib>
```

*Continued*

**Listing 3-3** *(Continued)*

```
    <security-constraint>
      <web-resource-collection>
        <web-resource-name>Protected Area</web-resource-name>
      <!-- Define the context-relative URL(s) to be protected. -->
        <url-pattern>/jsp/security/protected/*</url-pattern>
      <!-- If you list http methods,
          only those methods are protected. -->
      <http-method>DELETE</http-method>
        <http-method>GET</http-method>
        <http-method>POST</http-method>
      <http-method>PUT</http-method>
      </web-resource-collection>
      <auth-constraint>
        <!-- Anyone with one of the listed
            roles may access this area. -->
        <role-name>tomcat</role-name>
      <role-name>role1</role-name>
      </auth-constraint>
    </security-constraint>

    <!-- Default login configuration uses BASIC authentication -->
    <login-config>
      <auth-method>BASIC</auth-method>
      <realm-name>Example Basic Authentication Area</realm-name>
    </login-config>

    <!-- If you want to experiment with form-based logins, comment
        out the <login-config> element above and replace it with
        this one.  Note that we are currently using a nonstandard
        authentication method, because the code to support form
        based login is incomplete and only lightly tested.  -->
    <!--
    <login-config>
      <auth-method>EXPERIMENTAL_FORM</auth-method>
      <realm-name>Example Form-Based Authentication Area↵
</realm-name>
      <form-login-config>
        <form-login-page>/jsp/security/login/login.jsp↵
</form-login-page>
        <form-error-page>/jsp/security/login/error.jsp↵
</form-error-page>
      </form-login-config>
    </login-config>
    -->

</web-app>
```

Text between <!-- and --> tags are comments and are ignored by the XML parser.

The outermost set of tags in this file are <web-app> and </web-app> tags, so as you'd expect, this file is used to define behavior within this Web application. Take a look the following excerpt, which shows a set of tags that define a servlet:

```
<servlet>
        <servlet-name>
            snoop
        </servlet-name>
        <servlet-class>
            SnoopServlet
        </servlet-class>
</servlet>
```

The <servlet-name> tag defines an alias by which you can reference the servlet, while the <servet-class> tag defines the actual compiled servlet to be executed. As a result, you can use either

```
http://localhost:8080/examples/servlet/SnoopServlet
```

or

```
http://localhost:8080/examples/servlet/snoop
```

to execute this servlet.

Following several servlet definitions are some servlet mapping definitions. A *servlet definition* indicates which name belongs to which servlet. A *servlet mapping* lets you assign a directory or filename pattern to a servlet. The following code maps the /snoop directory to SnoopServlet:

```
<servlet-mapping>
        <servlet-name>
            snoop
        </servlet-name>
        <url-pattern>
            /snoop
        </url-pattern>
    </servlet-mapping>
```

Keep in mind that the paths here are in the context of the current Web application, which is in the examples directory, so the URL would look something like this:

```
http://localhost:8080/examples/servlet/snoop/thefileIwant.html
```

You can use servlet mapping if you want to intercept all requests for files in a particular directory. You then write code in the servlet to decide what action to take based on the URL of the request.

You can also map file name patterns. The following example shows a mapping for all files ending with the SNP extension (.snp).

```
<servlet-mapping>
      <servlet-name>
          snoop
      </servlet-name>
      <url-pattern>
          *.snp
      </url-pattern>
   </servlet-mapping>
```

This mapping is getting a bit trickier, because the `<servlet-name>` mapping doesn't point to an actual servlet; it points back to the snoop name defined for SnoopServlet. With this mapping in place, any request such as the following for a file ending in SNP results in a call to SnoopServlet:

```
http://localhost:8080/examples/anyoldpage.snp
```

If you try using a servlet mapping with a URL like the following, however:

```
http://localhost:8080/examples/servlet/anyoldpage.snp
```

you'll get a page not found error because the servlet directory is reserved for servlets, and pattern mapping doesn't apply here. On the other hand, this URL:

```
http://localhost:8080/examples/servlets/anyoldpage.snp
```

will work. The difference? If you look closely at the URL, you'll see I'm looking for a page in the `servlets` directory, not the `servlet` directory. Just keeping you on your toes.

## Servlet contexts

I've discussed servlet containers and Web applications. But how does a servlet container handle a Web application? The answer is something called a servlet context.

Quite often servlets need to communicate with each other. One of the things you could do with prior releases of the servlet specification was servlet chaining. You might want to have a set of servlets, each of which can apply different processing to a page request. One servlet might retrieve the data making up the page, and another translates that page into a different language. You could use servlet chaining to create a Web site devoted to VCR operation handbooks, or perhaps toy assembly instructions. Servlet chaining has been largely viewed with disfavor, in part because allowing any servlet to invoke any other servlet without any controls is a potential security risk.

Enter the servlet context. One or more servlet contexts exist inside the servlet container, and every servlet has to exist inside a servlet context. This implies that there's no way to run a servlet except inside a Web application, and in fact that's true. If you don't define a Web application, a default one is used. The relationship between contexts and servlets in a single container is shown in Figure 3-8. It's also possible, and even common, for a Web server to run multiple servlet containers at once, sometimes for security reasons, and to ensure that if one servlet container (and its Web applications) crashes, the other servlet containers continue to function.

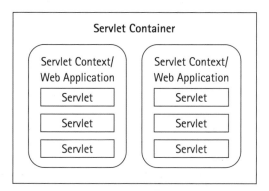

Figure 3-8: The relationship between contexts and servlets in a single container

When you want to exchange data between servlets, or pass requests from one servlet to another, you do it via the servlet context. For instance, you might want to have a servlet determine the content for a page, and then pass that information to a JSP for formatting using a RequestDispatcher object. The code to get the servlet context and request dispatcher, and then call the forward method on the request dispatcher, is shown here:

```
RequestDispatcher rd =
  getServletContext().getRequestDispatcher("results.jps");
rd.forward(request, response);
```

Because the servlet context functions as a repository for shared objects, you can use it as a basis for various kinds of interservlet communication. The main thing to keep in mind is that for all practical purposes a Web application and a servlet occupy the same space, and mean largely the same thing.

## The default web.xml

In addition to the Web application's web.xml file, there's another web.xml file in the Tomcat conf directory. This web.xml, shown in seriously abbreviated form in Listing 3-4, contains default settings for all Web applications.

**Listing 3-4: The conf/web.xml File and its Default Web Application Settings**

```
<?xml version="1.0" encoding="ISO-8859-1"?>

<!DOCTYPE web-app
    PUBLIC "-//Sun Microsystems, Inc.//DTD Web Application 2.2//EN"
    "http://java.sun.com/j2ee/dtds/web-app_2.2.dtd">

<web-app>
    <servlet>
        <servlet-name>
            default
        </servlet-name>
        <servlet-class>
            org.apache.tomcat.servlets.DefaultServlet
        </servlet-class>
    <load-on-startup>
        -2147483646
    </load-on-startup>
    </servlet>
    <servlet>
        <servlet-name>
            invoker
        </servlet-name>
<!--
            org.apache.tomcat.servlets.NoInvokerServlet
-->
        <servlet-class>
            org.apache.tomcat.servlets.InvokerServlet
        </servlet-class>
    </servlet>
    <servlet>
        <servlet-name>
            jsp
        </servlet-name>
```

```
        <servlet-class>
            org.apache.jasper.runtime.JspServlet
        </servlet-class>

<!-- uncomment the following to use Jikes for JSP compilation

        <init-param>
            <param-name>jspCompilerPlugin</param-name>
            <param-
value>org.apache.jasper.compiler.JikesJavaCompiler</param-value>
        </init-param>

-->

    <load-on-startup>
            -2147483646
    </load-on-startup>
    </servlet>
    <servlet-mapping>
        <servlet-name>
            invoker
        </servlet-name>
        <url-pattern>
            /servlet/*
        </url-pattern>
    </servlet-mapping>
    <servlet-mapping>
        <servlet-name>
            jsp
        </servlet-name>
        <url-pattern>
            *.jsp
        </url-pattern>
    </servlet-mapping>
    <session-config>
        <session-timeout>
            30
        </session-timeout>
    </session-config>
    <mime-mapping>
        <extension>
            txt
```

*Continued*

Listing 3-4 *(Continued)*

```
        </extension>
        <mime-type>
            text/plain
        </mime-type>
    </mime-mapping>
    <!-- numerous other mime-mapping entries removed for brevity -->
</web-app>
```

The servlets listed in the default `web.xml` file are there to handle core Tomcat operations. In Tomcat 3.1, `DefaultServlet` served up static files, but that's now handled by a `RequestInterceptor`, as declared in `server.xml`.

`InvokerServlet` has a mapping of `/servlet/*`, and it's this servlet that receives all URLs that point to the `/servlet` directory rather than to an existing servlet mapping (such as `.snp` for `SnoopServlet`). In a similar vein, all requests ending in `.jsp` are sent to `JspServlet`, which can then sort out whether a JSP needs to be compiled, or whether there's an already compiled version that can be run.

## Configuring it out

It is easy to become overwhelmed by the sheer number of Tomcat configuration options. Options in `server.xml`, the default `web.xml`, and the `web.xml` apply to each separate Web site. Remember that you should be able to use Tomcat out of the box. Just drop a Web application WAR file into a directory under `webapps`, fire up Tomcat, and you should be able to run your code. If you don't have a WAR file, you can just copy the required files to a directory under `webapps`.

You set up servlet mappings or make other changes for individual Web applications in the web.xml file that is in the Web application's `WEB-INF` directory. You set Tomcat-wide options either in the `conf/server.xml` file or in the `conf/web.xml` file. Use `conf/server.xml` to configure servlet or request interceptors, and `conf/web.xml` to set defaults for application `web.xml` files.

At the top of `server.xml` you'll see this line:

`<xmlmapper:debug level="0" />`

This determines how much information Tomcat writes to the server log. If you're having problems getting Tomcat to run, or you just want to see what's really going on, change the level to a value like 9, restart, and watch the log.

# Summary

To run servlets and JSPs, you need a standalone servlet container or one that's integrated into a Web server. This book assumes you're using the Tomcat reference implementation from Apache. You also need the Java SDK. Key points to remember include:

◆ Servlet containers (formerly called servlet engines) are responsible for creating, invoking, and destroying servlets.

◆ Containers integrated with Web servers can be in process with the Web server for maximum speed, or out of process for maximum reliability and scalability.

◆ You can use either JDK 1.$x$ or a Java2 SDK with Tomcat 3.I, but Tomcat 4.$x$ requires Java2.

◆ After installing Java, and before running Tomcat, create, compile, and run a "Hello World" class to ensure that Java is correctly installed.

◆ To test Tomcat, run the startup script and browse `http://localhost:8080/index.html` to see the Tomcat home page.

◆ The `server.xml` file in the `conf` directory contains Tomcat's configuration settings, including context and request interceptors and any predefined Web applications.

◆ There are two `web.xml` files, one in the `conf` directory, containing default values, and one in each Web application's WEB-INF directory, containing per-application servlet mappings.

# Chapter 4

# Servlet Fundamentals

## IN THIS CHAPTER

- Understanding the servlet life cycle
- Exploring the `GenericServlet` base class
- Exploring the `HTTPServlet` base class, from which most servlets are derived
- Understanding HTTP requests
- Calling servlet methods based on the request type
- Understanding request attributes

CHAPTER 3 COVERS HOW to install and run Tomcat and run the sample servlets and JSPs. That chapter also mentions that a JSP ultimately becomes a servlet, so whether your starting point is a servlet or a JSP, the server has to go through the same sequence of events for each request. First, the server has to create a servlet instance if it doesn't already have one. Then it passes the request to the servlet, and finally it obtains the servlet's output, which is usually an HTML page, and sends that output back to the user. In this chapter we take a look at what's happening under the covers when a servlet runs.

## The Servlet Life Cycle

All servlets have a well-defined life cycle. They are born either when the servlet container is started, on the first request, or on the first request after a change is made to the servlet's class file. They live, handling requests, and they die – hopefully not horribly – on exceptions, in preparation for reloading by the servlet container, when the servlet container shuts down, or if for any other reason the container decides they've outlived their usefulness.

So that the servlet container can manage this life cycle, all servlets must implement three standard methods: `init`, `service`, and `destroy`. When a servlet is loaded, the container automatically calls the servlet's no-parameter `init` method. This method allows the servlet to do any setup work such as read initialization parameters or create objects with class scope for later use by other methods in the servlet.

57

Whenever the servlet container receives a request directed at a particular servlet (which can come from its associated Web server or, in the case of a standalone container, an HTTP request), it calls that servlet's `service` method, passing an object that encapsulates all of the information about the particular request. This object could be something as simple as a page or as complex as a form with many field/value pairs.

When the servlet container wants to kill off the servlet, it calls its `destroy` method. The servlet can use this opportunity to clean up after itself, close any database connections, and so forth.

# The GenericServlet Class

The simplest of all possible servlets is `GenericServlet`. It's also an abstract class, which means you can't implement it directly. The `GenericServlet` class has some `getter` methods to retrieve `init` parameters and servlet information. It can also write messages to a servlet log file using the `log` method.

The `GenericServlet`'s `service` method follows. This is an abstract method that doesn't do anything; instead, it serves as a template for any derived class to implement.

```
public abstract void service(ServletRequest req,
    ServletResponse res) throws ServletException, IOException;
```

Since the container calls the servlet's `service` method whenever it receives a servlet request, and since `GenericServlet` doesn't implement any code for this method, `GenericServlet` on its own doesn't implement any service-related functionality at all. In fact, very few servlet developers use `GenericServlet`. It only exists in case developers need to use a protocol other than HTTP. A base `GenericServlet` provides a common ancestry for all servlets, whatever their protocol.

You call a servlet the same way you obtain a Web page from a server; you use the HyperText Transfer Protocol (HTTP). HTTP requests to a server usually come in one of two forms: a `GET` request, to retrieve a page, or a `POST` request, in which the user sends information to the server (which normally results in a page being sent back as well).

If you want, you can write the code to handle these kinds of requests, but that would be masochistic; the code has already been written for you. Instead of extending `GenericServlet`, extend `HTTPServlet`.

# The HTTPServlet Class

In almost all cases, servlets should extend `HTTPServlet`, or a class that has `HTTPServlet` in its hierarchy. The `HTTPServlet` class is a subclass of `GenericServlet`, and adds HTTP-specific capabilities. To see how `HTTPServlet` operates, you need to know a bit about HTTP.

The World Wide Web Consortium, also known as W3C, administers HTTP. The HTTP pages are listed at www.w3.org/Protocols/.

When a client (typically a Web browser) makes a request for a page, it sends one or more lines of text, followed by an empty line. If you're familiar with the telnet program, you can test this by opening a connection to your Web server (usually on port 80, or on port 8080 if you are running Tomcat standalone), typing the following line, and pressing Enter twice:

```
GET /path/index.html HTTP/1.1
```

The first line of text contains the method name – this is one of those shown in the example that follows – which is an extract from HTTPServlet. Additional lines contain information such as the browser version, the client computer, and so forth.

```
private static final String METHOD_DELETE = "DELETE";
private static final String METHOD_HEAD = "HEAD";
private static final String METHOD_GET = "GET";
private static final String METHOD_OPTIONS = "OPTIONS";
private static final String METHOD_POST = "POST";
private static final String METHOD_PUT = "PUT";
private static final String METHOD_TRACE = "TRACE";
```

The most common methods are GET and POST, which can both be used to pass information to the server, usually with the result that a different page is returned to the user's browser. Whatever method the request specifies, it's the servlet's service method that is called.

## The service method

There are two service methods in HTTPServlet. One overrides the declaration in GenericServlet and casts the ServletRequest and ServletResponse objects received by the service method to HTTPServletRequest and HTTPServletResponse objects. It then passes these to the second form of the service method, which is shown in Listing 4-1.

Listing 4-1: The HTTPServlet.service() Method

```
protected void service(HttpServletRequest req,
    HttpServletResponse resp)
    throws ServletException, IOException{
    String method = req.getMethod();
```

*Continued*

Listing 4-1 *(Continued)*

```
    if (method.equals(METHOD_GET)) {
        long lastModified = getLastModified(req);
        if (lastModified == -1) {
        // servlet doesn't support if-modified-since, no reason
        // to go through further expensive logic
        doGet(req, resp);
        } else {
        long ifModifiedSince =
             req.getDateHeader(HEADER_IFMODSINCE);
        if (ifModifiedSince < (lastModified / 1000 * 1000)) {
            // If the servlet mod time is later, call doGet()
                    // Round down to the nearest
                    //  second for a proper compare
                    // A ifModifiedSince of -1 will
                    //  always be less
            maybeSetLastModified(resp, lastModified);
            doGet(req, resp);
        } else {
            resp.setStatus(HttpServletResponse.SC_NOT_MODIFIED);
        }
        }

    } else if (method.equals(METHOD_HEAD)) {
        long lastModified = getLastModified(req);
        maybeSetLastModified(resp, lastModified);
        doHead(req, resp);

    } else if (method.equals(METHOD_POST)) {
        doPost(req, resp);

    } else if (method.equals(METHOD_PUT)) {
        doPut(req, resp);

    } else if (method.equals(METHOD_DELETE)) {
        doDelete(req, resp);

    } else if (method.equals(METHOD_OPTIONS)) {
        doOptions(req,resp);

    } else if (method.equals(METHOD_TRACE)) {
        doTrace(req,resp);

    } else {
```

```
        //
        // Note that this means NO servlet supports whatever
        // method was requested, anywhere on this server.
        //

        String errMsg = lStrings.getString("http.method_not_ ↵
implemented");
        Object[] errArgs = new Object[1];
        errArgs[0] = method;
        errMsg = MessageFormat.format(errMsg, errArgs);

        resp.sendError(
          HttpServletResponse.SC_NOT_IMPLEMENTED, errMsg);
    }
    }
```

The HTTPServletRequest parameter is an interface, not a class, so any class that implements HTTPServletRequest can be passed by the servlet context. The HTTPServletRequest parameter, which extends ServletRequest, provides access through getter methods to any information the client might pass, as well as information pertaining to the servlet context. This information includes the HTTP method, HTTP headers, the user's session, any cookies, the local host, the remote host, and much more.

As you can see in Listing 4-1, the key aspect of the service method is its call to the request's getMethod method. The value returned determines the kind of request made by the client, which results in another method call. In most cases, this method call is either doPost or doGet, and that's where you end up writing most of your servlet code.

## The doGet() method

The HTTP GET method is the most common HTTP request and is used (along with HEAD) for page requests where no parameters are specified. A simple page request would look something like this:

```
GET /index.html
```

In a situation like this, there's no need for POST at all. When you begin to use forms, or want to pass parameters for other reasons, however, you do have the choice between GET and POST.

The GET method is the simpler of the two requests. You can encode parameters into the URL when you make the request, in a link, or by using a form. To test this encoding, use SnoopServlet, which is part of the Tomcat examples Web application.

As you'll recall, the examples Web application web.xml contains a mapping for SnoopServlet that passes any page request ending in .snp to this servlet. You can use this servlet to examine the result of your parameter-passing experiments. Try the following URL (assuming you're running Tomcat standalone on your local machine):

```
http://localhost:8080/examples/test.snp?param=TestParameter
```

The `SnoopServlet` servlet retrieves a great deal of information about the servlet request, including any parameters that were passed.

## Experimenting with forms

Most of the time, parameters are passed by means of HTML forms. Listing 4-2 shows a simple form that submits two values.

**Listing 4-2: An HTML Form Using the GET Method**

```
<html>
<head>
<title>A Sample Form</title>
</head>
<body>
<p>Please fill in the following information and click on Submit ↵
Name.</p>
<form action="/servlet/ch04.GetFormFields" method="GET">
  <dl>
    <dd>
      <table>
        <tr>
          <td>Name
          <td><input type="text" size="35"
                maxlength="256" name="Username">
        </tr>
        <tr>
          <td>Tel
          <td><input type="text" size="35"
                maxlength="256" name="UserTel">
        </tr>
      </table>
    </dd>
  </dl>
  <p><input type="submit" value="Submit Name">
    <input type="reset" value="Clear Form"></p>
</form>
</body>
</html>
```

Enter the HTML in Listing 4-2 into a text file and save it as GetPostTest.html in the examples subdirectory. Listing 4-3 shows a small class that you can use to test the results of your GET and POST experiments.

**Listing 4-3: The GetFormFields Servlet Displays Form Data**

```java
import java.io.IOException;
import java.io.PrintWriter;
import java.util.Enumeration;
import javax.servlet.*;
import javax.servlet.http.*;

package ch04;

public class GetFormFields extends HttpServlet {

    public void doGet(HttpServletRequest request,⏎
HttpServletResponse response)
        throws ServletException, IOException
    {
        PrintWriter out = response.getWriter();
        response.setContentType("text/plain");
        out.println("<html>");
        out.println("<body>");
        out.println("<head>");
        out.println("<Title>Get/Put Test</Title>");
        out.println("<P>HTTP Method: " + request.getMethod()
            + "</P>");
        out.println("<P>Parameters Passed:</P>");
        Enumeration e = request.getParameterNames();
        while (e.hasMoreElements()) {
            String key = (String)e.nextElement();
            String[] values = request.getParameterValues(key);
            out.print("<P>    " + key + " = ");
            for(int i = 0; i < values.length; i++) {
                out.print(values[i] + " ");
            }
            out.println("</P>");
        }
        out.println("</body>");
        out.println("</html>");
    }
    public void doPost(HttpServletRequest request,
                       HttpServletResponse response)
        throws IOException, ServletException
    {
```

*Continued*

Listing 4-3 *(Continued)*

```
        doGet(request, response);
    }
}
```

The `GetFormFields` servlet uses the `request.getMethod` call to determine if this method was a `GET` or a `POST` and retrieves a list of parameter names using `request.getParameterNames`. If you've installed the accompanying Web application, you can find `GetFormFields.class` in the `examples/WEB-INF/classes/ch04` directory.

The form tag for `GetPostTest.html` specifies the URL the browser will use to submit the results of the form, and since the form and the class are in the same Web application, simply specifying the `/servlet` directory, which is mapped to `WEB-INF/classes`, and the class name is enough to get the job done.

```
<form action="/servlet/GetFormFields" method="GET">
```

The form, in action, is shown in Figure 4-1.

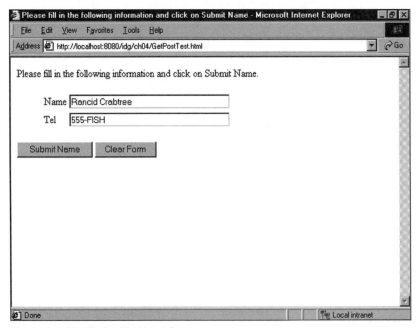

Figure 4-1: The GetPostTest.html form

When you complete the form by pressing the Submit Name button, the `GetFormFields` class returns the page shown in Figure 4-2.

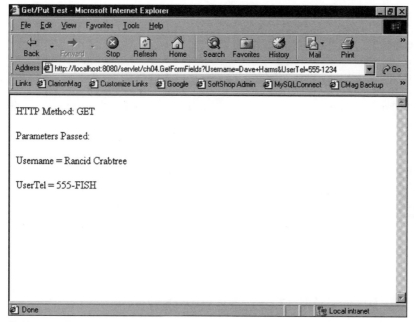

Figure 4-2: The results of the form submission, shown by the GetFormFields servlet

Figure 4-2 shows the HTTP method as GET, and the URL (confirmed by the servlet) is:

```
http://localhost:8080/servlet/ch04.GetFormFields?Username=Dave+Harms&
    UserTel=555-1234
```

A ? character separates the form data from the servlet and is arranged in field and value pairs, in the form:

```
field1=value1[+value2...]&field2=value1[+value2...] .
```

# The doPost() method

Suppose you go back to GetPostTest.html and change the form's method from GET to POST, as follows:

```
<form action="/servlet/GetFormFields" method="POST">
```

Now test the servlet again by bringing up the changed form and clicking on the Submit Name button. You won't notice any difference in the results, except that the URL for the servlet has changed. It is now:

```
http://localhost:8080/servlet/ch04.GetFormFields
```

The parameters have all disappeared because POST functions in quite a different way from GET. Instead of sending everything in one command line, POST first contacts the server, and then sends the parameters.

The GET method is limited to the maximum size of the command line and exposes the parameter string to the user's casual view. If you need to send large blocks of data, or don't want your user easily seeing what is sent, use POST. Otherwise, stick with GET. You can use GET, but remember that it's much more likely someone will either attempt to modify a GET request, or save it as a bookmark.

Even though the foregoing example demonstrated a POST request, I still coded the servlet to display the results of the request using the GET method. Since the only difference with POST is the mechanism for transmitting the form results, you often see POST requests simply handed off to the doGet() method.

## Infrequently used HTTP methods

And what about the other methods? Web servers do not generally permit the HTTP DELETE method, since you don't want just anyone deleting pages from your server! Tomcat implements DELETE as shown in Listing 4-4. For HTTP 1.1 requests, deleting pages is not allowed. For pre-HTTP 1.1 requests, the servlet returns a "bad request" error. You can, of course, override doDelete if you want to give your users the ability to delete pages.

Listing 4-4: The HTTPServlet.doDelete() Method

```
protected void doDelete(HttpServletRequest req,
    HttpServletResponse resp)
    throws ServletException, IOException {
      String protocol = req.getProtocol();
      String msg = lStrings.getString(
        "http.method_delete_not_supported");
      if (protocol.endsWith("1.1")) {
          resp.sendError(
            HttpServletResponse.SC_METHOD_NOT_ALLOWED, msg);
      } else {
          resp.sendError(HttpServletResponse.SC_BAD_REQUEST, msg);
      }
}
```

The HTTP HEAD method is used quite a lot when a client wants to just retrieve page header information. A browser usually uses HEAD to find out if the page has changed since the last time the browser requested the page; if not, the browser may display a cached copy of that page. The following example shows Tomcat's approach to HEAD requests, which is to create a NoBodyResponse object from response, and pass that to the doGet() method.

```
private void doHead(HttpServletRequest req,
   HttpServletResponse resp)
   throws ServletException, IOException {
     NoBodyResponse response = new NoBodyResponse(resp);
     doGet(req, response);
     response.setContentLength();
}
```

The OPTIONS method is a request for information about the communication options available either from the server, or from a resource specified in the OPTIONS request. Listing 4-5 shows Tomcat's approach to OPTIONS. First, the code obtains an array of methods in this and any parent classes. Then it defaults all methods except TRACE and OPTIONS to false. These methods are reset based on the names of the methods actually found in the object.

**Listing 4-5: The HTTPServlet.doOptions() Method**

```
protected void doOptions(HttpServletRequest req,
   HttpServletResponse resp)
   throws ServletException, IOException {
     Method[] methods = getAllDeclaredMethods(this.getClass());
     boolean ALLOW_GET = false;
     boolean ALLOW_HEAD = false;
     boolean ALLOW_POST = false;
     boolean ALLOW_PUT = false;
     boolean ALLOW_DELETE = false;
     boolean ALLOW_TRACE = true;
     boolean ALLOW_OPTIONS = true;
     for (int i = 0; i < methods.length; i++) {
         Method m = methods[i];
         if (m.getName().equals("doGet")) {
             ALLOW_GET = true;
             ALLOW_HEAD = true;
         }
         if (m.getName().equals("doPost"))
             ALLOW_POST = true;
         if (m.getName().equals("doPut"))
             ALLOW_PUT = true;
         if (m.getName().equals("doDelete"))
             ALLOW_DELETE = true;
     }
     String allow = null;
     if (ALLOW_GET)
```

*Continued*

Listing 4-5 *(Continued)*

```
            if (allow == null)
                allow = METHOD_GET;
    if (ALLOW_HEAD)
            if (allow == null)
                allow = METHOD_HEAD;
        else
                allow += ", " + METHOD_HEAD;
    if (ALLOW_POST)
            if (allow == null)
                allow = METHOD_POST;
        else
                allow += ", " + METHOD_POST;
    if (ALLOW_PUT)
            if (allow == null)
                allow = METHOD_PUT;
        else
                allow += ", " + METHOD_PUT;
    if (ALLOW_DELETE)
            if (allow == null)
                allow = METHOD_DELETE;
        else
                allow += ", " + METHOD_DELETE;
    if (ALLOW_TRACE)
            if (allow == null)
                allow = METHOD_TRACE;
        else
                allow += ", " + METHOD_TRACE;
    if (ALLOW_OPTIONS)
            if (allow == null)
                allow = METHOD_OPTIONS;
        else
                allow += ", " + METHOD_OPTIONS;
    resp.setHeader("Allow", allow);
}
```

Use the PUT method to update pages on a Web server. Again, this isn't something you want the general public to be able to do, and in Listing 4-6, you see that Tomcat's default approach is to disallow PUT just as it disallows DELETE.

### Listing 4-6: The HTTPServlet.doPut() Method

```
protected void doPut(HttpServletRequest req,
    HttpServletResponse resp)
    throws ServletException, IOException {
        String protocol = req.getProtocol();
```

```
String msg = lStrings.getString(
  "http.method_put_not_supported");
if (protocol.endsWith("1.1")) {
    resp.sendError(
      HttpServletResponse.SC_METHOD_NOT_ALLOWED, msg);
} else {
    resp.sendError(HttpServletResponse.SC_BAD_REQUEST, msg);
}
}
```

Tomcat handles the TRACE method according to the code in Listing 4-7. The TRACE method is just a loopback test, returning the requested URI and protocol, along with all of the header names and header elements. Since this request doesn't reveal anything new to the client, it's perfectly safe to do.

**Listing 4-7: The HTTPServlet.doTrace() Method**

```
protected void doTrace(HttpServletRequest req,
    HttpServletResponse resp)
    throws ServletException, IOException {
    int responseLength;
    String CRLF = "\r\n";
    String responseString = "TRACE "
        + req.getRequestURI() + " " + req.getProtocol();
    Enumeration reqHeaderEnum = req.getHeaderNames();
    while (reqHeaderEnum.hasMoreElements()) {
        String headerName = (String) reqHeaderEnum.nextElement();
        responseString += CRLF + headerName + ": "
            + req.getHeader(headerName);
    }
    responseString += CRLF;
    responseLength = responseString.length();
    resp.setContentType("message/http");
    resp.setContentLength(responseLength);
    ServletOutputStream out = resp.getOutputStream();
    out.print(responseString);
    out.close();
    return;
}
```

# What a Servlet Knows

Take a moment to look at the SnoopServlet sample servlet. Because SnoopServlet is, well, snoopy, it isn't something you want to leave available for the general public.

Depending on your setup, SnoopServlet could reveal database logon information or other security-related data.

If you haven't disabled SnoopServlet, you can run it using a URL such as http://localhost:8080/examples/test.snp, thanks to the web.xml mapping that translates any page request ending in SNP into a call to this servlet. Listing 4-8 shows the output from SnoopServlet on a Windows NT development machine, with Tomcat running under IBM's VisualAge for Java.

**Listing 4-8: The Information Retrieved by SnoopServlet**

```
Snoop Servlet

Servlet init parameters:

Context init parameters:

Context attributes:
   javax.servlet.context.tempdir =
      e:\IBMVJava\ide\project_resources\Apache
      Tomcat\.\work\localhost_8080%2Fexamples
   sun.servlet.workdir =
      e:\IBMVJava\ide\project_resources\Apache
      Tomcat\.\work\localhost_8080%2Fexamples


Request attributes:

Servlet Name: snoop
Protocol: HTTP/1.1

Scheme: http
Server Name: localhost
Server Port: 8080
Server Info: Tomcat Web Server/3.2 beta 2 (JSP 1.1; Servlet 2.2;
Java 1.1.7A; Windows NT 4.0 build 1381 Service Pack 5 x86;
java.vendor=IBM)
Remote Addr: 127.0.0.1
Remote Host: localhost
Character Encoding: null
Content Length: -1
Content Type: null
Locale: en_US
Default Response Buffer: 8192


Parameter names in this request:

Headers in this request:
```

```
Host: localhost:8080
Accept-Encoding: gzip, deflate
Cookie: JSESSIONID=q9ksi0ydv1
Accept: */*
Connection: Keep-Alive
User-Agent: Mozilla/4.0 (compatible; MSIE 5.5; Windows NT 4.0)
Accept-Language: en-us

Cookies in this request:
   JSESSIONID = q9ksi0ydv1

Request Is Secure: false
Auth Type: null
HTTP Method: GET
Remote User: null
Request URI: /examples/test.snp
Context Path: /examples
Servlet Path: /test.snp
Path Info: null
Path Trans: null
Query String: null

Requested Session Id: q9ksi0ydv1
Current Session Id: q9ksi0ydv1
Session Created Time: 967734566056
Session Last Accessed Time: 967734578884
Session Max Inactive Interval Seconds: 1800

Session values:
```

## Servlet initialization settings

The SnoopServlet servlet contains no meaningful servlet initialization parameters, but you can easily test this feature by adding some dummy parameters. In examples/WEB-INF/web.xml, look for this code:

```
<!--
      <init-param>
          <param-name>foo</param-name>
          <param-value>bar</param-value>
      </init-param>
-->
```

Uncomment the block in this example by removing the <!-- and --> comment delimiters. The settings in web.xml are read when Tomcat starts up, so you need to restart Tomcat to see the effect. Now when you run `SnoopServlet`, it reports the following:

```
Servlet init parameters:
    foo = bar
```

The servlet context's `getInitParameterNames` method retrieves this information as an enumeration. SnoopServlet then casts each element in the enumeration to a string, which corresponds to the name of the initialization parameter. The `SnoopServlet` servlet then passes this value to the servlet context's `getInitParameter` method, which retrieves the parameter's value.

In `SnoopServlet`, the point of the exercise is to print whatever parameters have been created. In a production servlet, you're probably not going to be that vague, and you know what parameters to expect. You also want to put this code in the servlet's `init` method, not in the `doGet` method. Your code is probably going to look more like this:

```
poolhandler.setDbName(getInitParameter("DbName"));
```

Here an object called `poolhandler` has one of its `setter` methods called with the value for the `DbName` parameter, as configured in the Web application's web.xml file. In this case, you don't need to call `getInitParameterNames` since you know the name of the attribute in which you're interested.

 **TIP**  Use servlet initialization parameters whenever the servlet contains information subject to change. It's far easier to make a slight modification to a text file than to locate, correct, compile, and deliver a Java class.

## Context initialization settings

If you have parameters you want available to all servlets in a Web application, you can set these in web.xml as context initialization parameters. An example, including the start of the web.xml file, follows.

```
<web-app>
    <context-param>
        <param-name>cfoo</param-name>
        <param-value>cbar</param-value>
    </context-param>
```

You can access these parameters in a similar manner to servlet initialization parameters, except you have to get the context first:

```
ServletContext context = getServletContext();
```

Now just call `context.getInitParameter`, passing in the name of the parameter you're after.

# Request Attributes

Web page requests can contain a lot of information, and generally more than you need to know about. This information includes the protocol, Web server name, port, the address and host name of the remote user, the character encoding used by the client browser, the length of any content accompanying the page request, the type of any accompanying content, the remote user's locale (for internationalization purposes), and more.

As I show in the `GetFormFields` servlet previously, you can use the request's `getParameterNames` and `getParameterValues` methods to retrieve form data posted to the servlet.

## Page compression

You have full access to the headers sent by the client browser. As Listing 4-8 shows, my browser accepts gzip and deflates encoded transmissions:

```
Accept-Encoding: gzip, deflate
```

If you're sending large, mainly text pages, compression can speed transmission considerably, yet you won't find a lot of Web sites compressing HTML pages. Images aren't generally affected, because most sites use compressed image formats. And compressing pages can be a hassle; if you compress on the fly, you increase the load on your server. If you compress ahead of time, you have to make sure you always keep your original pages and your compressed pages in sync. And remember that not everyone can handle the compressed format, so you do need both compressed and uncompressed pages.

## Cookies and session management

As Listing 4-8 shows, this browser is also returning a cookie:

```
Cookie: JSESSIONID=q9ksi0ydv1
```

The `SnoopServlet` servlet is showing a cookie because of this line of code in the `doGet` method:

```
HttpSession session = request.getSession();
```

That's all you need to place a cookie on the client's browser (assuming the client allows cookies). Cookies are the most common way of tracking a user through the various pages they may visit on the Web site.

For a simple Web site where you're just serving up Web pages, there isn't a lot of need for session tracking, unless you're particularly nosy and just want to see what the user is doing and when. In the good old days, you could probably accomplish this by tracking the IP address of the user, but it's quite possible for multiple users to be coming in on the same IP.

Session objects, whether associated with the user through the default cookie technique or by another means, are a generalized means of knowing which requests belong to which users. They really come into their own when you want to attach server-side information to individual users. The key methods here are `setAttribute`, `getAttribute`, and `removeAttribute`, which let you associate arbitrary objects with the user. In a shopping cart application, for example, a user might choose a forty-pound blue widget on one catalogue page, and a ratcheting reversible widget on a different page. Now the user heads for the checkout page. How can you be sure that the two widget orders are from the same person and that this is the person who has now arrived at the checkout?

The answer, if you're using session management, is to use `setAttribute` to associate a cart object with the user, and add the purchases to that cart object. A call to `request.getSession` at the checkout page returns this session object, from which you can obtain the cart and its contents.

## Detecting the browser

One of the biggest challenges facing Web developers is accommodating the wide variety of browsers extant on the Web. Not only is the official HTML specification evolving, with older browsers lacking support for newer features, but the speed at which the official specification evolves never seems to please the major browser vendors. The result is that some common features may not be part of the latest HTML specification and, if implemented on other browsers, may not be implemented consistently. And then there are just plain, old-fashioned bugs in HTML rendering engines, with older versions of Netscape being particularly notorious.

The result of all of this is that many Web sites version their content, providing different pages depending on the capabilities of the browser. Of course, you wouldn't want to have to ask a user which browser they're using. Fortunately, this information is contained in the header:

```
User-Agent: Mozilla/4.0 (compatible; MSIE 5.5; Windows NT 4.0)
```

## And all the other bits

You can retrieve a great many other morsels of information from a request object. These methods are all defined in the `HTTPServletRequest` interface and in the `Request` interface, which `HTTPServletRequest` extends.

**TIP** The Apache Turbine project (http://java.apache.org/turbine/index.html) has classes for automatic browser detection, along with a lot of other goodies.

# Summary

Servlets are the core technology for Java's Web strategy. Although the base class for servlets is GenericServlet, almost all servlets are derived from HTTPServlet, which implements the HTTP protocol. Key points to remember include:

◆ Servlets are created, initialized, and shut down by the servlet container.

◆ The servlet container calls the servlet's service method, passing in a request object and a response object.

◆ Most page requests are made with a GET request, and in HTTPServlet this request results in a call to the doGet method.

◆ A GET request passes parameters in the URL, so for long parameter values you want to use the POST method and either process the request in the doPut method or have doPut call doGet.

◆ Servlets have access to a wide variety of information through the request object, and the request's servlet context, including all HTTP headers, session data, cookies, and the like.

# Chapter 5

# Introducing JavaServer Pages

## IN THIS CHAPTER

◆ Understanding the JavaServer Pages solution

◆ Separating presentation and programming logic

◆ Including pages inside a JSP

◆ Understanding JSP actions

◆ Working with implicit JSP objects

◆ Understanding the JSP life cycle

◆ Determining the best place for your code

SERVLETS ARE AN EXCELLENT way to solve many server-side programming problems, but they're only one piece of the puzzle. If you decide to build an entire Web site using only servlets, you'll inevitably find yourself writing a lot of `println` statements to create HTML code. And that isn't a particularly brilliant thing to do, because the only way you can see the results is to run the servlet. The best WYSIWYG HTML editor in the world won't do you a lot of good in this scenario.

To get maximum productivity and flexibility out of your Web-design process, chances are you'll need a tool that enables you to visually design pages that include server-side Java code. There are several such tools available, and the best known is Sun Microsystems' JavaServer Page (JSP) technology.

## The JavaServer Pages Solution

Most of the time, writing server-side Java code and designing great Web pages are two separate disciplines and handled by two different people or groups of people. The challenge is to find a way to separate the presentation of the Web site, that is, the visual design, from the programming logic that determines how dynamic information arrives on the page. JavaServer Pages (JSP) are Sun's answer to that challenge.

77

JSPs are, in essence, HTML files with the extension JSP, which also contain special JSP tags. To deliver a JSP to a user your Web server must use or implement a JSP container, such as Tomcat. The JSP container reads the JSP and uses it as a template to create and compile a servlet (ah, back to servlets again!). The JSP container then invokes the temporary servlet, which creates the Web page that is sent back to the user. As with servlets, JSPs have both a request and a response, and similarly have access to all of the request and context/Web application data.

## Separating presentation and programming logic

Although JSPs end up as servlets, they start out as something much more like HTML, so they are easier to create with visual design tools. A Web designer can create the look and feel of the page without having to know programming, beyond the use of a few JSP tags or script elements. Meanwhile, the Java developer(s) can work out the code needed to support the Web page's dynamic portion without needing to know much about the Web page's graphics or layout. In reality these two disciplines often overlap, but the goal should be to avoid requiring Web designers to understand Java code and keep the Java coders from having to create HTML.

## Tag formats

As with HTML, all JSP code is contained within tags. JSP tags, however, are based on XML syntax, which is much more strictly enforced than HTML syntax. In HTML, tags do not necessarily have to be paired. To separate three paragraphs of text, you can enclose each paragraph in `<P>` and `</P>` tags, or you can just start each paragraph with `<P>` and omit the closing `</P>`. Both JSP and XML enforce closing tags, although you can combine both tags into a single line, as this example shows:

```
<TAG various parameters to the tag />
```

 Unlike HTML, JSP tags are case sensitive, and quote marks, where specified, are not optional as they are in HTML.

## Templates, directives, and actions

The template is the static HTML portion of a JSP, and when the servlet container compiles the JSP into a servlet, that servlet simply passes the HTML through to the response. The rest of the JSP code is made up of either directives or actions. Listing 5-1 shows a simple JSP.

**Listing 5-1: The basic.jsp Page That Displays the HTTP Request Method**

```
<html>
<head>
<title>A Simple JSP</title>
</head>
<body>
<%@ page language="java"%>
<P>The date and time: <%= new java.util.Date() %></P>
</body>
</html>
```

The `<%@ page language="java"%>` tag is a directive, which is an instruction to the servlet/JSP container about how to handle the JSP. The next tag is an element, and executes whenever a user requests the page:

```
<%= new java.util.Date() %>
```

If you call `basic.jsp` from the browser like this

```
http://localhost:8080/idg/ch05/basic.jsp
```

you see the current date and time displayed. Note also that each time you refresh the page, the time changes. This change happens because the container has compiled the JSP into a servlet, which is executing each time you refresh. Look in the Tomcat work directory for another directory related to the Web application name, and you find temporary JAVA and CLASS files. Listing 5-2 shows the source for the servlet automatically created from the JSP shown in listing 5-1.

**Listing 5-2: Automatically Generated Servlet Source for basic.jsp**

```
import javax.servlet.*;
import javax.servlet.http.*;
import javax.servlet.jsp.*;
import javax.servlet.jsp.tagext.*;
import java.io.PrintWriter;
import java.io.IOException;
import java.io.FileInputStream;
import java.io.ObjectInputStream;
import java.util.Vector;
import org.apache.jasper.runtime.*;
import java.beans.*;
import org.apache.jasper.JasperException;
```

*Continued*

**Listing 5-2** *(Continued)*

```
public class _0002fch_00030_00035_0002fbasic_0002ejsp_
0002fch05_0002fbasic_jsp_3 extends HttpJspBase {


    static {
    }
    public _0002fch_00030_00035_0002fbasic_0002ejsp_
0002fch05_0002fbasic_jsp_3( ) {
    }

    private static boolean _jspx_inited = false;

    public final void _jspx_init() throws JasperException {
    }

    public void _jspService(HttpServletRequest request,
        HttpServletResponse  response)
        throws IOException, ServletException {

        JspFactory _jspxFactory = null;
        PageContext pageContext = null;
        HttpSession session = null;
        ServletContext application = null;
        ServletConfig config = null;
        JspWriter out = null;
        Object page = this;
        String  _value = null;
        try {

            if (_jspx_inited == false) {
                _jspx_init();
                _jspx_inited = true;
            }
            _jspxFactory = JspFactory.getDefaultFactory();
            response.setContentType("text/html;charset=8859_1");
            pageContext = _jspxFactory.getPageContext(this, request, response,
                "", true, 8192, true);

            application = pageContext.getServletContext();
            config = pageContext.getServletConfig();
            session = pageContext.getSession();
            out = pageContext.getOut();

                out.write("<html>\r\n\r\n<head>\r\n<title>
                  A simple JSP</title>\r\n</head>\r\n\r\n<body>\r\n");
```

```
                    out.write("\r\n<P>The date and time: ");
                    out.print( new java.util.Date() );
                    out.write("</P>\r\n\r\n</body>\r\n\r\n</html>\r\n");

          } catch (Exception ex) {
             if (out.getBufferSize() != 0)
                out.clearBuffer();
             pageContext.handlePageException(ex);
          } finally {
             out.flush();
             _jspxFactory.releasePageContext(pageContext);
          }
     }
}
```

Now, aren't you glad you don't have to write that code by hand? And this is just a tiny JSP.

# Directives

Directives are instructions to the JSP container, and do not themselves create any page output, although they may certainly influence the final result. Directives have the syntax:

```
<%@ directive {attr="value"}%>
```

## The page directive

In Listing 5-1 you can see a page directive just after the <body> tag:

```
<%@ page language="java"%>
```

The language attribute tells the JSP container which language it should use to interpret scripts embedded in the page. Other page attributes are shown in Table 5-1.

---

TABLE 5-1 **ADDITIONAL PAGE DIRECTIVES**

---

| Directive | Description |
| --- | --- |
| extends="classname" | Specifies a different parent class for the JSP page. Not generally used. |

*Continued*

---

TABLE 5-1  ADDITIONAL PAGE DIRECTIVES *(Continued)*

| Directive | Description |
|---|---|
| `import="importlist"` | Provides a list of packages to import. By default, `java.lang.*`, `javax.servlet.*`, `javax.servlet.jsp.*`, and `javax.servlet.http.*` are all imported. |
| `session="true\|false"` | If true, the page has access to the implicit `session` variable, which references the page's current session. The default is `true`. |
| `buffer="none\|sizekb"` | Specifies the size of the output buffer. The default value is 8K, and when the buffer is full, the JSP either writes the output or raises an exception, depending on the `autoFlush` setting. |
| `autoFlush="True\|False"` | Determines whether the JSP automatically flushes the buffer when full, or raises an exception. The default is `true`. |
| `isThreadSafe="true\|false"` | Indicates if the servlet container should consider this page thread-safe. If `true`, then the container may deliver new requests to the page before existing requests have completed. It's still up to the developer to make sure that access to any shared objects (anything with page or larger scope) is synchronized. If this attribute is set to `false`, then requests to this page will be serialized, which may have performance implications. The default is `true`. |
| `info="info_text"` | Places a string, which you can retrieve by the `Servlet.getServletInfo` method. |
| `errorPage="error_url"` | If an uncaught exception occurs on this page, the container will forward to the page named here. |
| `isErrorPage="true\|false"` | If `true`, the exception implicit variable is made available to the page. The default is `false`. |
| `contentType="ctinfo"` | Defines the character encoding for the page. The default is text/html, with ISO-8859-1 character encoding. To change the value, specify TYPE or TYPE;charset=CHARSET with an optional space between the ; and the word charset. |

## The include directive

The `include` directive inserts a text file into the JSP at page translation time. The syntax of the directive is as follows:

```
<%@ include file="relativeURLspec" %>
```

The included file can contain text or code. Includes are useful for stock text such as copyright notices, navigation bars, or other headers and footers. You can nest `include` directives, which means that an included file can have its own `include` statements.

 Although any changes to a JSP with an `include` directive causes the servlet container to recompile that JSP, the container will not automatically compile any pages it includes.

## The taglib directive

The `taglib` directive tells the JSP container to evaluate tags with the specified prefix using the named `uutag` library. The syntax of the directive is:

```
<%@ taglib uri="tagLibraryURI" prefix="tagPrefix" %>
```

I'll have more to say about tag libraries in the next chapter. In short, they are a mechanism you can use to allow page designers to implement custom Java functionality in a page without having to learn Java. All the page designer needs is the definition of your tags, a tag library, and the custom JavaBeans your tag library uses.

# JSP Actions

Anything in a JSP that is not a directive is an action, and actions are dependent on the scripting language that the JSP is using. In JSP 1.1 the only officially supported language is Java. (You can find support for other languages elsewhere; Allair's JRun, for instance, supports JavaScript.) Actions can be in the form of tags, or they can be in the form of scriptlets, which are (in JSP 1.1) blocks of Java code. Tags have the following syntax:

```
<sometag attribute="some value" ...>
body
</sometag>
```

or if there is no body, just:

```
<sometag attribute="some value" .../>
```

Scriptlets have the basic syntax:

```
<% scriptlet source %>
```

or

```
<%= scriptlet source %>
```

In the latter example, the result of whatever output results from the scriptlet source is placed at that location in the JSP. What actually happens is the code is wrapped in a `println` statement in the resulting servlet.

 Scriptlets can extend over multiple lines, and because they're Java code, they conform to standard Java syntax rules.

To better illustrate how all of these aspects fit together, let's look at another concept: the implicit JSP object.

## Implicit JSP objects

All JSPs have certain objects available throughout the page. These implicit objects provide access to all aspects of the page, such as the request, response, page context, and so forth. All of these objects have a scope, which means they're visible only to certain objects and/or at certain times.

♦ Anything with page scope is only visible to code on that same page; you retrieve a page scope object using the `javax.servlet.jsp.PageContext.getAttribute` method. Once the page's request is completed, the servlet container discards the object's reference.

♦ An object with request scope is available via the page's `ServletRequest.getAttribute` method; once the request is completed, the servlet container discards the reference to this object.

♦ An object with session scope is associated with a user session; you retrieve such an object with the `HTTPSession.getAttribute`, and you get the session itself from the request object with the `getSession` method.

♦ An object with application scope is associated with the JSP's servlet context; you retrieve such an object with the `getAttribute` method.

Table 5-2 shows the implicit objects available in JSPs.

**TABLE 5-2 JSP IMPLICIT OBJECTS**

| Name | Scope | Description |
| --- | --- | --- |
| request | request | A ServletRequest object. |
| response | page | A ServletResponse object. |
| pageContext | page | The page's context — a wrapper class that insulates the JSP from the specifics of any given JSP implementation. The pageContext also provides a number of utility methods for retrieving implicit objects easily, including getOut, getException, getPage, getResponse, getRequest, getSession, getServletConfig, and getServletContext. |
| session | session | An HTTPSession object, if one has been created for this session. |
| application | application | The servlet context, which corresponds to the Web application. |
| out | page | The object to use to write output. |
| config | page | The ServletConfig object passed to the JSP. |
| page | page | An object reference to the compiled version of this page. When the page language is Java, page is a synonym for this. |

# Scriptlets

Scriptlets are units of code, normally Java, that execute in the context of the page. Listing 5-3 shows a JSP that displays the current date in default format.

**Listing 5-3: A JSP Containing a Java Scriptlet to Display the Current Date**

```
<html>
<head>
<title>Date Example</title>
</head>
<body>
```

*Continued*

**Listing 5-3** *(Continued)*

```
<%@ page language="java"%>
<P>Today's date: <%= java.text.DateFormat.getDateInstance().format(
    new java.util.Date()) %></P>
</body>
</html>
```

Listing 5-4 uses the `DateFormat` utility class to format the new `java.util.Date` object. If you just have a line or two of code, you may just want to use fully qualified class names as in the example. But if you have more than a few lines of code, using the page import directive relieves you of some typing. In Listing 5-3 I've used page import, and so I don't need to fully qualify the class names.

**Listing 5-4: Using the Page Import Directive**

```
<html>
<head>
<title>Date Example</title>
</head>
<body>
<%@ page language="java" %>
<%@ page import="java.util.*" %>
<%@ page import="java.text.*" %>
<P>Today's date: <%= DateFormat.getDateInstance().format(new ⏎
Date()) %></P>
</body>
</html>
```

 If you do find yourself writing a lot of Java code in a JSP, you may want to reconsider your strategy. JSPs are there to help in the separation of presentation and programming logic; the more code you incorporate into the JSP, the more difficult you make this task. Extensive scriptlets should be replaced with JavaBeans (discussed later in this chapter) and custom tag libraries (discussed in the next chapter).

You can, of course, use implicit objects in scriptlets as well, and one of the most used is the request object. Listing 5-5 shows a JSP containing an HTML form with a `GET` method. Because no action is specified, the browser will post the form results back to this same page, with the name parameter containing the value the user types. You can then retrieve this value from the request object.

**Listing 5-5: A JSP That Displays Text Conditionally**

```
<html>
<head>
```

```
<title>Implicit Variable Example</title>
</head>
<body>
<form method=get>
<table width="336">
<% String nameParam = request.getParameter("name");
if (nameParam != null && nameParam != "") { %>
<tr><td valign="top">
Last time you typed:
<td valign="top">
<%= nameParam %>
</tr>
<% } %>
<tr>
<td valign="top">
<P align="left">Type anything you like:  </P>
<P align="center">  </P>
<td valign="top">
 <input type="text" name="name" size="80">
</tr>
  <tr>
<td colspan="2">
<p align="center"><input type="Submit" value="submit">
</tr>
</table>
</form>
</body>
```

Not only does the JSP retrieve the name value with the `request.getParameter("name")` method call, it also conditionally includes the HTML following the call based on the name parameter it gets. This code is a lot easier to understand if you remember that the servlet container is compiling the JSP into a servlet with `out.write` statements for each block of static HTML. In a JSP, the tag delimiters (`<%` and `%>`) mark the Java code; the servlet container removes the tags when it compiles the JSP and wraps the remaining HTML code in `print` statements. As long as the Java code is good, the container will be able to compile the JSP.

## Declaring data

Because scriptlets are Java code, you can use them to declare data, just as you would in a Java class, as follows:

```
<% int counter=0; %>
```

You can now use this variable in other scriptlets on this page. Now take a look at the code in Listing 5-6.

**Listing 5-6: A JSP That Uses a Counter Variable**

```
<html>
<head>
<title>Experimenting with variables</title>
</head>
<body>
<%@ page language="java"%>
<% int counter=0; %>
<% counter ++; %>
<P>The counter is <%= counter %>.</P>
<% counter ++; %>
<P>The counter is <%= counter %>.</P>
<% counter ++; %>
<P>The counter is <%= counter %>.</P>
</body>
</html>
```

As you might expect, this page produces the following output.

```
The counter is 1.
The counter is 2.
The counter is 3.
```

If you refresh the page, you get exactly the same results each time. The counter begins at 1. Now take a look at Listing 5-7.

**Listing 5-7: A JSP That Implements a Page Counter**

```
<html>
<head>
<title>Experimenting with variables</title>
</head>
<body>
<%@ page language="java"%>
<%! int counter=0; %>
<% counter ++; %>
<P>This page has been viewed <%= counter %> times.</P>
</body>
</html>
```

When you run the JSP in Listing 5-7, something quite different happens. Each time you refresh this page, counter increments.

In Listing 5-6, I declared counter like this:

```
<% int counter=0; %>
```

In Listing 5-7, I declared `counter` with a ! character following the `<%`:

```
<%! int counter=0; %>
```

The extra ! makes all the difference in how the servlet container declares `counter` in the resulting servlet.

## Local and instance data

Without the !, `counter` is a local variable in the JSP servlet's `_jspservice` method. In the source for the servlet that the container creates from the JSP, you'll see the container has declared `counter` at the point in the code corresponding to the declaration's location in the JSP. With the !, the container declares `counter` as a class, or instance, variable. As an instance variable, `counter` has a different scope than it does as a local variable.

Each time the user requests the page, the servlet container calls the `_jspservice` method, and each method call gets its own copy of any variables declared in that method. Any variables declared as class variables are, in servlet parlance, instance variables. Remember that to conserve resources, a servlet container only creates one instance of any servlet name per Web application, so there's really just one JSP object for this page, and all the requests call the method associated with that object.

The bottom line is that if you want to share a variable among all instances of a particular JSP, declare that variable using the `<%! type label %>` syntax. But keep in mind that with concurrent calls to the JSP's `_jspservice` method, you may need to synchronize access to the variable.

## Declaring methods

You can declare methods as well as variables in a JSP. This makes perfect sense since the servlet container is going to translate the JSP into a servlet. Listing 5-8 shows a JSP that declares and uses a random number method.

**Listing 5-8: Using a Declared Method in a JSP**

```
<html>
<head>
<title>Declaring methods</title>
</head>
<body>
<%@ page language="java"%>
<%@ page import="java.util.Random" %>
<%! Random rand = new Random(); %>
<%! public double getRandomNumber() {
    return(rand.nextDouble() * 10000);
    } %>
<P>Here's a random number: <%=getRandomNumber() %></P>
```

*Continued*

Listing 5-8 *(Continued)*

```
<P>And another: <%=getRandomNumber() %></P>
<P>And one more: <%=getRandomNumber() %></P>

</body>
</html>
```

Because the Random instance, rand, must be visible anywhere in the class, you declare it as an instance variable. This declaration also ensures that the servlet won't reset the random numbers each time a user requests the page!

# The JSP Life Cycle

You've seen how the servlet container calls the _jspservice method whenever a user requests the JSP. There are two other methods you may find useful. Since JSPs are ultimately servlets, you might expect them to have a similar life cycle to regular servlets, and you'd be right. JSPs have initialization and destruction methods too, and you can put your own code in them by declaring the jspInit() and jspDestroy() methods, as shown in Listing 5-9.

Listing 5-9: A JSP with the jspInit() and jspDestroy() Methods

```
<html>
<head>
<title>Creating/Destroying A JSP</title>
</head>
<body>
<%@ page language="java"%>
<%! public void jspInit () {
    // Init code goes here
  } %>
<%! public void jspDestroy () {
    // Destroy code goes here
  } %>
<P>Look in the tomcat logs for the init/destroy messages.</P>
</body>
</html>
```

# Which Code Goes Where?

A lot more can be done with scriptlets, but before you start filling your JSPs up with embedded Java, ask yourself: is this really the best place to put my code? Remember that the problem Sun intended to solve with JSPs is that Web page designers have different skills, needs, and goals than do Web coders. JSPs are supposed to allow you to separate the business logic from the presentation of the business data.

If you fill up your JSPs with Java code, you're going to make it more difficult for a non-coder to make changes to the visual part of the JSP. Some Java code is going to have to make an appearance, but you want to keep its presence to an absolute minimum.

Even if you're the only person maintaining the JSP, and you're as comfortable with HTML as you are with Java, you've traded in your development environment for a JSP, which includes all sorts of things you really don't need to see when you're writing and debugging the Java code. Any way you look at it, the more Java scriptlets you add to a page, the greater the development and maintenance headaches.

Now, just because JSPs don't enforce a clean separation of logic and content doesn't mean they don't support such a development model. You really can have your Java mocha cake and eat it too.

What you need is the JSP tag-handling mechanism, which comes in two varieties. The original tag mechanism lets you move your Java code outside the page to classes called JavaBeans. That's adequate when you want to update bean properties and include bean output in pages. If you want a higher level of interaction between your Java code and the page, you can create custom tag libraries, which provide some significant advantages over simple bean handling. These techniques are the subject of the next chapter.

# Summary

JavaServer Pages enable you to keep the programming part of a Web application separate from the presentation part. Key points to remember include:

◆ JSPs are made up of template code, which gets passed through to the resulting page, and special instructions contained in tags.

◆ JSP code is made up of directives, which instruct the JSP container to do something, and actions, which the servlet container translates into Java code.

◆ The servlet container compiles the JSP into a servlet, and the servlet returns content (typically HTML) to the user.

◆ JSPs have access to several implicit objects such as the page context, which is the equivalent to a servlet context.

◆ Scriptlets are blocks of Java code that you can embed in the JSP, and that the servlet container inserts into the JSP's servlet code.

◆ You can declare data in a JSP and, depending on how you declare that data, you can share it between calls to a given page.

# Chapter 6

# JSPs, Beans, and Custom Tags

IN THIS CHAPTER

◆ Understanding the bean solution

◆ Loading JavaBeans and setting and getting properties

◆ Understanding the JavaBeans component model

◆ Knowing when to use JavaBeans and when to consider Enterprise JavaBeans

◆ Extending JSP tag capabilities with custom tag libraries

THE PREVIOUS CHAPTER discussed how to embed Java code in a JavaServer Page by using Java scriptlets. These Java code scriptlets become part of the servlet created when the servlet container compiles a JSP.

As powerful and useful as scriptlets are, there's something inherently dangerous about them. The more Java code you embed in your JSPs, the more often you, the Java developer, have to wrestle the page designer for access to the page. It's also much more difficult to read Java code when it's mixed in with HTML.

There are two ways you can keep your Java code separate from the JSP: one is to use JavaBeans, and the other is to use custom tags. In both approaches you use script statements to interact with your own Java classes.

## The Bean Solution

Since Java scriptlet code executes on the server, it's generally possible to put this code into its own class and call that class when necessary. For a class to be used this way, it has to conform to the standards established for JavaBeans, Java's component architecture. JavaBeans can be very simple. Listing 6-1 shows a small bean (okay, a jellybean) with one property.

Listing 6-1: The JellyBean Class

```
public class JellyBean {
    private String color;

    public JellyBean() {
    }
    public String getColor() {
        return color;
    }
    public void setColor(String newColor) {
        color = newColor;
    }
}
```

Although the JavaBean specification is extensive, for the purposes of servlet and JSP development only a few points are important:

◆ JavaBeans should not have any public properties. JellyBean's one property, its color, is marked `private` and, therefore, is only visible to this class; you could also give it the `protected` attribute, making the property visible to derived classes.

◆ Any of a JavaBean's properties that do need to be exposed should have getter and setter methods, as necessary. These properties have the form `getVariableName` and `setVariableName`.

◆ All JavaBeans must have a no-argument constructor method.

The first two points are good habits to get into in any case. In particular, the use of setter methods lets you control what values the caller can assign to the variable, which reduces the likelihood of bugs cropping up when someone sets a variable to a value you never anticipated. The no-argument constructor is a concession to the container, such as Tomcat, which will be creating the bean. The container shouldn't need to know anything about your bean ahead of time, but it still needs a way to invoke any needed initialization code. Now you know where to put that code.

# Using a JavaBean in a JSP

Once you've created your JavaBean, you'll want to use it in a JSP. The JSP specification defines three tags: one tag to locate or create a JavaBean in the specified scope, another tag to set a property on any JavaBean, and finally a tag to obtain a property from a JavaBean.

# Loading a JavaBean

The jsp:useBean tag has the following syntax:

```
<jsp:useBean id="name"
  scope="page|request|session|application" typeSpec />
```

The typeSpec can have several forms, but the most common is simply class="classname". For example, you can instantiate the JellyBean this way:

```
<jsp:useBean id="jb" scope="application"
  class="ch05.JellyBean" />
```

The id is the label you give the bean in your application, and it's how you refer to the bean within the page from this point forward. The scope attribute determines what object with which you're associating the bean. When you use the jsp:useBean tag, the compiled code first looks for an instance of it in the specified scope:

```
pageContext.getAttribute("jb",PageContext.REQUEST_SCOPE);
```

If the bean doesn't exist in the desired scope, the JSP creates an instance and adds it to that scope. If you don't specify a scope for the bean, it defaults to page, which is the most limited scope. Any bean referenced this way is visible only to code on this page.

A bean that has request scope associates the bean with the request that the servlet container passes to the JSP. If you forward to or include another page, that page receives the current request object as well as references to any beans associated with that request. Session scope associates beans with the current user session, which can be a useful way to link information with all the pages a user views over a specified period of time. And application scope makes the beans visible to all pages in this Web application.

# Setting a JavaBean property

Once you have the bean in hand, you can set its properties using the jsp:setProperty tag. You can use this tag several ways, including the following:

```
<jsp:setProperty name="beanName" property="propertyName"
  param="parameterName"/>
<jsp:setProperty name="beanName" property="propertyName"
  value="propertyValue"/>
```

To use setProperty with a parameter/value pair passed to a page using a GET or POST method, use the param="parameterName" form, specifying the name of the parameter whose value you want to pass to the bean. Without this shorthand method, you need to retrieve the parameter's value before storing it using the second form of `setProperty`.

Since storing data passed to a form is a common requirement, JSPs provide another, even faster way of setting properties:

```
<jsp:setProperty name="beanName" property="*">
```

The * character tells the `setProperty` method to match all request parameters with bean setter methods and pass the values across.

For automatic property setting to work, your method names need to adhere to some coding standards, since normally the variable names and the setter methods are different. Variables begin with a lowercase character, but you must capitalize the first character of the variable name in the set method. For example, if the variable is `beanTaste`, the servlet container will assume the setter is called `setBeanTaste`. If at least the first two letters of the variable name are uppercase, the servlet container assumes the setter method to be `get` with the exact name of the variable appended to it.

Listing 6-2 shows `setbeancolor.jsp`, which uses the `JellyBean` bean in session scope. It also contains a form that enables the user to choose a color for the bean. When the user clicks on the submit button, the browser posts this color back to the same page, where it assigns the new color to the bean. This isn't a completely useless function; as you'll see momentarily, another page can access this same bean and read the information set on this page.

**Listing 6-2: Setting a Bean Attribute for Access from Other Pages**

```
<html>
<head>
<title>Java Bean Setter Example</title>
</head>
<%@ page language="java"%>
<jsp:useBean id="jb" scope="session" class="ch05.JellyBean" />
<jsp:setProperty name="jb" property="color" param="newColor"/>
<body>
<form method=get>
<table width="336">
<tr><td valign="top">
The color has been set to:
<td valign="top">
<jsp:getProperty name="jb" property="color"/>
```

```
</tr>
<tr>
<td valign="top">
<P align="left">Choose a color: </P>
<P align="center">  </P>
<td valign="top">
 <input type="radio" value="Red" checked name="newColor">
Red <br>
 <input type="radio" value="Green" checked name="newColor">
Green <br>
 <input type="radio" value="Blue" checked name="newColor">
Blue
</tr>
  <tr>
<td colspan="2">
<p align="center"><input type="Submit" value="submit">
</tr>
</table>
</form>
</body>
```

Parameters passed to a page can have multiple values. The Checkbox example in the Tomcat demonstration Web application has multiple check boxes with the same value. The following shows the HTML check boxes with a common name.

```
<input TYPE=checkbox name=fruit VALUE=apples> Apples <BR>
<input TYPE=checkbox name=fruit VALUE=grapes> Grapes <BR>
<input TYPE=checkbox name=fruit VALUE=oranges> Oranges <BR>
<input TYPE=checkbox name=fruit VALUE=melons> Melons <BR>
```

Because all the check boxes have the same name attribute, the form data the browser sends back to the server will have just one parameter, but with multiple values possible. The jsp:setProperty tag handles this situation using the same syntax as for single values:

```
<jsp:setProperty name="foo" property="fruit" param="fruit" />
```

Because setProperty is now passing an array of strings, the CheckTest bean that receives the property via its setFruit method must declare the parameter as a String array, as shown in Listing 6-3.

### Listing 6-3: The CheckTest Bean

```
package checkbox;

public class CheckTest {
```

*Continued*

Listing 6-3 *(Continued)*

```
    String b[] = new String[] { "1", "2", "3", "4" };
    public String[] getFruit() {
     return b;
     }
    public void setFruit(String [] b) {
     this.b = b;
     }
}
```

# Getting a JavaBean property

To get a property from a JavaBean you use the getProperty method. This method has a much simpler syntax than setProperty:

```
<jsp:getProperty name="name" property="propertyName" />
```

Listing 6-4 shows the source for getbeancolor.jsp, which uses the getProperty tag to retrieve a bean property set by setbeancolor.jsp.

Listing 6-4: Reading a Bean Property Set by setbeancolor.jsp

```
<html>
<head>
<title>JavaBean Example</title>
</head>
<%@ page language="java"%>
<jsp:useBean id="jb" scope="session" class="ch05.JellyBean" />
<body>
<form method=get>
<table width="336">
<tr><td valign="top">
Another page has set the JellyBean color to:
<td valign="top">
<jsp:getProperty name="jb" property="color"/>
</tr>
  <tr>
<td colspan="2">
<p align="center"><input type="Submit"
  value="Get the bean color" name="submit">
</tr>
</table>
</form>
</body>
```

The bean is sharable between both pages provided the pages are in the same Web application, the same user is accessing both pages, and you're using some form of session tracking. If you look in the generated source for either JSP you see a call to the getSession method.

```
session = pageContext.getSession();
```

By default, Tomcat uses cookies for session tracking, so whenever the user requests one of these pages, the servlet looks for a cookie sent along with the page request. If the server doesn't find a cookie in the request, it adds a cookie to the response. Subsequent requests from the user will contain the cookie, provided the user isn't filtering cookies!

As you can probably guess, if this example doesn't work, then chances are you have cookies disabled in your Web browser. You can still experiment with shared beans by setting the scope to application, but if you do so all requests from all users for pages in this Web application have access to the same bean instance.

# The JavaBeans Component Model

JavaBeans fit nicely into a JSP-based development environment, but really they're part of a much larger concept: component-based development. The idea of functional, discreet units of code is an old one, certainly predating object-oriented development. Component-based development really took off with early versions of Microsoft's Visual Basic, which were able to use VBXs, the predecessor of today's ActiveX technology.

In a component-based development model each unit of code (typically a class) is both self-contained and reusable. You can then connect these components to each other to accomplish desired functionality. In most cases, components have a visual component. In fact, the JavaBeans specification provides this definition:

"A JavaBean is a reusable software component that can be manipulated visually in a builder tool."

This definition doesn't seem to apply to the JellyBean example, but if you read a little further in the specification you find that "invisible" JavaBeans, which have no visual representation, do have a purpose. The specification goes on to point out that JavaBeans aren't suitable for all situations; if the JavaBean has no visual component, a class library may be more appropriate.

## More beans, please

All of this may make you wonder why you need to bother with beans at all. The JavaBeans specification imposes several requirements that Web developers may find useful. As I pointed out at the beginning of this chapter, all beans must have a zero argument constructor, setter, and getter (also called accessor) methods, and should not expose any properties. These standards make it relatively easy to plug JavaBeans into a servlet-based Web environment.

The JavaBeans specification also deals at length with persistent storage. Although not required for JSP use, JavaBeans normally should implement the `Serializable` interface. Listing 6-5 shows the JellyBean class with this interface added.

**Listing 6-5: A JellyBean Class That Can Be Serialized**

```
import java.io.Serializable;

public class JellyBean implements Serializable{
    private String color;

    public JellyBean() {
    }
    public String getColor() {
        return color;
    }
    public void setColor(String newColor) {
        color = newColor;
    }
}
```

The `Serializable` interface doesn't have any methods that you have to implement. It simply serves as a marker indicating that you can convert this class into a serial byte stream for storage (usually on disk) using the `ObjectOutputStream.writeObject` method, and then reconstituted later with `ObjectInputStream.readObject`.

Bean persistence can be an issue depending on what kinds of information you're tracking on your Web site. Tomcat does use persistence to maintain session data in the event that you update a loaded servlet on a reloadable Web application. You might also want to implement persistence if you're using beans for things like shopping carts, and you want to ensure that no data is lost if the server or servlet/JSP container goes down for maintenance or for other less expected reasons.

## Enterprise JavaBeans

The next step up from *ordinary* JavaBeans is the Enterprise JavaBeans, or EJB, specification. While a JavaBean normally resides on the same machine as the code using the bean, EJBs support a more distributed, transactional multitier architecture. The EJB specification is also correspondingly more complex.

Just as JSPs and servlets need an appropriate container, so EJBs need an EJB container. And you need an EJB server to manage the EJB containers. The containers handle the EJB life cycle and requests for services.

EJBs embody a distributed component architecture, and so the EJB container/server moderates all access to an EJB, which means that you can reach the EJB anywhere you have network access to the server. The container also handles all system-level requirements, while the EJB itself focuses strictly on implementing business logic.

In particular, the specification defines two types of Enterprise JavaBeans. Session beans are, like servlet/JSP sessions, associated with a particular user's interaction with the system. Session beans run processes associated with that user, but on the EJB server. When a session terminates, the container no longer needs the session bean and no longer maintains its state. Entity beans are not linked to any one user and usually represent data on the server, such as a SQL database. These beans persist.

EJBs can be an essential part of a distributed Web environment but, because of its distributed nature, an EJB approach does add overhead. You have to take EJB server response times and network loading into account.

As of version 3.*x*, Tomcat does not directly support Enterprise JavaBeans, as this support would mean adding a whole raft of EJB services. Those services are beyond the scope of Tomcat's mission, which is to be the reference implementation for the Servlet and JSP specifications, not the EJB specification. However, since Tomcat is a freely available reference implementation, some vendors are integrating Tomcat into their EJB services.

## The non-EJB scalable Web server

If you need to spread your Web server across multiple machines, you may have options other than Enterprise JavaBeans. If your distributed application has a single Web server point of presence, but the back-end processing is spread over a number of machines, then EJB is probably the way to go. On the other hand, if your Web server is hitting its limits and you want to spread the load around, you may not need an EJB server (although it's still an option). Instead, you can handle multiple Web servers with a load-balancing switch or Web server, or by a round-robin Web server assignment.

You can configure a Domain Name System (DNS) server to respond to DNS server name requests with a round-robin list of Web server IP addresses, all of which carry the same content. This configuration helps spread the load, although if the client caches the DNS setting it received on the first request, it continues to use the same server. This round-robin configuration also doesn't normally do any server detection, so if one of the servers goes down, it doesn't take that IP address out of the rotation.

You can also configure some Web servers, like Apache, to distribute page requests, though in a somewhat different way. You can have Apache running as your front end Web server, but all requests for a specific Web application can go to a particular machine that runs a Tomcat servlet/JSP container.

Another option is the load balancing switch, which uses various algorithms to distribute loads. Such a switch can also ping destination servers and remove inactive hosts from the list.

## A sticky problem

Life is seldom really easy, and scaling a Web application by adding more hardware inevitably introduces other problems. One of the trickiest is what to do with user sessions in a distributed environment. The HTTPSession objects are not normally sharable across Web applications, much less across servers. In an ideal world, you want to keep the user coming back to the same server each time so you don't lose the session data.

Some switches offer a "sticky" option that attempts to route subsequent requests to the same server. Sometimes you can accomplish this routing by tracking the IP address or by using a cookie. Since IP addresses can change during a session (particularly for AOL users), and users can disable cookies, these are not guaranteed methods. You may find it necessary to use another mechanism to store session information, such as a distributed database, and then reload the session data when the user appears on another machine.

# Tag Libraries

JavaBeans make life a lot easier for Web developers by separating Java code from HTML and providing Web page designers with a simple set of tags for making use of those beans. What they don't do is give you any way to extend their capability. With jsp:useBean, jsp:setProperty, and jsp:getProperty you can pass parameters to a bean and retrieve output into a page. But that's all.

You can't make any changes to those three tags, but as of JSP 1.1 you can create your own custom tags. You can create tags that work just the way jsp:setProperty and jsp:getProperty work, but you can also create tags that conditionally process any HTML, tags, or other code that exists between the custom tag's start and end. You can decide whether the body should be output to the page, you can modify the contents of the body, and you can output the body any number of times.

## Tags without a body

The simplest custom tags are those without a body, and they have the following syntax:

```
<pre:tagname [id="someobject"] [attribute="value"...]  />
```

All custom tags have a prefix and a name. They can have attributes, and they can also declare an object that is then available in scriptlets following the tag.

Since custom tags are, well, custom, you also have to provide the compiler with some information telling it what the tag really means. There are thee parts to this information: the `taglib` directive, the tag library descriptor document, and the custom tag Java class.

# The taglib directive

For a JSP to interpret a custom tag, it needs a `taglib` directive, which has this syntax:

```
<%@ taglib uri="taglibdescriptor" prefix="prefix" %>
```

The `uri` points to an XML file that contains a description of the tags and their associated classes. Tag lib descriptor files normally have the extension TLD. You attach the `prefix` value to all tags, thereby differentiating same-named tags from different libraries. For example:

```
<%@ taglib uri="/WEB-INF/ch06/example.tld" prefix="act" %>
```

## THE TAG LIBRARY DESCRIPTOR

The tag library descriptor is an XML file that connects Java classes with the custom tags used in a JSP. At the top of the descriptor are a couple of tags that define the XML version and encoding. You'll also see the document type definition, which in most cases is the specification at `java.sun.com`. Listing 6-6 shows an example of a tag library descriptor.

### Listing 6-6: A Tag Library Descriptor

```
<?xml version="1.0" encoding="ISO-8859-1" ?>
<!DOCTYPE taglib
        PUBLIC "-//Sun Microsystems, Inc.//DTD JSP Tag Library ↵
1.1//EN"
      "http://java.sun.com/j2ee/dtds/web-jsptaglibrary_1_1.dtd">

<!-- a tag library descriptor -->

<taglib>
  <tlibversion>1.0</tlibversion>
  <jspversion>1.1</jspversion>
  <shortname>ch06</shortname>
  <uri></uri>
  <info>
     A tag library for Chapter 6 examples
  </info>

  <tag>
```

*Continued*

**Listing 6-6** *(Continued)*

```
    <name>repeat</name>
    <tagclass>ch06.VectorDataTag</tagclass>
    <teiclass>ch06.VectorDataTEI</teiclass>
    <info>Print repeating lines</info>
    <bodycontent>JSP</bodycontent>
    <attribute>
        <name>actor</name>
        <required>false</required>
    </attribute>
</tag>

<tag>
    <name>simple</name>
    <tagclass>ch06.SimpleTag</tagclass>
    <info>Print some text</info>
    <bodycontent>empty</bodycontent>
</tag>

</taglib>
```

The tag library definition itself begins with the `<taglib>` element, followed by several subelements that belong to the library as a whole. The `<tlibversion>` subelement is a library version number from 0.0.0.1 to 9.9.9.9. Right-hand zeros are optional.

The `<jspversion>` subelement indicates the version of the JSP specification to which this library conforms. The value in `<shortname>` is for the benefit of JSP page authoring tools that use this value to create unique names for tags. It can also be the default prefix value. The `<uri>` subelement is optional and often points to the home location of the tag library, that is, to the author's Web site.

Following the `<taglib>` subelements are one or more `<tag>` definitions. Each `<tag>` element corresponds to a Java class. The `<name>` subelement specifies the label the JSP code uses when referring to the class's object, and `<tagclass>` defines the actual class to use. The `<info>` element is simply descriptive text.

The `<bodycontent>` subelement can have one of three values. For single line tags, the value is always `empty`, because there is nothing between the start and end of the tag but the tag contents. Tags can also wrap around other text or code, in which case the `<bodycontent>` subelement is either `JSP` or `tagdependent`. More details about those settings will be discussed shortly.

## A SIMPLE TAG

In their simplest form, custom tags function much like the `jsp:getProperty` tag. Listing 6-6 shows a simple tag that returns a predefined string. The tag description for this class can be found in Listing 6-7.

**Listing 6-7: A Simple Custom Tag Class**

```
package ch06;

import javax.servlet.jsp.tagext.*;
import javax.servlet.jsp.*;
import javax.servlet.*;
import java.io.Writer;
import java.util.*;
import java.io.IOException;


public class SimpleTag extends BodyTagSupport {


    public int doStartTag() throws JspException {
        JspWriter out = pageContext.getOut();
        try {
            out.print("Outside of a dog, a book is " +
                "a man's best friend. Inside of a dog "
                + "it's too dark to read.");
        }
        catch(IOException e) {
            throw new JspTagException("I/O Exception");
        }
        return SKIP_BODY;
    }
}
```

The JSP that uses the tag class from Listing 6-7 is also quite simple, and is shown in Listing 6-8.

**Listing 6-8: A JSP That Uses SimpleTag**

```
<html>
<head>
<title>A simple custom tag</title>
</head>
<body>
<%@ page language="java"%>
<%@ taglib uri="/WEB-INF/ch06/example.tld" prefix="ch6" %>
<P>Here's one for you:</P><P>
<ch6:simple/>
</P>
</body>
</html>
```

The JSP that uses `SimpleTag` has just two lines that refer to the tag library. The line

```
<%@ taglib uri="/WEB-INF/ch06/example.tld" prefix="ch6" %>
```

tells the JSP container to look in the `/WEB-INF/ch06` directory (in the current Web application) for the tag library descriptor, which is in `example.tld`. It also defines the prefix for all tags defined in `example.tld`.

The tag `<ch6:simple/>` is an instruction to the JSP to find the tag definition in example.tld, which leads to the `ch06.SimpleTag` class. The JSP container then calls a series of methods in the tag class, most of which are not visible in `SimpleTag` but which the parent `TagSupport` class implements.

In `SimpleTag`, the `doStartTag` method contains all of the code. When you use a tag class in a JSP, the code generated for the JSP servlet first calls the `setPageContext` and `setParent` methods in `SimpleTag`. The page context is the equivalent to a servlet context, and by calling this method the JSP ensures that the tag class always has a valid reference to the page context.

The JSP servlet then calls the `doStartTag` method, which in the case of `SimpleTag` uses `pageContext.getOut` to obtain a `JspWriter` with which it can write to JSP output. After `doStartTag`, the JSP calls `doEndTag`.

## GETTING PARAMETERS

Listing 6-9 shows a tag handler that uses the page context to retrieve the page request, and then retrieves a request parameter that chooses the information to print to the page.

**Listing 6-9: A Tag Handler Class that Gets Request Parameters**

```
package ch06;

import javax.servlet.jsp.tagext.*;
import javax.servlet.jsp.*;
import javax.servlet.*;
import java.io.Writer;
import java.util.*;
import java.io.IOException;

public class GrouchoQuotes extends BodyTagSupport {

    public int doStartTag() throws JspException {
    String choice;
        JspWriter out = pageContext.getOut();
        ServletRequest request = pageContext.getRequest();
        choice = new String(request.getParameter("choice"));
        try {
            if (choice == "book")
```

```
                    out.print("Outside of a dog, a book is "
                    + "a man's best friend. Inside of a dog "
                        + "it's too dark to read.");
                else if (choice == "flies")
                    out.print("Time flies like an arrow. "
                        + "Fruit flies like a banana.");
                else if (choice == "principles")
                    out.print("Those are my principles. "
                        + "If you don't like them I have others.");
                else
                    out.print("Sorry, I can't find that quote.");
        }
        catch(IOException e) {
            throw new JspTagException("I/O Exception");
        }
        return SKIP_BODY;
    }
}
```

Listing 6-10 contains the JSP that uses this custom tag, and Figure 6-1 shows the JSP in action.

**Listing 6-10: A JSP That Passes Parameters to a Custom Tag**

```
<html>
<head>
<title>A simple custom tag</title>
</head>
<body>
<%@ page language="java"%>
<%@ taglib uri="/WEB-INF/ch06/example.tld" prefix="ch6" %>
<P>A Groucho Marx quote:</P><P><I>
<ch6:groucho/>
</I></P>
<P>Read some other quotes: </P>
<ul>
  <li><a href="groucho.jsp?choice=book">Man's best friend</a></li>
  <li><a href="groucho.jsp?choice=flies">Time flies</a></li>
  <li><a href="groucho.jsp?choice=principles">Principles</a></li>
  <li><a href="groucho.jsp?choice=evening">Wonderful ⏎
evening</a></li>
</ul>
</body>
</html>
```

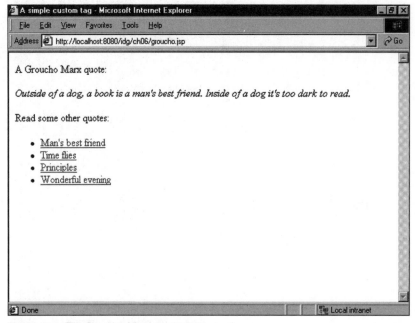

Figure 6-1: The Groucho Marx quote page

## A TAG WITH A BODY

Although tags without bodies can do a lot, they aren't quite as slick as tags with bodies. Listing 6-11 shows a small tag handler that conditionally displays text contained within the tag.

Listing 6-11: A Tag Handler for Including and Excluding Text

```
package ch06;

import javax.servlet.jsp.tagext.*;
import javax.servlet.jsp.*;
import javax.servlet.*;
import java.io.Writer;
import java.util.*;
import java.io.IOException;


public class Include extends TagSupport {
public int doStartTag() throws JspException {
    ServletRequest request = pageContext.getRequest();
    String include = request.getParameter("include");
    if ((include != null) && include.equalsIgnoreCase("true"))
```

```
            return(EVAL_BODY_INCLUDE);
        else
            return(SKIP_BODY);
}
}
```

The tag description for this class is slightly different from that of previous examples. In the following example, the <bodycontent> subelement now has a JSP attribute, which means that the JSP uses the tag to determine how to treat the tag body.

```
<tag>
    <name>include</name>
    <tagclass>ch06.Include</tagclass>
    <info>Optionally include some text</info>
    <bodycontent>JSP</bodycontent>
</tag>
```

Listing 6-12 shows an example of the include tag with a body. Here the tag is not all one line, but has separate start and end tags. In this case, the code between the tags is straight HTML, but you can include any valid JSP code in a tag, including scriptlets.

**Listing 6-12: A Custom Tag with a Body**

```
<html>
<head>
<title>Including/Excluding Text</title>
</head>
<body>
<%@ page language="java"%>
<%@ taglib uri="/WEB-INF/ch06/example.tld" prefix="ch6" %>
<p>Some of the text on this page only
appears when the page receives the command
?include=true</p>
<a href="includes.jsp?include=true">Include the text</a>
<p><a href="includes.jsp">Exclude the text</a>
<ch6:include>
<p><i>Strange things are done in the midnight sun<br>
by the men who moil for gold</i><br></p>
</ch6:include>
</body>
</html>
```

To display the text inside the tag, call the page with an `include` parameter of true:

```
includes.jsp?include=true
```

The listing includes links to display or hide the extra text.

So what's the secret? It all has to do with the sequence of tag handler methods called by the JSP and some special return values from those methods.

## THE TAG HANDLER METHODS

From this point on I focus on the life cycle of custom tags with bodies, since that's the more complex, and potentially useful, situation. Listing 6-13 shows the flow of code as generated from a JSP.

**Listing 6-13: Generated JSP Code for a Tag Handler with a Body**

```
ch06.VectorDataTag vectorDataTag = new ch06.VectorDataTag();
vectorDataTag.setPageContext(pageContext);
vectorDataTag.setParent(null);
// any attributes will be set here
try {
    int result= vectorDataTag.doStartTag();
    if (result!= Tag.SKIP_BODY) {
        try {
            if (result!= Tag.EVAL_BODY_INCLUDE) {
                out = pageContext.pushBody();
                vectorDataTag.setBodyContent((BodyContent) out);
            }
            vectorDataTag.doInitBody();
            do {
                // body appears here
            } while (vectorDataTag.doAfterBody()
                == BodyTag.EVAL_BODY_TAG);
        } finally {
            if (result!= Tag.EVAL_BODY_INCLUDE)
                out = pageContext.popBody();
        }
    }
    if (vectorDataTag.doEndTag() == Tag.SKIP_PAGE)
        return;
```

As you can see in Listing 6-13, after the JSP initializes the tag handler class it uses the result of `doStartTag` to determine if the rest of the code should execute. If `doStartTag` returns, `SKIP_BODY` execution goes straight to `doEndTag`. On all other valid values, the code obtains a writer, calls `setBodyContent`, and calls `InitBody` to set up processing for the body. The tag body can execute multiple times; the JSP will continue to call `doAfterBody` until that method returns a value of `EVAL_BODY_TAG`.

## A REPEATING TAG

Figure 6-2 shows a Web page that displays a list of names, using a repeating custom tag. The tag is simplicity itself:

```
<ch6:repeat><UL><LI><%= actor %></LI></UL></ch6:repeat>
```

Nothing about the tag itself indicates that it's repeating (except the name, which is arbitrary). The looping is totally under the control of the tag handler.

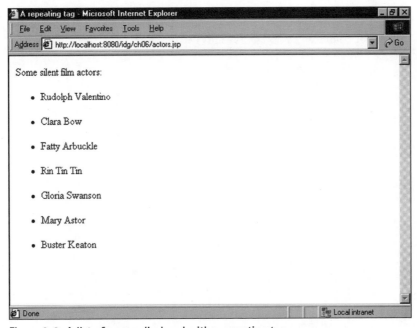

Figure 6-2: A list of names displayed with a repeating tag

Notice that the tag includes a scriptlet referencing something called `actor`. This is an object declared as part of the tag. It's a string that contains the value to be printed inside the tag body. The tag handler places this value in the `pageContext`, using `setAttribute`, and the page retrieves the value using `findAttribute`:

```
actor = (String) pageContext.findAttribute("actor");
```

Listing 6-14 shows the source for the `VectorDataTag` class, which displays a list of names. As you recall from Listing 6-13, after the JSP calls `doInitBody`, it calls doAfterBody repeatedly as long as that method returns EVAL_BODY_TAG. In this case, on each call doAfterBody sets actor with a value from the names vector and increments the counter until it reaches the maximum value.

**Listing 6-14: The VectorDataTag Tag Handler Class**

```
package ch06;

import javax.servlet.jsp.tagext.*;
import javax.servlet.jsp.*;
import javax.servlet.*;
import java.io.Writer;
import java.util.*;
import java.io.IOException;


public class VectorDataTag extends BodyTagSupport {
    protected Vector names;
    protected int index;
    protected BodyContent bodyContent;

public void addActor(String name) {
    names.addElement(name);
    }

public int doAfterBody() throws JspException {
    index++;
    if (index < names.size()) {
        pageContext.setAttribute("actor",
            (String)names.elementAt(index));
        return EVAL_BODY_TAG;
    }
    try {
        bodyContent.writeOut(bodyContent.getEnclosingWriter());
        return SKIP_BODY;
    }
    catch (IOException e) {
        throw new JspTagException(e.toString());
    }
}


    public void doInitBody() throws JspException {
        index = 0;
        names = new Vector(10);
        names.addElement("Rudolph Valentino");
```

```
            names.addElement("Clara Bow");
            names.addElement("Fatty Arbuckle");
            names.addElement("Rin Tin Tin");
            names.addElement("Gloria Swanson");
            names.addElement("Mary Astor");
            names.addElement("Buster Keaton");

pageContext.setAttribute("actor",(String)names.elementAt(0));
        }


    public int doStartTag() throws JspException {
        return EVAL_BODY_TAG;
    }
    public void setBodyContent(BodyContent bodyContent) {
        this.bodyContent = bodyContent;
    }
}
```

There's one problem with this scenario. How does the JSP know what type of object it's retrieving on that call to findAttribute? The answer lies in a helper class that you write and which the JSP container queries when it builds the JSP servlet.

## THE TagExtraInfo HELPER CLASS

Why go to all the hassle of setting up another class to define the objects a custom tag can present to a JSP? There are two answers to this question. One answer is that setting up another class enables you to expose a number of objects at once. With the custom tag format, you can expose only one object. The other is that you can use the tag extra info class to do runtime validation of objects.

To create an extra info class, you derive it from TagExtraInfo, as shown in Listing 6-15. By convention, such classes have names that end in TEI while the class they supplement ends in Tag.

**Listing 6-15: The Extra Info Class for VectorDataTag**

```
package ch06;

import javax.servlet.jsp.tagext.*;

public class VectorDataTEI extends TagExtraInfo {
    public VariableInfo[] getVariableInfo(TagData data) {
        return new VariableInfo[]
                {
                    new VariableInfo("actor",
                                        "String",
```

*Continued*

Listing 6-15 *(Continued)*

```
                                         true,
                                         VariableInfo.NESTED)
                    };
        }
}
```

One of the methods `TagExtraInfo` implements is `getVariableInfo`, which returns an array of `VariableInfo` objects. The `VariableInfo` method takes four parameters to its constructor: the object's label, it's data type, a flag indicating if this is a new variable or just an assignment of a new value to an existing variable, and a scope, which can be one of the following:

- `VariableInfo.AT_BEGIN` — The variable is in scope at the start tag.

- `VariableInfo.AT_END` — The variable is in scope at the end tag.

- `VariableInfo.NESTED` — The variable is in scope between the start and end tags.

You also have to declare the `TEI` class in the tag library descriptor, as shown in Listing 6-16.

**Listing 6-16: A Tag Library Descriptor Using a Tag Extra Info Class**

```
<tag>
    <name>repeat</name>
    <tagclass>ch06.VectorDataTag</tagclass>
    <teiclass>ch06.VectorDataTEI</teiclass>
    <info>Print repeating lines</info>
    <bodycontent>JSP</bodycontent>
    <attribute>
        <name>actor</name>
        <required>false</required>
    </attribute>
</tag>
```

Finally, Listing 6-17 shows the full text of the JSP that makes use of the repeating tag.

**Listing 6-17: A JSP That Uses the Repeating Tag**

```
<html>
<head>
<title>A repeating tag</title>
</head>
<body>
<%@ page language="java"%>
```

```
<%@ taglib uri="/WEB-INF/ch06/example.tld" prefix="ch6" %>
<P>Some silent film actors:</P>
<ch6:repeat>
<UL><LI><%= actor %></LI></UL>
</ch6:repeat>
</body>
</html>
```

The great benefit of repeating tags is that you can embody complex and powerful functionality in a simple tag. Keep in mind the mantra of separating presentation from business logic. It's much better to give your page designers a set of tags to work with than it is to expect them to remember all the peculiarities of Java syntax.

## Tag libraries and beans

Great things, tag libraries, but what about JavaBeans? Do tag libraries replace them? The short answer is no, beans still have an important role. For the sake of clarity I haven't used any beans in these tag library examples, but you should continue to hold the component model in high regard. The point of components is that they're self-contained and can be plugged into any situation. A tag handler is specific to a servlet/JSP environment. If you find yourself writing code in a tag handler that doesn't require that environment, and it makes sense as a component, split it out into a bean.

# Summary

Both JavaBeans and custom tag libraries have the effect of moving Java code out of the JSP itself and into a more programming-friendly environment. The result is a cleaner tag-based syntax that page designers can use to integrate custom Java functionality into the JSP. Key points to remember include:

- JavaBeans as used in servlets and JSPs follow less restrictive rules than beans used in a visual environment, with the main emphasis on protecting data behind accessor methods.

- The `jsp:setProperty` and `jsp:getProperty` tags enable you to set values in and extract data from the bean.

- In a distributed system you may want to consider using Enterprise JavaBeans, although they use additional communication overhead, and Tomcat doesn't support them directly (and isn't likely to); if EJB is a requirement consider using an EJB server that implements Tomcat.

◆ Custom tags add considerable new functionality to JSPs as they have ready access to the page context; you can use these tags in a similar way to bean tags.

◆ Custom tags with a body can conditionally process that body by modifying the body contents, printing or not printing the body, and by printing the body repeatedly until a given condition occurs.

◆ Custom tags can expose a single object to the JSP, or they can expose multiple objects using tag extra info classes.

◆ Custom tags do not replace beans; they just provide another way to implement bean code in a JSP.

# Part II

## Web Sites and Databases

# Chapter 7

# Introducing Relational Databases

## IN THIS CHAPTER

♦ Learning the origins of relational databases

♦ Understanding SQL databases

♦ Diagramming databases

♦ Creating relationships between tables

♦ Learning normalization the easy way

ALL COMPUTER PROGRAMS USE data in some format or another, and in most cases some of this information is persistent; that is, it continues to exist even when the program is not running. Most commonly, persistent data is stored in files on hard disks, and in its simplest form these files are flat text files.

Text files are just fine for small amounts of information, but really aren't designed for efficient storage or fast retrieval of information. They aren't particularly compact, are too easily read and/or modified by other programs, and don't provide any level of control over what kinds of information they hold. Besides that, it is time consuming to insert or delete data from a text file, since all the surrounding text has to move for each insertion or deletion.

Efficient, useful data storage generally depends on some sort of binary file format and some means of indexing data, and many products over the years have attempted, with varying degrees of success, to solve data storage problems. Knowing you need a relational database management system (RDBMS) is one thing; designing and using a relational database is another. In this chapter I'll cover some of the common terminology, and go through some of the fundamentals of database design.

# A Popular History of Databases

For those of us, hoary with age, who participated in the early years of the personal computer revolution, databases were once synonymous with dBASE and its many variants and competitors (collectively called "xBASE"). dBASE was a database management system, or DBMS, which included not only the ability to create data files but software to manipulate the contents of the files. dBASE still lives on, though in greatly modified form, and dBASE data files are still relatively common.

dBASE lets you define various files in which to store different kinds of data. If you were writing a course management system for a school, you might have one file for student information, another for courses, another for instructors, and so forth. Each file would contain zero or more records comprised of fields. The data from such a file could appear in table form, as shown in Table 7-1.

TABLE 7-1  DATA FROM A DBASE FILE

| Course ID | Title | Level | Credits |
|-----------|-------|-------|---------|
| UWBW | Underwater Basket Weaving | 101 | 4 |
| IDB3 | Introduction to dBASE III | 203 | 1 |
| APN | Armpit Noisemaking | 300 | 5 |

In addition to data files, dBASE lets you define a number of indexes per file. You could use these indexes to find data quickly, or to sort the data for reporting/ processing purposes. And because dBASE was a DBMS, you could use it on its own to create and maintain a database, create forms that let users update data, and generate reports on the data.

dBASE certainly wasn't the only product of its type. Some competitors, such as Clipper and Foxbase, used the dBASE file format. Others, like R:BASE used their own file format.

dBASE is the best-known example of a flat-file DBMS. In a flat-file system, the data storage is separate from the code that manages access to the data files. That means that you could have a database made up of a set of dBASE files, yet several different applications could manipulate that data, perhaps using completely different rules for how that data is managed.

For instance, dBASE II had no date field format, so you might define a date field as an eight-character field, using the format MMDDYYYY. Another programmer, knowing this to be a date field, might look at the data to determine the format and wrongly assume that the format you used is DDMMYYYY. That's just fine until one program attempts to read or update data written by the other program. Ouch! And problems aren't limited to field formats. What happens when two programs take different approaches to treating related records? One program may allow a customer to be removed from a database only if that customer has not made any purchases; the other program allows the delete without making the check, leaving orphaned invoice and payment records.

## Relational database management systems

Flat-file databases certainly weren't the only option available in the '80s, but most vendors developing alternative databases were doing so for the big iron. In the mainframe world the move was on to relational database management systems that enforced certain rules for data storage and integrity.

The impetus for this move came from a now-famous paper published by Dr. E. F. Codd, an IBM researcher, entitled "A Relational Model of Data for Large Shared Data Banks." Codd laid out a set of rules for how databases could be designed, and how a database system should manage the relationships between various data. Codd's article also laid the groundwork for a large number of books and other articles on relational database design.

## Then came SQL and client/server

What the relational model needed to become a success was a suitable implementation. In the mid seventies, IBM began a project called System/R, which had its genesis in Codd's article. One of the products of System/R was a language called SEQUEL, meaning Structured English Query Language. SEQUEL was eventually shorted to SQL. (Both the original pronunciation and the "ess-queue-ell" pronunciation are common.)

As the name suggests, SEQUEL (or SQL) lets you write queries in relatively understandable terms. For example, the query:

```
SELECT LASTNAME,FIRSTNAME,ADDRESS FROM STUDENTS;
```

would, as you'd assume, retrieve all the name and address information from the STUDENTS file, as shown in Listing 7-1. Only it wasn't called a file anymore, but a table.

Listing 7-1: First and Last Names Selected from the STUDENTS Table.

```
+-----------+-----------+
| FIRSTNAME | LASTNAME  |
+-----------+-----------+
| Morton    | Salter    |
| Jimi      | Filmore   |
| Eustace   | Shoe      |
| Archy     | Roche     |
| Catherine | LaGrande  |
| asdf      | asdf      |
+-----------+-----------+
```

## SQL/RELATIONAL TERMINOLOGY

In the flat-file PC world, databases are often simple files, and within those files are fields, such as FirstName, LastName, and City. In a SQL world, data storage concepts become just a little more abstract. It is, after all, the job of the SQL RDBMS to manage the actual storage of the data, and when you're using a SQL database you don't need to know or care where that data is actually stored (unless, of course, you're the database administrator). A collection of related information is now a table instead of a file, and within that table you have columns of data. This is, in fact, just how you're probably accustomed to thinking about data, especially when it's shown as it is in Table 7-1.

Relational Software shipped Oracle, the first commercially available SQL database, in 1979. Two years later IBM debuted its own SQL product. Although Oracle ran on minicomputers rather than mainframes, it was still a long step down to the PC world.

## SQL ON PERSONAL COMPUTERS

As the mainframe/minicomputer world realized the value of a common database language, it also bumped up against the limitations of flat-file databases on PCs. More powerful personal computers made it possible to use larger databases, and many flat-file systems weren't up to the task. At the same time, software began to evolve in the direction of client/server, where a smart/fat client talked across the network to a database server. SQL fit perfectly with this arrangement for several reasons.

In a client/server environment, network traffic is a limiting factor, and in the early years of the networked PC, bandwidth was certainly at a premium. Flat-file databases had a tendency to choke the network because all of the involved data had to be shuttled back and forth between the database server and the client PC. SQL databases eliminated a lot of this network traffic, since the SQL server handled many of the required operations, particularly batch operations like deletes and updates, in a very efficient way. Only the SQL commands needed to travel the network.

Besides giving developers a way to optimize network loading, SQL provided a common language for accessing a variety of databases. In 1986, the American National Standards Institute (ANSI) and the International Standards Organization (ISO) published a SQL standard definition, which was updated in 1992 (SQL2), and again in 1999 (SQL99).

SQL databases have become enormously successful on PC-based systems, and on workstations as well as on servers. Some of the smaller-footprint SQL databases are taking over territory previously held by flat-file databases, and you can even find SQL on handheld devices. The reasons are largely the same as for server-based SQL: SQL provides a common and efficient way of administering and accessing relational databases.

# What is a SQL database really?

A SQL database is a collection of tables and indexes. The database isn't the same thing as the database server, which is the software that manages access to the database (or databases, because in most cases you can have more than one). Of course, just to confuse things, the term database server is also used to refer to the physical machine that holds the database and the database server software.

A SQL database is more than just a simple collection of data, however. Each table contains columns, and each column has a data type (string, integer, BLOB, and so on) and possibly a default value. The column can also have a NOT NULL requirement, which means that you can't add a row that contains no value in this column, or perhaps the column must have a unique value. These limited means of ensuring data validity are part of the original (SQL1) standard.

The SQL2 standard expands the concept of data integrity to include relationships between tables. You can optionally store referential integrity rules in the database; these rules define what action the server should take when it updates or deletes a row and there are related rows in other tables. The server can restrict changes to one row if related rows would be affected by the change/delete, or it can cascade changes/deletes to the related rows. If you have a restrict rule on customer deletes, you won't be able to delete any customer rows if the database contains order rows for that customer. If you have a cascade rule on customer deletes, then the server will delete all of that customer's order rows as well (not usually a good idea).

A SQL database can also contain user-defined SQL code. This code isn't stored in the user-defined tables, so I'm not talking about object-relational databases (yet). Rather, this is SQL code that is called automatically under certain conditions, or when the user or application invokes the code directly. The former is called a trigger, and the latter a stored procedure. Neither of these is a defining requirement of a SQL database, but they are commonly implemented and can help enforce the database's data model.

It's not vital that you know the details of what a particular SQL database does at this point; it's more important that you know that a SQL database *manages* its own data, rather than simply contains it.

It's important to note that SQL isn't a requirement for a relational model. Some vendors build an RDBMS on top of a flat-file database, but the RDBMS has to mediate control of the data. A number of hybrid systems out there allow SQL access to flat-file databases, or which otherwise handle relational integrity in code without preventing other systems from accessing the data in a nonrelational way.

## Current developments

To hear some developers talk, relational databases are already going the way of the dinosaur, replaced by the warm-blooded, fur-bearing object-relational and object databases. I think that sentiment is a bit premature, but object technology is making its way into SQL and other database systems.

### OBJECT DATABASES

Object databases are still databases, but instead of storing raw data, they store objects. This makes a lot of sense when you're working in an object-oriented programming environment. Your application is modeling its world using objects, yet when it stores the data about that world, it has to reduce it back to a form the relational database understands (this difference between data structures is often called impedance mismatch). It makes more sense to store the object directly.

Widespread acceptance of object databases has several impediments, not the least of which is education. Developers need to learn how to use object databases. But the relational database model is still in far greater use, and is also understood well enough by many nondevelopers. SQL makes it relatively easy to retrieve information without having a great deal of technical knowledge.

### OBJECT-RELATIONAL DATABASES

Many vendors are beginning to bridge relational and object technology by mapping relational database concepts to object concepts. This approach retains the strength of relational DBMS querying while allowing the use and storage of objects. Some vendors also provide object-mapping tools, which make it easier to store objects in traditional relational databases.

### WHAT'S NEXT?

For the near future, object-relational databases seem more likely to succeed in most applications than pure object databases. As the technology still has a ways to go before it reaches maturity, and as most developers are still using relational database systems, I'll focus on the SQL RDBMS approach in this book.

# Designing Relational Databases

Creating a database is a bit like writing software. It's common for a software project to begin with a small, realistic goal of providing some basic functionality. Then one requirement leads to another. As you add more code, you begin to stress the underlying structure of the program. The greater the distance between your original design and your current implementation, the greater the risk that your application will break under the stress.

Relational database design isn't any different. If you don't give much thought to your database before you begin writing the application, you'll quickly outgrow your original design, or lack thereof. However, by following a few well-established design principles, you can create a solid database that you can readily adapt to changes in your application. You'll also find that understanding your database design can make some significant differences to how you design the application itself.

## How many tables do I need?

When you begin designing a database, one of the first tasks is to begin grouping the data you're dealing with into tables. Some of these groupings seem immediately obvious. Consider a database that is used to manage an online magazine. At a minimum, this database contains information about articles. At first blush, you might think about an Articles table that looks like the one shown in Figure 7-1.

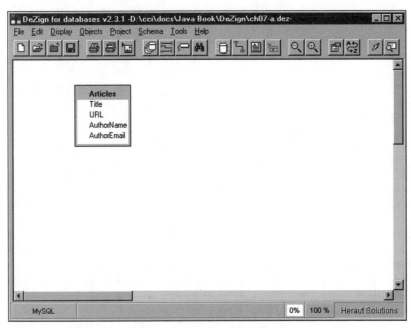

Figure 7-1: A table for online magazine article information

The table shown in Figure 7-1 would be fine if each author only had one article. But as soon as an author writes a second article, you're faced with duplication of data. Now you have to enter the author's name and e-mail address twice or more, and when the author changes ISPs, you have to locate all instances of that e-mail address and update them accordingly.

While it's true that SQL makes mass updates fairly easy to do, this design doesn't do a good job of modeling the data. It's better to split this table into two, one for authors, and one for articles. Figure 7-2 shows two such tables.

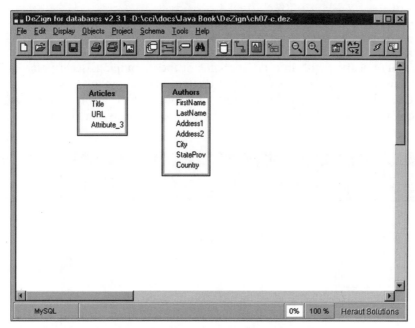

Figure 7-2: Storing article and author information in separate tables

The tables shown in Figure 7-2 are headed in the right direction, but they still have a few problems. One is that you don't have a way to link the information in the Authors table with the information in the Articles table.

One of the requirements of a SQL database is that you must be able to uniquely identify any row in a table. This is actually a requirement of all databases, but in non-SQL databases, that identifier may be something like an internal counter or the byte offset of the start of the row in the data file. In SQL, you normally set aside one column in the table to provide this unique ID. This column is called the *primary key*.

You can use any column as the primary key, provided it's a unique and, preferably, unchanging value. As a matter of principle, you should define the primary key column as soon as possible in the table design process. Figure 7-3 shows the Article and Author tables, each with the addition of an integer ID field that is used as the primary key.

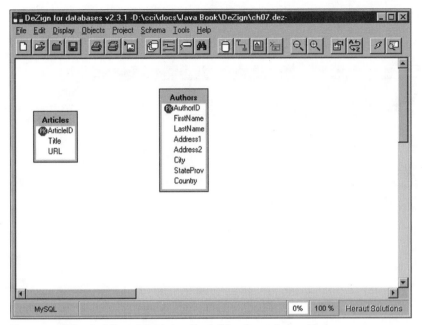

Figure 7-3: The Article and Author tables with primary keys added

## Creating table relationships

To link an author to an article, you need to create a relationship between the two tables. If each author can have multiple articles, and each article has one author, then you can create the relationship by adding a column to the Articles table, giving it a suitable name (such as `AuthorID`). You then store the primary key of the appropriate Author row in each row of the Articles table. When you store that primary key value in the Articles table, it is called a *foreign key*, because the information comes from a different table.

The terms *key* and *index* may cause some confusion. Indexes are physical structures in the database that the server creates to speed access to information. If you want to locate your customers readily by company name, for instance, you want to define an index on the company name column. Keys, whether foreign or primary, are not physical structures. They're simply a *definition* of which columns identify the current row or a row in another table. To make things just slightly bewildering to the SQL newcomer, when you define a primary key, the SQL database automatically creates an index for it, but the same isn't true for foreign keys. If indexes are necessary (and they usually are), you have to define them yourself.

Figure 7-4 shows the updated table definition along with an indicator of the relationship between the tables.

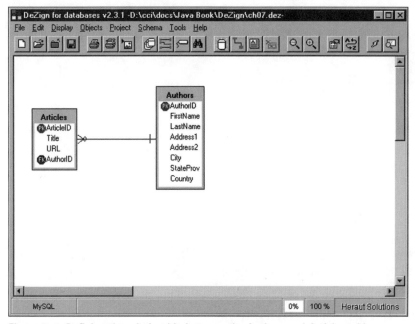

Figure 7-4: Defining the relationship between the Authors and Articles tables

You can define three different kinds of relationships between two tables: one-to-many, one-to-one, and many-to-many. To make understanding these relationships easier, many developers diagram databases using Entity Relationship Diagrams.

## Drawing databases with Entity-Relationship Diagrams

A number of different ways of diagramming relational databases have evolved over the years, and one of the most common is the ERD, or Entity-Relationship Diagram. All of the database diagrams in this book are ERDs. None of these diagrams use particularly complex symbology: They show tables, or entities, as boxes with a title and a list of columns, also called attributes, and relationships between tables as lines with special terminators, as shown in the following table.

**Symbol  Description**

————————— The "one" side of the relationship

≻————— The "many" side of the relationship

In addition to indicating the one or many side, the relationship line can also indicate whether the linking value is required or not. These symbols are shown in the following table.

| Symbol | Description |
| --- | --- |
| —0— | Zero or one row may exist. |
| —┼— | Exactly one row must exist. |
| >0— | Zero to many rows may exist. |
| >┼— | At least one row must exist, and many may exist. |

## ONE-TO-MANY RELATIONSHIPS

In a one-to-many relationship, you link a row of data in one table to multiple rows of data in the other table. In Figure 7-4, the Author table is on the one side of the relationship, and the Articles table is on the many side of the relationship. Since the Articles table has a column for the Author ID value, any number of articles can point to one author. One-to-many relationships (or many-to-one relationships, depending on your point of view) are the most common type of relationship (at least among data files), and are easy to manage.

## ONE-TO-ONE RELATIONSHIPS

One-to-one relationships are the least common type of relationship and are also easy to manage, but often difficult to justify. If one row from one table will always point to only one row from another table, why not combine the two tables? Sometimes you'll use one-to-one relationships to make data storage more efficient, as when most rows in a table don't need to store information in the second table.

## MANY-TO-MANY RELATIONSHIPS

Many-to-many relationships present a special problem. In the Authors/Articles example I've been careful so far to state that each article can have only one author. But in the real world, authors collaborate all the time, and an article can have more than one author. This changes the relationship between Authors and Articles from one-to-many to many-to-many.

Your first impulse might be to add an AuthorID2 column to the Articles table. It's a common enough idea, but you must resist! Adding a second linking column creates two serious problems (and a host of irritations): the second column wastes space, since most rows won't need it; and it provides no way of dealing with the inevitable article with three or four authors. The more columns you add to deal with contingencies, the more wasted space you have. You'll also have to write code to look in the additional columns for links to authors, which is where the irritations begin to appear.

The standard way to deal with many-to-many relationships is to introduce a third, linking table, as shown in Figure 7-5.

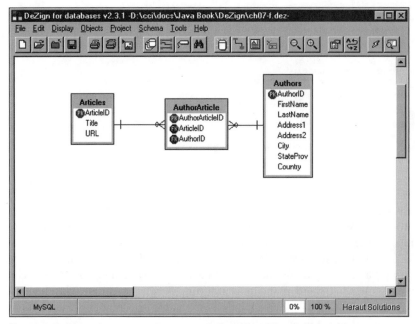

Figure 7-5: Managing a many-to-many relationship with a linking table

The database in Figure 7-5 is able to deal with any number of articles for a given author, and any number of authors for a given article. For each combination of author and article you will have one row in the AuthorArticle table.

Also, note that I defined AuthorArticle as having a primary key column called ID. This column isn't strictly necessary because for any row, the combination of author and article ID should be unique. Nonetheless, I created a separate primary key, in part because I prefer to use a single column for a primary ID and in part because it's my habit to start any table definition with the primary ID, no matter what comes next. I think it's a good habit to have.

# Normalization

If you've done any work on databases, you've probably heard the term *normalization*, perhaps *third normal form*, or *3NF*. Normalization theory is the study of optimizing relational databases.

There are five normal forms, with the first being most generally applicable and the last the most esoteric. Normal forms one through three are the forms most commonly applied to database designs, which is why you often hear of a design conforming to third normal form, or perhaps just that it is "normalized." This section provides an overview of normal forms, rather than a detailed treatment.

# First normal form

In essence, first normal form says "don't use arrays or other repeating fields." In the Authors/Articles example given earlier in this chapter, I pointed out that while it's possible to manage a many-to-many relationship by creating additional foreign keys in the linking table, these keys cause a variety of problems, including waste of space, limited flexibility, and a more complex coding requirement. Whether you use arrays or extra columns, this arrangement clearly violates first normal form.

The same is true of something like a product order table. While you could create an order table with a whole set of columns such as `ProductID1`, `ProductPrice1`, `ProductID2`, `ProductPrice2`, `ProductID3`, `ProductPrice3`, and so forth, this approach suffers from the same problems as the incorrect many-to-many linking solution. Instead, you would want to create an Item table with the Order row's primary key as its foreign key.

# Second normal form

For a table to qualify for second normal form, it must be in first normal form (1NF), and all of the data in the table must be dependent on the value of the primary key (which is typically some sort of ID field). The primary key stands for whatever "thing" you're storing in that row in that table, and there should only be one such "thing." That's why I created an Author and an Article table; these are really two separate things, rather than one entity. If each author had one and only one article, then I could probably say that the article information was dependent on the author primary key, although even then common sense would probably kick me in the shins and tell me that even though at that point I had only one article per author, that might change.

By splitting out the Author table, I was forced to create one additional linking field (the `AuthorID` column), but in the long run I reduced data storage requirements, and I avoided unnecessary duplication of data, which is one of the key benefits of adhering to 2NF.

# Third normal form

For a table to qualify for third normal form (3NF) it must be in 2NF (and, therefore, 1NF) and each of the columns in that table, except those used as keys, must not be interdependent. Another way to say this is that you don't want a table to contain information already defined somewhere else, or which can be calculated from existing values.

I've designed the database shown in Figure 7-6 to store information about online articles. To make it easier for search engines to locate these articles, I would probably want to add some keywords to the article definition, and automatically generate these into the article's HTML page at request time. I also want to keep track of the type of article.

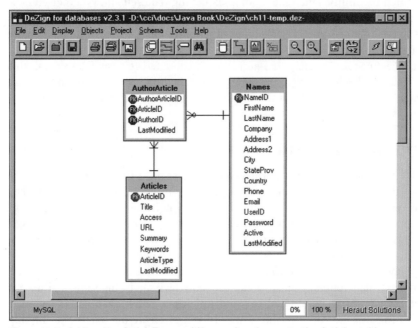

Figure 7–6: Adding the ArticleType and Keywords columns to the Articles table

If you think about the ArticleType and Keywords columns, you'll soon realize that there's some overlap in the kind of information they contain. The ArticleType groups similar articles, say, all those about servlet programming, or perhaps about hair loss encountered while servlet programming. Similarly, the Keywords field contains information about what kind of article this is. Keywords and ArticleType are not mutually exclusive.

A solution to this problem is to split the keywords information into another table, and to link by article type, as shown in Figure 7-7.

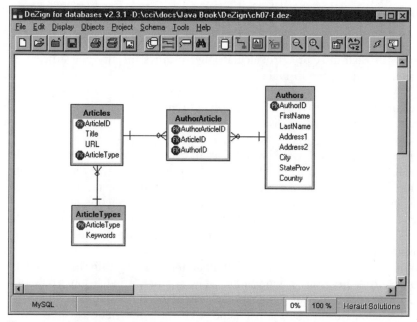

Figure 7-7: Adding an ArticleTypes table to achieve third normal form

Now all of the non-key columns in the Articles table are mutually exclusive, and the database doesn't duplicate information. In fact, if you keep this concept of avoiding duplication of information in mind, and you follow 2NF, your designs generally conform to 3NF.

The database design powers that be have extended normalization to fourth and fifth normal forms, but if you've achieved 3NF, you'll have dealt with most of the problems that plague database designers.

## Breaking the rules

The reality of database design is that many, if not most, databases do not strictly conform to third normal form. Oftentimes the designers simply don't understand the principles involved, but other times, they have reasons for violating one of the normal forms. The most important rule is to know the rules before you decide to break them!

Strict conformance to 3NF (which, of course, means adherence to 1NF and 2NF) means that under some circumstances you may be compromising performance. For example, let's say you're using your database to keep track of Web site users.

Additionally, you're charging a fee for certain articles on the site. It's common practice to restrict access to Web site pages on a directory-by-directory basis, so you set up a table to keep track of the directories and how many subscriptions you've sold for each directory. To calculate the earnings for any one article you need to apply the following formula:

```
value of article = total of all subscriptions for this directory /
    number of articles in this directory
```

A strict adherence to 3NF would mean that for every article you need to find the corresponding record in a directory table, and then retrieve all of the subscriptions for that directory, sum them, and then count the number of related articles and use that to determine the value of each article. You could write a function or a SQL trigger to do this, but if you attempt to use this function to create a report on the value of each and every article, you're going to have to read a lot of records, many of them repeatedly.

The problem is that the appropriate technique for updating information related to one article isn't necessarily appropriate when running a batch job. You could write much more efficient code to update the article cost information for all articles at once. If you don't always need a real-time calculation of a value, it can be more convenient, for reporting purposes, to periodically run a process that updates a lot of values and stores those calculated values (in violation of 3NF) in a column.

The downside to breaking the normalization rules is that you typically have to write code to ensure that data integrity is maintained. After all, one of the reasons for normalization is to avoid writing all that code.

# Summary

Relational databases are at the heart of most business applications, and many Web applications, and the most common way to access these databases is with SQL. A number of techniques and tools exist to make the design and management of relational SQL databases easier. Key points to remember include:

- Although object databases and object-relational databases are on the way, most applications still use traditional relational databases.

- SQL is a powerful tool not just for querying data, but also for updating and for performing administrative tasks.

- The first task in designing a database is grouping data into tables.

- Tables are related to one another through fields called keys.

- Relationships can be one-to-one, many-to-one, or many-to-many, but many-to-many relationships require the addition of a linking table.

◆ Normal forms are standards for database design.

◆ For a table to qualify for first normal form, it must not have any arrays or repeating fields.

◆ For a table to qualify for second normal form, it must be in first normal form and all of the data in the table must be dependent on the table's primary key.

◆ For a table to qualify for third normal form, it must be in second normal form and all non-key columns must be mutually independent.

◆ In general, if you avoid duplicating any data, you are well along the road to third normal form.

◆ Occasionally, you may wish to break normalization rules for performance or convenience reasons, but doing so typically requires you to write more code to maintain data integrity.

# Chapter 8

# Getting Started with MySQL

## IN THIS CHAPTER

- ◆ Learning the strengths and limitations of MySQL's SQL implementation

- ◆ Understanding the benefits of MySQL for Web development

- ◆ Installing and starting MySQL

- ◆ Creating permissions by adding/updating tables

- ◆ Creating permissions with GRANT and REVOKE statements

NOW THAT YOU HAVE a handle on what a SQL database server is, and how tables can be used, you'll want to start creating and using tables. In this chapter you'll learn how to use the popular MySQL database server, which is available at no charge, and runs on numerous hardware platforms and operating systems. Whether you use MySQL or some other server, you'll be faced with some common tasks. You'll need to install the server, and you'll need to set up permissions so you can go about creating and using tables and indexes. If you already have a SQL database server set up, you can skip to the next chapter.

## The MySQL Database Server

Databases are becoming a big part of Web-site development, and one of the most popular products is MySQL, from MySQL AB (www.mysql.com). Recently released as open source under the General Public License, MySQL has in the neighborhood of one million installations worldwide. Let's take a look at some of its strengths and limitations.

## SQL strengths

MySQL is popular with ISPs and Web developers because of its speed and reliability and the flexibility of its access control system. In fact, MySQL was originally designed for speed (if not always for comfort) when using very large databases.

As MySQL's popularity (and funding) has grown, the MySQL developers have lengthened the list of features currently being, or soon to be, added. As of this writing, the feature list includes:

- Multithreading using kernel threads

- Numerous APIs, including C, C++, Java, Perl, PHP, Python, and TCL

- Support for a large number of platforms, including Windows, Linux, and most variants of Unix

- Very fast joins

- Optimized SQL functions

- Left outer join support

- Multidatabase query

- An ODBC driver

- Fixed and variable length records

- In-memory tables

- SQL92 aliases on tables and columns

- Multiple language support

- Client connection via TCP/IP or Unix sockets, or using named pipes under Windows NT

- A SHOW command that retrieves information about databases, tables, and indexes

- An EXPLAIN command that shows how the optimizer optimizes a query

- Transaction support (a relatively new feature)

## SQL limitations

MySQL doesn't yet provide all the features many SQL developers have come to expect, although the documentation states that the developers intend to make MySQL fully SQL92/SQL99 compliant. Some of the features still missing, or not fully implemented, are:

- Subselects — a SELECT statement inside another SELECT statement, but you can often work around this with a JOIN

- SELECT ... INTO TABLE — MySQL does support the equivalent INSERT INTO ... SELECT ...

- Stored procedures — on the MySQL to-do list

◆ Triggers – The developers have no plans to add triggers, as they feel these impose too great a performance penalty

◆ Foreign keys – support for these is coming, but slowly

◆ Views

Perhaps the biggest concern for most developers is the lack of support for foreign keys, as used to enforce referential integrity. I deal with some of the ways to get around this limitation in Chapter 10.

# Why MySQL?

Given that MySQL is still missing some features common to most other SQL databases, and only now getting others (like transactions), why should you use it? Well, it's free, but that's not really a compelling reason. Reliability, speed, access control, and the availability of key development tools are all vital.

## Reliability

It won't do you a lot of good to have a database-using or database-centered Web site if your database suffers a lot of downtime, and, unless you're the mythical perfect programmer, you'll have enough worries without wondering if the database server itself is bug-ridden. MySQL has proven itself in numerous installations around the world and has a deserved reputation for reliability.

## Speed, speed, speed

To some extent MySQL owes its existence to the need of its developers for a database that could work with very large databases with excellent performance. The need for speed is the main reason MySQL doesn't support foreign keys and triggers, and why it's taken a long time for the developers to add support for transactions. Foreign keys demand automatic lookups of related data, and triggers must be checked for before any eligible database action. The MySQL developers do intend to add support for foreign keys, but only as an informational tool. In other words, MySQL will store the information that a relationship exists, but won't enforce that relationship.

## Capacity

In general, MySQL's database capacity is limited by the maximum size of files allowed by the operating system. On a PC running Linux, for instance, you can create a single table of up to two gigabytes, or four gigabytes if you're using the Reiserfs file system. On Linux-Alpha, however, maximum table size is eight terabytes. If you're coming up against a table size limit, you can use the merging library to treat two tables as one, but MySQL doesn't fully support merged table indexing as of this writing.

## Access control

MySQL's highly configurable permission system enables you to control access not just based on the user ID and password, but also on the connecting host. You can control permissions down to table and column levels. In most Web development cases it's the server, not the user, that connects to the database, but even there you may wish to give server code (such as a servlet) access only to the data it needs. ISP can easily set MySQL permissions to allow each customer their own database or databases.

## Development tools

If you're developing your MySQL applications using only Java, you have ready access to JDBC MySQL database drivers. Many other languages, including Perl and PHP, also have interfaces to MySQL.

# Installing MySQL

You can download versions of MySQL for many different platforms, including Windows 95/98/NT/2000, Mac OS X, Linux, Solaris, and just about any other Unix variant you can think of. Your first task, then, is to find a version of MySQL for your machine. For all MySQL versions and documentation, your first stop should be www.mysql.com. Click on the Downloads link for a list of available versions.

## Choosing a release

At any given time, a number of releases of MySQL are available, including: the latest beta release, which may or may not contain some significant bugs; the previous stable release (which is the safest bet if you don't need the most recent features); a previous stable release; and probably at least one older and unsupported release. All of these are available from the Downloads page at the MySQL Web site.

If for some reason you need a version not shown on the Downloads page, do anonymous FTP to ftp.mysql.com and look in the Old-Versions directory. Downloads are available in source and binary formats.

## Interpreting the version naming scheme

MySQL versions have a well-defined naming scheme. At the time of this writing, the current MySQL Windows version has this name:

```
mysql-3.23.27-beta-win.zip
```

Each file name contains three numbers, separated by decimal points.

◆ The first number indicates the file format. When this number changes, you have to convert all tables from previous numbered versions to the new format.

◆ The second number is the release level. Usually at least two versions are available at any time, the current beta and the previous stable release.

◆ The third number is the release version number. This version is updated with each released build.

Following the version number is one of the following:

◆ Alpha – This build includes code that may not be fully tested, but there should be no known bugs.

◆ Beta – This build contains fully tested code. Versions are moved from alpha to beta status when there have not been any fatal bugs reported for at least a month.

◆ Gamma – This is a stable release.

The last part of the file name indicates the platform and, of course, the install file type.

## Installing MySQL binaries

It's generally preferable to install a binary version of MySQL if that's possible. If you have an unsupported operating system, or the version you want to use isn't yet available in binary format, or you want to configure MySQL in a particular way, you need to do a source install and compile MySQL yourself, as described in the next section.

On a recent visit to the MySQL Downloads page I found numerous binary installs of MySQL. For Unix and Unix-like systems, these are in the form of gzipped TAR files, or tarballs. Red Hat Linux users can download RPMs, and Windows users can download a ZIP file. In addition to the official downloads, you can find many links to user-contributed files.

I advise using a MySQL mirror site whenever possible. There are many of these; you can find a listing in Chapter 4 of the MySQL online manual.

## Installing Unix binaries

To install MySQL on Unix or Linux (although you may prefer to use RPMs on Linux) you need the gunzip and tar programs.

 The Solaris tar program has known problems, so you should use GNU tar instead when installing MySQL.

Use the following sequence of commands to install and run MySQL:

```
groupadd mysql
useradd -g mysql mysql
```

The groupadd and useradd commands create a mysql user on the system, in the user group mysql.

```
cd /usr/local
gunzip < /path/to/mysql-VERSION-OS.tar.gz | tar xvf -
```

Change to the /usr/local directory and then unzip/untar the MySQL tarball. The files are placed in a subdirectory automatically with the name mysql followed by the version number. On some systems, you may also be able to use the following form of the command:

```
tar zxvf  /path/to/mysql-VERSION-OS.tar.gz
```

This form of tar unzips as well as unpacks the tarball.

```
ln -s mysql-VERSION-OS mysql
```

The ln command creates a symbolic link named mysql that points to the actual directory where MySQL is installed. This link is a convenience that makes changing to that directory easier (who can remember version numbers?) and also provides a logical location for MySQL no matter which version you're using.

```
cd mysql
scripts/mysql_install_db
```

Change to the mysql directory (using the symbolic link, which you can use exactly the same way as a normal directory name) and run the install script. This script creates the core permissions database and establishes some initial values so you can log onto the database.

```
chown -R mysql /usr/local/mysql
chgrp -R mysql /usr/local/mysql
```

Set the owner and group of all files in the `mysql` directory to the `mysql` user.

```
bin/safe_mysqld --user=mysql &
```

Start the MySQL server as the `mysql` user. Don't forget that & on the end of the command line!

## Installing RPMs on Linux

If you're running Linux, you can do so using an RPM. RPM stands for Red Hat Package Manager and is a now standard format for Linux installs. RPMs are generally easier to use than tarballs because, in addition to copying files, they can handle any needed setup chores.

Unlike the single tarballs, the RPM installation is broken up into several files, including the following:

- ◆ MySQL-VERSION.i386.RPM — the MySQL database server.

- ◆ MySQL-client-VERSION.i386.RPM — The MySQL client programs that you use to administer the MySQL server, create tables, and so on.

- ◆ MySQL-bench-VERSION.i386.RPM — various tests and benchmarks. This RPM requires Perl and MySQL Perl modules.

- ◆ MySQL-devel-VERSION.i386.RPM — libraries and include files. You may need these if you have to compile any MySQL-related tools or products, but they're not essential for getting MySQL up and running.

- ◆ MySQL-VERSION-src.rpm — MySQL source code. This RPM isn't needed unless you want to do development or compile MySQL for other platforms or with non-default options.

For a basic MySQL installation, download the MySQL and MySQL-client RPMs, and execute the following command:

```
rpm -i MySQL-VERSION.i386.rpm MySQL-client-VERSION.i386.rpm
```

This command installs both the server and the client programs. The RPM starts the MySQL server, and also creates the necessary setup information in `/etc/rc.d/` to load MySQL each time the computer is started.

## Installing Windows binaries

To install the Windows version, extract the install files from the zip to a temporary directory and run setup.exe. This command runs the Installshield installation program. Figure 8-1 shows the Destination Folder dialog box.

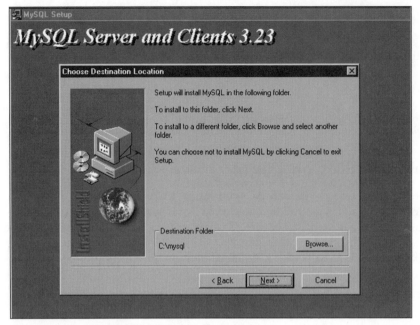

Figure 8-1: The Windows MySQL installation program

If you wish to install MySQL somewhere other than `c:\mysql`, you're advised to use the default directory and then move the installation later manually.

For Windows 95 and Windows 98, you have two MySQL servers to choose between. You can use mysqld, which as of this writing is compiled with full debugging capability, or mysqld-opt, which is optimized for Pentium processors. Both should work on a computer with a 386 or newer processor. Simply execute

```
c:\mysql\bin\mysqld
```

or

```
c:\mysql\bin\mysqld-opt
```

On Windows NT and Windows 2000 you have the option of running MySQL as a service:

```
c:\mysql\bin\mysqld-nt --install
```

To remove the service use the `--remove` option:

```
c:\mysql\bin\mysqld-nt --remove
```

To start and stop the server once you've installed it, use the NET command:

```
NET START mysql
NET STOP mysql
```

You can also run the server standalone rather than as a service:

```
c:\mysql\bin\mysqld-nt --standalone
```

## Source installation

You need a source distribution of MySQL if you want to develop on the source code, if you want to explore options not available in the precompiled versions, or if you can't get a precompiled version for your platform. You can find the source distributions via the MySQL Download page.

In addition to whatever tools you need to unpack the source distribution (as for binary installations), you also need an ANSI C++ compiler and a good make program. Check the MySQL installation documentation for the minimum version requirements for your platform.

If compiling MySQL sounds intimidating, you can relax (somewhat). In most cases compiling MySQL involves running a few commands from the shell (usually configure, make, and make install) and setting some file attributes. See the installation documentation for details.

## Directory structure

Any directory into which you install MySQL will have the following subdirectories:

- bin — contains the MySQL server and client programs

- data — contains log files and databases

- scripts — on non-Windows systems contains the mysql_install_db script, which is used to create the default databases

- doc — on Windows systems contains documentation

- share/mysql — subdirectories that contain language-specific error message files

# Testing Your Installation

Once you have MySQL installed, the next step is to make sure that everything is working properly. One way to do this is by executing the mysqlshow command, which displays the databases available to MySQL, as follows:

```
c:\mysql\bin\mysqlshow
+-----------+
| Databases |
+-----------+
| mysql     |
| test      |
+-----------+
```

When you install MySQL, the installation script or program automatically creates two databases, test and mysql. The mysql database (now there's a name choice bound to confuse) actually contains tables used to define user permissions. You can use mysqlshow to describe the tables in that database, as shown in Listing 8-1.

**Listing 8-1: The Output from mysqlshow mysql**

```
c:\mysql\bin\mysqlshow mysql
Database: mysql
+--------------+
|    Tables    |
+--------------+
| columns_priv |
| db           |
| func         |
| host         |
| tables_priv  |
| user         |
+--------------+
```

You can further expand the explanation by adding the table name, as shown in Listing 8-2.

**Listing 8-2: Using mysqlshow to Describe the User Table**

```
c:\mysql\bin\mysqlshow mysql user
Database: mysql  Table: user  Rows: 9
+----------------+----------------+------+-----+---------+-------+
| Field          | Type           | Null | Key | Default | Extra |
+----------------+----------------+------+-----+---------+-------+
| Host           | char(60)       |      | PRI |         |       |
| User           | char(16)       |      | PRI |         |       |
| Password       | char(16)       |      |     |         |       |
| Select_priv    | enum('N','Y')  |      |     | N       |       |
| Insert_priv    | enum('N','Y')  |      |     | N       |       |
| Update_priv    | enum('N','Y')  |      |     | N       |       |
| Delete_priv    | enum('N','Y')  |      |     | N       |       |
| Create_priv    | enum('N','Y')  |      |     | N       |       |
| Drop_priv      | enum('N','Y')  |      |     | N       |       |
```

```
| Reload_priv      | enum('N','Y') |      |    | N |    |    |
| Shutdown_priv    | enum('N','Y') |      |    | N |    |    |
| Process_priv     | enum('N','Y') |      |    | N |    |    |
| File_priv        | enum('N','Y') |      |    | N |    |    |
| Grant_priv       | enum('N','Y') |      |    | N |    |    |
| References_priv  | enum('N','Y') |      |    | N |    |    |
| Index_priv       | enum('N','Y') |      |    | N |    |    |
| Alter_priv       | enum('N','Y') |      |    | N |    |    |
+-----------------+---------------+------+----+--------+------+
```

Listing 8-3 shows all of the command-line parameters you can use with mysqlshow. To see this list use the -? option.

**Listing 8-3: mysqlshow's Command-Line Options**

```
mysqlshow  Ver 6.2 Distrib 3.22.19a, for pc-linux-gnu (i586)
TCX Datakonsult AB, by Monty
This software comes with ABSOLUTELY NO WARRANTY


Shows the structure of a mysql database (databases,tables and
fields)

Usage: mysqlshow [OPTIONS] [database [table [field]]]

   -#, --debug=...         output debug log. Often this is
                           'd:t:o,filename`
   -?, --help              display this help and exit
   -C, --compress          Use compression in server/client protocol
   -h, --host=...          connect to host
   -k, --keys              show keys for table
   -p, --password[=...]    password to use when connecting to server
                           If password is not given it's asked from the
                           tty.
   -P  --port=...          Port number to use for connection
   -S  --socket=...        Socket file to use for connection
   -u, --user=#            user for login if not current user
   -V, --version           output version information and exit

If last argument contains a shell wildcard (* or ?) then only what's
matched by the wildcard is shown.
If no database is given then all matching databases are shown.
If no table is given then all matching tables in database are shown
If no field is given then all matching fields and fieldtypes in
table are shown
```

# Other Utilities

Realistically, you probably won't use mysqlshow a whole lot, but a number of other utilities come with MySQL. A partial list is shown in Table 8-1.

## TABLE 8-1  A PARTIAL LIST OF MYSQL UTILITY PROGRAMS

| Program | Description |
|---|---|
| mysqldump | Dumps a MySQL database to a text file |
| mysqlimport | Imports a text file into a database |
| myisamchk | Checks, optimizes, and repairs MySQL tables |
| mysqladmin | Performs various administrative tasks such as creating or dropping databases, reloading grant tables, and so on |
| replace | Replaces strings in files or in standard input (used by msql2mysql) |
| msql2mysql | Converts mSQL programs to MySQL |
| mysql | Executes SQL statements against MySQL databases in a command line SQL shell that can also be used for administrative functions |
| myisampack | Compresses tables, after which they are read-only |

One of the most-used utilities is mysqladmin, which has various important administrative functions. For the complete mysqladmin command syntax see Tables 8-2 and 8-3.

## TABLE 8-2  MYSQLADMIN [OPTIONS] COMMANDS

| Option | Description |
|---|---|
| -#, --debug=... | Outputs a debug log; often this is 'd:t:o,filename' |
| -f, --force | Doesn't ask for confirmation on drop database; with multiple commands, continues even if an error occurs |
| -?, --help | Displays this help and exits |
| -C, --compress | Uses compression in the server/client protocol |

| Option | Description |
| --- | --- |
| -h, --host=# | Connects to a host |
| -p, --password[=...] | Uses the password when connecting to a server; if a password isn't given, it's asked for from the tty |
| -P --port=... | Uses the port number for a connection |
| -i, --sleep=sec | Executes commands again and again with a sleep between |
| -r, --relative | Shows the difference between current and previous values when used with -I; currently this works with extended-status only |
| -s, --silent | Silently exits if one can't connect to a server |
| -S, --socket=... | Uses the socket file for a connection |
| -t, --timeout=... | Uses a timeout for a connection to the mysqld server |
| -u, --user=# | Uses the user for login, if it's not the current user |
| -V, --version | Outputs version information and exits |
| -w, --wait[=retries] | Waits and retries if the connection is down |

### TABLE 8-3 MYSQLADMIN COMMANDS

| Command | Description |
| --- | --- |
| create databasename | Creates a new database |
| drop databasename | Deletes a database and all its tables |
| extended-status | Returns an extended status message from the server |
| flush-hosts | Flushes all cached hosts |
| flush-logs | Flushes all logs |
| flush-status | Clears status variables |
| flush-tables | Flushes all tables |
| flush-privileges | Reloads grant tables (same as reload) |
| kill id,id,... | Kills mysql threads |

*Continued*

TABLE 8-3 MYSQLADMIN COMMANDS *(Continued)*

| Command | Description |
| --- | --- |
| password new-password | Changes the old password to a new password |
| ping | Checks if mysqld is alive |
| processlist | Shows a list of active threads in the server |
| reload | Reloads grant tables |
| refresh | Flushes all tables and closes and opens log files |
| shutdown | Takes the server down |
| status | Returns a short status message from the server |
| variables | Prints available variables |
| version | Gets version information from the server |

Now that you have MySQL up and running, the next step is to configure MySQL to suit your particular situation. That's the subject of the next chapter.

# Summary

Although MySQL lacks a few of the standard features of a SQL database (such as triggers and foreign keys), it is a popular choice for Web development because of its speed, reliability, and highly configurable access control system. As an open source database, MySQL is freely available and actively developed. Key points to remember include:

- ◆ MySQL is now under the GNU General Public License (GPL).

- ◆ MySQL is optimized for accessing very large databases very quickly.

- ◆ Numerous tools, drivers, and APIs exist for integrating MySQL with other products and languages.

- ◆ MySQL is available in binary and source versions for most platforms, but binaries are usually the easiest with which to work.

- ◆ You can test your MySQL installation using mysqlshow to display available databases and tables.

- ◆ mysqladmin is one of the most-used MySQL utilities and can perform a number of administrative tasks such as creating databases and shutting down the server.

# Chapter 9

# Configuring MySQL

## IN THIS CHAPTER

- ◆ Running the `mysql` client
- ◆ Viewing database and table structures
- ◆ Viewing, updating, and deleting table data
- ◆ Understanding the access control system
- ◆ Setting the root password
- ◆ Setting permissions with `INSERT`, `UPDATE`, and `DELETE`
- ◆ Setting permissions with `GRANT` and `REVOKE`

BY NOW YOU SHOULD have MySQL installed in its default configuration. The next step is to set some minimal permissions and create a database that can house your own tables using the `mysql` client program. Using the mysql client is a little like using a text mode editor — it may not be the prettiest tool for the job, but it's always there. In this chapter you'll use the `mysql` client program to set user permissions, create databases and tables, and update table data.

## The mysql Client

To run the `mysql` client program just type `mysql` at the command prompt. If you're working with a default installation, and no permissions have been changed, you should be able to connect to the database server without specifying the password. If you're working on a Unix installation, and you are not logged in as root, you may need to specify the root user:

```
$ mysql -u root
```

If you're successful in connecting to the database, you see the `mysql` prompt. At this point you can execute only a limited number of commands. One of these is `SHOW DATABASES`, which lists all of the databases to which this MySQL server has access:

```
SHOW DATABASES;
+----------+
| Database |
+----------+
| mysql    |
| test     |
+----------+
2 rows in set (0.00 sec)
```

If this is your first time working with a SQL server, then congratulations, you've just executed your first SQL statement! Okay, so it wasn't that much of a thrill.

As is generally the case, the SQL statement ends with a semicolon. If you leave the semicolon off and press the Enter key, mysql responds with a new line and a slightly changed prompt, as follows:

```
SHOW DATABASES
    ->
```

This feature enables you to split a SQL statement over multiple lines, which can be helpful when you're dealing with long or complicated statements. You could complete the command this way:

```
SHOW DATABASES
;
```

Press Enter and the interpreter reads the semicolon and understands you've completed the statement. It reads the input, ignoring the line breaks. You cannot, however, split words across lines.

The SHOW DATABASES statement indicates that you have two databases available: mysql and test. The test database isn't of any concern at this point because, in a new installation, it's simply an empty database that you can use to create your own tables. If it weren't there, many users would think they needed to create their tables inside the mysql database. Do not do this! The mysql database is for administrative purposes only.

## The mysql database

Although you don't want to add new tables to the mysql database, you or your database administrator has to update information in this database to allow you or other users access to any databases you create.

When you first start the mysql client, you're not able to modify any databases because mysql doesn't know which database you want to work with. You give it this information with the USE statement:

```
USE mysql;
```

MySQL responds with the message:

```
Database changed
```

 Although I've shown the USE mysql statement terminated with a semi-colon, USE is one of the few commands that doesn't require the terminator. But there's no harm in using it, either.

Now that you're actually using the mysql database, you can get some further information about it. Try the SHOW TABLES statement:

```
SHOW TABLES;
+-----------------+
| Tables in mysql |
+-----------------+
| columns_priv    |
| db              |
| func            |
| host            |
| tables_priv     |
| user            |
+-----------------+
6 rows in set (0.00 sec)
```

You can get further details with the DESCRIBE statement, as follows:

```
DESCRIBE user;
```

An example of the output for this statement is shown in Listing 9-1.

**Listing 9-1: Using the DESCRIBE Statement**

| Field | Type | Null | Key | Default | Extra |
|-------|------|------|-----|---------|-------|
| Host | char(60) | | PRI | | |
| User | char(16) | | PRI | | |
| Password | char(16) | | | | |
| Select_priv | enum('N','Y') | | | N | |
| Insert_priv | enum('N','Y') | | | N | |
| Update_priv | enum('N','Y') | | | N | |
| Delete_priv | enum('N','Y') | | | N | |
| Create_priv | enum('N','Y') | | | N | |

*Continued*

**Listing 9-1** *(Continued)*

```
| Drop_priv       | enum('N','Y') |       | N      |       |
| Reload_priv     | enum('N','Y') |       | N      |       |
| Shutdown_priv   | enum('N','Y') |       | N      |       |
| Process_priv    | enum('N','Y') |       | N      |       |
| File_priv       | enum('N','Y') |       | N      |       |
| Grant_priv      | enum('N','Y') |       | N      |       |
| References_priv | enum('N','Y') |       | N      |       |
| Index_priv      | enum('N','Y') |       | N      |       |
| Alter_priv      | enum('N','Y') |       | N      |       |
+-----------------+---------------+-----+-----+--------+-------+
17 rows in set (0.00 sec)
```

As you may recall, the `mysqlshow` utility is capable of producing pretty much the same output.

## Viewing data with the SELECT statement

To actually view the data in the user file described in Listing 9-1, use the SQL `SELECT` statement, as follows:

```
SELECT User,Host,Password,Select_priv,Insert_priv FROM user;
```

This `SELECT` statement returns a data set something like the following:

```
+------+-----------+------------------+-------------+-------------+
| User | Host      | Password         | Select_priv | Insert_priv |
+------+-----------+------------------+-------------+-------------+
| root | localhost | 162eebfb6477e5d3 | Y           | Y           |
|      | %         |                  | N           | N           |
|      | localhost |                  | Y           | Y           |
| root | %         |                  | Y           | Y           |
+------+-----------+------------------+-------------+-------------+
```

This `SELECT` statement shows the `User`, `Host`, and `Password` fields from the user table, along with a few permission flags that indicate if the user can select or add data.

You can return all of the data in the table with this form of `SELECT`:

```
SELECT * FROM user;
```

You can also restrict the records with a `WHERE` clause:

```
SELECT User,Host,Password,Select_priv,Insert_priv
```

```
FROM user WHERE Host='localhost';
```

You can also use logical conditions in a WHERE statement:

```
SELECT User,Host,Password,Select_priv,Insert_priv
FROM user WHERE Host='localhost' and Insert_priv = 'Y';
```

## SQL case sensitivity

It's customary to use all caps for SQL statements, but MySQL understands SQL keywords regardless of capitalization. The same is true of field names. Database and
table names, however, may be case sensitive, because databases are stored in directories and tables are stored as files. If the OS uses case-sensitive file names, as do
Unix and Linux, then your SQL statements will have to match case on database and
table names exactly. On case-insensitive file systems, such as Windows, this is not
necessary.

# The Access Control System

The key to using MySQL is understanding its access control system. The three main
tables involved are user, db, and host. These tables represent a hierarchy of access
control. When MySQL receives a SQL statement, it looks first in the user table for
a record matching the host from which the connection is made, the user, and, if
used, the password. If it finds no matching record, it refuses to execute the SQL
statement. Table 9-1 shows the user table fields with some sample data and the
purpose of the field. Table 9-2 provides similar information about the db table.

TABLE 9-1  THE USER TABLE FIELDS

| Field Name | Sample Data | Purpose |
| --- | --- | --- |
| Host | localhost | The computer from which the user is connecting |
| User | root | User ID |
| Password | 02ad42c52176de17 | Password (usually encrypted) |
| Select_priv | N | Select records |
| Insert_priv | N | Add records |
| Update_priv | N | Update records |

*Continued*

TABLE 9-1  THE USER TABLE FIELDS *(Continued)*

| Field Name | Sample Data | Purpose |
|---|---|---|
| Delete_priv | N | Delete records |
| Create_priv | N | Create tables and databases |
| Drop_priv | N | Drop tables and databases |
| Reload_priv | N | Execute mysqladmin reload, refresh, flush-privileges, flush-hosts, flush-logs, and flush-tables |
| Shutdown_priv | N | Shut down the server |
| Process_priv | N | Execute mysqladmin processlist, kill |
| File_priv | N | Read/write files on the server! |
| Grant_priv | N | Give others the same privileges as yourself |
| References_priv | N | Not implemented? |
| Index_priv | N | Create/drop indexes |
| Alter_priv | N | Alter tables |

TABLE 9-2  THE DB TABLE

| Field Name | Sample Data | Purpose |
|---|---|---|
| Host | 192.168.100.1 | The computer from which the user is connecting |
| Db | testdb | Database |
| User | prefect | User |
| Select_priv | Y | Select records |
| Insert_priv | Y | Add records |
| Update_priv | Y | Update records |
| Delete_priv | Y | Delete records |
| Create_priv | Y | Create tables |

| Field Name | Sample Data | Purpose |
|---|---|---|
| Drop_priv | Y | Drop tables |
| Grant_priv | Y | Give others the same privileges as yourself |
| Index_priv | Y | Create/drop indexes |
| Alter_priv | Y | Alter tables |

If MySQL does find a matching record in the user table, it checks the appropriate permission flag in that record. If the statement is not permitted, MySQL next checks the db table for a record that matches the user, host, and database (the password, if required, has already been verified in the first step). If a matching db record exists, and MySQL still doesn't permit the operation, MySQL checks the hosts table for a record that matches the host and database.

In most cases, you need to concern yourself with user and db permissions only, not host permissions. However, if you wish, you can restrict access not just on a per-host basis (different hosts having different permissions, using the host table), but also by table and by column (using the columns_priv and tables_priv tables).

Any connection to the MySQL server involves at a minimum a host name (the computer from which you're connecting) and a user ID. If you're connecting from the computer on which the MySQL server is running, then the host and user default to localhost and whatever user you're logged in as.

## Setting the root password

Take another look at the subset of fields selected earlier from the user table:

```
+------+-----------+-----------------+-------------+-------------+
| User | Host      | Password        | Select_priv | Insert_priv |
+------+-----------+-----------------+-------------+-------------+
| root | localhost |                 | Y           | Y           |
|      | localhost |                 | Y           | Y           |
+------+-----------+-----------------+-------------+-------------+
```

Select and Insert aren't the only privileges, and you can assume that the other permissions have the same values as those shown in this example. In addition, in two of these records the Host field has a value of %, which is a wildcard meaning that any host matches.

Privileges granted in the user table are effectively superuser privileges and apply to all databases. That means if you grant Update rights to a user, that user can now update all tables in all databases, *including the* `mysql` *database.* Such a user is effectively a MySQL administrator/superuser and can change any and all information including root passwords and so forth. So be very careful about which user records have database privileges.

Anyone who logs in with superuser privileges has complete control over the MySQL database, can set permissions at will, and can modify any database records anywhere. This is not a good situation. You can set the root password (if you're logged in as root) from outside MySQL with the following statement:

```
mysqladmin password mynewpassword
```

Follow this line with a `reload` command to put the new password into effect.

```
mysqladmin reload
```

You'd better write that password down in a safe place, because you need it to get access! If you forget it, you need to restart `mysqld` with the `-skip-grant-tables` option to log in.

Once you set the root password, you need to specify it whenever you connect to MySQL. You do this with the `-p` option. For instance, if your password is "mypassword," then call `mysqlshow` this way (you can dispense with the `-uroot` option if you're already logged in as root):

```
mysqlshow -uroot -p
```

and type the password when prompted, or type:

```
mysqlshow -uroot -pmypassword
```

or

```
mysqlshow -password=mypassword
```

The last two options display your password on screen, of course. Perhaps no one is looking over your physical shoulder. Even so, someone could be looking over your virtual shoulder. For instance, the Unix `ps` command lists any currently executing processes along with their command-line parameters, so in theory someone could telnet in, run `ps`, and see your password, although it would only be visible momentarily.

Similarly, if you're logged in to your server through a publicly visible connection (say, over the Internet), someone could be eavesdropping on your communication with the MySQL server. You should seriously encrypt your telnet session with a protocol like SSH2. Installing and configuring SSH2 is beyond the scope of this book, but you can find more information about free implementations of the SSH2 protocol at `www.openssh.org`. You can either use SSH as secure telnet, or tunnel your MySQL connection through SSH2.

## Using the INSERT statement to add new permissions

After you install MySQL you can, as you might expect, access the MySQL databases from that machine, because the install script or program creates permissions for the host `localhost`. To access MySQL from another machine, you need to set up some permissions. You can do this with the `mysql` client. On the database server machine type

```
mysql
```

   or

```
mysql -p
```

   if you've assigned a root password. Then create a database:

```
create database testdb;
```

   You get a response similar to the following:

```
Query OK, 1 row affected (0.01 sec)
```

   Remember that when you start the `mysql` client, no database is selected, so specify the `mysql` database:

```
use mysql;
```

   You can now update the `mysql` database and create the necessary records to allow another user to connect to the database from another machine.

   Let's say your database server and the machine from which you want to access the database are both on a local network, and their IP addresses are, respectively, 192.168.100.1 and 192.168.100.9. First, create a user record:

```
INSERT INTO user (host,user,password)
VALUES('192.168.100.9','prefect',password('megadodo'));
```

   This `INSERT INTO` statement specifies only three fields in the user file. All the remaining fields default to N, which again is a good idea unless you want to give this user superuser privileges. Note the use of the password function to do the encryption. Next, add a db record:

```
INSERT INTO db (host,db,user,Select_priv,Insert_priv,
Update_priv,Delete_priv, Create_priv,Drop_priv)
VALUES ('192.168.100.9','testdb','prefect',
'Y','Y','Y','Y','Y','Y');
```

Before these values take effect, you need to do one of two things. You can reload the privileges from `mysql`:

```
FLUSH PRIVILEGES;
```

Alternately, you can use the `QUIT` statement to exit `mysql`, then run `mysqladmin` to reload the grant tables:

```
mysqladmin reload
```

MySQL keeps the privilege settings in memory rather than reading them from disk each time a request is made, and you have to tell it explicitly to reload this information from the database.

## Using the UPDATE statement to change permissions

Once you reload the grant tables, you should be able to log in to the database from the client machine. If you are still unable to do so, run `mysql` on the database machine and use the `SELECT` statement to view and verify the data from the `user` and `db` tables. If you've made a mistake, such as incorrectly typing a user id, you can fix this with the SQL `UPDATE` statement. For example:

```
UPDATE db SET user='me' WHERE user='you';
```

Don't forget the `WHERE` clause! If you execute a statement such as

```
UPDATE db SET user='me';
```

you update *all* the rows in that table. And there's no undo.

## Using the DELETE statement to remove permissions

If you need to remove permissions, you have two choices. Either you can set all of the user's access flags to `N` in all of that user's rights records in the `user` and `db` (and if necessary, `host`) tables, or you can delete the `users` records:

```
DELETE FROM user WHERE user='prefect';
DELETE FROM db WHERE user='prefect';
```

As with the `UPDATE` statement, be sure to use the `WHERE` clause or you will delete *all* rows in the table.

SQL is a powerful language, and if you have superuser privileges, you can easily wreak havoc on a database. It's not necessarily that difficult if you don't have superuser privileges, either. As long as you have DELETE or UPDATE privileges, you can affect massive numbers of records with a single statement.

# Using the GRANT and REVOKE statements to set permissions

It's good to know how to set permissions in MySQL by creating, updating, and, if necessary, deleting records. But setting permissions is also a tedious and error-prone process. Happily, as of version 3.22.11, MySQL provides two commands that make life a little easier by adding the permission records for you.

## HOW TO GRANT PERMISSIONS
The GRANT statement has the following syntax:

```
GRANT <permissions> ON <table(s)> TO <user[@domain]>
    [IDENTIFIED BY '<password>']
```

To give the user prefect viewing permission on the tables in the testdb database, from localhost, you would use the statement:

```
GRANT SELECT ON testdb.* TO prefect;
```

By not specifying a host domain, you're allowing this user to connect from anywhere, which may not be a wise move, particularly since you haven't specified a password either. All anyone needs to guess is the user ID. It's better, if you know the domain, to specify it:

```
GRANT SELECT ON testdb.* TO prefect@localhost;
```

This GRANT statement is an improvement, but it doesn't yet include a password. To apply a password, use IDENTIFIED BY:

```
GRANT SELECT ON testdb.* TO prefect@localhost
IDENTIFIED BY 'megadodo';
```

The combination of host domain and password make these permissions fairly difficult to compromise. If the user is coming from a network where IP addresses are assigned as needed, you may need to specify a wildcard in the host domain name. MySQL does allow you to use the % (any characters) and _ (any one character) wildcards for hosts (names or IP addresses), but you should be careful when doing this as it greatly decreases the security of your system.

The following GRANT statement restricts access to the user prefect coming from the class C subnet 192.168.34:

```
GRANT SELECT ON testdb.* TO prefect@'192.168.34.%'
IDENTIFIED BY 'megadodo';
```

 When using wild cards, you have to put the host name in quotes.

You can use a combination of the permissions listed in Table 9-3 immediately after the GRANT statement.

TABLE 9-3 PERMISSIONS THAT CAN BE GRANTED

| Privilege | Description |
|---|---|
| ALL PRIVILEGES | Allows the user to do anything |
| FILE | Imports data from or exports data to a disk file |
| RELOAD | Reloads the grant tables and flushes logs |
| ALTER | Alters the table structure |
| INDEX | Adds or removes indexes |
| SELECT | Views table data |
| CREATE | Creates databases, tables, or indexes |
| INSERT | Adds table data |
| SHUTDOWN | Shuts down the MySQL server |
| DELETE | Deletes data |
| PROCESS | Runs processlist and kill to manage server threads |
| UPDATE | Updates table data |
| DROP | Drops tables or databases |
| USAGE | Provides a synonym for INSERT UPDATE DELETE |

## HOW TO REVOKE PERMISSIONS

To remove permissions, whether they are created manually or with the GRANT statement, you can use the REVOKE statement. The syntax is similar to GRANT except that no password is ever needed, and instead of granting TO you revoke FROM:

```
REVOKE SELECT ON testdb.* FROM prefect@'192.168.34.%';
```

 All of the GRANT and REVOKE examples shown here deal with entire databases. You can also use GRANT and REVOKE to set table- and column-specific permissions. See the MySQL documentation, section 7.33, for more information.

## DANGER AHEAD!

Apply the "less is more" principle to your permission granting. It's best to start with the most restrictive permissions and then grant more as needed than to discover you allowed a user to modify someone else's data, or compromised your system by permitting easy access for an intruder. In particular, be careful of the following rights:

◆ GRANT – allows users to assign their own level of permission to others, which may result in dangerous combinations of privileges.

◆ FILE – effectively allows users to read any world-readable file anywhere on your server (including other MySQL databases) by importing the file into a table.

◆ PROCESS – may allow users to snoop on passwords and other valuable information.

◆ ALTER – by renaming tables users may be able to bypass access restrictions.

◆ SHUTDOWN – allows users to terminate the server.

# Summary

The key to using MySQL safely is understanding the access control system. With MySQL you can tightly control which users get access to which parts of the database, and from which hosts. To set permissions, you need to learn only a few basic SQL statements. Key points to remember include:

♦ Before you can work with a database you need to issue the use <databasename> statement.

♦ Although a few statements (such as use) do not need a terminating semicolon, you can always use one.

♦ In most cases you need to add information only to the user and db tables.

♦ You can use SQL INSERT, UPDATE, and SELECT statements to update user permissions.

♦ You have to use the FLUSH PRIVILEGES statement or execute mysqladmin reload before privilege changes take effect.

♦ Always set the root password.

♦ The easiest way to set or change permissions is with the GRANT and REVOKE statements.

♦ Be very careful when allowing GRANT, FILE, PROCESS, ALTER, and SHUTDOWN permissions.

Chapter 10

# Working with SQL Tables

## IN THIS CHAPTER

◆ Creating and removing databases

◆ Creating tables

◆ Choosing data types

◆ Understanding indexes and foreign keys

◆ Changing table definitions

DATABASE ADMINISTRATORS, or DBAs, are responsible not just for setting user access rights, but also for creating and maintaining databases. In a large organization, getting the DBA to add just one field to a table or create an index may involve a lot of politics and perhaps some begging. If you've installed MySQL, however, you are your own DBA, and you can create and modify databases at will. Therefore, you'll need to know a few of the fundamentals. In this chapter you'll learn how to create and remove databases, and how to create, modify, and remove tables and indexes.

## Creating Databases

A database is a collection of tables, and a SQL server can normally handle more than one database at a time. This is not only possible, but in most cases desirable, particularly for ISPs that often use MySQL to provide individual databases to customers. Certainly if you're just starting to experiment with SQL, you should create at least one new database for this purpose. You don't want to risk messing up existing data.

 You may be tempted to use the database called "mysql" for test purposes. Don't! This database exists strictly for MySQL administrative purposes. Do not create any new tables for this database, and don't modify any of the existing administrative tables. Any servlet you create should not even be allowed read access to this database, as you'd be just asking for a security problem.

## Creating a database

There are two ways to create a database: you can use a graphical client like MySQLGUI or MySQL Administrator for Windows, or you can create the database using direct SQL statements, either in a SQL client or in a servlet. Even if a graphical client is easier to use, you should familiarize yourself with the underlying SQL statements. In either case, to create a database you need to create (Create_priv) rights.

 For a discussion about setting rights in MySQL, see Chapter 9.

To use the `mysql` client to create a test database, use this statement:

```
CREATE DATABASE test;
```

You'll need the semicolon at the end of the statement. If you forget it, the line simply breaks, and you'll get a chance to type it again, so no worries.

## Removing a database

Removing a database deserves a word of caution up front. The DROP DATABASE statement is an *extremely* dangerous statement to execute, and is not unlike deleting an entire directory of important data. In most cases, a lot of work has gone into creating a SQL database, and it should only be dropped with the greatest of care. It's also a good idea not to give two databases with similar names, or you may drop the wrong one. You can use the DROP DATABASE statement to remove an entire database, as follows for a database named Test:

```
DROP DATABASE Test;
```

## Case sensitivity

Although SQL is traditionally written in all caps, it can be lower or mixed case. In MySQL, database names and table names are case sensitive when MySQL is installed on an operating system that uses case-sensitive file names. This case sensitivity is because creating a database creates a directory, and creating a table creates a file in that directory to store the table. Field names are not case sensitive, since they're just a structure within the table.

# Creating Tables

Creating a table is a bit more complicated than creating a database. First, you need to make sure that you're using the database where you want the table created:

```
USE test;
```

Now you can issue the table creation statement. Listing 10-1 shows an example of a CREATE statement that adds a table with three fields to the current database (test, in this case).

**Listing 10-1: Using the CREATE Statement to Make a New Names Table**

```
CREATE TABLE Names (
ID INT AUTO_INCREMENT PRIMARY KEY,
FirstName CHAR(30) NOT NULL,
LastName CHAR(30) NOT NULL,
INDEX LastNameKey (LastName,FirstName)
);
Query OK, 0 rows affected (0.00 sec)
```

The SQL code in Listing 10-1 is shown on multiple lines, but it is still a single statement. The statement could also have been written all on one line, but that's a little hard on the eyes, and it gets worse when you're dealing with large table structures. Use line breaks to improve readability.

## Using the CREATE syntax

Listing 10-1 shows one of the simplest table creation statements you're likely to see, but it illustrates the essentials. The CREATE statement begins as CREATE TABLE <tablename>, followed by a create definition in parentheses. Listing 10-2 shows the MySQL CREATE TABLE syntax.

**Listing 10-2: The MySQL CREATE TABLE Syntax**

```
CREATE [TEMPORARY] TABLE
[IF NOT EXISTS] tbl_name
[(create_definition,...)]
[table_options]
[select_statement]

create_definition:

col_name type [NOT NULL | NULL] [DEFAULT default_value]
   [AUTO_INCREMENT] [PRIMARY KEY] [reference_definition]
or PRIMARY KEY (index_col_name,...)
```

*Continued*

Listing 10-2 *(Continued)*

```
or KEY [index_name] (index_col_name,...)
or INDEX [index_name] (index_col_name,...)
or UNIQUE [INDEX] [index_name] (index_col_name,...)
or FULLTEXT [INDEX] [index_name] (index_col_name,...)
or [CONSTRAINT symbol]
FOREIGN KEY index_name (index_col_name,...)
[reference_definition]
or CHECK (expr)
```

Each element in a table is, by convention, written on its own line. Immediately following the CREATE TABLE statement are the column definitions. Column definitions can vary slightly between vendors; in MySQL, each column has the form:

```
col_name type
[NOT NULL | NULL]
[DEFAULT default_value]
[AUTO_INCREMENT]
[PRIMARY KEY]
[reference_definition]
```

Immediately after the column name is the column's data type. There are a lot of these, and MySQL's available data types are shown in Table 10-1.

TABLE 10-1 DATA TYPES AVAILABLE TO MYSQL

| Type | Optional attributes | Description |
| --- | --- | --- |
| TINYINT | UNSIGNED<br>ZEROFILL | A signed integer from –128 to 127, or unsigned from 0 to 255 (the default is signed); if ZEROFILL is used, values are displayed padded with zeroes instead of spaces. |
| SMALLINT | UNSIGNED<br>ZEROFILL | A signed integer from -32768 to 32767, or unsigned from 0 to 65535 (the default is signed). |
| MEDIUMINT | UNSIGNED<br>ZEROFILL | A signed integer from 8388608 to 8388607, or unsigned from 0 to 16777215. The default is signed. |
| INT | UNSIGNED<br>ZEROFILL | A signed integer from 2147483648 to 2147483647, or unsigned from 0 to 4294967295 (the default is signed). |

| Type | Optional attributes | Description |
|------|--------------------|-------------|
| INTEGER | | A synonym for INT. |
| BIGINT | UNSIGNED ZEROFILL | A signed integer from 9223372036854775808 to 9223372036854775807, or unsigned from 0 to 18446744073709551615 (the default is signed). |
| FLOAT (precision) | ZEROFILL | A signed floating point number: single precision if the precision value is up to 24, or double precision for values from 25–53. |
| FLOAT | (M,D) ZEROFILL | A floating point single precision signed number; M is the display width, and D is the number of decimal places. |
| DOUBLE | (M,D) ZEROFILL | A floating point single precision signed number; M is the display width, and D is the number of decimal places. |
| DOUBLE PRECISION | (M,D) ZEROFILL | A synonym for DOUBLE. |
| REAL | (MD,) ZEROFILL | A synonym for DOUBLE. |
| DECIMAL | (M[,D]) ZEROFILL | An unpacked, signed floating point number stored as a string with one character for each digit. |
| NUMERIC | (M,D) ZEROFILL | A synonym for DECIMAL. |
| DATE | | A date from 1000-01-01 to 9999-12-31. |
| DATETIME | | A combination of date and time from 1000-01-01 00:00:00 to 9999-12-31 23:59:59 |
| TIMESTAMP | (M) | A combination of date and time from 1970-01-01 00:00:00 to a day in the year 2037 (can you say Y2.037K bug?).<br><br>If present, this column automatically sets to the current date and time whenever an INSERT or UPDATE happens on the record. |

*Continued*

TABLE 10-1 DATA TYPES AVAILABLE TO MYSQL *(Continued)*

| Type | Optional attributes | Description |
| --- | --- | --- |
| | | The M value indicates how the date/time is displayed. |
| TIME | | A time value from –838:59:59 to 838:59:59 — that's plus or minus a little over 838 hours, which is a bit more than a month. |
| YEAR | (2\|4) | A year value in two-digit (1970–2069) or default four-digit (1901–2155) format. |
| CHAR(M) NATIONAL CHAR(M) | BINARY | A fixed length string (1(255), right padded with spaces — the NATIONAL attribute is prefixed to the declaration, as in NATIONAL CHAR(20); indicates the current character set should be used; and is the default. |
| | | The CHAR(0) function can be used as a kind of boolean, as it takes only NULL or empty ("") values. |
| | | If the BINARY attribute is not used, comparisons are case insensitive. |
| VARCHAR(M) NATIONAL VARCHAR(M) | BINARY | Variable length string from 1–255 characters; a VARCHAR of less than four characters is converted to a CHAR. |
| | | If a MySQL table has at least one VARCHAR (of 4+ chars), TEXT, or BLOB field, the record is variable length and all CHAR fields of more than four characters are treated as VARCHAR. |
| | | If the BINARY attribute is not used, comparisons are case insensitive. |
| TINYBLOB TINYTEXT | | A text or BLOB (binary large object) field of up to 255 characters. |
| BLOB TEXT | | A text or BLOB (binary large object) field of up to 65535 characters. |
| MEDIUMBLOB MEDIUMTEXT | | A text or BLOB (binary large object) field of up to 16777215 characters. |

| Type | Optional attributes | Description |
|------|---------------------|-------------|
| LONGBLOB<br>LONGTEXT | | A text or BLOB (binary large object) field of up to 4294967295 characters. |
| ENUM<br>('value1',<br>'value2',...) | | A string field that can have only one of a predefined set of up to 65535 possible distinct values. |
| SET<br>('value1',<br>'value2',...) | | A string that can have zero or more values from a predefined set of up to 64 values. |

As you can see in Table 10-1, MySQL, like other SQL databases, offers a wide variety of data types. How do you choose which data type to use?

## Choosing data types

The rule of thumb in choosing a data type for a column is to not use anything bigger than you need. If you need a field for the day of the week, use a TINYINT, not an INT. But be sure you do choose something that's large enough. If you think you may need values from 1–200 for a field, perhaps you're better off with a SMALLINT, or you may find that you're crowding 255 before you know it. Similarly, make sure that you use a signed or unsigned value as appropriate.

Floating point numbers can be problematic. Intel's famous Pentium math error aside, floating point arithmetic is by nature imprecise. If you're working with currencies where absolute precision is essential, you should probably consider storing values in DECIMAL fields.

String type choices usually come down to CHAR and VARCHAR for values of under 255 characters. Fixed-length fields are generally faster, so all VARCHAR fields of under four characters are converted to CHAR. But a mix of longer CHAR and VARCHAR fields can be dealt with more easily if all are the same type, so if you're using any VARCHAR (of more than four characters), TEXT, or BLOB fields, all CHAR fields in the table are converted to variable length VARCHAR fields, and the entire record becomes variable length. You may wish to simply stick with VARCHAR for all string declarations of up to 255 characters.

For very large text fields or large binary fields, you have a selection of data types, all the way up to the 4GB LONGBLOB and LONGTEXT. SQL has good support for date and time formats. Take special note of the TIMESTAMP type that automatically tracks the last inserted/modified date and time.

# Column attributes

Take another look at the column declaration syntax, which shows optional attributes in square brackets:

```
col_name type
[NOT NULL | NULL]
[DEFAULT default_value]
[AUTO_INCREMENT]
[PRIMARY KEY]
```

## NULLS

The concept of NULL is an important one in SQL. The NULL value is distinct from a zero numeric value or an empty string. A NULL value means that no value has been set. After all, a zero or an empty string could easily be important data, especially if it stands for the money you owe or the name of the person to whom you owe the money. Unless you specify a default value for a column, NULL will be the default.

In the column declaration, NULL means that you can insert a null value into this column. A NOT NULL value means that you must supply a non-NULL value.

```
FirstName CHAR(30) NOT NULL,
```

## DEFAULT VALUES

You can specify a default value for the field, as in this example of an enumerated field:

```
Contacted ENUM('Y','N') DEFAULT 'N')
```

You can also use numeric default values:

```
CallsMade SMALLINT DEFAULT 0)
```

## PRIMARY KEYS AND AUTO INCREMENT FIELDS

As explained in Chapter 7, the server uses primary keys to uniquely identify each row within a table. To mark a column as the primary key, simply use the PRIMARY KEY attribute.

You can use primary keys in conjunction with automatically incremented fields to assign a default unique ID to each record:

```
ID INT NOT NULL AUTO_INCREMENT PRIMARY KEY
```

Each time you add a record, the server will give the ID field as defined here a value equal to the highest ID value in the table, plus one. The first record entered will have an ID value of 1.

There is another way to define a primary key in the CREATE TABLE statement:

```
PRIMARY KEY (index_col_name,...)
```

As this alternate syntax makes plain, you can have more than one column in the primary key.

## Viewing an existing table definition

If you want to know the structure of tables already in a database, you can use the SHOW and DESCRIBED statements. The SHOW TABLES statement entered as:

```
SHOW TABLES;
```

displays a list of all of the tables in the currently selected database, as shown here:

```
+----------------+
| Tables in test |
+----------------+
| Names          |
+----------------+
1 row in set (0.00 sec)
```

For details on the table's structure use the DESCRIBE statement, as shown here:

```
DESCRIBE Names;
```

to obtain ouput such as this:

```
+-----------+----------+------+-----+---------+----------------+
| Field     | Type     | Null | Key | Default | Extra          |
+-----------+----------+------+-----+---------+----------------+
| ID        | int(11)  |      | PRI | 0       | auto_increment |
| FirstName | char(30) |      |     |         |                |
| LastName  | char(30) |      | MUL |         |                |
+-----------+----------+------+-----+---------+----------------+
3 rows in set (0.00 sec)
```

Note the three fields in the Names table. Two are as you'd expect: one for first name and the other for last name. The third (well, first) field is a unique field used as a primary key to make it easy to link data in other tables to this table.

# Indexes and Foreign Keys

As pointed out in Chapter 7, keys are a logical definition of fields that link tables, while indexes are a structure the server uses to quickly locate records. The keys, not the indexes, define the relationship. Figure 10-1 shows a diagram of the relationship between the `Authors` and `Articles` tables discussed in that chapter.

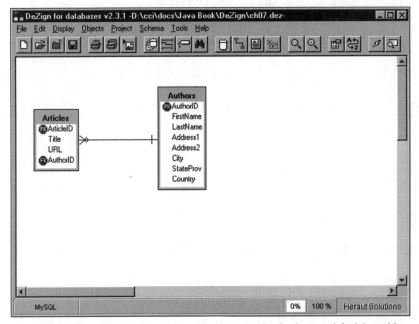

Figure 10-1: Diagramming the relationship between the Authors and Articles tables

In Figure 10-1, the ID field in the Articles table is a primary key used to uniquely identify each row. When an article is linked to an author, the `AuthorID` field in the `Articles` table is set to the value of the `Authors ID` field. Fields used to refer to another primary key are called foreign keys, because they link to some data that is outside of, or foreign to, this table.

A key is just a logical construct – there's nothing at this point that supports the quick retrieval of related records. If I have thousands of author records and tens of thousands of article records, it may take the MySQL server a noticeable period to locate all of the articles for a particular author.

To speed things up, you can create an index on the foreign key. The syntax, within the `CREATE TABLE` definition, is this:

```
INDEX [index_name] (index_col_name,...)
```

Creating indexes is easy. Just specify the name of the index and one or more columns to index. If you're indexing CHAR or VARCHAR fields, the index will not be case sensitive unless you specify the BINARY attribute on the field definitions (not the index definition).

To index on the LastName and FirstName fields, you create an index this way:

```
INDEX LastFirstIDX (LastName,FirstName)
```

 To get some insight into which indexes MySQL is or isn't using, use the EXPLAIN command followed by the statement. The EXPLAIN command will show you the indexes and fields the server uses to evaluate your statement.

## Keys

In MySQL, KEY is just a synonym for INDEX. Unfortunately this synonym only makes it more difficult to differentiate between keys (which are a logical construct) and indexes (which are a physical construct). But in reality a lot of people use the two terms interchangeably.

## Unique indexes

Indexes by default allow duplicates. If you want a unique index, use the UNIQUE keyword instead of INDEX. You can also use UNIQUE INDEX if you wish, but that doesn't add any functionality. Since a unique key can have only unique values, you'll get an error if you attempt to add or update a record that would cause a duplicate key.

## Text indexes

In addition to the usual kind of indexing, MySQL can also index very large text fields (up to 4GB). As of this writing, MySQL's matching algorithm is designed for natural language searches, where the value of any word is related to the number of times it appears in a given block of text. Boolean searches are under development and may be available by the time you read this. See the MySQL documentation for more information on full text indexing.

# Changing Table Definitions

Databases tend to be Darwinian, evolving constantly, and hopefully adapting to changing conditions (although if you've been writing database software for a few years, you've probably seen at least one evolve itself right into extinction). You might need to add a field, change the type of a column, or add an index. You can do all this with the ALTER TABLE statement.

## Using the ALTER TABLE statement

You can use ALTER TABLE to change field names and data types, set new default values, add new fields, drop fields, and generally cause all kinds of chaos. Remember that SQL is a very powerful language, and there's a reason large organizations restrict this kind of activity to well-paid and (hopefully) highly trained DBAs.

The ALTER TABLE statement has the syntax shown in Listing 10-3. When you execute ALTER TABLE on a MySQL table, the server creates a temporary copy of the table, makes changes on that copy, and then deletes the original and renames the copy.

**Listing 10-3: The ALTER TABLE Statement Syntax**

```
ALTER [IGNORE] TABLE tbl_name alter_spec [, alter_spec ...]

alter_specification:
        ADD [COLUMN] create_definition [FIRST | AFTER column_name ]
  or    ADD [COLUMN] (create_definition, create_definition,...)
  or    ADD INDEX [index_name] (index_col_name,...)
  or    ADD PRIMARY KEY (index_col_name,...)
  or    ADD UNIQUE [index_name] (index_col_name,...)
  or    ADD FULLTEXT [index_name] (index_col_name,...)
  or    ALTER [COLUMN] col_name {SET DEFAULT literal | DROP DEFAULT}
  or    CHANGE [COLUMN] old_col_name create_definition
  or    MODIFY [COLUMN] create_definition
  or    DROP [COLUMN] col_name
  or    DROP PRIMARY KEY
  or    DROP INDEX index_name
  or    RENAME [TO] new_tbl_name
  or    table_options
```

When you use ALTER TABLE to change a column's data type, MySQL attempts to convert the data. Don't attempt something like this without backing up first! You might even want to create a test table, add some representative data, and try converting that table's columns first.

## Adding columns and indexes

You use the ADD alter specification to add columns and indexes to a table. For columns, the syntax is:

```
ALTER TABLE ADD [COLUMN] create_definition
  [FIRST | AFTER column_name ]
```

or

```
ALTER TABLE ADD [COLUMN] (create_definition, create_definition,...)
```

The `create_definition` attribute is the same as when creating tables:

```
col_name type [NOT NULL | NULL] [DEFAULT default_value]
[AUTO_INCREMENT] [PRIMARY KEY]
```

You can use the `FIRST` and `AFTER column_name` forms if you want to locate the new column at a specific place in the table. If you omit these, the column is created at the end of the table.

Similarly, add an index by following the `CREATE TABLE` syntax:

```
ALTER TABLE ADD INDEX [index_name] (index_col_name,...)
```

As with `CREATE TABLE`, you can create unique and full text indexes.

## Modifying columns

It's a bit trickier modifying columns than adding or removing them, and of course you need to pay attention to what's going to happen to the data as a result of the change! If you want to change the default value for a column, use the `ALTER` column statement.

```
ALTER TABLE ALTER [COLUMN] col_name
{SET DEFAULT literal | DROP DEFAULT}
```

 You can write `ALTER  COLUMN` if it makes you feel better; it won't affect the end result at all.

If you need to change the name or type of the column, use `ALTER  TABLE` *tablename* `CHANGE` or `MODIFY`.

```
ALTER TABLE CHANGE [COLUMN] old_col_name create_definition
ALTER TABLE MODIFY [COLUMN] create_definition
```

There's a subtle difference between the `CHANGE` and `MODIFY` statements. With the `CHANGE` statement, you specify the old column name, so you can use this instruction to rename the column, whether or not you change its data type. With MODIFY you can change column attributes other than the column's name. For instance, to change a column from a CHAR(30) to a VARCHAR(30), use the following:

```
ALTER TABLE Authors MODIFY Address VARCHAR(30)
```

This statement changes the data type to a VARCHAR(30), but because of MySQL's optimization rules, you may be surprised to discover that all of your other CHAR fields of more than three characters length are now also VARCHAR instead of CHAR. You will also have some difficulty changing these back to CHAR, because MySQL ignores any attempts to change a single field to CHAR, if there is at least one other VARCHAR in the table.

## Removing columns and indexes

You can remove columns, primary keys, or indexes from a table using the ALTER TABLE *tablename* DROP statement.

```
ALTER TABLE DROP [COLUMN] col_name
ALTER TABLE DROP PRIMARY KEY
ALTER TABLE DROP INDEX index_name
```

Dropping a column can, of course, have some drastic consequences. Similarly, dropping a primary key may cause problems because any related tables use (or should use) the primary key value as a foreign key. Dropping an index is a safe thing to do by comparison, because it really only affects how quickly the server can locate data. That may cause a mild to severe inconvenience, but it shouldn't break anything.

# Summary

SQL servers such as MySQL can support a large number of databases, so you have lots of room to play when you're getting started. Just set up a new database (or several) and start creating tables and indexes. Key points to remember include:

- ◆ Never put your tables in the mysql database; that's for administrative purposes only.

- ◆ Be careful about dropping an entire database, especially if it contains production data — once it's gone, it's gone.

- ◆ When choosing currency data types, be aware of floating point inaccuracies; you may wish to use a decimal field instead.

- ◆ Don't use unnecessarily large data types.

◆ Don't worry if you don't have the table exactly right at the start; you can always modify the table structure later.

◆ MySQL attempts to convert data when you change a column's data type, but as there's no guarantee the conversion will be successful, you should always back up important data first.

# Chapter 11

# Designing a Database:
# A Case Study

**IN THIS CHAPTER**

◆ Introducing a rudimentary database requirement

◆ Creating the core tables

◆ Clarifying the design requirements

◆ Establishing relationships between tables

◆ Implementing the requirements

◆ Using indexes effectively

◆ Running table creation scripts

IF YOU WANT YOUR database-enabled Web applications to have long and productive lives, you need to design your database with due care and attention. The case study I present in this chapter deals with a small database containing ten tables. Ten tables may seem like a lot if you're used to working with just two or three tables, but in SQL database terms it's small potatoes. Scores, or even hundreds of tables, are not uncommon for a SQL database.

As you become more experienced with database applications, you'll find that even for what seems like simple applications, you can quickly come up with twenty tables or more. In this chapter I'll walk you through a case study, and show you how to design a practical, useful Web-application database.

## The Database Requirement

Sometimes you receive a formal specification for a database, and you can just start creating the tables. Other times you have a rough idea of the task you want to accomplish, and you need to create the database as you go. In this chapter, I use the example of an online magazine Web application. As the database designer, I'm working with a rough specification I've received from the application designer (also me, but wearing another hat). I see that the (very) rough design specification identifies the following requirements:

◆ Maintain information on articles and authors

◆ Authenticate users for specified pages on the site

◆ Track subscription orders

Those are some of the sketchiest requirements you're ever likely to see, but every database has to begin somewhere. And if you can create a database from almost no information, you'll be well equipped to handle more specific database design requirements.

## Tools that make the job easier

Any time you get beyond one or two tables, it's best to begin diagramming the database, paying particular attention to the relationships between the tables. I'll demonstrate this process using Herault System's DeZign, a relatively inexpensive tool for drawing Entity-Relationship Diagrams (ERDs).

A great many diagramming tools are available at a wide range of prices. Generally the more you pay, the more you get, particularly if you're looking at a tool that can do database administration as well as help you with your diagrams. You'll also find that there are a lot of variations on the ERD, depending on how much detail you want to record in the diagram, and which symbol set you prefer to use.

## Unified Modeling Language

Although the many varieties of ERDs are still the mainstay of database design, more and more designers are using Unified Modeling Language (UML) tools to diagram databases. UML is more common in object-oriented software development, but as the object model permeates database development, more designers are seeing the benefits of using a tool that is designed to explain object-oriented systems.

Unless you have a lot of experience with UML, I think you'll be better off creating ERDs at first. As you become more comfortable with database design, you can experiment with UML database drawings.

# Deciding the Core Tables

The first step in database design is to begin some grouping of data together into tables. At first you'll find it easy to group data; some bits of information, such as a name and address, just naturally belong together. A bit of general knowledge about the system you're designing takes you through the first few tables.

You can start by taking a *noun list* approach to the specification. Nouns describe things, and in a specification they often indicate the core tables you need. One of the nouns listed in the specification is *user*, which suggests a table to keep track of users' personal information.

## The Names table

My first impulse is to create a table called User or perhaps Subscriber, but past experience tells me that it's good to think about all the possible uses a table may have. A user is really a role someone has when at the Web site. Another possible role is administrator. And you may want to keep some information in the database that doesn't relate to users. For instance, you might want to store some information about authors. Since there's little to distinguish these different kinds of people, I'll call the table Names. Figure 11-1 shows a first cut of the Names table.

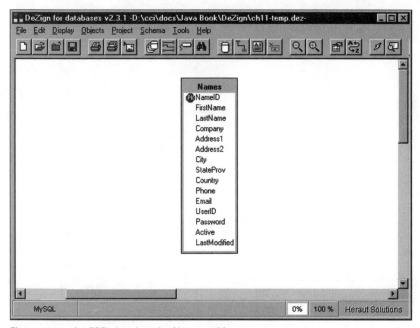

Figure 11-1: An ERD showing the Names table

As Figure 11-1 shows, the Names table contains typical information such as first name, last name, address, e-mail address, and so forth. It also contains user ID and password fields. The assumption here is that almost all records in the Names table will be actual users. Since each user never has more than one user ID and password, it makes sense to group the user's security information with the more general user information.

## The Articles table

The specification also mentions articles. Basic information to be stored about articles, after further discussion with the design team, includes the article URL, the title (for display in menus), an article summary, and a flag indicating if this article requires a subscription for access. Note that this table, like all others, has a `LastModified TIMESTAMP` field, which the server automatically updates. Figure 11-2 shows the Articles table added to the ERD.

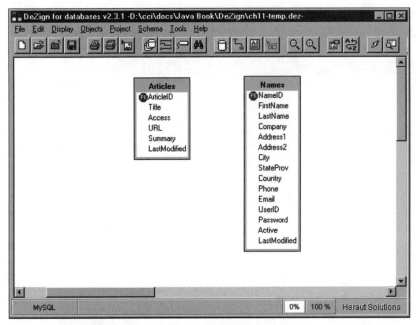

Figure 11-2: An ERD showing the Names and Articles tables

So far, so good. The database design is, however, about to get a bit more complicated.

# Establishing Relationships

Although the primitive requirements list discussed at the beginning of this chapter doesn't say so explicitly, it's obvious that articles and authors are related pieces of information, since authors write articles. Chapter 7 covers relationships in some detail. This chapter doesn't duplicate that discussion here, except to highlight the three kinds of relationships: one-to-many, one-to-one, and many-to-many.

◆ *One-to-many relationships* – In a one-to-many relationship, you link a row of data in one table to multiple rows of data in the other table. One-to-many relationships (or many-to-one relationships, depending on your point of view) are the most common type of relationship and are easy to manage.

◆ *One-to-one relationships* – One-to-one relationships, where one record has zero or one related record in another table, are the least common type of relationship. Sometimes you'll use one-to-one relationships to make data storage more efficient, as when most rows in a table do not need to store information in the second table.

◆ *Many-to-many relationships* – Many-to-many relationships occur when table A has a many-to-one relationship to table B, and table B also has a many-to-one relationship to table A. In other words, more than one record in table A is related to more than one record in table B. Many-to-many relationships are more difficult to handle than one-to-many and one-to-one relationships.

## The Authors–Articles relationship

As indicated in Chapter 7, at first blush there would seem to be a one-to-many relationship between authors and articles, since one author can write many articles. Whenever you see a one-to-many relationship, ask yourself or any other people involved whether there's a possibility that this could be a many-to-many relationship. In this case, you know that one author can write many articles; what you need to know next is whether multiple authors can write one article. If the answer is yes, then you have a many-to-many relationship.

The problem is it's difficult (and certainly not advisable) to model a many-to-many relationship with just two tables. While you can represent a many-to-many relationship with two tables, the result can be pretty ugly. You would have to create additional foreign keys within one table, and the number of keys you create would determine the number of relations. Then you would have to write some kludgy code to retrieve related records. You really don't want to go there. Instead, take the advice provided in Chapter 7 and create a linking table, as shown in Figure 11-3.

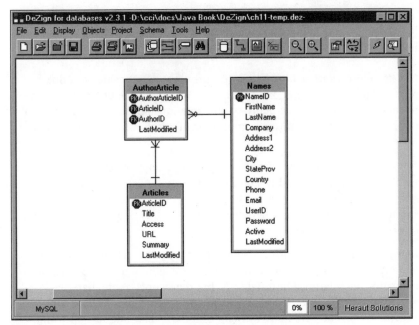

Figure 11-3: The AuthorArticle table links the Names and Articles tables.

The `AuthorArticle` table contains four fields. The first is marked as the primary key. It isn't strictly necessary to have a separate field for the primary key in this case. Any guide to relational database design will tell you that the combination of `ArticleID` and `AuthorID` is unique, and so you can use those two fields together as the unique key.

I've added the `AuthorArticleID` primary key out of habit, really. It's the first step I take when I create a table. I may remove it later if it becomes obvious that a different field or combination of fields is the logical primary key. I also have a `LastModified TIMESTAMP` in the table, as I do in all the tables. Again, it's not necessary for the design, but it does give me an audit trail of sorts.

The `AuthorID` and `ArticleID` fields are the foreign keys that link the `AuthorArticle` record back to the `Names` and `Articles` tables, which forms an intermediary link defining the many-to-many relationship. For each combination of author and article you will need to create one row in the `AuthorArticle` table. To retrieve all the authors for a given article, use the `ArticleID` to look up the related records in `AuthorArticle`, and then use the `AuthorID` from each record to obtain the author record. Similarly, you can retrieve all articles by a given author by obtaining all the `AuthorArticle` records that match the `AuthorID`, and then look up each article.

## Adding article type information

Chapter 7 introduces an `ArticleTypes` table to store article keyword information. Figure 11-4 shows the ERD with the addition of the `ArticleTypes` table. You may remember from that earlier discussion of database design that many articles may have the same type and keywords, and so it makes sense to break that information out into its own table, and link it by storing `ArticleType` in the `Articles` table.

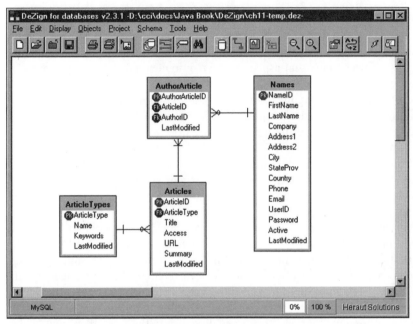

Figure 11–4: Adding the ArticleTypes table with type and keyword information

   At this point, the database design supports the storage of author information, articles, type and keyword information related to articles, and a link between articles and authors.

# Implementing the Requirements

Now that you've dealt with the most obvious data storage requirements, it's time to start thinking about some of the less clear specifications, including access control and subscription order tracking. Still, the same principles used to determine how to store user and article information apply. You need to know what information you're tracking, how to retrieve that information, and you also need to define the relationships between sets of data.

# Implementing access control

The access control requirement specifies that you will only allow users with a valid user ID and password to access specific pages on the site. You might think that this requirement isn't really a database requirement at all, but a user interface design issue, since the problem seems to be how to ask the user for an ID and password. But before you assume that you don't need to worry about access control in your database design, get a little more information.

## START ASKING QUESTIONS

Never assume that any part of an application requirements document doesn't apply to the database. Always ask yourself, the other people on the design team, and most importantly the users, how that aspect of the requirements document will play out in the real world.

You know that the Web application will prompt the user for an ID and password. You've anticipated the need to store this information with the user data, so pat yourself on the back and ask the next question: how will the Web application ask the user for an ID and password? You probably have at least two options; use the standard browser authentication window, or display an HTML form to the user.

Neither the standard authentication window nor a security form necessarily requires changes to the database design. But how does the Web application know that it's supposed to prompt the user to log in?

Having worked with password-protected Web sites, I know that Web servers commonly provide directory-based authentication. Is an approach like this adequate? That depends on whether a page is always restricted, or sometimes not restricted. If a page's security requirements never change, then you can use the page's URL as a security descriptor. But if the page's security clearance will change (say the page is freely available for several days as part of a promotional effort) and you don't want to move that page from one directory to the next, then you need to use a data store for that information.

## PERSISTENCE PAYS OFF

You're probably getting an idea of the kinds of permissions you'll need to assign to a Web page, but you'll have a better handle on the design if you flesh out the requirements a bit more. By discussing the potential subscriber rights situations with other design team members and with the users, you learn the following:

◆ Usually, a subscriber buys a subscription for a certain period of time, and has permanent rights to read all articles published during that time. If the subscription is for March 2001, the subscriber can always read articles that were published in that month.

◆ Subscribers can buy individual articles.

◆ Subscribers can buy special groups of articles.

This is what usually happens in a specification. Something that seemed quite simple, on the surface, is rapidly becoming more complex. Now there are three ways that the subscriber can get access: by a subscription over a period of time, by a single article purchase, or by a purchasing a predefined group of articles.

The specification is getting more complex, but as you add new requirements, you'll also begin to see ways to create generalized solutions. For instance, if the user can buy a predefined group of articles, you can probably treat a timed subscription as a predefined group of articles also, and save yourself a bit of coding. Perhaps you can even treat a single article as a "group" of one article.

## CONSIDERING A SOLUTION

You've established that users can buy access to articles one at a time, by groups of articles, and by date ranges. One subscriber can buy access to multiple articles, and any one article can be read by multiple subscribers. This situation is really another many-to-many relationship. However, if you tried to create a linking table between Names and Articles you'd have to deal with a massive number of records, and it would be something of a maintenance headache.

As mentioned previously, you can think of any subscription as the sale of a group of articles. If you create a table for groups of articles, then you have a many-to-many relationship between the groups of articles and the subscribers, as shown in Figure 11-5.

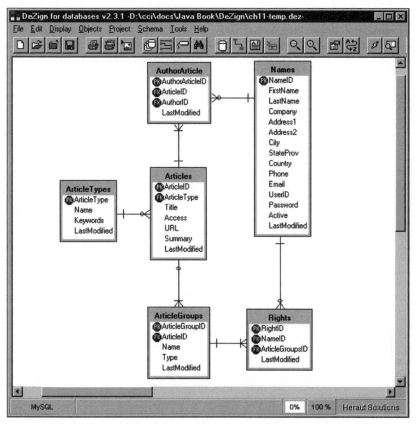

Figure 11-5: You can use a Rights table to link groups of articles to subscribers.

The problem with the scenario shown in Figure 11-5 is that it assumes each article belongs to only one group. That isn't going to be the case if, for instance, someone wants to sell access to a special promotions package made up of selected articles. So create another table to mediate the many-to-many relationship between groups and articles, as shown in Figure 11-6.

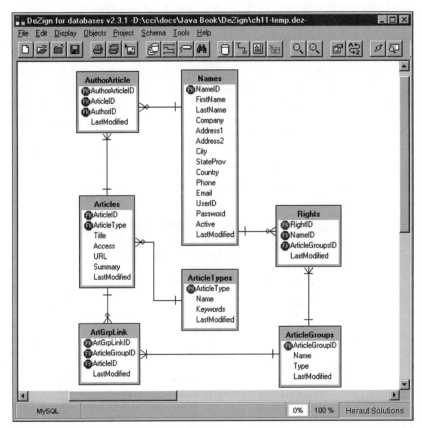

Figure 11-6: Defining two sets of many-to-many relationships to manage user access rights

## THE DESIGN SO FAR

Take a moment to make sure you understand the database design. You've created tables to control access to groups of articles, whether these groups are weekly issues or promotional groupings or whatever. An administrative person will have to group the issues manually, or perhaps an automated process can do this based on publication dates and so on. In any case, one ArticleGroup record will define a group of articles to which user access rights can be assigned.

You assign user rights by creating records in the `Rights` table that links the user (`Names`) record with the `ArticleGroup` record. You link the `ArticleGroup` record to multiple Articles records by creating records in the linking `ArtGrpLink` table.

## WHAT ABOUT SPEED?

How effective will this design be in a real-world situation? Any time a user requests an article, you have two pieces of information you can use to assess the rights: the user's ID and the article's URL. In the current design, you can start by looking up the user's primary key and the article's primary key. Armed with these, you can find the rights records (you may have several) for the user and then inspect each of the `ArticleGroups` records. From there, get the `ArtGrpLink` records and look for a match on the article's primary key. That's a lot of work just to check rights on one article!

This illustrates the kind of tradeoff that you're faced with continually when designing databases. A logically clean, maintainable design isn't always the fastest, and vice versa. The fastest way to look up rights would be to have a simple linking table between articles and names. That way you only have to do two lookups: one to get the article's primary key from the article, and another to get the matching record from the linking table. Well, actually you would have to do three lookups, but being a good programmer you saved the user's primary key value on login so you don't have to go get it again now. At most you're retrieving two records as opposed to possibly dozens or even hundreds.

It's true that read operations are very fast in MySQL. The slowest MySQL server in my office is running on a lowly P100, and MySQL can still retrieve a thousand records of comparable size to the linking tables in .04 seconds. Depending on the number of records you're retrieving, you may not be concerned about the overhead.

If the number of records you're reading is an issue, and you don't want to lose the flexibility that the article grouping design affords, you can choose to denormalize your database and duplicate the linking information in a table that sits between Articles and Names. Call this table something like `RightsCache`, and do not allow an administrator to update this information directly. Instead, use the article grouping scheme to assign rights to users (by associating an article group with a user in a `Rights` record), and when this information changes, execute a routine that updates the `RightsCache` records to reflect the current state of the user's rights.

Oh yes, you still have to deal with the individual article rights. Since discussion with the design team and the users has revealed that individual article sales are the minority, I've decided to implement individual article sales exactly the same as groups of articles, except that in these cases the groups will only have one article. On its own, this wouldn't be the most efficient solution, but there are great advantages to reusing existing tables where appropriate. As it is, tables proliferate like rabbits.

# Implementing subscription order tracking

The remaining database-related requirement listed at the beginning of this chapter is that of tracking subscription orders. Since a subscription is often a single-item purchase, you might be tempted to use a single table to keep track of subscription orders. Again, find out whether purchases will always be single items. What happens when the site begins selling access to individual articles, and a user makes a purchase of three or five articles?

## PURCHASE HEADER AND DETAIL TABLES

The standard approach to handling purchases is to have one table for a header record that keeps track of when the purchase was made, who placed the order, shipping status, and so on, and another for the purchase details, or line items. The products for sale are kept in a third table. Figure 11-7 shows one such design.

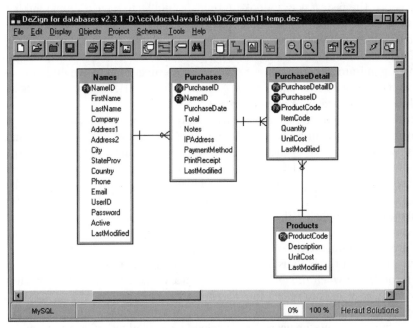

Figure 11-7: Purchase header and detail tables, and a products table

Figure 11-7 shows a one-to-many relationship between the Purchases header table and the PurchaseDetail table. The PurchaseDetail table is also related to the Products table, on ProductCode.

You may think that this design unnecessarily duplicates data, because Products and PurchaseDetail both have a UnitCost field. Although you could get the cost from the Products table, doing so causes problems if you update the price of the product at a later date. You really don't want the cost of the product to the user to be changed after the order is completed!

## THE WHOLE ENCHILADA

Figure 11-8 shows the database diagram in its entirety. This database is by no means a large one, and it can (and will) grow considerably larger. As of yet, the design doesn't provide for logging user access, sending e-mail, or any of the myriad other features that could be added to this Web site. Still, it's a fair start.

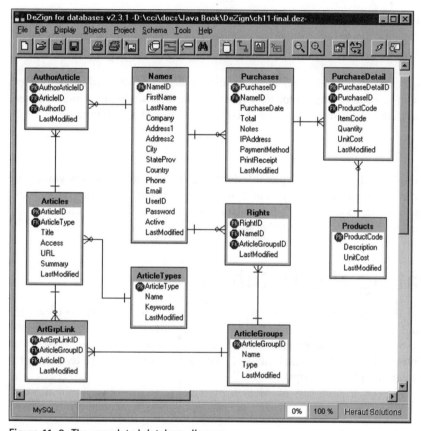

Figure 11-8: The completed database diagram

# Effective Use of Indexes

Figure 11-8 shows the relationships between the various tables, but doesn't give any indication of indexes (other than primary keys). Indexes are an important part of all but the smallest databases, since efficient operation means the server needs a way of locating the desired records as quickly as possible.

The first place to think about indexes is on foreign keys. To find all rights records for a user, the server has to match the `User.NameID` field to the `Name.NameID` field. It can do this search a lot faster if it has an index on `User.NameID`. To create an index on `NameID`, you add this to the `Rights CREATE TABLE` statement:

```
INDEX IDX_NameID (NameID)
```

You can also create the index after you've created the `Rights` table:

```
ALTER TABLE Rights ADD INDEX IDX_NameID (NameID);
```

The other place you want an index is on any field you regularly use to select data. If you want to be able to locate a record in the `Names` table by e-mail address, you'll want an `INDEX` line in your table-creation statement as follows:

```
INDEX IDX_Email (Email)
```

You don't need to create all possible indexes, and the more indexes you create the greater the overhead when you add or update a record, since that necessitates changes to the index(es) as well. But if you're noticing performance problems, the first thing to check is whether you've indexed the foreign key fields.

# Creating the Database

To create the database, change to the database in which you want to create the tables and execute the appropriate `CREATE TABLE` statements. Save yourself some grief and do not attempt to enter these statements by hand. Instead, put these statements into a file, and then either cut and paste them into the `mysql` terminal program, or run the file as a script.

You can feed a text file of MySQL statements to the `mysql` client using redirection:

```
mysql < createscript
```

If you've set the root password (which you should have done), you need to specify some or all of the following parameters:

```
mysql -h host -u user -p < createscript
```

If you use the `-p` parameter, the `mysql` client will ask you for your password. Listing 11-1 shows a `CREATE` statement for the tables shown in Figure 11-8.

**Listing 11-1: A Script to Create a Database and the Tables Shown in Figure 11-8**

```
CREATE DATABASE ch12;

USE ch12;

CREATE TABLE Names(
NameID INT DEFAULT 0 AUTO_INCREMENT NOT NULL,
FirstName VARCHAR(30) NOT NULL,
LastName VARCHAR(30) NOT NULL,
Company VARCHAR(30) NOT NULL,
Address1 VARCHAR(30),
Address2 VARCHAR(30),
City VARCHAR(30),
StateProv VARCHAR(10),
Country VARCHAR(20) NOT NULL,
Phone VARCHAR(30),
Email VARCHAR(60) NOT NULL,
UserID VARCHAR(20),
Password VARCHAR(20),
Active ENUM('Y','N') DEFAULT 'N',
LastModified TIMESTAMP,
PRIMARY KEY (NameID),
INDEX IDX_Names_LastFirst (LastName,FirstName),
INDEX IDX_Names_Company (Company),
INDEX IDX_Names_Email (Email),
INDEX IDX_Names_FirstLast (FirstName,LastName),
INDEX IDX_Names_Country (Country));


CREATE TABLE Products(
ProductCode VARCHAR(6) NOT NULL,
Description VARCHAR(255),
UnitCost VARCHAR(10),
LastModified TIMESTAMP,
PRIMARY KEY (ProductCode),
INDEX IDX_Products_ProductCode (ProductCode));


CREATE TABLE ArticleTypes(
ArticleType VARCHAR(8) NOT NULL,
Name VARCHAR(30) NOT NULL,
Keywords VARCHAR(255),
LastModified TIMESTAMP,
```

*Continued*

**Listing 11-1** *(Continued)*

```
PRIMARY KEY (ArticleType),
INDEX IDX_ArticletType_Name (Name));


CREATE TABLE Articles(
ArticleID INT DEFAULT 0 AUTO_INCREMENT  NOT NULL,
ArticleType VARCHAR(8) NOT NULL,
Title VARCHAR(200) NOT NULL,
Access ENUM('R','P') DEFAULT 'R' NOT NULL,
URL VARCHAR(255),
Summary TEXT,
LastModified TIMESTAMP,
PRIMARY KEY (ArticleID),
INDEX IDX_Articles_TypeCode (ArticleType),
INDEX IDX_Articles_Title (Title));


CREATE TABLE ArticleGroups(
ArticleGroupID INT DEFAULT 0 AUTO_INCREMENT NOT NULL,
Name VARCHAR(60) DEFAULT '' NOT NULL,
Type ENUM('R','M') DEFAULT 'R' NOT NULL,
LastModified TIMESTAMP,
PRIMARY KEY (ArticleGroupID),
INDEX IDX_ArticleGroups_Name (Name));


CREATE TABLE ArtGrpLink(
ArtGrpLinkID INT DEFAULT 0 AUTO_INCREMENT NOT NULL,
ArticleGroupID INT NOT NULL,
ArticleID INT NOT NULL,
LastModified TIMESTAMP,
PRIMARY KEY (ArtGrpLinkID),
INDEX IDX_ArtGrpLink_Article (ArticleID,ArticleGroupID),
INDEX IDX_ArtGrpLink_GroupID (ArticleGroupID,ArticleID));


CREATE TABLE Rights(
RightID INT DEFAULT 0 AUTO_INCREMENT NOT NULL,
NameID INT NOT NULL,
ArticleGroupsID INT NOT NULL,
LastModified TIMESTAMP,
PRIMARY KEY (RightID),
INDEX IDX_Rights_NameID (NameID),
INDEX IDX_Rights_ArticleGroupsID (ArticleGroupsID));
```

```
CREATE TABLE Purchases(
PurchaseID INT DEFAULT 0 AUTO_INCREMENT NOT NULL,
NameID INT NOT NULL,
PurchaseDate DATE NOT NULL,
Total DECIMAL(10,2),
Notes TEXT,
IPAddress VARCHAR(20),
PaymentMethod VARCHAR(20),
PrintReceipt ENUM('Y','N','P'),
LastModified TIMESTAMP,
PRIMARY KEY (PurchaseID),
INDEX IDX_Purchases_NameID (NameID,PurchaseDate));


CREATE TABLE PurchaseDetail(
PurchaseDetailID INT DEFAULT 0 AUTO_INCREMENT NOT NULL,
PurchaseID INT NOT NULL,
ProductCode VARCHAR(6) NOT NULL,
ItemCode VARCHAR(6),
Quantity TINYINT,
UnitCost DECIMAL(10,2),
LastModified TIMESTAMP,
PRIMARY KEY (PurchaseDetailID),
INDEX IDX_PurchaseDetail_PurchaseID (PurchaseID));


CREATE TABLE AuthorArticle(
AuthorArticleID INT DEFAULT 0 AUTO_INCREMENT NOT NULL,
ArticleID INT NOT NULL,
AuthorID INT NOT NULL,
LastModified TIMESTAMP,
PRIMARY KEY (AuthorArticleID),
INDEX IDX_AuthorArticle_Author (AuthorID,ArticleID),
INDEX IDX_ArticleAuthor_Article (ArticleID,AuthorID));
```

# Summary

Database design is as much art as it is science. Although the rules of normalization go a long way toward defining what is good, a lot depends on the designer's experience and ability to anticipate what the database might be used for in the future. Key points to remember include:

◆ Choose a good diagramming tool, whether ERD, UML, or some other methodology.

◆ Work out the easy table definitions first.

◆ Ask lots of questions, of yourself and anyone involved in the application design.

◆ Sometimes data that appears to be duplicated really isn't.

◆ Aim for a normalized data structure; if performance is an issue, evaluate the real-world (not estimated) performance penalties against maintenance issues.

◆ Use indexes to optimize record access times.

# Chapter 12

# Working with SQL Data

## IN THIS CHAPTER

- ◆ Adding data to a table
- ◆ Retrieving and sorting data
- ◆ Deleting rows from tables
- ◆ Updating data
- ◆ Understanding SQL functions and operators

MYSQL, LIKE OTHER SQL databases, provides a rich environment for creating, manipulating, and deleting data. This environment provides statements to directly manipulate rows in tables, as well as a number of standard functions and operators. An exhaustive treatment of SQL data handling could (and often does) take up a book on its own; this chapter is meant only as a brief introduction to retrieving and updating SQL data. In this chapter you'll learn how to use the INSERT statement to add data to tables, the UPDATE statement to change data, the DELETE statement to remove data, and the SELECT statement to return data. The chapter also discusses using functions and operators in your SELECT statements.

## Creating Data

When adding data to a SQL table, you have two options: you can fill in all of the fields in the row, or you can fill in fields selectively. You might wonder why you would ever want to only partially fill in a row of data. Some fields may have default values set that you may not need to override. Also, TIMESTAMP fields are updated automatically, as are any integer AUTO_INCREMENT fields.

### Inserting data

To add data to a table use the INSERT statement, with the following syntax:

```
INSERT [LOW_PRIORITY | DELAYED] [IGNORE]
       [INTO] tbl_name [(col_name,...)]
       VALUES (expression,...),(...),
```

The first three flags indicate to the MySQL server when it should attempt to add the row. If `LOW_PRIORITY` is used, MySQL waits until it has completed any other requested reads of this table. The user has to wait until the server completes the `INSERT`.

If you use the `DELAYED` flag, MySQL again waits, but returns control to the client. You can expect a delay of uncertain length before the record that appears to have been written to the database is actually committed. Using the `IGNORE` flag makes MySQL ignore an `INSERT` that would otherwise create a duplicate primary key or other unique key. A typical `INSERT` statement looks something like this:

```
INSERT INTO Products
(ProductCode,Description,UnitCost)
values ('1YRSUB','One year subscription',225.00);
```

That statement adds the following data to the `Products` table:

```
+-------------+----------------------+----------+----------------+
| ProductCode | Description          | UnitCost | LastModified   |
+-------------+----------------------+----------+----------------+
| 1YRSUB      | One year subscription | 225     | 20001109002523 |
+-------------+----------------------+----------+----------------+
```

As you may recall from Chapter 11, the `LastModified` field is a `TIMESTAMP`, which is updated automatically with the current date and time.

You can omit the column list from the `INSERT` statement, but if you do this, you need to put all the column values in `VALUES()` and in the same order as the table. Use `DESCRIBE tablename` if you're not sure what the column order is.

This statement does not work:

```
INSERT INTO Products
values ('1YRSUB','One year subscription',225.00);
```

and yields the following:

```
ERROR 1136: Column count doesn't match value count at row 1
```

In this case, the problem is the missing `TIMESTAMP`. You don't want to set that anyway, but if you use a `NULL` value, the `TIMESTAMP` is correctly set:

```
INSERT INTO Products
VALUES ('1YRSUB','One year subscription',225.00,NULL);
```

The `REPLACE` statement is a variation on the `INSERT` statement. You can use the `REPLACE` statement in exactly the same way as the `INSERT` statement; the only difference is that REPLACE looks for and deletes any record that matches it on a unique key before inserting data.

# Deleting data

To remove one or more rows from a table, use the DELETE statement:

```
DELETE [LOW_PRIORITY] FROM tbl_name
    [WHERE where_definition] [LIMIT rows]
```

For example, to delete all purchases over $300 from the Purchases table, execute the following:

```
DELETE FROM Purchases WHERE Total > 300;
```

This example might return the following:

```
Query OK, 1 row affected (0.00 sec)
```

When used without a WHERE clause, the DELETE statement removes *all* records from a table, without warning (unless you use the LIMIT clause). Actually, MySQL does this by simply deleting and recreating the table, which is far faster than deleting the individual rows.

# Updating data

To modify existing data, you use the UPDATE statement, which has the following syntax:

```
UPDATE [LOW_PRIORITY] [IGNORE] tbl_name SET
    col_name1=expr1,col_name2=expr2,...
    [WHERE where_definition] [LIMIT rows]
```

Just as with DELETE, an UPDATE statement without a WHERE clause updates all of the specified columns in the table, unless you use the LIMIT clause. If for some reason you decide to change a product code, and you have existing orders, you need to execute two UPDATE statements:

```
UPDATE Products
set ProductCode = 'ANNSUB'
WHERE ProductCode='YRSUB';
UPDATE PurchaseDetail
set ProductCode = 'ANNSUB'
WHERE ProductCode='YRSUB';
```

# Querying Data

Once you have data in a table, you need some way to get that data back, and in SQL you do this with the SELECT statement. With SELECT you can query a single table, or you can query multiple related tables according to join conditions you define. You can restrict the result set to only certain records with a WHERE clause, and you can also limit the number of returned records and decide the order in which you want the records displayed. Listing 12-1 provides the syntax for MySQL's SELECT statement.

**Listing 12-1: MySQL's SELECT Statement**

```
SELECT [STRAIGHT_JOIN] [SQL_SMALL_RESULT] [SQL_BIG_RESULT] [SQL_BUFFER_RESULT]
      [HIGH_PRIORITY]
      [DISTINCT | DISTINCTROW | ALL]
   SELECT_expression,...
   [INTO {OUTFILE | DUMPFILE} 'file_name' export_options]
   [FROM table_references
      [WHERE where_definition]
      [GROUP BY {unsigned_integer | col_name | formula}]
      [HAVING where_definition]
      [ORDER BY {unsigned_integer | col_name | formula} [ASC | DESC] ,....]
      [LIMIT [offset,] rows]
      [PROCEDURE procedure_name] ]
```

That's a nasty-looking syntax specification, so you can simplify it just a bit. To see all the data in, for example, the Products table, you can execute the following:

```
SELECT * FROM Products;
```

That statement returns the following:

```
+-------------+------------------------+----------+----------------+
| ProductCode | Description            | UnitCost | LastModified   |
+-------------+------------------------+----------+----------------+
| 1YRSUB      | One-year subscription  | 225      | 20001109002523 |
| 2YRSUB      | Two-year subscription  | 400      | 20001109004619 |
| 1MOSUB      | One-month subscription | 20       | 20001109004652 |
| LIFSUB      | Lifetime subscription  | 2500     | 20001109010219 |
+-------------+------------------------+----------+----------------+
```

That wasn't too painful, was it? Queries using SELECT statements can be simple, or they can be quite complex. To get just a bit more sophisticated, use a SELECT statement to view only the ProductCode and Description columns, as follows:

```
SELECT ProductCode,Description FROM Products;
```

That statement can return a result such as this:

```
+-------------+-----------------------+
| ProductCode | Description           |
+-------------+-----------------------+
| 1YRSUB      | One-year subscription |
| 2YRSUB      | Two-year subscription |
| 1MOSUB      | One-month subscription|
| LIFSUB      | Lifetime subscription |
+-------------+-----------------------+
```

## Sort orders

Besides choosing which columns to display, you can also specify the display order using the ORDER BY clause. You can use any field in the table (or tables) in the ORDER BY clause, whether or not that field is part of the SELECT statement. The following ORDER BY clause sorts product orders by the product description:

```
SELECT ProductCode,Description FROM Products
ORDER BY Description;
```

which returns the following:

```
+-------------+-----------------------+
| ProductCode | Description           |
+-------------+-----------------------+
| LIFSUB      | Lifetime subscription |
| 1MOSUB      | One-month subscription|
| 1YRSUB      | One-year subscription |
| 2YRSUB      | Two-year subscription |
+-------------+-----------------------+
```

You can list multiple fields in an ORDER BY clause; just separate the fields with commas, and MySQL will sort the query by all the fields in the order you've listed them. You can also append the DESC keyword to use a descending sort order.

## Restricting result sets

All the example SELECT statements discussed so far have returned all of the rows in the table. That's not a problem with four rows, but in many circumstances you want a strictly limited number of records, or you want only records that meet a certain condition.

## USING THE LIMIT CLAUSE

You can use the LIMIT clause to set the maximum number of rows the server will return. The LIMIT clause is particularly useful when you're dealing with large data sets; if there are several thousand records in a table, you probably don't want to retrieve all of those records at once.

```
SELECT ProductCode,Description FROM Products
ORDER BY Description LIMIT 2;
```

That SELECT statement returns:

```
+-------------+------------------------+
| ProductCode | Description            |
+-------------+------------------------+
| LIFSUB      | Lifetime subscription  |
| 1MOSUB      | One-month subscription |
+-------------+------------------------+
```

**TIP**

If you just want to look at the ten most recently modified records in a table, and your table has a TimeStamp field, end your SELECT statement with ORDER BY TimeStampField DESC LIMIT 10;.

## USING THE WHERE CLAUSE

You can select subsets of table data using the WHERE clause. A SQL WHERE clause tests each retrieved record according to the SELECT statement you define, and if the statement returns a true value, the server includes the row in the result set. For instance, to find only those products with a cost under $300 dollars, use the following:

```
SELECT Description,UnitCost FROM Products
WHERE UnitCost < 300;
```

which returns:

```
+------------------------+----------+
| Description            | UnitCost |
+------------------------+----------+
| One-year subscription  | 225      |
| One-month subscription | 20       |
+------------------------+----------+
```

The WHERE clauses can contain multiple conditions and operators, and can become complex. They are also an enormously powerful tool for extracting meaningful data from your database.

# Multitable SELECT statements

SQL's SELECT statements can work with one table, or with a number of tables. Consider the following SELECT statement:

```
SELECT Total,PaymentMethod,NameID
FROM Purchases;
```

that returns this single row in the Purchases table:

```
+--------+---------------+--------+
| Total  | PaymentMethod | NameID |
+--------+---------------+--------+
| 225.00 | VISA          |      2 |
+--------+---------------+--------+
```

This data indicates that one purchase was recorded, and the foreign key NameID points to a row in the Names table. That table, which results from this statement:

```
SELECT ID,LastName,FirstName FROM Names;
```

contains the following data:

```
+----+----------+-----------+
| ID | LastName | FirstName |
+----+----------+-----------+
|  1 | Salter   | Morton    |
|  2 | Filmore  | Jimi      |
|  3 | Shoe     | Eustace   |
|  4 | Roche    | Archy     |
|  5 | LaGrande | Catherine |
+----+----------+-----------+
```

It's often convenient to obtain related data from two or more tables as a single row in a result set. To retrieve combined tables, you have to tell the server how it should match up, or join, records from those tables.

## THE INNER JOIN

To retrieve just the related data from these two tables, use the following form of the SELECT statement:

```
SELECT LastName,FirstName,Total
FROM Names,Purchases
WHERE Purchases.NameID = Names.ID;
```

to return this table:

```
+----------+-----------+--------+
| LastName | FirstName | Total  |
+----------+-----------+--------+
| Salter   | Morton    | 225.00 |
+----------+-----------+--------+
```

This last SELECT statement *joins* two tables, and is sometimes called an equijoin since it displays records that are related by common data. Since multiple tables are involved, you might run into name clashes. To resolve these, you may need to use the table name as well as the field name:

```
Purchases.NameID
```

Because typing out so much can get a bit tedious, SELECT allows you to create table aliases, which are typically single characters. The previous SELECT statement with aliases looks like this:

```
SELECT n.LastName, n.FirstName, p.Total
FROM Names n, Purchases p
WHERE n.ID=p.NameID;
```

All the following examples use table aliases, if for no reason other than to save my typing fingers.

## THE LEFT, OR OUTER, JOIN

Another form of the table join is the left join, which you create with the LEFT JOIN statement:

```
SELECT LastName,FirstName,Total
FROM Names left join Purchases
on Names.ID = Purchases.NameID;
```

to produce this result:

```
+----------+-----------+--------+
| LastName | FirstName | Total  |
+----------+-----------+--------+
| Salter   | Morton    |   NULL |
| Filmore  | Jimi      | 225.00 |
```

```
| Shoe     | Eustace   |  NULL |
| Roche    | Archy     |  NULL |
| LaGrande | Catherine |  NULL |
+----------+-----------+-------+
```

Instead of displaying only those rows where data matches in both tables, the left join substitutes null values where the joined row does not exist.

If you switch the table names around the left join, you get a slightly different result, because now you're selecting from the Purchases table and looking for matching records in the Names table:

```
SELECT n.LastName, n.FirstName, p.Total
FROM Purchases p LEFT JOIN Names n
on p.NameID = n.ID;
```

That statement produces this result:

```
+----------+-----------+--------+
| LastName | FirstName | Total  |
+----------+-----------+--------+
| Filmore  | Jimi      | 225.00 |
+----------+-----------+--------+
```

## INNIE OR OUTIE?

In SQL1 the only kind of join available was the inner join, where the server retrieved only those rows with matching data on both sides. If you want to show only those names with orders, an inner join is perfect. In many cases, however, it's helpful to see all of the rows from a given table whether or not they have related joined rows. For general display of data, the outer, or left join, wins hands down.

## SUPPRESSING DUPLICATE ROWS

Sometimes you want to remove duplicate rows from your result sets. If a user has more than one purchase, and you request an outer join on Names and Purchases, as follows:

```
SELECT n.LastName, n.FirstName, p.Total
FROM Names n LEFT JOIN Purchases p
ON p.NameID = n.ID;
```

you may get duplicate records, like this:

```
+----------+-----------+--------+
| LastName | FirstName | Total  |
+----------+-----------+--------+
```

```
| Salter   | Morton    |  NULL  |
| Filmore  | Jimi      | 225.00 |
| Filmore  | Jimi      | 400.00 |
| Shoe     | Eustace   |  NULL  |
| Roche    | Archy     |  NULL  |
| LaGrande | Catherine |  NULL  |
+----------+-----------+--------+
```

You can remove the duplicates with the DISTINCT keyword. However, DISTINCT only works when the duplicate happens across all columns. Adding the DISTINCT keyword to the above statement like this:

```
SELECT DISTINCT n.LastName, n.FirstName,
p.Total FROM Names n LEFT JOIN Purchases p
ON p.NameID = n.ID;
```

makes no difference, as you see here:

```
+----------+-----------+--------+
| LastName | FirstName | Total  |
+----------+-----------+--------+
| Salter   | Morton    |  NULL  |
| Filmore  | Jimi      | 225.00 |
| Filmore  | Jimi      | 400.00 |
| Shoe     | Eustace   |  NULL  |
| Roche    | Archy     |  NULL  |
| LaGrande | Catherine |  NULL  |
+----------+-----------+--------+
```

The problem is the Total column—it still shows unique values for both "Filmore" records. Remove this column and try again with this statement:

```
SELECT DISTINCT n.LastName, n.FirstName,
p.Total FROM Names n LEFT JOIN Purchases p
ON p.NameID = n.ID;
```

and you'll see a result like this:

```
+----------+-----------+
| LastName | FirstName |
+----------+-----------+
| Salter   | Morton    |
| Filmore  | Jimi      |
| Shoe     | Eustace   |
```

```
| Roche     | Archy     |
| LaGrande  | Catherine |
+-----------+-----------+
```

This time, the server suppresses the duplicate row.

# SQL Functions and Operators

SQL is a lot more than just retrieving data. It's a fairly well-equipped programming language. In many SQL implementations, you can write procedures in SQL and store them on the server, calling them manually or when certain conditions (triggers) occur. While this isn't possible with MySQL, at least not yet, it does have a library of functions that you can use in SELECT statements and WHERE clauses. You can use some of these to assist in the retrieval of data, and some you can use without reference to table data.

## Operators

MySQL has a wealth of operators that you can use in your SQL statements. You can use these operators, constants, and fields in your SQL statements. Comparison operators are listed in Table 12-1.

TABLE 12-1 COMPARISON OPERATORS

| Operator | Description |
| --- | --- |
| ! or NOT | a logical NOT |
| \|\| or OR | a logical OR |
| && or AND | a logical AND |
| = | the values are equal |
| <> or != | the values are not equal |
| <= (less than or equal) | the left value is less than or equal to the right value |
| < (less than) | the left value is less than the right value |
| >= (greater than or equal) | the left value is greater than or equal to the right value |
| > (greater than) | the left value is greater than the right value |
| <=> (null safe equal) | the values are equal, but both can also be NULL |

*Continued*

TABLE 12-1 COMPARISON OPERATORS *(Continued)*

| Operator | Description |
| --- | --- |
| IS NULL | the value is NULL |
| IS NOT NULL | the value is not NULL |
| expression BETWEEN min AND max | the value is within a range |
| expression IN (value,...) | the value is in a list of values |
| expression NOT IN (value...) | the value is not in a list of values |
| ISNULL(expression) | returns true if the expression evaluates to NULL |
| COALESCE(list) | returns the first non-null element in the list |
| INTERVAL(N,N1,N2...) | returns 0 if N is less than N1, 1 if N1 is less than N2, and so on. |

## String comparisons

String comparisons are among the most useful operators in running database queries, since they enable you to look for approximate matches in the data. You can perform substring matches, full text pattern matching, and even regular expressions.

To look for a string inside a string, use the LIKE operator. For example, to find all names with the string "er" in the first or last name, use this SELECT statement:

```
SELECT FirstName,LastName
FROM Names WHERE LastName like('%er%')
OR FirstName like('%er%');
```

to obtain a result like this:

```
+-----------+----------+
| FirstName | LastName |
+-----------+----------+
| Morton    | Salter   |
| Catherine | LaGrande |
+-----------+----------+
```

You can use either of two wildcards in a LIKE test. To represent any single character, use an underscore (_), and to represent multiple characters, use a percent sign. You can also make an inverse match as follows:

```
SELECT FirstName,LastName FROM Names
WHERE LastName not like('%a%');
```

to get a result like this:

```
+-----------+----------+
| FirstName | LastName |
+-----------+----------+
| Jimi      | Filmore  |
| Eustace   | Shoe     |
| Archy     | Roche    |
+-----------+----------+
```

MySQL provides regular expression support with the regexp and rlike operators (your choice). Regular expressions give you extensive pattern-matching capabilities, a discussion of which is well beyond the scope of this chapter. See the MySQL documentation for more information.

You can compare strings using the strcmp(expression1,expression2) operator, which returns a value of 0 if the strings are the same, -1 if the first string comes before the second, and 1 if the first string comes after the second, using the current sort order.

In conjunction with VARCHAR and TEXT fields and full text indexes, the MATCH operator returns a relevance indicator in the specified column(s) against a given expression, using this syntax:

```
MATCH (col1,col2,...) AGAINST (expr)
```

MySQL's full text matching is designed to work with large collections of words. In general, the more often a less common word is found in the text, the greater the relevance of the match.

MySQL does basic four-function match; you can use the *, /, +, and – operators in your SQL statements. MySQL also has an extensive math library and can do bitwise operations on 64-bit numbers.

# What, there's more?

I've only touched on MySQL's ability to manage and manipulate data. Take some time to review MySQL's online documentation, particularly Chapter 7, the MySQL Language Reference. You may also want to read up on SQL; there are a number of good books available, including *MYSQL/PHP Database Applications* by Jay Greenspan and Brad Bulger (Hungry Minds, 2001).

Although you can get started writing SQL code and maintaining SQL databases with just a little information, you can easily make a career out of it without running out of things to do.

# Summary

Although SQL is often thought of as a query language, it's also very good at inserting and updating table data. Adding data is the simplest operation, followed by updates and deletes. You can use complex WHERE clauses to restrict the update action to only the desired records. And, of course, SQL querying is immensely capable, with various ways of relating data from multiple tables. Key points to remember include:

◆ When adding a row to a table, you may not need to supply all of the data, depending on what default values and auto_increment fields the table contains.

◆ Deletes and updates are batch operations; when used without a WHERE clause, they can easily wipe out or modify the entire table.

◆ Use the ORDER BY clause to specify the sort order of the resulting set.

◆ Inner joins retrieve only rows where a match exists in the joined table.

◆ When a joined table has no matching row, outer joins supply null values.

◆ MySQL's SQL is a capable programming language with numerous operators, functions, and string-matching capabilities.

# Part III

## Delivering Content

# Chapter 13

# Using JDBC

INCREASINGLY, WEB SITES NEED to connect to back-end data sources. The servlet and JSP specifications don't have anything to say on this subject, but that isn't a problem, because Sun provides the Java Database Connectivity (JDBC) API. JDBC is in many ways similar to Microsoft's Open Database Connectivity (ODBC); both are based on the X/Open Call Level Interface (CLI) specification. ODBC and JDBC function as a translation layer between the application and the data source and provide a standard way of connecting with a variety of SQL relational databases. ODBC is also used to connect to flat-file databases.

With ODBC already in the market, why create another API? Because ODBC uses platform-specific C code, which would tie any Java application, applet, or servlet to a specific hardware implementation, defeating Java's write once, run anywhere mandate. The use of C code also opens up some safety issues, as C doesn't share Java's security model. And ODBC uses C programming techniques, such as pointers, not supported in Java. Porting ODBC to Java isn't an option.

In this chapter you'll learn how to create a servlet that connects to a MySQL database using JDBC and returns data from that database to the user.

## A JDBC Overview

JDBC was one of the first APIs to be added to the Java family, and it's not difficult to see why. Few programs do anything meaningful without storing some sort of persistent data, and as applications grow in complexity, text files just don't make the grade.

215

Figure 13-1 shows the overall structure of JDBC. The application makes calls to the JDBC API to open a connection with the database, retrieves and updates data, executes commands on the data source, and closes the connection. At the other end, the database drivers connect either to a specific database, or to another protocol (such as ODBC or a middleware product). Since databases vary in their support of SQL, the database driver needs to handle any translation issues between the JDBC commands and the database engine. Databases also vary widely in the protocols used to connect to the engine.

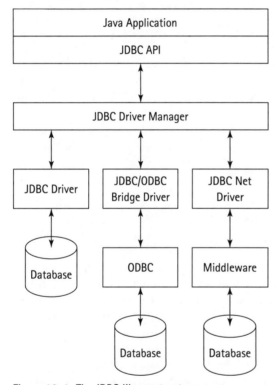

Figure 13-1: The JDBC library structure

The JDBC API and driver manager are part of the Java Development Kit. You can get JDBC drivers from the database vendor or third parties. You can also find open source drivers, particularly for open source databases, as you'd expect.

# Driver types

As Figure 13-1 suggests, JDBC makes it possible to connect a Java servlet to a wide variety of data sources in a number of different ways. The driver you choose can have a significant impact on performance and capability. JDBC drivers are classified in four types.

## TYPE 1: THE JDBC-ODBC BRIDGE

The only Type 1 driver is the JDBC-ODBC bridge driver, which lets you connect to an ODBC driver manager, which can then connect to a back-end database by whatever means available. The bridge driver represents potentially the most convoluted approach to database access. Your application talks to JDBC, JDBC talks to ODBC, ODBC talks to a driver, and the driver might talk to several layers of middleware before reaching the actual database. In general, the more layers you have, the greater the performance penalty, the greater likelihood of errors, and the more exposure to security risks.

The JDBC-ODBC bridge is sometimes the only shot you have, and it can be a useful tool especially when accessing older corporate databases; but it was conceived as an interim solution while other drivers were being prepared, and it shouldn't be your first choice.

 Although you could access MySQL on Windows via the JDBC-ODBC driver connecting to MySQL through the MyODBC driver, there is a much better solution. See the upcoming section on Type 4 drivers.

## TYPE 2: NATIVE BINARY CODE

Type 2 JDBC drivers plug in some native binary code, which is called by Java code. As with any time you're mating Java and native code, you run the risk of compromising Java's security, and certainly platform independence goes out the window. You get better performance with a Type 2 driver than with the JDBC-ODBC bridge driver since you've eliminated the ODBC driver manager; native code isn't generally the preferred solution either.

## TYPE 3: MIDDLEWARE

Type 3 JDBC drivers are a pure Java solution, involving a complex design. These drivers encompass both a Java driver client and a Java driver server, which communicate using a network protocol. Figure 13-2 shows the client (which is connected to the application via the driver manager, as with other drivers), the server, and a variety of databases.

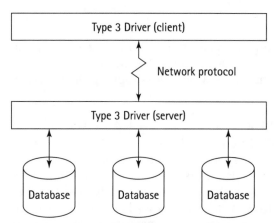

Figure 13-2: Type 3 JDBC drivers use a network protocol to communicate between the server and the client.

Type 3 drivers put all the responsibility for the connection to the back-end database on the Type 3 server, which reduces client-side maintenance. The client can now connect to the database, and it's up to the server part of the driver to determine how that connection happens. These drivers are particularly well suited to multitier enterprise solutions.

### TYPE 4: PURE JAVA

Like Type 3 drivers, Type 4 drivers are pure Java, but provide a direct connection between the JDBC Driver Manager and the SQL database. No middleware is involved. Type 4 drivers are well suited to servlets that connect to a database server on the same hardware or local network. Since these are pure Java drivers, whatever connection they have to the database must be through a protocol rather than a direct library call.

The servlet examples in this book that connect to a database do so using the MM. MySQL Type 4 driver. I cover the installation details for that driver shortly.

## Choosing a driver

If you're following the examples in this book strictly and using the MySQL driver, then I've already made your choice for you. The MM (for Mark Matthews) driver isn't the only JDBC driver available for MySQL, but it's under the GNU LGPL (the library version of the GPL open source license); is actively developed by its author; and is popular, reliable, and fast.

As unlikely as it may seem, you could have another database (or driver) in mind. Keep in mind the following points when looking for a driver:

- **Reliability** – Reliability is paramount. You have enough issues to deal with in a Web site environment without worrying about your database driver flaking out. You can get reliability information from product reviews, but I also always look in the usenet newsgroup archives at `http://www.deja.com/usenet` to find out what other developers are saying about a product.

- **Availability** – Who produces the driver? Generally – though not always – larger, older companies are more reliable sources. Vendors of major relational databases (such as IBM, Oracle, Microsoft, and Sybase) are about as reliable as you can get. If you're dealing with a driver from a very small company or an individual, you should be looking for source code as well.

- **Speed** – You may start out thinking of speed, but if your driver isn't reliable, and you don't have any guarantee of access to future releases, a fast driver just means you have a better head of speed up when you hit the wall.

You'll want to test any driver against the conditions you expect it to encounter. But you need to think about more than just the driver itself. How fast is your database? If the Web server and the database are on different machines, what's the network connection like? Is the bottleneck really in your JDBC driver (actually a pretty good place to look) or is your server maxing out just serving pages?

You need to use the driver in an efficient way. The first examples I show are most emphatically *not* optimized for speed. You really don't want each servlet establishing a connection to your database because that can take a long time (although with MySQL this does happen quite quickly). A better idea is to use a database connection pool. This way you incur the connection overhead only at startup and, occasionally, as the load increases and the pool has to grow.

If you have a busy site, or you need redundancy, you may be looking at load balancing, where requests for one site are handled by more than one server box. Here you'll almost certainly have a separate database server, and, as you add more Web servers, you need to monitor the database server load and the ability of your local network to handle the traffic.

## Installing the MM.MySQL driver

Begin the installation of the MM.MySQL driver by going to Mark Matthews' Web site at `http://www.worldserver.com/mm.mysql`. I suggest you go with the latest stable release (you have many releases to choose from). Depending on your personal risk comfort level, you may wish to go with the latest beta release and do your bit to further development. The 2.0 and later releases support scrollable cursors and transactions.

The MM Web site includes some useful information, including online documentation, benchmarking data, and links to tools such as connection pools.

All you really need to download to use the MM driver is the JAR file, which contains the compiled classes. Source is, of course, also available. Having downloaded the JAR file, just put it in your CLASSPATH, or unpack the JAR file into a directory in your CLASSPATH. In particular, you don't need to import anything into your servlets.

# A MySQL Servlet

One of the easiest ways to get started with MySQL and JDBC is with a servlet. You can write a simple servlet with just one method and still deal with all the essentials: creating an instance of the driver, connecting to the driver, executing SQL statements, retrieving data from the result set, closing the connection, and delivering data to the user.

Listing 13-1 shows a small test servlet that connects to a MySQL database, retrieves a few records, and formats them as an HTML table. The servlet's output is shown in Figure 13-2.

Listing 13-1: A Simple Servlet to Test MySQL Access

```
package ch13;

import java.io.*;
import java.util.*;
import javax.servlet.*;
import javax.servlet.http.*;
import java.sql.*;


public class MySQLNamesTest extends javax.servlet.http.HttpServlet {

public void doGet(HttpServletRequest request, HttpServletResponse
response)
    throws IOException, ServletException {
    response.setContentType("text/html");
    PrintWriter out = response.getWriter();
    out.println("<html>");
    out.println("<head>");
    out.println("<title>MySQL Test</title>");
    out.println("</head>");
```

```
out.println("<H1>A list of names from a <br>MySQL table</H1>");
out.println(
    "<table border=\"1\" cellpadding=\"5\""
    + " cellspacing=\"0\" width=\"300\">");
out.println(
    "<tr><td><b>First Name</b></td><td><b>"
    + "Last Name</b></td></tr>");
/* WARNING! The following code demonstrates connecting
   to a MySQL database. In a real world implementation you
   would want to use connection pooling and also specify the
   connection information as initialization parameters.
   Connecting to the server on each servlet request can
   result in delays (although the mm driver does
   establish a connection quite quickly).*/
String connectionURL = "jdbc:mysql://localhost:3306/test";
Connection connection = null;
Statement statement = null;
ResultSet resultSet = null;
try {
    Class.forName("org.gjt.mm.mysql.Driver").newInstance();
    connection = DriverManager.getConnection(connectionURL,
        "servlet", "yowza");
    statement = connection.createStatement();
    resultSet = statement.executeQuery(
            "SELECT FirstName,LastName FROM Names "
            + "ORDER BY LastName,FirstName");
    while (resultSet.next()) {
        out.println(
            "<tr><td>"
                + resultSet.getString("FirstName")
                + "</td><td>"
                + resultSet.getString("LastName")
                + "</td></tr>");
    }
    if (resultSet != null) {
        resultSet.close();
    }
} catch (ClassNotFoundException e) {
    System.err.println(
        "Couldn't find the mm " + "database driver: "
        + e.getMessage());
} catch (InstantiationException e) {
    System.err.println(e.getMessage());
} catch (IllegalAccessException e) {
```

*Continued*

Listing 13-1 *(Continued)*

```
        System.err.println(e.getMessage());
    } catch (SQLException e) {
        System.err.println("SQL Problem : " + e.getMessage());
        System.err.println("SQL State   : " + e.getSQLState());
        System.err.println("Vendor Error: " + e.getErrorCode());
    } finally {
        try {
            if (connection != null) {
                connection.close();
            }
        } catch (SQLException e) {
            System.err.println(e.getMessage());
        }
    }
    out.println("<body>");
    out.println("</body>");
    out.println("</html>");
}
}
```

The servlet in Listing 13-1 is an example demonstrating how to connect to a MySQL database. The method used is expedient, but can incur significant performance and resource usage penalties because of the way it creates a database connection. Use this approach for in-house testing, and possibly in low-load situations.

To run this servlet on your system, at a minimum you probably need to do the following:

- ◆ Create the table.
- ◆ Give your servlet access to the table.
- ◆ Change the IP address, user ID, and password to those accepted by your MySQL server.

## Giving the servlet access

Use the GRANT statement to give your servlet access to the database. Assuming your database is installed on localhost, and you're using the user ID and password as coded in Listing 13-1, your GRANT statement would look like this:

```
GRANT SELECT ON test.Names to
servlet@localhost IDENTIFIED BY 'yowza';
```

In this case, GRANT gives the servlet rights to select data only from the Names table in the test database. While these rights are fairly restrictive rights, they are quite safe. Following the GRANT statement, you need to update the in-memory permissions, or the changes won't take effect:

```
FLUSH PRIVILEGES;
```

That's all you need to give this servlet sufficient rights to do its job.

## CREATING THE TABLE AND ADDING TABLE DATA

You can create a simple Names table with this SQL statement:

```
CREATE TABLE Names(
NameID INT AUTO_INCREMENT NOT NULL,
FirstName VARCHAR(30) NOT NULL,
LastName VARCHAR(30) NOT NULL,
PRIMARY KEY (NameID));
```

This table is just for demonstration purposes; in most cases, you'd want quite a bit more information in the table, such as address, phone number, and so forth. The table does have a primary key, as should all your tables.

I've made both FirstName and LastName NOT NULL, which means that you will need to supply values for these fields when you insert a record. You might think a NOT NULL requirement could cause a problem in the real world. After all, you might have Cher, Madonna, or the artist formerly known as the artist formerly known as Prince in your names list (well, maybe not, but it's good to be prepared). In fact, you probably do want to require a value, since you can't have an INDEX on a field that allows NULL values. Keep in mind that an empty string is not a null. You should also consider adding an index on LastName, FirstName if that's how you expect to be commonly ordering the records, or if you want to locate a record by last name. You would declare a table with such an index like this:

```
CREATE TABLE Names(
NameID INT AUTO_INCREMENT NOT NULL,
FirstName VARCHAR(30) NOT NULL,
LastName VARCHAR(30) NOT NULL,
PRIMARY KEY (NameID),
INDEX IDX_Names_LastFirst (LastName,FirstName));
```

Also note the creation of an INDEX on the last name and the first name. For a small number of records, you really don't need an index like this. In a large database, if you use a SELECT statement such as:

```
SELECT FirstName,LastName FROM Names ORDER BY LastName,FirstName
```

the server uses the existing index to speed the retrieval of the data. You can, of course, modify tables at any time and add indexes as they become necessary.

Next, use the INSERT statement to add some table data:

```
INSERT INTO Names (FirstName,LastName) VALUES ('Morton','Salter');
INSERT INTO Names (FirstName,LastName) VALUES ('Jimi','Filmore');
INSERT INTO Names (FirstName,LastName) VALUES ('Eustace','Shoe');
INSERT INTO Names (FirstName,LastName) VALUES ('Archy','Roche');
INSERT INTO Names (FirstName,LastName) VALUES
        ('Catherine','LaGrande');
```

### RUNNING THE SERVLET

Now you're ready to run the servlet. If you're running Tomcat on localhost, the URL is as follows:

```
http://localhost:8080/hungryminds/servlet/ch13.MySQLNamesTest
```

This URL assumes that you're running the hungryminds Web application that is available from www.covecomm.com/java.

In keeping with the other examples in this book, classes specific to each chapter are in their own packages. In this case, the package is ch13, which is why the servlet is referred to as ch13.MySQLNamesServlet. The actual MySQLNamesServlet. class file is located in /hungryminds/WEB-INF/classes/ch13. When you run the servlet, you should see something like the browser window shown in Figure 13-3.

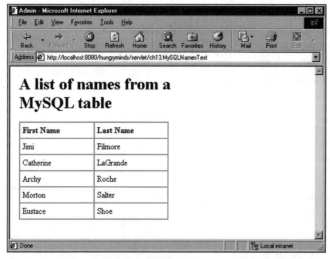

Figure 13-3: Running the MySQLNamesTest servlet from a browser

**TIP**  If all you see when your servlet runs is the "A list of names from a MySQL table" header, then for one reason or another the servlet is not able to connect to the database. Look in tomcat.log for a possible cause. The two most likely reasons are a missing file driver or incorrect permissions. Are you certain the MM driver JAR file is on the path? You should have it in the Tomcat lib directory, where the Tomcat startup script can add it to the path. If the MM driver is available, you're probably getting a "Server configuration denies access to data source" error. Try logging on to the MySQL server locally using the mysql client and the ID and password the servlet is using.

## Preparing the page

One of your primary goals as a server-side Java developer should be to separate presentation from content. That means keeping HTML out of your Java code. Unfortunately, my goal right now is to explain how this servlet works, and that's easiest to do if you can see all of the relevant code. As a result, this servlet does generate some HTML directly. The following example shows the code used to create the beginning of an HTML table to hold the results of the query.

```
out.println("<table border=\"1\" cellpadding=\"5\""
    + " cellspacing=\"0\" width=\"300\">");
out.println("<tr><td><b>First Name</b></td><td><b>"
    + "Last Name</b></td></tr>");
```

## Creating an instance of the driver

Notice that the beginning of the MySQLNamesTest class doesn't have an import statement for the driver. You don't need or want it because the code

```
Class.forName("org.gjt.mm.mysql.Driver").newInstance();
```

creates and loads a new instance of the MM driver (located on the CLASSPATH), which registers itself with the JDBC DriverManager object so it can be used for subsequent data requests.

# Working with SQL Data

After the servlet loads the MM driver, you're ready to start talking to the MySQL database server. The first step is to establish a connection with the server, which the MM driver does using TCP, by default on port 3306. After that, you can create a

SQL statement, execute the statement on the server, and extract data from the result set the server sends back to your application.

## Connections, statements, and result sets

A number of errors can occur while you are connecting to a database and retrieving data. Because of this, you need to enclose all of the code that manages the data connection in a try{} block. In a production system using a connection pool, the connection will open and close the connections in its own try{} block.

```
connection = DriverManager.getConnection(
    connectionURL,"servlet", "yowza");
```

The connection URL in this case contains the following information:

```
jdbc:mysql://localhost:3306/test
```

The first part of the connection URL is the JDBC driver identifier, telling DriverManager which of its (hopefully) registered drivers to use. After the driver identifier, you add driver-specific information. In the case of the MM JDBC driver, you need to include the IP address (or name) of the server and the TCP port on which to attempt the connection. MySQL uses port 3306 by default, but you can configure the server to use a different port. After the port comes the name of the database to use.

The second and third parameters are the user ID and password, both of which you specify in plain text. In a production system you should not code these directly into a servlet; instead, define these values as servlet initialization parameters in the application's web.xml configuration file. Once you have a connection to a database, you can pass it a query and get back a result set.

## Executing a query

In JDBC, you execute queries to a data source in the context of a Statement object. Notice that I've placed a null Statement reference at the method's start to ensure that the statement object is created in a known state:

```
Statement statement = null;
```

Next, the Connection object creates a Statement object and assigns it to the statement reference:

```
statement = connection.createStatement();
```

Finally, it's time to execute a query and pass the results back to a ResultSet:

```
resultSet = statement.executeQuery("SELECT "
    + "FirstName,LastName FROM Names ORDER BY LastName,FirstName");
```

When you execute a JDBC query, you get back a ResultSet, which initially sets a cursor to point before the first row of data. You can then use the next() method to retrieve successive rows. Result sets also contain a number of methods for retrieving the individual fields (columns). The MySQLNamesTest servlet uses the getString() method to retrieve string field values by column name, but if you don't know the name or the data type, you can use the getMetaData() method to return a ResultSetMetaData object, which has detailed information on all the columns returned in a ResultSet.

Since the MySQLNamesTest servlet knows which fields it wants, it doesn't use getMetaData to inspect the returned fields. Instead, it makes a request for field data using getString and dumps that data into an HTML table, as shown in this example:

```
while (resultSet.next()) {
    out.println("<tr><td>"
        + resultSet.getString("FirstName")
        + "</td><td>"
+ resultSet.getString("LastName")
        + "</td></tr>");
}
```

The while loop terminates when next() returns a false value. Go ahead and close the result set, but make sure that you really do have a result set to close, and make sure that there's something there to close. If resultSet is null because of an earlier error, it won't take kindly to having a nonexistent close method called.

After a try{} block, you have to catch any non-thrown exceptions. This servlet tests for a missing MM driver, instantiation or illegal access problems, and any SQL problems. That means if you misspell a column name, or use an invalid SQL statement, none of the out.println statements in the try{} block executes, and you end up with an empty table. In this case, all error messages in this example are sent to the Tomcat log, rather than to the Web page. In a production setting, you probably do want to alert the user that something has gone wrong, and that the Web administrator has been notified and will take care of the problem.

# And finally, finally{}

After you attempt the database connection and/or operation in a try{} block and catch any exceptions, clean up after yourself by closing the connection. The MySQLNames test example creates a connection as needed, so you have to dispose of that connection. In a real-world setting, you'll most likely use a connection pool, in which case you get a connection from the pool when you need it and return it to the pool when you're done, and the connection pool itself takes care of creating and disposing of connections as needed.

In either case, you don't want to leave database connections open. MySQL defaults to a maximum of 100 simultaneous connections, so if you don't close your connections when you're done, after only 100 requests, your servlet won't be able to return any data from the database.

One more small item: The `Connection` object's `close` method can throw an exception too, but at this point the exception is meaningless.

## Remove that HTML

The `MySQLNamesTest` servlet in this chapter is only an example; I wouldn't suggest that you ever build a real-world servlet this way. The problem, as you've no doubt noticed, is that the servlet hard codes the HTML portion of the page, making page design and maintenance quite difficult.

Rewriting this servlet as a JavaServer Page would make the visual design a lot more manageable but raises other problems. The `MySQLNamesTest` servlet contains some moderately involved code to retrieve names from the database. You could embed this code as scriptlets, but while you've solved the visual design problem, you've created a code maintenance problem, because JSPs really aren't an ideal environment for writing Java code. JavaBeans are another possibility, but the standard `jsp:useBean`, `jsp:setProperty`, and `jsp:getProperty` syntax doesn't seem to allow for things like iterating through a result set.

This problem does have a solution, involving a combination of servlets, JSPs, custom tags, and JavaBeans, and that's the subject of the next chapter.

# Summary

Connecting the JDBC API to a SQL database is easy, and with the freely available MM.MySQL driver you have speedy access to one of the preferred Web databases. You do have to check for exceptions when accessing a database, and it's vital you clean up any connection even if an exception should occur. This chapter discussed connecting to and using a SQL database. Key points to remember include:

♦ In most cases, a Type 4 driver is your best choice for working with MySQL.

♦ You have to give the servlet permission to connect; use the `GRANT` and `FLUSH PRIVILEGES` statements.

♦ Don't give the servlet any more rights than it needs.

♦ You execute all SQL statements in the context of a `Statement` object.

♦ Statements return query results in a `ResultSet`.

♦ Always close your result sets and connections when done.

♦ Even though this example generates HTML directly from the servlet, that isn't something you should make a habit of doing!

# Chapter 14

# A Web Site Strategy

## IN THIS CHAPTER

- ◆ Understanding the limitations of servlets and JSPs

- ◆ Applying design patterns to dynamic Web-site development

- ◆ Understanding the Model-View-Controller design pattern

- ◆ Managing user input by using servlets

- ◆ Displaying data by using views

- ◆ Implementing the application's logic by using beans

- ◆ Understanding the role of custom tag libraries

No MATTER HOW SIMPLE or complex the Web site, users make requests to the server, and the server returns pages to the user. Throw a database into the mix, and the content of those pages inevitably becomes dynamic, and sometimes even the choice of pages becomes dynamic. So what's the best way to present this kind of dynamic data to the user? Is it with servlets? With JSPs? With JavaBeans? How do you create a home page for your site with customized or other dynamic menus? How do you manage the user's access to your Web site?

In this chapter, you'll learn how to blend servlets, JSPs, JavaBeans, and custom tags into a database-enabled Web application. You'll understand how to use servlets to manage user input to an application, how to model the application's state with JavaBeans, and how to deliver information back to the user with a combination of JSPs and custom tag libraries.

## The Challenge of Java Web-Site Development

The previous chapter introduced a simple servlet that queried a database and returned an HTML table populated with names from a table in that database. That example showed that it's possible to extract data from a database and return it as a Web page, but it also demonstrated the limitations of a strictly servlet-based solution. Because the servlet generates its entire HTML via `println` statements, designing the page becomes a tedious process of trial and error. And each time the servlet container calls the servlet's doGet() method, that method has to create a database connection. While that's not a particularly expensive operation with a MySQL database, it can cause lengthy delays with some other database servers. Listing 14-1 shows the MySQLNamesTest servlet.

**Listing 14-1: A Simple Servlet to Test MySQL Access**

```
package ch13;

import java.io.*;
import java.util.*;
import javax.servlet.*;
import javax.servlet.http.*;
import java.sql.*;


public class MySQLNamesTest extends javax.servlet.http.HttpServlet {

public void doGet(HttpServletRequest request, HttpServletResponse
response)
    throws IOException, ServletException {
    response.setContentType("text/html");
    PrintWriter out = response.getWriter();
    out.println("<html>");
    out.println("<head>");
    out.println("<title>MySQL Test</title>");
    out.println("</head>");
    out.println("<H1>A list of names from a <br>MySQL table</H1>");
    out.println(
        "<table border=\"1\" cellpadding=\"5\""
        + " cellspacing=\"0\" width=\"300\">");
    out.println(
        "<tr><td><b>First Name</b></td><td><b>"
        + "Last Name</b></td></tr>");
    String connectionURL = "jdbc:mysql://localhost:3306/test";
    Connection connection = null;
    Statement statement = null;
    ResultSet resultSet = null;
    try {
        Class.forName("org.gjt.mm.mysql.Driver").newInstance();
        connection = DriverManager.getConnection(connectionURL,
            "servlet", "yowza");
        statement = connection.createStatement();
        resultSet = statement.executeQuery(
                "SELECT FirstName,LastName FROM Names "
                + "ORDER BY LastName,FirstName");
```

```java
            while (resultSet.next()) {
                out.println(
                    "<tr><td>"
                        + resultSet.getString("FirstName")
                        + "</td><td>"
                        + resultSet.getString("LastName")
                        + "</td></tr>");
            }
            if (resultSet != null) {
                resultSet.close();
            }
        } catch (ClassNotFoundException e) {
            System.err.println(
                "Couldn't find the mm " + "database driver: "
                + e.getMessage());
        } catch (InstantiationException e) {
            System.err.println(e.getMessage());
        } catch (IllegalAccessException e) {
            System.err.println(e.getMessage());
        } catch (SQLException e) {
            System.err.println("SQL Problem : " + e.getMessage());
            System.err.println("SQL State   : " + e.getSQLState());
            System.err.println("Vendor Error: " + e.getErrorCode());
        } finally {
            try {
                if (connection != null) {
                    connection.close();
                }
            } catch (SQLException e) {
                System.err.println(e.getMessage());
            }
        }
        out.println("<body>");
        out.println("</body>");
        out.println("</html>");
    }
}
```

Servlets are an excellent way of intercepting a user request for a page or other data. Servlet mapping makes it easy to redirect all requests that match a specified pattern to a given servlet, and this servlet can examine all of the request information and make a decision about what to do next. However, servlets aren't a great way of presenting data back to the user, unless your users are extraordinarily easy to please.

## The problem with JSPs

JavaServer pages handle the design aspect of HTML pages nicely, and you can create these pages with just about any visual HTML editor. You can redirect page
requests to a central JSP in various ways (using URL rewriting, or perhaps forwarding from a mapped servlet) so you can use that JSP as a servlet-style gateway to
your Web site. In this scheme, the JSP examines the request and then either displays appropriate information, or forwards the request to a more appropriate page.

On the face of it, the JSP approach to mediating a user's experience of the Web
site sounds ideal. You can design the page visually, and you can insert code to handle the logic. But that, of course, is the problem. JSPs have a bad rap in a lot of
shops because it's too easy to insert code into a JSP, and the more code you have in
a JSP, the more difficult it is to maintain. For instance, you will commonly see this
kind of database access code in a JSP:

```
<jsp:useBean id="someData" class="TableData"/>
<% while(someData.next()) { %>
<p><jsp:getProperty name="someData" property="someField"/>
<% } %>
```

You need to be a Java developer to create a page like this, because everything
enclosed in the <% %> tags is Java code, not some more easily understood script
language. If the Web developer and the Java coder are the same person, this can
work, although even then a JSP is a far from ideal environment in which to edit
and test Java code.

## The problem with beans

What about JavaBeans? A JavaBean is a Java class that conforms to a set of minimum requirements, none of which preclude your using a JavaBean as part of a Web
application. But you can't build a Web site out of just beans either, because the JSP
and Servlet specification don't provide a way for a user to directly execute a
JavaBean's methods via HTTP, so JavaBeans have to exist in conjunction with JSPs
and/or servlets. JavaBeans also have a particular role in Web-site development, and
I'll get to that a little later in this chapter.

# Designing Dynamic Web Sites

If you're reading this book, you're not interested in creating traditional Web sites
with static pages. On static pages you worry about presentation, but not really
about the user's interaction with the site. Once all the links are in place, the user
can traverse the site at will, hopping from page to page in the true spirit of the
hyperlinked document.

Once you begin adding dynamic content, you're on the way to a development process that looks a lot more like that associated with traditional application development, but with a few twists.

One of the things that makes Web site development different from desktop development is the document-centric nature of the Web. Users work with a finite number of desktop applications, and these applications generally look different enough from each other that it's not hard to differentiate between them. You know whether that's your word processor you have in front of you, or your spreadsheet, or your email program. On the Web, however, everything's a document. And that means the documents have to differentiate themselves.

## Web-page layouts

Over the years, a few de facto standards have emerged for Web site design. Figure 14-1 summarizes standard approaches to locating Web-page information.

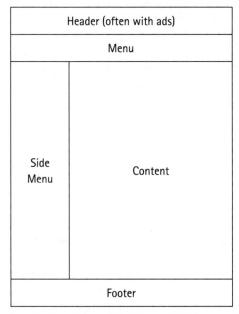

Figure 14-1: Common locations of Web-page elements

Designing Web pages has evolved over the years. At one time it was common to have a simple menu across the top of the page, perhaps under a logo. The rest of the page was given over to text and graphics — in other words, the content. At the bottom of the page, you could find another copy of the top menu.

Many business sites still use this kind of approach, but increasingly the space on the left side of the page is set aside for a site menu and sometimes ads. Sometimes a similar area on the right side of the page is also used for menu and ad space. Typically the various areas of the Web page are laid out using HTML tables.

All of this has an important bearing on your choice of Web application architecture. If you have what is essentially repeating data on most pages (like a menu), you really only want to create that data once, in its own file, and then include that file where needed.

## Including other pages

You can include repeated page components at compile time with a `<%@include file="nameoffile">` directive, or at runtime with `jsp:include`. Compile time includes are faster, but if you change the included file, you have to recompile the JSP to make the changes take effect.

An important consideration is how many pages you expect to create. In a static site you might create a sort of template page with `include` directives for headers, footers, sidebar menus, and so forth. Besides the `include` directives, this page would contain the overall structure of the page and the main content. It isn't practical to build each Web page by including header, footer, and other content if your site presents a lot of content using JSPs. If you need to change the width of a sidebar menu, then the pages that include that sidebar menu will probably suffer some unwanted side effects; perhaps the right side of the content area will no longer line up with the right side of the header. If you have a large number of pages, each of those pages will have to be recompiled whenever you change the page structure.

## An approach to delivering dynamic Web sites

The approach to delivering Web pages using a standard layout is very close to a good solution. All you really need to do is take a slightly different perspective on how you separate the standard, mostly unchanging parts of a Web page from the changing part. Don't try to attach your entire standard formatting information to each and every Web page; instead, create just one (or several) standard Web page(s), and include whatever page the user has requested in the content area.

Now you have a limited number of display pages, with which you can display all of your site's content. Your page designer is happy because she has a small, fixed number of pages to maintain. Of course, you still have a lot of content to deliver. If you have 3,000 pages of content, and only three possible JSPs users can use to view that content, how do you translate a page request into the appropriate display?

Happily, this sort of wheel has already been invented a number of times. It turns out that managing a dynamic Web site isn't that different from developing a lot of other application, and a solution is ready at hand.

# Applying Design Patterns

Object-oriented programming design patterns have become common currency in recent years, and a number of books on the subject are available. A design pattern is just a formalization of an approach OO developers can use to solve a programming problem. Software developers have defined a great many design patterns; the following are just a few examples:

- **Adapter** – a class that functions as an intermediary between two classes with incompatible interfaces

- **Facade** – a class that provides a high-level interface to a system with multiple interfaces

- **Singleton** – a class that has only one instance, and can be accessed globally

- **Flyweight** – a system using a shared class to support common functionality for a large number of very small objects

As you can see from these examples, design patterns describe what OO programmers already do, and even if you don't have any prior knowledge of design patterns, you're undoubtedly using them all the time.

Formally described design patterns come from the knowledge and experiences of many people, and are an important resource for object-oriented software development. By learning about existing design patterns and applying them to your development you're leveraging that skill and knowledge.

## The Model-View-Controller design pattern

Although design patterns often model a small part of an application system, they can also model the application as a whole. This modeling is what the Model-View-Controller, or MVC pattern, does.

MVC is also sometimes referred to as Model 2.

The MVC design pattern divides an application into three component areas:

- The Model is the application's business logic and data. This code and data is conceptually independent of the View and the Controller, and in fact you could have one Model supporting both desktop and Web applications.

- The View is the part of the application that displays information to the user. In a desktop application the view is the on-screen display. In a Web application, the display is on the screen of the remote user, so the view is in effect the Web page returned to the user following the request.

◆ The Controller is that part of the application that manages user input. In a desktop application, input can be keystrokes or mouse clicks. In a Web application, input is most likely an HTTP request.

Figure 14-2 shows the MVC design pattern as applied to one style of Java-based Web development.

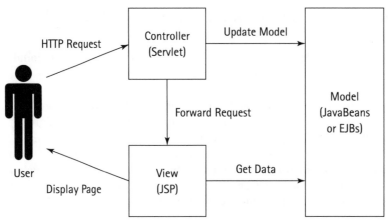

Figure 14-2: A Model-View-Controller pattern for Java-based, Web-site development

Leaving aside for the moment the question of whether Figure 14-2 represents the ideal way to structure a Web application, consider the benefits of the MVC architecture.

The part most likely to change in any relatively mature application is the user interface. Perhaps you need to display an additional table field, or you need your application installed to a client in another country, and you have to change all of the prompts on the screens into another language. It could even be that you're porting the application to another platform, with subtly different user interface requirements, such as a one-button mouse instead of a two-button mouse.

If you can keep the user interface separate from the application's business logic, then changes to the user interface don't of themselves run the risk of breaking that logic (provided you clearly define, and strictly control, the interface to the business logic).

Sometimes it becomes necessary to change the application's underlying operation as well. If the task is to redesign a set of tables so that information can be presented more quickly to the user, the user won't care how it happens, but is pleased with the increase in speed.

And speaking of tables, in most cases an application has a data store, which you can diagram as a separate entity, as shown in Figure 14-3.

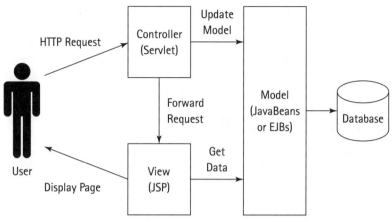

Figure 14-3: An MVC pattern for Web applications, with a database

If, as is likely, the Model portion of your MVC application becomes more complex, you can deconstruct the Model into any number of objects, each with its own function. In a distributed Web application, you can deploy the model across multiple servers. Enterprise JavaBeans are well beyond the scope of this book, but even without EJBs you can have multiple servers involved, with the Web application making use of remote components using Java's Remote Method Invocation (RMI).

## Controlling inputs by using servlets

In Figure 14-2, the user provides inputs to the browser, which makes an HTTP request at the server. A servlet receives this input, examines the request object, and determines what action to take next.

Since Web applications can map various kinds of requests to specific servlets, you can easily channel all requests for, say, HTML pages to a particular servlet. Just include something like the following in the Web application's web.xml:

```
<servlet-mapping>
    <servlet-name>
        traffic
    </servlet-name>
    <url-pattern>
        *.html
    </url-pattern>
</servlet-mapping>
```

This servlet mapping assumes that you have previously declared a servlet with the name traffic. With this mapping, all requests to this Web application that end in .html are sent to the appropriate method in the traffic servlet (usually doGet or doPut).

Once the servlet has the request, it can examine all of the request's information, including the URL, the location, any parameters, and any additional header information such as cookies or authentication data. The servlet can then decide what to do with the request. It may communicate with one or more JavaBeans, which represent the state of the Web application. At some point, it will most likely need to pass control to a JSP, which can send a page back to the user.

# Viewing the data with JSPs

For a servlet to function as a controller in a MVC configuration it has to be able to trigger the display of a JSP. You can do this two ways. One is to send an HTTP redirect request back to the user, indicating which page the user's browser should now request. Redirecting a request is *not* a particularly good idea in most situations. First, a redirect requires an additional request by the user's browser, which takes extra time. Second, and even more critically, if you want to pass any information from the first request to the second, you will probably have to encode that data into the redirected URL, which is cumbersome.

If, for instance, a user requests /webapp/dummypage.html, and you want to display dummypage.html inside /webapp/main.jsp, just sending a redirect back telling the user to go to main.jsp won't do any good, because main.jsp won't have any way of knowing that dummypage.html is the page it should display. Some kludgy ways to deal with this are setting a cookie on the user's machine and using session tracking, but you really shouldn't give these approaches serious consideration.

### USING REQUESTDISPATCHER

The second, and far superior, way to call a JSP is to use a RequestDispatcher. First, save the original request URI as an attribute in the request object, so that the JSP that receives the forwarded request can extract this information later:

```
request.setAttribute("URI",request.getRequestURI());
```

Now get a RequestDispatcher object from the servlet's context (in other words, the Web application), specifying the page to which you are forwarding:

```
RequestDispatcher dispatcher =
    getServletContext().getRequestDispatcher("/main.jsp");
```

Finally, call the dispatcher's forward method to execute the JSP:

```
dispatcher.forward(request,response);
```

Inside the JSP, you need to call request.getAttribute to retrieve the stored URI, and then pass that information to the jsp:include tag:

```
<% String URI = (String)request.getAttribute("URI");%>
<jsp:include page="<%=URI%>" flush="true"/></td>
```

This JSP excerpt contains some of that deadly scriptlet code. Sometimes this code is unavoidable, but in this case, you can convert the code to a custom tag. I take care of that in the next chapter.

### ENDLESS LOOP, SEE LOOP, ENDLESS

If you are paying close attention, you may notice a problem with the preceding example. The `web.xml` setting maps all requests for `.html` files to the `traffic` servlet, and the servlet sends these requests to the JSP. When the JSP executes the `jsp:include` tag, the `traffic` servlet will pick up the `.html` request and call the JSP again. And that most definitely isn't what you want, because you either get an endless loop, or more likely an exception. In either case you shouldn't be surprised, because all requests for a mapped servlet, whether internally or externally generated, should always go through that servlet.

One way to fix this problem is to make the extension of the actual file different from that of the request. If your files are saved as `.htm`, but your links to that file all specify `.html`, you can just strip off the last character.

```
url = url.substring(0,url.length()-1);
```

Now the file extension is changed from `.html` to `.htm`, and the new URL is saved as a request attribute and retrieved by the JSP for use in the `jsp:include` directive.

 When including a relative URL, the current page's location is the one to which that included URL is relative. So if the JSP to which you send your URL is in a different directory, you may need to adjust the URL. Any relative URLs inside the included page are affected as well.

All of the links pointing to pages that you wish to route to a servlet must, of course, be links to `.html` pages, not `.htm` pages, or you may find that Tomcat is serving raw pages, rather than including them inside a JSP. Assuming you have a separate working copy of the Web site, you can work with `.html` pages and only rename the pages to `.htm` (or vice versa) when you copy these pages to the production Web server.

## Modeling the application with JavaBeans

Servlets are ideal for intercepting HTTP requests, and JSPs are a convenient way to display data back to the user. But they're only a part of the story, and sometimes a very small part.

## Other Uses for Servlet Mapping

You can use servlet mapping for purposes other than providing JSP wrappers for `.html` pages. Instead of mapping all request URLs ending in `.html`, you might want to map all request URLs ending in `.frm` to a servlet that can read form fields and take appropriate action, such as writing values to a database or validating form content.

```
<servlet-mapping>
   <servlet-name>
      formshandler
   </servlet-name>
   <url-pattern>
      *.frm
   </url-pattern>
</servlet-mapping>
```

To call the servlet from a form, specify a URL with the `.frm` extension in the form's action property:

```
<form action="newuser.frm" method="POST">
```

When the user completes the form and submits the results to the server as `newuser.frm`, the servlet container will forward the request to the `formshandler` servlet. Note that you don't need a document with the name `newuser.frm` anywhere on the Web site — all you need is a URL that the servlet container has a mapping for; it's up to the servlet to know what to do with the URL. You can use the name portion of the URL to further tell the handling servlet what action it should take, because it can obtain this information with a call to `request.getRequestURI()`.

All applications have internal logic, and when doing Java-based Web development you have choices to make as to where you implement this logic. You don't want to put it all in the servlet because that forces the servlet to generate HTML, and you don't want to put it in a JSP because the MVC police hang you by your toenails. The logical place to put most of your application logic is in JavaBeans.

I said *most* of your application logic should go into JavaBeans, because it can't, and shouldn't, all go there. Here's a breakdown of what code goes where:

♦ **JavaBeans** — all code that isn't dependent on your Web application. If you could usefully call the code from another application (whether or not that seems likely), put it in a JavaBean.

♦ **Servlets** — all non-JavaBean code related specifically to the Web application but not related to any display of information to the user.

♦ **JavaServer Pages** – all non-JavaBean, non-servlet code. This is code that displays to the user. In fact, you should almost never put this code directly into a JSP; instead, you put it in a custom tag, and use the custom tag in the JSP.

The JavaBeans portion of your Web application is the business logic. You may have any number of JavaBeans to handle functions like authentication, session tracking, shopping carts, user preferences, and so forth. By keeping all of this code in JavaBeans, you make your application logic as flexible and portable as possible.

Similarly, you should never include any Web-specific code in a JavaBean. If a JavaBean needs to know something from a request object, then you need to change either the JavaBean (or a part thereof) into a servlet, or you need to pass in just the requested information from the request object, provided that information isn't specific to the Web component.

## Message flow in MVC

In an MVC application, when the controller (in this case a servlet) receives an HTTP request, it typically makes calls to JavaBeans to update the state of the application. After the servlet finishes calling the JavaBeans, it forwards the request to an appropriate JSP using a request dispatcher, as shown in Figure 14-4.

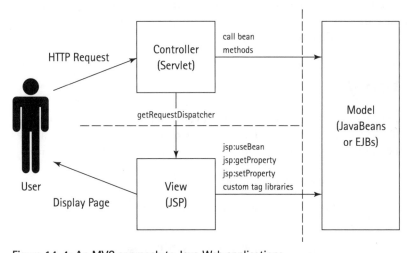

Figure 14-4: An MVC approach to Java Web applications

For example, in a shopping cart application a servlet responding to a form completion (perhaps using the .frm mapping discussed earlier in this chapter) could pass along information about the form action to a JavaBean, which would update the user's shopping cart information accordingly. If the next step is to display the user's current selections, the servlet can forward the request to an appropriate JSP.

That JSP obtains the user's shopping cart information from the model (JavaBeans) and displays it to the user. It's also possible that the servlet may pass some information directly to the JSP by setting attributes in the forwarded request.

Figure 14-4 shows the view making both `jsp:GetProperty` and `jsp:SetProperty` calls on the model. You might think from this figure that the view is updating the model, but normally the only reason the view sets a property in a Model JavaBean is to indicate that the JavaBean is to return a particular subset of the Model's state information.

Setting and getting JavaBean properties has its limits, particularly in a JSP context, since these tags take strings as input and produce strings as output. The view JSP inevitably needs to work more closely with objects. Although you can manipulate objects in a JSP using scriptlet code, custom tag libraries provide a more powerful and appropriate means of using custom objects inside a JSP.

## The role of custom tag libraries

Custom tag libraries are in many ways the glue that binds JSPs to the JavaBean application model. If you find scripting code showing up in your JSPs, it's a sure sign that somewhere there's a custom tag waiting to be written.

Custom tags are Java classes you derive from core classes known to the JSP context, and that have set behaviors useful for conditionally including output in a JSP. Custom tags are the appropriate place for any code that is tightly bound to the Web application itself, and that bridges the display of data and the application's model.

Custom tags are a key part of any Java Web development strategy, and I cover this subject in detail in Chapter 17.

# Summary

Successful Java-based, server-side, Web-site development requires a combination of servlet, JSP, and JavaBean technologies, with the addition of custom tag libraries to remove the burden of script code from JSPs. Key points to remember include:

◆ Servlets alone make HTML maintenance difficult.

◆ JSPs alone require extensive scripting, which makes Java code maintenance difficult.

◆ Servlets can intercept user requests via servlet mapping.

◆ JSPs are a convenient tool for presenting data to users.

◆ JavaBeans can model an application's business logic.

◆ Whenever you're tempted to place script code in a JSP, consider adding that code to a custom tag library instead.

◆ The combination of servlets, JSPs, JavaBeans, and custom tag libraries can make for a robust, maintainable, and powerful MVC Web application.

# Chapter 15

# Designing a Web Application's Model and Controller

IN THIS CHAPTER

- ◆ Reviewing the database layout
- ◆ Designing classes for an MVC-based Web application
- ◆ Designing from the core class perspective
- ◆ Designing from a high-level perspective
- ◆ Handling connection pools
- ◆ Creating menu JavaBeans
- ◆ Using a controller servlet to forward requests

THE MODEL-VIEW-CONTROLLER (MVC) design pattern is an established approach to developing many kinds of programs, including Web applications. In a Java Web application, you can use a servlet to intercept or control requests for Web pages, model the application's state with JavaBeans, and present the information back to the user with JSPs and custom tag libraries.

In this chapter you'll learn how to design a controller servlet and a set of classes to model an application's menus. You'll also learn how to develop a database that supports an MVC Web application.

## Design Requirements

The demonstration application in this chapter is a continuation of the online magazine application from Part 2, where database design issues were discussed. For the purposes of this chapter, the application needs to do the following:

- ◆ Show an index page with a menu of articles taken from the database.
- ◆ Display the selected articles in a JSP.

243

◆ Show a left-side menu of commonly used pages on the index and article pages, again taken from the database.

In keeping with the discussion in Chapter 14, I use a mapped servlet to intercept all requests for HTML pages, and redirect these to a JSP. So for starters, this Web application requires two JSPs and one servlet.

You could create an application using just these three files, a database, and a whole lot of script code inside the JSPs. By now you're probably getting tired of my beating the drum about scriptlets in JSPs, so just take it as read that there won't be any, or they'll only be a temporary substitute for something more reusable and friendlier to page designers.

So far, the only pure Java component is the mapped servlet. In theory you could stuff just about all of the necessary code into the servlet. The logic would go something like this:

1. Find out which kind of page the user has requested.

2. Query the database for all the necessary bits of information, assemble the data into text strings, and stuff it into the request object.

3. Forward the request to the JSP.

4. Have the JSP extract the information from the request and place it on the page.

An approach like this *would* work, but that's about the only good thing I can say about it. The problems are legion. All of the code is in one place, and monolithic code blocks are more difficult to debug and extend. Code that isn't tied to the Web application at all is included in the servlet, so it can't be reused elsewhere. The JSP designer has to request servlet changes to update the appearance of the JSP. There's more, but you get the idea.

## The component approach

Discard the monolithic, servlet-driven approach; instead, look at ways of breaking the Web application down into a set of classes. Object-oriented design, like relational database design, is as much art as science.

My own preference when designing a set of classes to address some requirements is to work from both ends toward the middle. By that I mean I try both to determine the fundamental, most base classes needed, where a lot of lines of code are required to do a particular task, and to imagine how I would like to use those classes in their most abstracted form, where one line of code (say a custom tag) does a tremendous amount of work.

### THE CORE CLASSES
One useful way to begin class design is called the noun-list approach. You read (or if necessary write) a requirements document for your project, and then you extract

from that document all of the nouns. Write them down on cards if it helps, and shuffle them around to see which of these represent unique "things" in your system, which are variations on other things, and which make use of, or are composed of, other things.

You may find some correspondence between your database design and your class design, particularly if you've used an OO design tool to diagram your database. Then again, subtle differences may surface. The following is a partial noun list for the pages this Web application displays.

◆ Links – Many links are on each page, particularly in the menus.

◆ Articles – By and large, articles are represented as links, except on the index page where a summary may follow a link.

◆ Authors – Display as links.

◆ Menus – These are groups of links.

◆ Banners – These are fixed images at present, but you need to think about rotating ad banners for the future.

◆ Header – There may be another menu across the top of the page.

◆ Footer – There may be a footer across the bottom of the page.

The concept of the link figures heavily in almost all of these nouns, so go ahead and create a class that represents a link. Some of the components of a link are the link's text, its URL, and perhaps some associated descriptive text. In fact, you can present most of the dynamic content on both pages using a link class.

You can group links into menus, such as the sidebar menu. In the case of the main page, you can have multiple link groups on a page – one for the sidebar and another for the list of current articles.

## DATABASE LAYOUT

Keeping in mind your initial thoughts on class design, begin to think about the database design. You'll recall that the online magazine database already contains tables for authors and articles, and a linking table that associates authors with articles. Figure 15-1 shows the portion of that database design.

The tables shown in Figure 15-1 include the following:

◆ Names – contains the names of authors as well as users of the Web site (if you are controlling access to the site).

◆ Articles – contains the articles (Web pages) that the users can view.

◆ AuthorArticle – is a linking table to manage the many-to-many relationship between authors and articles; each author might have written multiple articles, and an article can have multiple authors.

◆ ArticleTypes – is a table to store keyword information that may be common to a set of articles.

◆ `ArticleGroups` — is a table for grouping articles, such as all articles on a particular topic, or all articles released during a given month.

◆ `ArtGrpLink` — manages the many-to-many relationship between `Articles` and `ArticleGroups`; one article might be in multiple groups, and each group normally contains multiple articles.

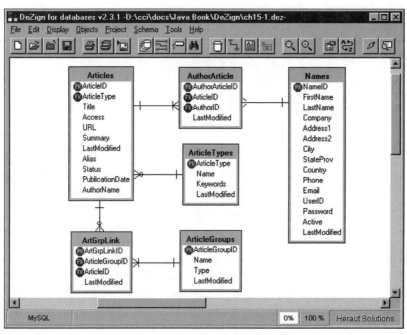

Figure 15-1: The magazine database showing name and article-related tables

For more information on the database design, see Chapter 11.

As Figure 15-1 illustrates, groups of articles are an important part of the data design, and it seems likely that a class to model these groups is a useful addition.

## Creating the database

Listing 15-1 shows the SQL script used to create the database tables. Note that the script begins by creating a database called `ch15`, and then switching to that database before creating the tables.

**Listing 15-1: The Script for Creating Tables**

```
CREATE DATABASE ch15;
USE ch15

CREATE TABLE Names(
NameID INT DEFAULT 0 AUTO_INCREMENT NOT NULL,
FirstName VARCHAR(30) NOT NULL,
LastName VARCHAR(30) NOT NULL,
Company VARCHAR(30) NOT NULL,
Address1 VARCHAR(30),
Address2 VARCHAR(30),
City VARCHAR(30),
StateProv VARCHAR(10),
Country VARCHAR(20) NOT NULL,
Phone VARCHAR(30),
Email VARCHAR(60) NOT NULL,
UserID VARCHAR(20),
Password VARCHAR(20),
Active ENUM('Y','N') DEFAULT 'N',
LastModified TIMESTAMP,
PRIMARY KEY (NameID),
INDEX IDX_Names_LastFirst (LastName,FirstName),
INDEX IDX_Names_Company (Company),
INDEX IDX_Names_Email (Email),
INDEX IDX_Names_FirstLast (FirstName,LastName),
INDEX IDX_Names_Country (Country));


CREATE TABLE ArticleTypes(
ArticleType VARCHAR(8) NOT NULL,
Name VARCHAR(30) NOT NULL,
Keywords VARCHAR(255),
LastModified TIMESTAMP,
PRIMARY KEY (ArticleType),
INDEX IDX_ArticletType_Name (Name));


CREATE TABLE Articles(
ArticleID INT DEFAULT 0 AUTO_INCREMENT  NOT NULL,
ArticleType VARCHAR(8) NOT NULL,
Title VARCHAR(255) NOT NULL,
Access ENUM('R','P') DEFAULT 'R' NOT NULL,
URL VARCHAR(255),
Summary TEXT,
```

*Continued*

**Listing 15-1** *(Continued)*

```
LastModified TIMESTAMP,
Alias VARCHAR(255),
Status CHAR(1),
PublicationDate DATETIME,
AuthorName VARCHAR(100),
PRIMARY KEY (ArticleID),
INDEX IDX_Articles_TypeCode (ArticleType),
INDEX IDX_Articles_Title (Title));


CREATE TABLE ArticleGroups(
ArticleGroupID INT DEFAULT 0 AUTO_INCREMENT NOT NULL,
Name VARCHAR(60) DEFAULT '' NOT NULL,
Type ENUM('R','M') DEFAULT 'R' NOT NULL,
LastModified TIMESTAMP,
PRIMARY KEY (ArticleGroupID),
INDEX IDX_ArticleGroups_Name (Name));


CREATE TABLE ArtGrpLink(
ArtGrpLinkID INT DEFAULT 0 AUTO_INCREMENT NOT NULL,
ArticleGroupID INT NOT NULL,
ArticleID INT NOT NULL,
LastModified TIMESTAMP,
PRIMARY KEY (ArtGrpLinkID),
INDEX IDX_ArtGrpLink_Article (ArticleID,ArticleGroupID),
INDEX IDX_ArtGrpLink_GroupID (ArticleGroupID,ArticleID));


CREATE TABLE AuthorArticle(
AuthorArticleID INT DEFAULT 0 AUTO_INCREMENT NOT NULL,
ArticleID INT NOT NULL,
AuthorID INT NOT NULL,
LastModified TIMESTAMP,
PRIMARY KEY (AuthorArticleID),
INDEX IDX_AuthorArticle_Author (AuthorID,ArticleID),
INDEX IDX_ArticleAuthor_Article (ArticleID,AuthorID));
```

After you create the database, you need to set permissions so your JDBC driver can connect to the server and work with this database:

```
GRANT SELECT,INSERT,UPDATE,DELETE
ON ch15.* TO ch15@207.161.247.82
identified by 'ch15';
```

After granting privileges, remember to flush the privileges table so that your changes take effect:

```
FLUSH PRIVILEGES;
```

You're now ready to enter the data. Or, if you'd like to create the sample data, use the `createch15.sql` script, which is in the `ch15/WEB-INF/sql` directory. This script creates the necessary tables and table data. I created this script using the `mysqldump` utility, which is a useful tool for backing up and copying databases.

## A high-level look at classes

So far, the class design includes a way to model links and groups of links. That's a good start on the low-level end of things. But before getting too far along in designing the class library, think a bit about how you want to be able to use classes at the highest level.

I often find imagining how I will use the result of my class designs useful. I've identified the display of groups of links as one of the key requirements. How am I likely to do this in a JSP?

Ideally, JSPs get runtime text from JavaBeans, using the `jsp:getProperty` syntax. The trick, in this case, is that JavaBeans don't by themselves provide a way of iterating their content into a page. Because my list of links is coming out of a database, and is therefore variable, I can't make a specified number of `jsp:getProperty` calls looking for a sequential number of entries. What I really want is a loop. I need to iterate through the available links, whether the list contains no links, or a hundred.

Since I've sworn off JSP scriptlet code, the logical place to look is in custom tags, because they can be made to iterate. I might use such a tag this way:

```
<mytags:menu menuName="mainmenu" >
    <p align="left"><font size="1">
        <jsp:getProperty name="thisMenu" property="link"/></p>
</mytags:menu>
```

In this (imaginary) tag, I pass in the name of the menu I want to display ("mainmenu"). I then hard code (warning bells!) into this tag an object of a known type called `thisMenu`, which the menu tag exposes to the JSP using the a `TagExtraInfo` class. The menu tag iterates through its list of menu items, and on each iteration it creates or obtains the `thisMenu` object and makes it available to the JSP.

You might be thinking that rather than stuffing the `thisMenu` object into the page context, you can just put a link string there. And you can do this. I recommend you stick with objects and `jsp:getProperty` for two reasons. First, you avoid name collisions; two objects can have properties with the same name. Second, you don't have to change the tag library each time you want to access a different property on the object.

## A generalized iterate tag

A single tag for looping through menu items is a nifty idea, but I find it helpful to break down the tag's functionality a little further. Iteration is something that happens a lot on Web pages. Right now you're just using the iterate tag for a menu, but in the future, you may want to display some table data, or some other repeating information. A better approach would be to separate the iteration functionality from the rest of the tag so you can use it with any other tag or JavaBean. Such code might look like the following:

```
<ch15:menu menuName="leftside">
    <ch15:iterate collection="leftside"
iteratedItemName="menuItem"
iteratedItemClass="HttpLinkBean">
        <p align="left"><font size="1"><jsp:getProperty
name="menuItem" property="url"/></font></p>
    </ch15:iterate>
</ch15:menu>
```

Now the outer tag supplies the menu object, while the inner iterate tag obtains an `Iterator` from the menu object and presents a series of objects of the specified class and name to the JSP. You can then work with these objects using `jsp:getProperty`. I cover the implementation of this iterator tag in detail in Chapter 17.

# Support Classes

The online Web application consists of a servlet, two JSPs, a class representing an HTTP link, a class for groups of links (a menu or other list), and two tags: one for managing collections of links stored as a JavaBean, and another for iterating through JavaBeans. You need to define three other pieces of this application, and they relate primarily to the database operations.

## A connection pool

Almost all Web applications that use databases can benefit from a connection pool because establishing a connection with the database involves a certain amount of handshaking and permission checking. If you can reuse a connection, you avoid having to go through this for each request. MySQL typically handles connections very quickly, but even so you should consider a connection pool. I don't suggest you write one, as there are a number of free and commercial products available. In the examples for this book I used the Java Exchange `DbConnectionBroker`, available at `http://www.javaexchange.com`.

To use the connection broker, you need to create an instance of DbConnection-Broker, using a command such as the following:

```
dbPool
    new DbConnectionBroker(driverName,connectionURL,
        userID,password,minConnections,
        maxConnections,logFile,daysBetweenResets)
```

You could hard code the various parameters to DbConnectionBroker, but that seriously limits the flexibility of your code. So you want to load those values from an outside source. You need a place from which to call this code as well. You can take care of both requirements by using an initialization servlet. The DbConnectionBroker connection pool is a single java class file, so to use it you need to place it under a directory in your CLASSPATH environment variable.

## An initialization servlet

You can use an initialization servlet to create objects and store them in the Web application's context where you can readily retrieve them. Do this with the load-on-startup setting:

```
<servlet>
    <servlet-name>
        setup
    </servlet-name>
    <servlet-class>
        ch15.WebAppSetup
    </servlet-class>
    <load-on-startup>1</load-on-startup>
</servlet>
```

When set to 1, load-on-startup makes the servlet context load the servlet at the earliest opportunity and call its init method.

While the initialization servlet approach is usually reliable under Tomcat, the servlet 2.2 specification doesn't really provide a good way of ensuring that the servlet container leaves a servlet in memory until the container is shut down. The 2.3 specification addresses this by providing Web application startup and shutdown events, which you can use to trigger setup code.

## A menu cache JavaBean

The last item to be added to this design is a class to keep a cache of groups of links. You probably don't want to be going to the database every time you create a menu (or other group of links), and you want these menus to be available to JSPs, so this class needs to be a JavaBean.

# Writing the Application

Finally, it's time to crank out some code. Of course, I've already done the development work and some testing, so I'm presenting the following as a bit of a fait accompli. Still, plenty of rough edges need to be smoothed. First, you'll need some code to initialize the Web application and create any necessary objects such as those that model the application's menus. For the menus you'll also need to connect to the database and retrieve the menu data. You'll also want to write a controller servlet that can intercept all Web-page requests and take appropriate action so that the users see the pages you want them to see.

## Initializing the application

In addition to loading on startup, you want to pass the initialization servlet any other information such as that needed to create the connection pool. Listing 15-2 shows the `WebAppSetup` servlet definition from `ch15/WEB-INF/web.xml`.

Listing 15-2: Init Parameters for the WebAppSetup Servlet

```
<servlet>
    <servlet-name>
        setup
    </servlet-name>
        <servlet-class>
            ch15.WebAppSetup
        </servlet-class>
        <init-param>
            <param-name>DriverName</param-name>
            <param-value>org.gjt.mm.mysql.Driver</param-value>
        </init-param>
        <init-param>
            <param-name>DriverType</param-name>
            <param-value>jdbc:mysql</param-value>
        </init-param>
        <init-param>
            <param-name>DbName</param-name>
            <param-value>ch15</param-value>
        </init-param>
```

```
        <init-param>
            <param-name>Host</param-name>
            <param-value>207.161.247.94</param-value>
        </init-param>
        <init-param>
            <param-name>Port</param-name>
            <param-value>3306</param-value>
        </init-param>
        <init-param>
            <param-name>UserID</param-name>
            <param-value>ch15</param-value>
        </init-param>
        <init-param>
            <param-name>Password</param-name>
            <param-value>ch15</param-value>
        </init-param>
        <load-on-startup>1</load-on-startup>
    </servlet>
```

Listing 15-3 shows the code for the WebAppSetup servlet. It contains the following methods:

◆ init — is called when the servlet container first creates the servlet (in this case, when the Web application starts); it calls createDbPool and createMenus.

◆ destroy — is called when the servlet container destroys the servlet, normally when the Web application shuts down.

◆ createDbPool — creates a connection pool.

◆ createMenus — searches the database for menu information and creates corresponding objects for later use.

◆ doGet — lets you use the servlet for administrative purposes such as refreshing menu information from the database.

**Listing 15-3: The WebAppSetup Servlet**

```
package ch15;


import java.sql.*;
import java.io.*;
import javax.servlet.*;
import javax.servlet.http.*;
```

*Continued*

Listing 15-3 *(Continued)*

```java
import sun.misc.*;
import java.util.*;
import com.javaexchange.dbConnectionBroker.*;

public class WebAppSetup extends HttpServlet {
    DbConnectionBroker dbPool;
    HttpLinksCacheBean linksCache;


    protected void createDbPool() throws ServletException {
        if (dbPool == null) {
            try {
                dbPool =
                    new DbConnectionBroker(
                        getInitParameter("DriverName"),
                        getInitParameter("DriverType")
                            + "://"
                            + getInitParameter("Host")
                            + ":"
                            + Integer.parseInt(getInitParameter
                                ("Port"))
                            + "/"
                            + getInitParameter("DbName"),
                        getInitParameter("UserID"),
                        getInitParameter("Password"),
                        5,
                        50,
                        "dbconn.log",
                        1.0);
            } catch (IOException e) {
throw new ServletException(e);
            }

        }
        if (dbPool != null) {
            getServletContext().setAttribute("dbPool", dbPool);
} else
            throw new ServletException("ch15: Unable to create
                dbPool");

    }

    protected void createMenus() throws ServletException {
        if (dbPool == null)
```

```java
            throw new ServletException("No dbPool, can't create
                menus");
        if (linksCache == null)
            linksCache = new HttpLinksCacheBean();
        linksCache.init(dbPool);
        getServletContext().setAttribute("linksCache", linksCache);
    }
    public void destroy() {
        super.destroy();
        try {
            // give the pool 10 seconds to shut down
            dbPool.destroy(10000);
        } catch (SQLException e) {
            System.out.println("One or more database "
                + "pool connections left open");
        }
    }
    public void doGet(HttpServletRequest request,
        HttpServletResponse response)
        throws IOException, ServletException {
        response.setContentType("text/html");
        PrintWriter out = response.getWriter();
        out.println("<html>");
        out.println("<head>");
        out.println("<title>Admin</title>");
        out.println("</head>");
        out.println("<body>");
        String cmd = request.getParameter("cmd");
        if (cmd != null) {
            try {
                if (cmd.equals("refreshmenus")) {
                    createMenus();
                    out.println("Admin action: Refresh menus");
                }
            } catch (Exception e) {
                System.out.println("Error initializing "
                    + "the web application " + e);
            }

        }
        out.println("</body>");
        out.println("</html>");
    }
```

*Continued*

**Listing 15-3** *(Continued)*

```
public void init(ServletConfig config)
    throws ServletException {
    super.init(config);
    try {
        createDbPool();
        createMenus();
    } catch (ServletException e) {
        throw new ServletException(e);
    }
}
}
```

## CREATING THE CONNECTION POOL

The `createDbPool` method uses the `getInitParameter` method to obtain the parameter values specified in `web.xml`, and passes the results directly to the `DbConnectionBroker` constructor. Assuming your setup servlet has successfully created the connection pool, it next stores the pool in the Web application context:

```
getServletContext().setAttribute("dbPool", dbPool);
```

The `setAttribute()` method places the pool reference in the Web application's context. Any object with access to the application context (such as a JSP or other servlet) can then retrieve the pool reference with the `getAttribute()` method:

```
DBConnectionBroker pool =
(DbConnectionBroker)getServletContext().getAttribute("dbPool");
```

Since `getAttribute` returns an `Object`, you have to cast that object back to its original type before you can call its methods.

## CREATING THE MENUS

After the initialization servlet creates the connection pool, it creates the menu objects, but rather than doing so directly it creates an object that can cache all of the menu objects, and then it tells that object to initialize itself. Listing 15-4 shows the code for this class, called `HTTPLinksCacheBean`.

**Listing 15-4: The HTTPLinksCacheBean Class**

```
package ch15;


import com.javaexchange.dbConnectionBroker.*;
import java.util.*;
import java.sql.*;
```

```java
public class HttpLinksCacheBean {
    Map linksMap;
    protected DbConnectionBroker dbPool;

    public HttpLinksCacheBean() {
        super();
    }

    public HttpLinksBean getLinks(String listName) {
        HttpLinksBean links = (HttpLinksBean)
            linksMap.get(listName);
        return links;
    }

    public void init(DbConnectionBroker newDbPool) {
        // Assign the connection pool reference
        if (dbPool == null)
            dbPool = newDbPool;
        HttpLinksBean thisList = null;
        // create or clear the list of lists of
        // Http links
        if (linksMap == null)
            linksMap = new HashMap();
        else
            linksMap.clear();
        /* select all of the database records which
           correspond to Http links. Data returned includes:
           listName - the list this link belongs to
           URL - the raw URL
           Name - the link text
           Text - descriptive text associated the the link
                  (such as an article summary)
        */
        String listName = "";
        String name = "";
        String url = "";
        String text = "";
        String style = "";

        Connection conn = null;
        Statement stmt = null;
        try {
            conn = dbPool.getConnection();
```

*Continued*

**Listing 15-4** *(Continued)*

```java
        stmt = conn.createStatement();
        ResultSet rs =
            stmt.executeQuery(
                "select g.Name, "
                    + "a.Title, "
                    + "a.URL, "
                    + "a.Summary, "
                    + "a.PublicationDate "
                    + "from Articles a, "
                    + "ArtGrpLink l, ArticleGroups g "
                    + "where a.ArticleID = l.ArticleID "
                    + " and g.ArticleGroupID = l.ArticleGroupID "
                    + " order by g.Name");
        while (rs.next()) {
            // linksMap stores multiple lists of links,
            // so first try to get this list
            listName = rs.getString("Name");
            thisList = (HttpLinksBean) linksMap.get(listName);
            // if the list doesn't exist, create it
            if (thisList == null) {
                thisList = new HttpLinksBean(listName);
                linksMap.put(listName, thisList);
            }
            // create a new HttpLlink object and add it to the
                list
            HttpLinkBean link =
                new HttpLinkBean(
                    rs.getString("URL"),
                    rs.getString("Title"),
                    rs.getString("Summary"),
                    rs.getDate("PublicationDate"));
            thisList.add(link);

        }

    } catch (SQLException e1) {
        System.out.println("ch15:SQL Error: " + e1);
    } finally {
        try {
            if (stmt != null) {
                stmt.close();
            }
        } catch (SQLException e2) {
```

```
        };

        // Return the connection to the Broker
        if (dbPool != null)
            dbPool.freeConnection(conn);


    }

  }

}
```

The `HTTPLinksCacheBean` `init` **method takes a** `DbConnectionBroker` **instance** as its single parameter. You don't want to require a JavaBean to have knowledge about the Web application itself, and the connection pool could be coming from anywhere.

The `init` method begins by obtaining a connection from the connection pool. If the connection pool doesn't have a free connection on hand, it creates one, unless it has already reached its own maximum number of connections.

```
conn = dbPool.getConnection();
```

From the connection, the code next creates a statement object:

```
stmt = conn.createStatement();
```

The `ResultSet` object contains the results of the query, which is a join on the `Names`, `ArtGrpLink`, and `ArticleGroups` tables. Listing 15-5 shows the query.

**Listing 15-5: A Query to Retrieve All of the Menu Items**

```
ResultSet rs =
    stmt.executeQuery(
        "select g.Name, "
        + "a.Title, "
        + "a.URL, "
        + "a.Summary, "
        + "a.PublicationDate "
        + "from Articles a, "
        + "ArtGrpLink l, ArticleGroups g "
        + "where a.ArticleID = l.ArticleID "
        + " and g.ArticleGroupID = l.ArticleGroupID "
        + " order by g.Name");
```

Listing 15-6 shows the query as executed from the command line, along with the result set, except that it leaves off the `Summary` and `PublicationDate` fields. You can see that the items to display are in two groups: `current` is the list of article links to display on the main page, and `leftsidemenu` is the list of page links to display on the left side menu on each page.

**Listing 15-6: A Query Returning Data to be Used in the Creation of Links**

```
SELECT g.Name,a.Title,a.Url FROM Articles a,
ArtGrpLink l, ArticleGroups g WHERE a.ArticleID = l.ArticleID
AND g.ArticleGroupID = l.ArticleGroupID ORDER BY g.Name;
+--------------+----------------------------+------------------+
| Name         | Title                      | Url              |
+--------------+----------------------------+------------------+
| current      | Experiences of a Bandmaster | /sousa.html     |
| current      | 20,000 Leagues Under the Sea | /leagues.html  |
| current      | Zanoni                     | /zanoni.html     |
| current      | The Scarlet Pimpernel      | /scarlet.html    |
| current      | Shin-Bones                 | /shinbones.html  |
| current      | White Fang                 | /whitefang.html  |
| leftsidemenu | Home Page                  | /index.html      |
| leftsidemenu | Subscribe                  | /subscribe.html  |
+--------------+----------------------------+------------------+
```

The job of `HttpLinksCacheBean` is to keep a cache of JavaBeans that represent the various groups of links. The links management involves two kinds of JavaBeans:

- `HttpLinkBean`—models a single link.

- `HttpLinksBean`—models a group of links.

The `HttpLinksCacheBean` class has a collection (a `HashMap`) called `linksMap`. Each time it retrieves a record from the database, it searches `linksMap` for an `HttpLinksBean` instance that matches the `Name` field. If `HttpLinksCacheBean` doesn't find the `HttpLinksBean` it's looking for, it creates a new `HttpLinksBean` and adds it to `linksMap` using the `Name` value as the key.

```
listName = rs.getString("Name");
    thisList = (HttpLinksBean) linksMap.get(listName);
    // if the list doesn't exist, create it
    if (thisList == null) {
        thisList = new HttpLinksBean(listName);
        linksMap.put(listName, thisList);
    }
```

With a new or existing `HttpLinksBean` (`thisList`) in hand, the servlet next creates a new instance of a single link (`HttpLinkBean`) and adds it to `thisList`.

After the servlet reaches the end of the result set, it closes the statement and releases the connection back to the pool. Both of these actions are essential!

The initialization servlet has now created the connection pool and the menu objects, so its work is done. The Web application starts and prepares to receive requests.

# The controlling servlet

You map the controlling servlet to intercept all requests for HTML files. Listing 15-7 shows that part of web.xml that declares the servlet and does the mapping.

**Listing 15-7: Declaring and Mapping the Controller Servlet in web.xml**

```
<servlet>
    <servlet-name>
        controller
    </servlet-name>
    <servlet-class>
        ch15.ControllerServlet
    </servlet-class>
</servlet>

<servlet-mapping>
    <servlet-name>
        controller
    </servlet-name>
    <url-pattern>
        *.html
    </url-pattern>
</servlet-mapping>
```

Listing 15-8 shows the code for ch15.ControllerServlet. This servlet is relatively simple; it simply looks at the requested URI and forwards the request to an appropriate JSP.

**Listing 15-8: The ch15.ControllerServlet Manages All Requests for HTML Pages**

```
package ch15;


import java.io.IOException;
import java.io.PrintWriter;
import java.util.Enumeration;
import javax.servlet.*;
import javax.servlet.http.*;


public class ControllerServlet extends HttpServlet {

    public void doGet(HttpServletRequest request, HttpServletResponse response)
        throws ServletException, IOException {
        String forwardTo;
```

*Continued*

**Listing 15-8** *(Continued)*

```
        String URI = request.getServletPath();
        if (URI.equalsIgnoreCase("/index.html"))
            forwardTo = "/index.jsp";
        else {
            forwardTo = "/article.jsp";
            request.setAttribute("includePage", URI);
        }
        RequestDispatcher dispatcher =
            getServletContext().getRequestDispatcher(forwardTo);
        dispatcher.forward(request, response);

    }


    public void doPost(HttpServletRequest request, HttpServletResponse response)
        throws IOException, ServletException {
        doGet(request, response);
    }
}
```

The `ControllerServlet` servlet uses the `request.getServletPath` method to obtain the actual page the user requested. If the user enters a URL such as `http://localhost:8080/ch15/moreau.html`, then `getServletPath` returns `/moreau.html` which is the URI of the article in the context of the Web application. If you have a link on any page in this application to `moreau.html`, that link must be relative to the root Web application, not the current Web application (unless the root application is the current application, of course). If you put a link of `/moreau.html` in the `ch15` Web application, Tomcat sends that request to the root Web application.

Web application URIs can be confusing because when the time comes to include an article HTML page in the article JSP for display, the `include` method expects a URI that's relative to the current Web application, not the root Web application. You do use `/moreau.html` in that case. I come back to this in the next chapter.

In Listing 15-8, I've hard coded the JSP to which the servlet forwards control, sending all `/index.html` requests to `index.jsp`, and everything else to `article.jsp`. I'll be adding some flexibility a little later on. In fact, you'd probably want to do a lookup in the database to make sure the user is requesting an actual article, and perhaps you may want to modify the database so you can assign each article a specific target JSP.

If the controller servlet sends the request to `index.jsp`, `index.jsp` just displays the Web application's home page. There's no practical difference between the user requesting `/index.html` and `/index.jsp`. If the request is for an article, however, `article.jsp` needs to know which page it is supposed to display. The code

```
request.setAttribute("includePage", URI);
```

creates a String attribute containing the value of URI in the request object with the key `includePage`. Now any object that receives the request can look for this parameter.

## Forwarding the request

Finally, the controller uses a `RequestDispatcher` to send the request on to the appropriate JSP. You can use a `RequestDispatcher` in two ways. You can forward, as the controller servlet does. Once you forward a request, all control passes to that JSP (or servlet). Alternatively, you can call the `RequestDispatcher's` include method, which incorporates the output of the dispatcher into the current servlet or JSP. Since the purpose of the controller is to send requests on, the controller uses the `forward` method.

```
RequestDispatcher dispatcher =
    getServletContext().getRequestDispatcher(forwardTo);
    dispatcher.forward(request, response);
```

 Once the controller calls the `RequestDispatcher`'s `forward()` method, the View part of the Web application takes over. In this example, the controller servlet really hasn't updated the data part of the Web application, but that's only because the Web application doesn't contain any significant data to update as yet. As a next step you could enhance the controller to log the user's request to the database, or to check the user's access.

At this point, the Web application knows how to create the JavaBeans it will use to represent the application's data and logic, and it can intercept and forward requests as needed. That leaves only the View part of the model, which is the subject of the next chapter.

# Summary

Java Web development readily lends itself to a MVC approach to application development. You can use JavaBeans to model the application's state and business logic, and servlets to intercept user input (as requests), update the model's state, and forward the request to the View (JSPs). Key points to remember include:

♦ You can begin designing classes by looking at the "things" represented by the specification.

- ◆ Thinking about a class design from the perspective of its highest-level use (where the smallest line of code accomplishes a great deal) can be helpful.

- ◆ The design of classes to model the application often has parallels in the database design.

- ◆ A number of lists of links in this Web application should suggest to you the need for a generalized iterator function.

- ◆ Use JavaBeans to model the application's state.

- ◆ Use a servlet as the Controller part of the application.

# Chapter 16

# Designing a Web Application's View

IN AN MVC-BASED Web application, the view is usually the HTML page you return to the user. You seldom return a static HTML page; instead, you use one or more JSPs to create the HTML page based on the state of the application (the Model). In this chapter you'll learn how to create two view JSPs, one to display an index of articles available on the site, and another to display any article the user selects. You'll also use custom tags to create the article index and to include a static page in a JSP.

## Creating index.jsp

Your Web site should have a home page that provides access to the rest of your Web site. It's common practice among Web developers to use /index.html or /index.htm as the home page. As a Java developer, you could also use /index.jsp. As with most Web servers, you can configure Tomcat to default to a particular URL when the user doesn't specify one.

In this example Web application, the home page is /index.html, but you're going to use /index.jsp to display that page. Remember that you've mapped all .html requests to the controller servlet, and that servlet will forward a request for /index.html to /index.jsp.

Your users will not see the /index.jsp URL; you could forward the /index.html request to another servlet or to any JSP and the URL on the client browser will not change.

Figure 16-1 shows the proposed JSP layout for both articles and the main page.

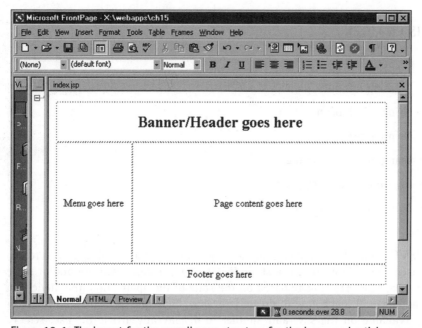

Figure 16-1: The layout for the overall page structure for the home and article pages

As you can see in Figure 16-1, the top part of the page is reserved for a banner or header, the left side for a sidebar menu, and the bottom for a footer. The remaining part of the page will display either an article (the articles page), or a list of currently available articles (the main index page). Listing 16-1 shows the HTML code that makes use of HTML tables to arrange these elements on the page. The index and article pages share some similar HTML code, and in a production system you want to avoid this kind of duplication. You can reuse HTML by placing common code in separate, included files (many HTML editors support this feature) or you can use a template system as discussed in Appendix A.

As this chapter is a continuation of Chapter 15, the Web application is still ch15, and all of the classes are in the ch15 package.

Listing 16-1: The HTML Code for the Page Shown in Figure 16-1

```
<html>
<head>
<meta http-equiv="Content-Type"
content="text/html; charset=iso-8859-1">
<title>Magazine Main Page</title>
</head>
<body>
<table border="0" width="525">
  <tr>
    <td width="525" align="center" colspan="2">
<h2>Banner/Header goes here</h2>
    </td>
  </tr>
  <tr>
    <td width="120" align="center" valign="middle">
    Menu goes here
    </td>
    <td width="405" align="center">
    <p>Page content goes here</p>
  </td>
  </tr>
  <tr>
    <td width="525" valign="middle"
    align="center" colspan="2">
    <p>Footer goes here </p>
    </td>
  </tr>
</table>
</body>
</html>
```

Figure 16-1 and Listing 16-1 represent just the bare essentials of this particular design. I am, after all, a software developer, not a graphic artist. Not that you probably had any doubt.

# Designing index.jsp

I begin with index.jsp, because it's the simpler of the two pages. At a minimum, I want index.jsp to display a menu of choices along the left side of the page, a list of current articles, and perhaps a menu across the top (this menu could be slightly different from the side menu, although for simplicity's sake I make them the same for now). Figure 16-2 shows the general idea of what I'm aiming at.

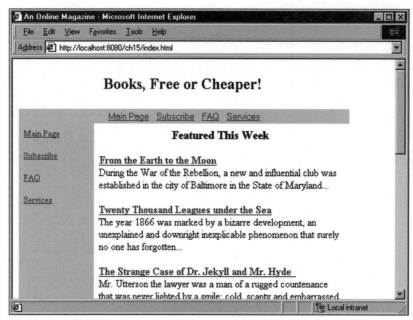

Figure 16-2: What index.jsp is supposed to look like

As you can see, Figure 16-2 contains two varieties of lists of links. The two menus have links only, while the list of articles includes a summary. You recall from the previous chapter that a class called HttpLinkBean models an individual link; another class called HttpLinksBean (note the plural Links) models a list of links, such as the menu or the current articles; and a third class called HttpLinksCacheBean creates and manages the lists of links. The strategy is to make a call to the HttpLinksCacheBean instance (the Web application has only one) and request the HttpLinksBean instance that represents whatever list of links I want to display. I can then iterate through this list and place the links on the page.

## Using custom tags

You can make any object created in a Web application available throughout that application. All you need to do is create the object in, say, a servlet, and then use the getServletContext().setAttributeservlet method to place that object in the Web application's context. From that point forward any servlet or JSP can retrieve the object and use it. You can also store objects in requests, pages, and sessions.

In theory, I could embed a bunch of scriptlet code in a JSP to obtain the necessary objects and insert my menu code. I won't do that because it's messy and because it means the code isn't going to be particularly easy to reuse. I already have three places on just this one page where I'm going to need to iterate through a list of links, and that makes it pretty obvious that scriptlet code isn't going to cut it.

# Using a link bean

Listing 16-2 shows a nested pair of tags displaying menus. I explain how to use these tags, starting from the inside and working out.

**Listing 16-2: A Set of Tags for Displaying a Menu**

```
<ch15:menu menuName="leftsidemenu">
    <ch15:iterate collection="leftsidemenu"
        iteratedItemName="menuItem"
        iteratedItemClass="ch15.HttpLinkBean">
        <p align="left"><font size="2">
        <jsp:getProperty name="menuItem" property="link"/>
        </font></p>
    </ch15:iterate>
</ch15:menu>
```

At the center of the code in Listing 16-2 is a line that creates an actual link via a jsp:getProperty tag:

```
<jsp:getProperty name="menuItem" property="link"/>
```

This jsp:getProperty tag is requesting data from an object called menuItem. The servlet generated from the JSP at translation time declares menuItem like this:

```
ch15.HttpLinkBean menuItem = null;
menuItem = (ch15.HttpLinkBean)
    pageContext.findAttribute("menuItem");
```

You can see that menuItem is an object of type ch15.HttpLinkBean, which is the class that models a single link. The generated JSP servlet, first creates menuItem as a null object, and then looks in the pageContext for an attribute of this name. If the generated JSP servlet finds such an object, it assigns that object to menuItem. Assuming that this process has been successful, you can see how the jsp:getProperty tag is able to retrieve the link field (by using the property naming conventions to call the object's getLink method).

## The iterate tag

Where did the menuItem object come from? The jsp:getProperty code is wrapped in the iterate tag. This iterate tag creates the menuItem object. Looking up one level in Listing 16-2 you can see the following code for the ch15:iterate tag:

```
<ch15:iterate collection="leftsidemenu"
        iteratedItemName="menuItem"
        iteratedItemClass="ch15.HttpLinkBean">
```

The iterate tag uses classes from the Java2 Collection package. You will not be able to use this tag with Java 1.x.

I discuss exactly how the iterate tag works in Chapter 17. But here's the overview. The iterate tag takes three parameters:

◆ collection — is an object that contains a list or group of other objects, and which has a special getIterator method you can use to extract a single object from that set.

◆ iteratedItemName — is the name of the single object extracted from the collection.

◆ iteratedItemClass — is the type of the single object extracted from the collection.

It isn't essential that you understand right now exactly how the iterate tag does what it does; I'll explain the inner workings of iterate in the next chapter. What's important is that the iterator tag is able to take a known collection object and, using a method with a known name (getIterator), extract from that object, in turn, each of the objects contained in the collection. (I'm using the term *collection* generically, rather than referring to the Java2 Collection package.)

The generated servlet code creates the leftsidemenu object as follows:

```
ch15.HttpLinksBean leftsidemenu = null;
leftsidemenu = (ch15.HttpLinksBean)
    pageContext.findAttribute("leftsidemenu");
```

Now something a bit curious is happening. The code creates the leftsidemenu object not as ch15:HttpLinkBean (note the singular Link) but as ch15:HttpLinksBean (note the plural Links). These objects are two separate and distinct objects with different purposes. The Ch15.HttpLinksBean object contains a list of links, each modeled by an instance of Ch15.HttpLinkBean.

## The menu tag

There's one more layer to the code in the JSP that creates the list of article links. The outermost tag is the menu tag, and this tag places an object called menuItem in the page context.

```
<ch15:menu menuName="leftsidemenu">
    <ch15:iterate collection="leftsidemenu"
        iteratedItemName="menuItem"
```

```
        iteratedItemClass="ch15.HttpLinkBean">
        <p align="left"><font size="2">
        <jsp:getProperty name="menuItem" property="link"/>
        </font></p>
    </ch15:iterate>
</ch15:menu>
```

You might think from looking at the tag code that the iterate tag is creating an object called menuItem, of type ch15.HttpLinkBean. This isn't the case. The menu tag creates an appropriate menuItem object based on the menuName attribute, which is "leftsidemenu" in this example. The iterate tag can work with any object that has a getIterator method that returns an iterator, while the menu tag creates a very specific object that has that all-important getIterator method. Listing 16-3 shows the code for MenuTag, and its accompanying tag extra info class, MenuTEI.

**Listing 16-3: Source Code for the MenuTag and MenuTEI Classes**

```
package ch15;


import javax.servlet.jsp.tagext.*;
import javax.servlet.jsp.*;
import javax.servlet.*;
import java.io.Writer;
import java.util.*;
import java.io.IOException;
import com.javaexchange.dbConnectionBroker.*;
import java.sql.*;

public class MenuTag extends TagSupport {
    protected String menuName;
    public int doStartTag() throws JspException {
        ServletRequest request = pageContext.getRequest();
        HttpLinksCacheBean linksCache =
            (HttpLinksCacheBean) pageContext.getAttribute(
                "linksCache",
                pageContext.APPLICATION_SCOPE);
        if ((linksCache != null) && (menuName != null)) {
            HttpLinksBean menu = linksCache.getLinks(menuName);
            if (menu != null) {
                pageContext.setAttribute(menuName, menu);
                return (EVAL_BODY_INCLUDE);
            }

        }
```

*Continued*

**Listing 16-3** *(Continued)*

```
        return (SKIP_BODY);
    }

    public java.lang.String getMenuName() {
        return menuName;
    }

     public void setMenuName(java.lang.String newMenuName) {
        menuName = newMenuName;
    }
}


import javax.servlet.jsp.tagext.*;
import java.util.*;

public class MenuTEI extends TagExtraInfo {
    public VariableInfo[] getVariableInfo(TagData data) {
        return new VariableInfo[] {
            new VariableInfo(
                data.getAttributeString("menuName"),
                "ch15.HttpLinksBean",
                true,
                VariableInfo.NESTED)
            };
    }
}
```

The core of the menu tag is the doStartTag() method. First, the code searches the Web application's context for a reference to the HttpLinksCacheBean instance created by the initialization servlet:

```
(HttpLinksCacheBean)
    pageContext.getAttribute("linksCache",
    pageContext.APPLICATION_SCOPE);
```

If the code finds the object, it tries to get a menu corresponding to the name passed to the menuName property.

```
HttpLinksBean menu =
    linksCache.getLinks(menuName);
```

If this passing is successful, the code places that bean into the page context where the `iterator` tag can work with it:

```
pageContext.setAttribute(menuName, menu);
```

The iterator then extracts the individual `HttpLinkBean` instances so you can extract properties using `jsp:getProperty`.

Because all of `HttpLinkBean`'s properties are available, you have flexibility in the information you display. The list of articles is similar to the menu, but with the addition of the bold attribute and the text property, as shown in Listing 16-4.

**Listing 16-4: Creating the List of Current Articles**

```
<ch15:menu menuName="current">
    <ch15:iterate collection="current"
        iteratedItemName="menuItem"
        iteratedItemClass="ch15.HttpLinkBean">
    <p align="left"><b>
    <jsp:getProperty name="menuItem" property="link"/>
    </b><br>
    <jsp:getProperty name="menuItem" property="text"/>
    </p>
    </ch15:iterate>
</ch15:menu>
```

Note that in the Listing 16-4 example, `menuName` is doing double duty. It becomes the name of the `HttpLinksBean` instance, but it is also the name of the `ArticleGroups` record in the database. Each ArticleGroups record corresponds to a menu. Among other things, this means that you cannot have any characters (such as spaces) in the `ArticleGroup` name, which would be invalid for a Java class name. If you want to have menu names with spaces, create a separate column in the `ArticleGroups` table and call it something like "Title."

# A header menu

In addition to the sidebar menu, `index.jsp` also has a header menu. You could define the header menu as a separate ArticleGroups record, but for the sake of simplicity I've simply duplicated the sidebar menu. The difference is that this menu doesn't put each link into its own paragraph.

```
<ch15:menu menuName="leftsidemenu">
    <ch15:iterate collection="leftsidemenu"
      iteratedItemName="menuItem"
      iteratedItemClass="ch15.HttpLinkBean">
        <jsp:getProperty name="menuItem"
```

```
            property="link"/>   
    </ch15:iterate>
</ch15:menu>
```

Keep in mind that because the database accommodates many-to-many relationships, where an article can be in many groups and many articles can be in one group, you can have some menu items in several or all menus and some in just one menu. All you need to do is create the necessary linking records in the ArtGrpLink table.

## The tag library definition

Before you can use the tag libraries, you have to define them in a tag library descriptor. Listing 16-5 shows ch15.tld, which contains the descriptors for the iterate and menu tags, as well as the include tag used by article.jsp.

**Listing 16-5: The Tag Library Definition (ch15.tld)**

```
<?xml version="1.0" encoding="ISO-8859-1" ?>
<!DOCTYPE taglib
        PUBLIC "-//Sun Microsystems, Inc.//DTD JSP Tag Library
1.1//EN"
    "http://java.sun.com/j2ee/dtds/web-jsptaglibrary_1_1.dtd">

<!-- a tag library descriptor -->

<taglib>
  <!-- after this the default space is
    "http://java.sun.com/j2ee/dtds/jsptaglibrary_1_2.dtd"
  -->

  <tlibversion>1.0</tlibversion>
  <jspversion>1.1</jspversion>
  <shortname>cmag</shortname>
  <uri></uri>
  <info>
        A tag library various functions
  </info>


    <tag>
        <name>iterate</name>
        <tagclass>ch15.IterateTag</tagclass>
        <teiclass>ch15.IterateTEI</teiclass>
        <bodycontent>JSP</bodycontent>
```

```
        <attribute>
            <name>collection</name>
            <required>true</required>
            <rtexprvalue>false</rtexprvalue>
        </attribute>
        <attribute>
            <name>iteratedItemName</name>
            <required>true</required>
            <rtexprvalue>false</rtexprvalue>
        </attribute>
        <attribute>
            <name>iteratedItemClass</name>
            <required>true</required>
            <rtexprvalue>false</rtexprvalue>
        </attribute>
    </tag>

    <tag>
        <name>menu</name>
        <tagclass>ch15.MenuTag</tagclass>
        <teiclass>ch15.MenuTEI</teiclass>
        <bodycontent>JSP</bodycontent>
        <attribute>
            <name>menuName</name>
            <required>true</required>
            <rtexprvalue>false</rtexprvalue>
        </attribute>
    </tag>

    <tag>
        <name>includePage</name>
        <tagclass>ch15.IncludePageTag</tagclass>
        <bodycontent>JSP</bodycontent>
    </tag>
</taglib>
```

To use the tag library in a Web page, include a page directive specifying the tag library descriptor file and the prefix to use for all tags. The prefix makes possible the use of multiple tag libraries in a page without having naming conflicts.

```
<%@ taglib uri="/WEB-INF/ch15.tld" prefix="ch15" %>
```

Listing 16-6 shows the complete source code for index.jsp.

**Listing 16–6: The Source Code for index.jsp**

```
<html>
<head>
<meta http-equiv="Content-Type" content="text/html; charset=iso-
8859-1">
<title>An Online Magazine</title>
</head>
<body bgcolor="#FFFFFF">
<%@ page language="java" %>
<%@ taglib uri="/WEB-INF/ch15.tld" prefix="ch15" %>

<table border="0" width="525" cellspacing="0" cellpadding="0">
  <tr>
    <td width="525" valign="middle" align="center" height="62"
colspan="2">
      <h2>Books, Free or Cheaper!
  </h2>
    </td>
  </tr>
  <tr>
    <td width="525" valign="middle" align="center"
     height="22" bgcolor="#CCCCCC" colspan="2" >
    <font face="MS Sans Serif" align="center" size="2"
         color="#FFFFFF">   
    <ch15:menu menuName="leftsidemenu">
       <ch15:iterate collection="leftsidemenu"
             iteratedItemName="menuItem"
             iteratedItemClass="ch15.HttpLinkBean">
       <jsp:getProperty name="menuItem"
             property="link"/>   
       </ch15:iterate>
    </ch15:menu>
    </font>
    </td>

  </tr>
  <tr>
    <td width="120" valign="top" align="left" height="32"
bgcolor="#CCCCCC" >

    <table border="0" cellpadding="0" width="100%" cellspacing="8">
      <tr>
        <td width="100%">
           <ch15:menu menuName="leftsidemenu">
        <ch15:iterate collection="leftsidemenu"
              iteratedItemName="menuItem"
              iteratedItemClass="ch15.HttpLinkBean">
           <p align="left"><font size="2">
```

```
                    <jsp:getProperty name="menuItem" property="link"/>
                    </font></p>
                </ch15:iterate>
            </ch15:menu>

</td>
         </tr>
      </table>

      </td>
      <td width="405" height="32" valign="top" align="left">
      <table border="0" cellpadding="0" width="100%" cellspacing="8">
         <tr>
            <td width="100%">
               <h3 align="center">Featured This Week</h3>
               <ch15:menu menuName="current">
               <ch15:iterate collection="current"
iteratedItemName="menuItem"
               iteratedItemClass="ch15.HttpLinkBean">
               <p align="left"><b>
                        <jsp:getProperty name="menuItem"
property="link"/>
                        </b><br>
               <jsp:getProperty name="menuItem"
                        property="text"/></p>
            </ch15:iterate>
         </ch15:menu>

            </td>
         </tr>
      </table>
</td>

  </tr>
  <tr>
    <td width="525" valign="middle" align="center" height="32"
colspan="2">

    </td>
  </tr>
  <tr>
    <td width="525" valign="middle" align="center" height="32"
colspan="2">
    </td>
  </tr>
</table>

</body>
</html>
```

# The Articles Page

With the index page up and running, all that remains is to create `article.jsp`. Much of `article.jsp` is the same as `index.jsp`, with the exception that instead of a list of current articles, this page will include another HTML page, so it looks something like Figure 16-3.

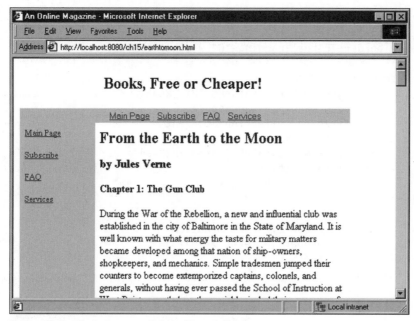

Figure 16–3: Displaying an article inside article.jsp

## Including the article text

Remember from Chapter 15 that the controller servlet stores the URI of the requested page in a request attribute called `includePage`.

```
request.setAttribute("includePage", URI);
```

All you need inside the JSP is the following tag:

```
<ch15:includePage/>
```

# The IncludePageTag

Since request attributes are available from inside custom tags, you can easily write a tag that looks for this value and then includes the specified page. Listing 16-7 shows the source code for IncludePageTag.

**Listing 16-7: The Source Code for IncludePageTag**

```
package ch15;

import javax.servlet.jsp.tagext.*;
import javax.servlet.jsp.*;
import javax.servlet.*;
import java.io.Writer;
import java.util.*;
import java.io.IOException;

public class IncludePageTag extends TagSupport {
    public int doStartTag() throws JspException {
        ServletRequest request = pageContext.getRequest();
        String includePage =
            (String) request.getAttribute("includePage");
        int i = includePage.lastIndexOf(".");
        if (i > 0) {
            includePage = includePage.substring(0, i) + ".zzz";
            try {
                pageContext.include(includePage);
            } catch (IOException e1) {
                throw new JspException(e1.getMessage());
            } catch (ServletException e2) {
                throw new JspException(e2.getMessage());
            }
        }
        return EVAL_BODY_INCLUDE;
    }
}
```

The doStartTag() method retrieves the URI to include from the request attribute:

```
ServletRequest request = pageContext.getRequest();
```

## Using an alternate file extension

The doStartTag() method next looks for the last period in the URI and exchanges the old extension for a new extension, in this case .zzz:

```
includePage = includePage.substring(0, i) + ".zzz";
```

The .zzz extension is completely arbitrary, and is just a convenient way of hiding the actual HTML from the user. You can simply copy all files with the extension .html to the extension, and then you're ready to roll. You don't even need to get rid of the HTML files because the servlet mapping prevents Tomcat from ever serving those .html files directly. If you want to be a bit more obtuse about the new extension, you can use something like .34zkGFiw98Dsls-esf87cHs, which no user is likely to guess.

Next, the tag attempts to include the specified page using the pageContext. include() method.

```
try {
    pageContext.include(includePage);
}
```

Finally, the tag returns EVAL_BODY_INCLUDE to tell the JSP to incorporate the results of the include in the JSP.

## Improving the tag

You can make several improvements to this tag. Although the tag is simple to use, it necessarily makes some assumptions. The servlet must store the include page with the name includePage, but what happens when you want to include two different documents on the same page, using two instances of the tag? You need a way to specify the attribute the tag should search for in the request:

```
<ch15:includePage includeAttribute="firstInclude"/>
<ch15:includePage includeAttribute="secondInclude"/>
```

Similarly, you may want to specify a different alternate extension for the included file:

```
<ch15:includePage newExtension="abcd"/>
```

Listing 16-8 shows the updated tag with two new properties for the include attribute and the extension. The tag provides both properties with default values and the tag definition from ch15.tld (see Listing 16-9) adds these as optional attributes.

**Listing 16-8: The Source Code for IncludePageTag with Include Page and Extension Attributes**

```
package ch15;

import javax.servlet.jsp.tagext.*;
import javax.servlet.jsp.*;
```

```java
import javax.servlet.*;
import java.io.Writer;
import java.util.*;
import java.io.IOException;

public class IncludePageTag extends TagSupport {
    protected String includeAttribute = "includePage";
    protected String newExtension = "zzz";
    public int doStartTag() throws JspException {
        ServletRequest request = pageContext.getRequest();
        String includePage =
            (String) request.getAttribute(includeAttribute);
        int i = includePage.lastIndexOf(".");
        if (i > 0) {
            includePage = includePage.substring(0, i + 1)
                + newExtension;
            try {
                pageContext.include(includePage);
            } catch (IOException e1) {
                throw new JspException(e1.getMessage());
            } catch (ServletException e2) {
                throw new JspException(e2.getMessage());
            }
        }
        return EVAL_BODY_INCLUDE;
    }

    public java.lang.String getIncludeAttribute() {
        return includeAttribute;
    }

    public java.lang.String getNewExtension() {
        return newExtension;
    }

    public void setIncludeAttribute(java.lang.String
newIncludeAttribute) {
        includeAttribute = newIncludeAttribute;
    }

    public void setNewExtension(java.lang.String newNewExtension) {
        newExtension = newNewExtension;
    }
}
```

**Listing 16-9: The Updated Tag Library Definition for IncludePageTag**

```
<tag>
    <name>includePage</name>
    <tagclass>ch15.IncludePageTag</tagclass>
    <bodycontent>JSP</bodycontent>
    <attribute>
        <name>includeAttribute</name>
        <required>false</required>
        <rtexprvalue>false</rtexprvalue>
    </attribute>
    <attribute>
        <name>newExtension</name>
        <required>false</required>
        <rtexprvalue>false</rtexprvalue>
    </attribute>
</tag>
```

# Summary

JSPs are well suited to the View portion of an MVC application, and judicious use of custom tags can eliminate most if not all scriptlet code, increasing code reuse and maintainability. Key points to remember include:

- Web pages commonly use lists of links, which can be stored as beans.

- With the generic `iterator` tag you can easily loop through the list of links stored in a bean.

- The `iterator` exposes a JavaBean representing the link, which provides data the page designer can wrap in HTML.

- The article display page uses an `include` tag to include a page determined by the controller servlet.

- To hide raw HTML pages that you include in the articles view JSP, change the file extension to something difficult to guess.

# Chapter 17

# Using Beans in JSPs

## IN THIS CHAPTER

- ◆ Understanding the Collections API
- ◆ Using Collections utility classes
- ◆ Understanding Java interfaces
- ◆ Using collections to store page data
- ◆ Creating a tag to iterate a collection

ONE OF THE REALLY nice features of Java2 is its extensive support for collections of objects. From a Java Web developer's perspective, objects can represent many of the components of a Web page. I've created beans to represent links to articles, and these can be grouped (collected) into menus. Similarly, a form contains a group or collection of fields.

If, for instance, you've created a collection of links to be displayed as a menu, you need a way to extract the individual objects so you can use their properties inside a JSP. Since collections present some standard ways to handle groups of data, it follows that you can create a custom tag to do the same. In this chapter, I'll explain collections and tag-to-iterate collections.

## Understanding Collections

In Chapter 16, the custom `menu` and `iterate` tags are used – and they are in the example that follows – to repeatedly extract data from a bean for presentation on the page. As you can see, the `ch15:menu` and `ch15:iterate` tags are nested. The purpose of the `ch15:menu` tag is to expose a bean containing a collection of menus to the `ch15:iterate` tag. The `ch15:iterate` tag then takes this collection and exposes the individual beans for use by `jsp:getProperty`.

```
<ch15:menu menuName="leftsidemenu">
    <ch15:iterate collection="leftsidemenu"
        iteratedItemName="menuItem"
        iteratedItemClass="ch15.HttpLinkBean">
        <p align="left"><font size="2">
        <jsp:getProperty name="menuItem"
```

```
        property="link"/>
      </font></p>
    </ch15:iterate>
</ch15:menu>
```

Chapter 16 covers the menu tag; in this chapter, I explain how the iterating tag class, called `IterateTag`, works.

I've designed the `IterateTag` to be used with JavaBeans that make use of the Java2 Collections API. Collections are a way of representing groups, or lists, of objects. Earlier versions of Java did have support for vectors and arrays, which are useful ways of handling such object groupings. However, Java2's Collections framework greatly simplifies these kinds of tasks and provides a number of useful collection implementations.

## The interface concept

Java collections are not defined as classes, as you might expect. Instead, they're defined as interfaces. Interfaces are often confusing to new Java programmers, in part because the term interface is so heavily overloaded in computer usage. In Java, an interface is a bit like an abstract class. It's declared with a structure like a class, and the interface's methods have no code. The following example shows the `java.util.Iterator` interface.

```
package java.util;

public interface Iterator {
    boolean hasNext();
    Object next();
    void remove();
}
```

As an interface has no code, it also wouldn't appear to have a lot of use. Yet it's one of the most useful and powerful aspects of the Java language, and it solves one of the most common problems in object-oriented programming, which is this: how do you create an object that can perform a known set of actions (method calls) on any of a great variety of objects it might receive?

Imagine a problem faced by the Rocks and Animals Store. They have a system for keeping track of the rocks in stock, and the animals in stock. They have one class for each, as shown in Listing 17-1.

**Listing 17-1: The Rocks and Animals Classes**

```
public class Rock {
    protected int quantity = 0;
    protected String type;
```

```java
    public Rock() {
        super();
    }

    public int getQuantity() {
        return quantity;
    }

    public java.lang.String getType() {
        return type;
    }

    public void setQuantity(int newQuantity) {
        quantity = newQuantity;
    }

    public void setType(String newType) {
        type = newType;
    }
}

public class Animal {
    protected String species;
    protected int quantity;

    public Animal() {
        super();
    }

    public int getQuantity() {
        return quantity;
    }

    public String getSpecies() {
        return species;
    }

    public void setSpecies(String newSpecies) {
        species = newSpecies;
    }

    public void setQuantity(int newQuantity) {
        quantity = newQuantity;
    }
}
```

Both the Rock and Animal classes have a quantity property, and the store owner wants to use this property to accumulate totals using the Totals class from Listing 17-2.

**Listing 17-2: The Totals Classes**

```
public class Totals {
    protected int total = 0;

    public Totals() {
        super();
    }

    public void clearTotal() {
        total = 0;
    }
    public void sum(Object o) {
        total += o.getQuantity();
    }
}
```

The idea is that the Totals class is able to obtain current quantities from any object passed to its sum() method. The only problem is that Object doesn't have a method signature of getQuantity, so the code

```
total += o.getQuantity();
```

won't compile. How do you solve this problem?

You could derive both Animal and Rock from a common class, called Thing perhaps, and then give Thing a getQuantity method, and prototype the sum() method this way:

```
public void sum(Thing t)
```

That would work, but it only partly addresses the issue. You may in fact not want to have Animal and Rock share a common base class. The more levels you have in a class hierarchy, the more difficult the class library is to manage, and the more fragile it becomes, because bugs in parent classes will most likely show up in child classes. If the bug is some distance up the inheritance chain, it can be difficult to track down.

Even if you decide to derive Animal and Rock from a base Thing class that has a Sum() method, there may be yet another class you want to pass to sum() that already has its own base class. Now you have to find the topmost class in that hierarchy and make its parent class Thing. Forcing compatibility by the use of base classes generally leads to complex and difficult-to-maintain class hierarchies.

## Multiple inheritance

Some OO languages, like C++, address the Animal/Rock/Totals type of problem
with multiple inheritance, where a single class can be derived from more than one
class. Unfortunately, multiple inheritance makes code more difficult to understand
and maintain, since the class is typically gaining a lot of functionality, not just a set
of method signatures that another class can understand.

## Interfaces

Java's approach to solving the Animal/Rock/Totals problem involves interfaces.
Define a Quantity interface like this:

```
public interface Quantity {
    public int getQuantity();
}
```

Listing 17-3 shows the Animal, Rock, and Totals classes updated to use the new
Quantity interface.

**Listing 17-3: Using the Quantity Interface**

```
public class Rock implements Quantity {
    protected int quantity = 0;
    protected String type;

    public Rock() {
        super();
    }

    public int getQuantity() {
        return quantity;
    }

    public java.lang.String getType() {
        return type;
    }

    public void setQuantity(int newQuantity) {
        quantity = newQuantity;
    }

    public void setType(java.lang.String newType) {
        type = newType;
    }
}
```

*Continued*

**Listing 17-3** *(Continued)*

```java
public class Animal implements Quantity {
    protected String species;

    public Animal() {
        super();
    }

    public int getQuantity() {
        return quantity;
    }

    public java.lang.String getSpecies() {
        return species;
    }

    public void setSpecies(java.lang.String newSpecies) {
        species = newSpecies;
    }
    protected int quantity;

    public void setQuantity(int newQuantity) {
        quantity = newQuantity;
    }
}

public class Totals {
    protected int total = 0;
    public Totals() {
        super();
    }

    public void clearTotal() {
        total = 0;
    }

    public int getTotal() {
        return total;
    }
    public void sum(Quantity q) {
        total += q.getQuantity();

    }
}
```

Now both `Animal` and `Rock` implement the `Quantity` interface and `sum()` receives a type of Quantity. That means that `sum()` knows that whatever object the compiler allows to be passed to, it will have a `getQuantity` method as defined in the `Quantity` interface, and it can safely call that method. The following code tests the new design:

```
Rock r = new Rock();
Animal a = new Animal();
r.setQuantity(11);
a.setQuantity(42);
Totals t = new Totals();
t.sum(r);
t.sum(a);
System.out.println("There are "
    + t.getTotal()
    + " rocks and animals");
```

The `sum()` method receives a `Rock` instance and an `Animal` instance and can deal with each, or with any other object that implements the `Quantity` interface.

Since classes can implement multiple interfaces, you can use them to adapt an existing class to work with a variety of other classes. It's still up to the author of each of those classes to implement correct code for the interface's methods, of course.

Interfaces are a powerful feature of the Java language, and heavily used throughout the Java APIs, including the Collections API.

## The Collection interfaces

There are four interfaces in the Java2 Collections API:

- ◆ `Collection` – is the root interface from which the other collections interfaces are derived, defining method signatures for adding, removing, comparing, converting, and iterating objects in a group.

- ◆ `Set` – is a collection that cannot have duplicates (a `SortedSet` is also available).

- ◆ `List` – is an ordered collection that can have duplicates.

- ◆ `Map` – is a collection that maps keys to values (like `HashTable`) (a `SortedMap` is also available).

Java2 Collections API also contains six general-purpose implementations of these interfaces; that is, these implementations are classes that contain code to implement the interfaces. Of the six, you are most likely to need these three:

- ◆ HashSet — an implementation of Set using a hash table

- ◆ ArrayList — an implementation of List using a resizable array

- ◆ HashMap — an implementation of Map using a hash table

The HashSet implementation also has a balanced tree counterpart called TreeSet; HashSet is much faster, but doesn't guarantee the order of its elements, while TreeSet does. The ArrayList implementation has a linked list counterpart called, appropriately enough, LinkedList; ArrayList is the faster of the two, but less flexible. The balanced tree version of HashMap is called TreeMap. The TreeMap implementation is slower than HashMap but provides sorted maps.

## A set of menus

In Chapter 16, you can see how to use MenuTag and IterateTag to display a menu of links. Listing 17-4 shows the HttpLinksBean class, one instance of which contains a menu.

**Listing 17-4: The HttpLinksBean class**

```
package ch15;

import java.util.*;

public class HttpLinksBean {
    protected Set links;
    protected String linksName = "default";

    public HttpLinksBean() {
        super();
        links = new HashSet();
    }

    public HttpLinksBean(String linksName) {
        this();
        setLinksName(linksName);
    }
    public void add(HttpLinkBean link) {
        links.add(link);
    }

    public java.util.Iterator getIterator() {
        if (links == null)
            links = new HashSet();
        return links.iterator();
    }
```

```
public java.lang.String getLinksName() {
    return linksName;
}

public void setLinksName(java.lang.String newLinksName) {
    linksName = newLinksName;
}
}
```

The HttpLinksBean class contains a Set object called links. The Set object is one of the utility implementations in the Collections framework and models a unique set of elements. The HttpLinksBean class has an add method you can use to add objects to its links Set, and a getIterator method that returns an Iterator. IterateTag will use the Iterator to present each of the links objects in turn.

Similarly, HttpLinksCacheBean has a Map called linksMap, as shown in Listing 17-5. I've used a Map here rather than a Set because the HttpLinksCacheBean class will need to look up collections of links by name.

**Listing 17-5: The HTTPLinksCacheBean Class**

```
package ch15;


import com.javaexchange.dbConnectionBroker.*;
import java.util.*;
import java.sql.*;

public class HttpLinksCacheBean {
    Map linksMap;
    protected DbConnectionBroker dbPool;

    public HttpLinksCacheBean() {
        super();
    }

    public HttpLinksBean getLinks(String listName) {
        HttpLinksBean links = (HttpLinksBean)
            linksMap.get(listName);
        return links;
    }

    public void init(DbConnectionBroker newDbPool) {
        // Assign the connection pool reference
```

*Continued*

**Listing 17-5** *(Continued)*

```java
        if (dbPool == null)
            dbPool = newDbPool;
        HttpLinksBean thisList = null;
        // create or clear the list of lists of
        // Http links
        if (linksMap == null)
            linksMap = new HashMap();
        else
            linksMap.clear();
        /* select all of the database records which
           correspond to Http links. Data returned includes:
           listName - the list this link belongs to
           URL - the raw URL
           Name - the link text
           Text - descriptive text associated the the link
                  (i.e. an article summary)
        */
        String listName = "";
        String name = "";
        String url = "";
        String text = "";
        String style = "";

        Connection conn = null;
        Statement stmt = null;
        try {
            conn = dbPool.getConnection();
            stmt = conn.createStatement();
            ResultSet rs =
                stmt.executeQuery(
                    "select g.Name, "
                        + "a.Title, "
                        + "a.URL, "
                        + "a.Summary, "
                        + "a.PublicationDate "
                        + "from Articles a, "
                        + "ArtGrpLink l, ArticleGroups g "
                        + "where a.ArticleID = l.ArticleID "
                        + " and g.ArticleGroupID = l.ArticleGroupID
"

                        + " order by g.Name");
            while (rs.next()) {
                // linksMap stores multiple lists of links,
                // so first try to get this list
```

```
                        listName = rs.getString("Name");
                        thisList = (HttpLinksBean) linksMap.get(listName);
                        // if the list doesn't exist, create it
                        if (thisList == null) {
                            thisList = new HttpLinksBean(listName);
                            linksMap.put(listName, thisList);
                        }
                        // create a new HttpLlink object and add it to the
list
                        HttpLinkBean link =
                            new HttpLinkBean(
                                rs.getString("URL"),
                                rs.getString("Title"),
                                rs.getString("Summary"),
                                rs.getDate("PublicationDate"));
                        thisList.add(link);

                }

            } catch (SQLException e1) {
                System.out.println("ch15:SQL Error: " + e1);
            } finally {
                try {
                    if (stmt != null) {
                        stmt.close();
                    }
                } catch (SQLException e2) {
                };

                // The connection is returned to the Broker
                if (dbPool != null)
                    dbPool.freeConnection(conn);

            }
        }
    }
```

# Creating the Iterate Tag

The iterate tag itself doesn't contain a collection, because it's a general-purpose tag that could apply to any class. All it needs is something called an Iterator, which is defined by the Iterator interface:

```
public interface Iterator {
    boolean hasNext();
    Object next();
    void remove();
}
```

The three methods in this interface enable you to navigate a group of objects. Now a group of objects sounds a lot like a collection, right? And in fact the Collection interface just happens to have a method with the following signature:

```
Iterator iterator();
```

Since HashSet, HashMap, and the other utility implementations are all ultimately implementations of Collection, it follows that you can call the iterator method to get access to the list of objects stored internally in that collection.

I can now define the requirements for the iterate tag as follows:

◆ Get an object from a tag attribute.

◆ Get that object's Iterator.

◆ Get each object from the Iterator, in sequence.

◆ Place each of the Iterator's objects in the page context in turn so you can get information from the object using jsp:getProperty.

## Iterate tag attributes

Recall that the tag usage inside the JSP, as shown in Listing 17-6, prepares a JavaBean for use by the iterate tag.

**Listing 17-6: A Set of Tags for Displaying a Menu**

```
<ch15:menu menuName="leftsidemenu">
    <ch15:iterate collection="leftsidemenu"
        iteratedItemName="menuItem"
        iteratedItemClass="ch15.HttpLinkBean">
        <p align="left"><font size="2">
        <jsp:getProperty name="menuItem"
            property="link"/>
        </font></p>
    </ch15:iterate>
</ch15:menu>
```

The code to create the bean is as follows:

```
ch15.HttpLinksBean leftsidemenu = null;
leftsidemenu = (ch15.HttpLinksBean)
    pageContext.findAttribute("leftsidemenu");
```

The menu tag in the JSP specifies the object `leftsidemenu` of type `ch15.HttpLinksBean` (note the plural). This object, which provides an `Iterator`, is now available to the `iterate` tag.

The first attribute of the `iterate` tag is the collection attribute, which in the example code shown in Listing 17-6 is as follows:

```
collection="leftsidemenu"
```

The generated code looks something like this:

```
_jspx_th_ch15_iterate_0.setCollection("leftsidemenu");
```

The `iterate` tag stores the `"leftsidemenu"` value in it's `collection` property, which is a `String`. This value is next used in the `doStartTag` method, which is where the tag library prepares the task of looping through an iteration of objects. Since the tag has only the name of the object, it has to retrieve the actual object by name, using the `pageContext getAttribute` method:

```
Object object = pageContext.getAttribute(collection);
```

If the object is not available, `doStartTag` throws an exception.

## Getting a method by reflection

Assuming the `iterate` tag has found a suitable object, it next needs to call a `getIterator` method on that object. The problem is that it doesn't know the object's type. Fortunately, it doesn't need to. Java has a Reflection API that allows a class to inspect another class and determine at runtime that class's methods (among other useful pieces of information).

 The use of a `getIterator` method is completely arbitrary in this design. If you want to use a class with the `iterate` tag, it *must* have a `getIterator` method that takes no parameters and returns an object that implements the `Iterator` interface. The name of the method could just as easily, and just as arbitrarily, be called `getWombat`.

The first step is to attempt to obtain a `Method` object from the object. The path to `getMethod` is a bit convoluted. You need to prepare an empty array of objects; the `getIterator` method doesn't take any parameters, but `getMethod` expects an array of objects just in case. And `getMethod` doesn't exist in the object, but it does exist in the Class instance, and you can get that by calling the object's `getClass` method. Whew!

```
Class[] params = new Class[0];
Method method = object.getClass().getMethod("getIterator", params);
```

Once you have the method object, create another empty array of objects for the nonexistent parameters to the method, and invoke the object. The result must be cast back to the `Iterator` type.

```
Object[] args = new Object[0];
iterator = (Iterator) method.invoke(object, args);
```

A number of exceptions can occur in this process, including `NoSuchMethodException`, `InvocationTargetException`, `IllegalAccessException`, and `ClassCastException`. You must handle these exceptions in your code.

Assuming the JSP writer and the JavaBean writer have followed the fairly simple rules for using this tag, all should be well, and the tag should have an object implementing `Iterator` in hand.

Both the `doStartTag` and `doAfterBody` methods call the `iterate` method. Assuming the `Iterator` object is not null and it has another element, it obtains that object and stuffs it back into the page context under the name determined by the `iteratedItemName` tag attribute value:

```
Object element = iterator.next();
pageContext.setAttribute(iteratedItemName, element);
```

At this point in the code, the `IterateTag` code doesn't need to know the type of the object being placed in the page context. The generated JSP code, however, declares the object this way:

```
ch15.HttpLinkBean menuItem = null;
menuItem = (ch15.HttpLinkBean)
    pageContext.findAttribute("menuItem");
```

The complete source to `IterateTag` is shown in Listing 17-7.

### Listing 17-7: The IterateTag Class

```
import javax.servlet.jsp.tagext.*;
import javax.servlet.jsp.*;
import javax.servlet.*;
import java.io.Writer;
import java.util.*;
import java.io.IOException;
```

```java
import java.lang.reflect.*;
import java.sql.*;

public class IterateTag extends BodyTagSupport {
    protected Object collectionBean;
    protected Iterator iterator;
    protected String iteratedItemName;
    protected String iteratedItemClass;
    protected String collection;

    public int doAfterBody() throws JspException {

        if (iterate() == SKIP_BODY) {

            try {
                bodyContent.writeOut(
                    bodyContent.getEnclosingWriter());
                return SKIP_BODY;
            } catch (IOException e) {
                throw new JspTagException(e.toString());
            }
        }
        return EVAL_BODY_TAG;
    }

    public int doStartTag() throws JspException {
        try {
            Object object = pageContext.getAttribute(collection);
            if (object == null)
                throw new JspException("IterateTag could not find "
                    + "the object to iterate");
            Class[] params = new Class[0];
            Method method =
object.getClass().getMethod("getIterator", params);
            Object[] args = new Object[0];
            iterator = (Iterator) method.invoke(object, args);
        } catch (NoSuchMethodException e1) {
            System.out.println("Exception " + e1);
        } catch (IllegalAccessException e2) {
            System.out.println("Exception " + e2);
        } catch (InvocationTargetException e3) {
            System.out.println("Exception " + e3);
        } catch (ClassCastException e4) {
```

*Continued*

**Listing 17-7** *(Continued)*

```java
            System.out.println("Exception " + e4);
        }
        return iterate();
    }

    public String getCollection() {
        return collection;
    }

    public String getIteratedItemClass() {
        return iteratedItemClass;
    }
    protected int iterate() {
        if ((iteratedItemName != null) && (iterator != null)
                && (iterator.hasNext())) {
            Object element = iterator.next();
            pageContext.setAttribute(iteratedItemName, element);
            return EVAL_BODY_TAG;
        } else {
            return SKIP_BODY;
        }

    }

    public void setCollection(String newCollection) {
        collection = newCollection;
    }

    public void setIteratedItemClass(String newIteratedItemClass) {
        iteratedItemClass = newIteratedItemClass;

    }

    public String getIteratedItemName() {
        return iteratedItemName;
    }

    public void setIteratedItemName(String newIteratedItemName) {
        iteratedItemName = newIteratedItemName;
    }
}
```

If `IterateTag` doesn't know the name and type of the object it's placing in the page context, then how does the JSP engine know what name and type to give the object? The answer is in the `IterateTEI` class, which accompanies `IterateTag`.

## The IterateTEI Class

Tag classes can have an optional accompanying class derived from `TagExtraInfo`. Such classes, by convention, have TEI as the last three letters of their names. Listing 17-8 shows the code for the `IterateTEI` class.

**Listing 17-8: The IterateTEI Tag Extra Info Class**

```
import javax.servlet.jsp.tagext.*;
import java.util.*;

public class IterateTEI extends TagExtraInfo {
public VariableInfo[] getVariableInfo(TagData data) {
    String objectType =
        data.getAttributeString("iteratedItemClass");
    if (objectType == null)
        objectType = "java.lang.Object";
    return new VariableInfo[] {
        new VariableInfo(
            data.getAttributeString("iteratedItemName"),
            objectType,
            true,
            VariableInfo.NESTED)
        };
    }
}
```

TEI classes are a bit unusual in that they're not used at all while the JSP is executing on the Web server. Instead, they exist to provide information used at JSP generation time. The `VariableInfo` class contains the following elements, which determine what will be declared in the JSP, and where:

```
private String varName;
private String className;
private boolean declare;
private int scope;
```

The JSP will use `varName` and `className` for the name and type of the variable in the page context. The `declare` flag indicates if the variable is new or already existing in the page. The scope will be one of the following:

- ◆ VariableInfo.AT_BEGIN — The variable is in scope at the start tag.

- ◆ VariableInfo.AT_END — The variable is in scope at the end tag.

- ◆ VariableInfo.NESTED — The variable is in scope between the start and end tags.

In many cases, a TEI class contains all static information, with the varName and className hard coded. In IterateTEI, however, the getVariableInfo method returns data based on attributes specified in the iterate tag used in the JSP. For instance, in the following example IterateTEI sets objectType to whatever value has been specified for the iteratedItemClass property in the JSP:

```
String objectType =
    data.getAttributeString("iteratedItemClass");
```

The JSP engine uses IterateTEI to examine the iterate tag's attributes. The JSP can then create a suitable object, like this:

```
ch15.HttpLinkBean menuItem = null;
menuItem = (ch15.HttpLinkBean)
    pageContext.findAttribute("menuItem");
```

Whether a TEI provides static or dynamic information, it's how the JSP knows what kind of objects to create in the JSP page.

# Summary

Web sites that work with databases frequently have to display repeated blocks of information from that database. You can store this data in collections inside JavaBeans and display it on the Web page using an iterate tag. Key points to remember include:

- ◆ The Collections API is new to Java2.

- ◆ Java2 defines Collections as interfaces, which are particularly useful as a means of allowing one object to interact with different objects in a common way.

- ◆ A variety of utility classes are available that implement the different collection interfaces.

- ◆ To use an object with the IterateTag class, just implement the Iterator interface in that object.

- ◆ The IterateTEI class provides information back to the JSP about the objects that the JSP should expose.

# Chapter 18

# Performance and Design Issues

DESIGNING FOR A WEB-APPLICATION environment is quite a bit different from designing for a desktop-application environment. In a standalone desktop application, there is only one user and only one data source. Concurrent access to data isn't an issue. In a Web application, you can have users contending for the same data, and you need to take this into account in your database and application design. In this chapter, you'll learn how to create Java Web applications that gracefully handle concurrent requests for data.

## Data Concurrency

Database-enabled Web applications have a lot in common with client/server applications, because a number of users have shared access to a database. Data concurrency becomes an issue when more than one person is capable of updating a single record in the database at one time. Approaches to data concurrency usually take one of two approaches: pessimistic or optimistic.

### Pessimistic concurrency

*Pessimistic concurrency* says that when more than one user can have access to some data, you have to lock that data before the update begins. The underlying assumption is that someone else will want to update a record that's already in use. If you and I are on two terminals on a network, sharing the same user records, and I decide to update one of those records, the first thing the code has to do is determine that no one else has locked that record. If that's the case, the code locks the record, performs the update, and releases the record.

You have a number of ways to deal with other requests against a locked record. You may allow read-only access to anyone who is not the one that locked the record. Or, you may disallow access and notify the user that someone else is modifying the record.

All of this sounds straightforward, but that's because this example involves only a single record. What if the user is updating a vendor record and the system currently has a few hundred related purchase order records in process? Do you lock all of those records? Then what happens when a user brings up a form to update a record and inadvertently leaves that record on screen, locked, and calls in sick the next day? Although pessimistic concurrency ensures data integrity, it's difficult to implement well.

## Optimistic concurrency

Some developers, whether because of their sunny dispositions or their dislike for the hassles of pessimistic concurrency, choose *optimistic concurrency*, which assumes that a record in use by one user is unlikely to undergo updating by a different user at the same time. A typical scenario for optimistic concurrency is to retrieve a record, make the changes, and then write the record back (in a transaction) if there have been no other changes to the record in the meantime. Detection of the changed record could be by timestamp, or by comparing a saved copy of the original record with a refresh of the record from the database. If the record has changed in the interim, redisplay it to the user and inform them that another user changed the record.

Both approaches have their places, but my own feeling is that in most cases optimistic concurrency is a safer approach, since it locks records for a shorter period. In addition, some older (typically non-SQL) database systems may permit only table or page-level locking, not row-level locking. Table locking means the INSERT, UPDATE, or DELETE statement requires exclusive access to the entire table. In a page-locking scheme, the server locks a block of disk space that usually contains multiple rows.

MySQL was originally designed for high speed with large data sets, not transaction-intensive processing, so it locks tables for updates. Because of MySQL's speed this isn't as much of a drawback as it would be in a lower database system, but in some situations a table lock in one process will cause problems in another process. To get around the problem for noncritical tasks such as logging, you can use delayed inserts. A *delayed insert* returns control to the calling program immediately but doesn't actually happen until the next table unlock.

When you begin coding at a Web application level with Java, concurrency issues quickly go beyond the problem of what to do about database access.

# Multithreading and Servlets

If you've been in the computing industry since the early days of personal computers, you'll remember single-tasking operating systems like DOS. Under DOS, you could run just one application, and that application could have only one block of code executing at one time.

In today's world of multitasking operating systems, a single tasking system seems like a quaint and constricting concept. No doubt you're so accustomed to being able to print a document in the background while downloading files and replying to e-mail that you never give it a moment's thought. Yet it's all too easy to fall back into the old single-task, single-thread mindset when writing code, because that's how the code seems to present itself. When you trace a possible path of execution through a servlet, where one method calls another, or the method works with some class data, you may be tempted to assume that the code executes just the way you step through it. This assumption is not necessarily the case.

When a user calls a servlet (or a JSP) on a Web server, the server creates a new instance of the servlet either at Web-application startup, or when a user first requests the servlet. The server reuses this servlet, creating a new thread of execution for each request. That thread executes the servlet's methods as necessary.

In a Web-server environment, each user request can generate a separate thread. Those threads can call methods on the servlet simultaneously. On servers with multiple CPUs, threads may literally execute at the same time. However, on any server, the operating system may interrupt one thread and allow another thread to execute. The new thread may well be executing the same part of the program as the interrupted thread.

To be accurate, the Web server will only create one instance of a *named* servlet. A servlet class can have multiple instances declared under different names in web.xml.

In this multithreaded context, servlets are shared resources with the following characteristics:

◆ All threads share class data, that is, data that you declare outside of methods.

◆ Threads do not share data you declare inside a method – each thread has its own unique copy of this data.

If two threads call the same servlet method, each thread has its own copy of that method's data, but both have access to any class data. Consider the servlet in Listing 18-1, which displays a series of ten numbers.

**Listing 18-1: The ThreadTest Servlet**

```
package ch18;

import java.io.IOException;
import java.io.PrintWriter;
import javax.servlet.*;
import javax.servlet.http.*;
import java.util.*;

public class ThreadTest extends HttpServlet {
    public void doGet(HttpServletRequest request,
        HttpServletResponse response)
        throws ServletException, IOException {
        count = 0;
        Random rand = new Random();
        response.setContentType("text/html");
        PrintWriter out = response.getWriter();
        out.println("<html>");
        out.println("<head>");
        out.println("<title>Admin</title>");
        out.println("</head>");
        out.println("<body>");
        for (int i = 0; i < 10; i++) {
            try {
                synchronized (this) {
                    this.wait(rand.nextInt(1000));
                }
            } catch (InterruptedException e) {
            }
            count++;
            out.println(count + "<br>");
        }
        out.println("</body>");
        out.println("</html>");
    }

    protected int count = 0;
}
```

The ThreadTest servlet simply displays a series of ten numbers beginning with one. To slow things down to a human timescale, I've introduced a random wait of up to one second between increments of the count integer, so the servlet will take a few seconds to return a result.

Run the `ThreadTest` servlet by itself, and you see a display similar to the one shown in Figure 18-1.

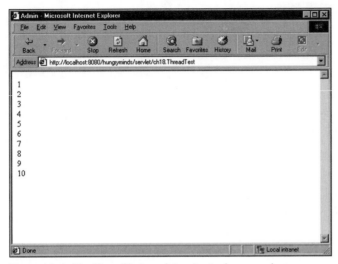

Figure 18-1: The ThreadTest servlet output when run alone

If, however, you access the servlet at the same time in two browsers, you see a different result, as shown in Figures 18-2 and 18-3.

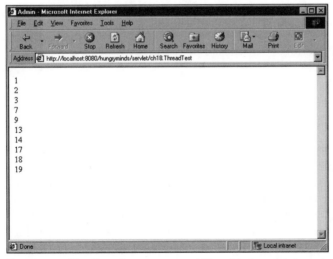

Figure 18-2: The first of two concurrent ThreadTest servlet requests

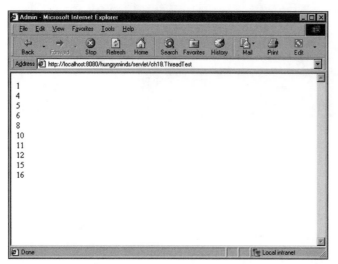

Figure 18-3: The second of two concurrent ThreadTest servlet requests

As Figures 18-2 and 18-3 show, this servlet gives some unsatisfactory results when two browsers request it at the same time – it hasn't learned to count! The problem is that the count property is only declared once for the class as a whole. The two requests each run the doGet() method at the same time, and because of the delays between incrementing the counters (introduced by the wait method), they interfere with each other's incrementing of count.

The general rule of thumb is that if you have any data you want to be specific to a single page request, you declare that data inside a method. You can test this in ThreadTest by changing one line in the doGet() method from:

```
count = 0;
```

    to

```
int count = 0;
```

The redeclaration of count as a local variable takes precedence over the class count variable and each instance of ThreadTest returns the numbers 1 to 10.

Of course, declaring data in the method means that you cannot share this data between methods, unless you pass the data directly to the other methods. If your methods do need to work with shared data, you really have two choices: implement your servlet so that the container does not share instances, or use synchronization.

## SingleThreadModel

If you declare a servlet that implements SingleThreadModel, the servlet container creates new instances of this servlet as needed to service requests. At least you hope this is the case; the Servlet Specification doesn't require the servlet container to create the new instance, but in the event that you do get a unique servlet for each request, you can treat the servlet as a self-contained unit with no outside forces acting on it.

You won't see SingleThreadModel used very often, in part because the servlet specification is a little vague on whether the container really has to implement support, which may affect portability, and in part because of the cycles and resources SingleThreadModel can consume. Java Web applications can have a light footprint precisely because they share resources as much as possible.

# Synchronization

In almost all circumstances where multiple simultaneous accesses to a servlet (or a JSP) would cause problems with shared data, the best approach is to make sure that only one thread can access that data at a given time. Listing 18-2 shows a version of ThreadTest, called ThreadTestSync, which adds a synchronized block around the for loop.

**Listing 18-2: The ThreadTestSync Servlet**

```
package ch18;

import java.io.IOException;
import java.io.PrintWriter;
import javax.servlet.*;
import javax.servlet.http.*;
import java.util.*;

public class ThreadTestSync extends HttpServlet {
    public void doGet(HttpServletRequest request,
        HttpServletResponse response)
        throws ServletException, IOException {
        count = 0;
        Random rand = new Random();
        response.setContentType("text/html");
        PrintWriter out = response.getWriter();
        out.println("<html>");
        out.println("<head>");
        out.println("<title>Admin</title>");
        out.println("</head>");
        out.println("<body>");
        synchronized (this) {
            for (int i = 0; i < 10; i++) {
                try {
                    this.wait(rand.nextInt(1000));
```

*Continued*

Listing 18-2 *(Continued)*

```
                } catch (InterruptedException e) {
                }
                count++;
                out.println(count + "<br>");
            }
        }
        out.println("</body>");
        out.println("</html>");
    }

    protected int count = 0;
}
```

A synchronized block of code must specify an object that the virtual machine can use as a *monitor* to control access to this code. The monitor can have only a single user at a time, and in this case, the monitor is the current instance of ThreadTestSync:

```
synchronized (this) {
    // some code
}
```

(If you compare Listing 18-2 with Listing 18-1, you'll notice a synchronized block already around the wait method — this is a requirement of wait.)

If you rerun the two-browser test on ThreadTestSync, you find that where previously both browsers returned a result in about five seconds, the first request takes about five seconds, and the second request takes an additional five seconds. The reason is the synchronized block prevents the second thread from executing until the first thread has completed executing the code in that block.

Synchronization serializes requests for a given block of code, which means that any time you have synchronization your scalability is in danger. If a synchronized block of code in a servlet takes five seconds to process, and ten users descend on your site at once and request that servlet, the last user has to wait almost a minute for a result.

If synchronization presents such potential for disaster, you might be thinking that SingleThreadModel is the way to go. The problem, assuming the servlet container implements SingleThreadModel, is that you run into scalability problems when you create a new servlet instance for each request. The more requests you get, the more memory and CPU time goes to creating instances of the servlet.

The moral of the story is that if your processing makes SingleThreadModel sound appealing, you probably have design problems anyway.

# Designing for scalability

To make your applications scale well, stick with the default servlet model, which allows multiple threads to use a single instance of the servlet. Identify those areas that absolutely must have exclusive access to some data, and synchronize *only* what's necessary. Remember that any single block of synchronized code is a bottleneck through which all requests that need that code will have to funnel.

You can often find alternatives to synchronizing code. Consider the HttpLinksCacheBean from Chapter 17. As the code in Listing 18-3 shows, this JavaBean has a method called getLinks that retrieves an HttpLinksBean instance.

**Listing 18-3: The HTTPLinksCacheBean Class**

```
package ch15;


import com.javaexchange.dbConnectionBroker.*;
import java.util.*;
import java.sql.*;

public class HttpLinksCacheBean {
    Map linksMap;
    protected DbConnectionBroker dbPool;

    public HttpLinksCacheBean() {
        super();
    }

    public HttpLinksBean getLinks(String listName) {
        HttpLinksBean links = (HttpLinksBean)
            linksMap.get(listName);
        return links;
    }

    public void init(DbConnectionBroker newDbPool) {
        // Assign the connection pool reference
        if (dbPool == null)
            dbPool = newDbPool;
        HttpLinksBean thisList = null;
        // create or clear the list of lists of
        // Http links
        if (linksMap == null)
            linksMap = new HashMap();
        else
            linksMap.clear();
```

*Continued*

**Listing 18-3** *(Continued)*

```
/* select all of the database records which
   correspond to Http links. Data returned includes:
    listName - the list this link belongs to
    URL - the raw URL
    Name - the link text
    Text - descriptive text associated with the link
          (i.e., an article summary)
*/
String listName = "";
String name = "";
String url = "";
String text = "";
String style = "";

Connection conn = null;
Statement stmt = null;
try {
    conn = dbPool.getConnection();
    stmt = conn.createStatement();
    ResultSet rs =
        stmt.executeQuery(
            "select g.Name, "
                + "a.Title, "
                + "a.URL, "
                + "a.Summary, "
                + "a.PublicationDate "
                + "from Articles a, "
                + "ArtGrpLink l, ArticleGroups g "
                + "where a.ArticleID = l.ArticleID "
                + " and g.ArticleGroupID = l.ArticleGroupID "
                + " order by g.Name");
    while (rs.next()) {
        // linksMap stores multiple lists of links,
        // so first try to get this list
        listName = rs.getString("Name");
        thisList = (HttpLinksBean) linksMap.get(listName);
        // if the list doesn't exist, create it
        if (thisList == null) {
            thisList = new HttpLinksBean(listName);
            linksMap.put(listName, thisList);
        }
        // create a new HttpLlink object and add it to the
            list
```

```
                    HttpLinkBean link =
                        new HttpLinkBean(
                            rs.getString("URL"),
                            rs.getString("Title"),
                            rs.getString("Summary"),
                            rs.getDate("PublicationDate"));
                    thisList.add(link);

                }

        } catch (SQLException e1) {
            System.out.println("ch15:SQL Error: " + e1);
        } finally {
            try {
                if (stmt != null) {
                    stmt.close();
                }
            } catch (SQLException e2) {
            };

            // The connection is returned to the Broker
            if (dbPool != null)
                dbPool.freeConnection(conn);

        }
    }
}
```

Since menu links change from time to time, it's possible that you'll need to replace a links JavaBean at exactly the same time the controller servlet is calling the getLinks() method, resulting in a null menu. This could happen if you call the WebAppSetup servlet's doGet() method to refresh all menus from the database. See Listing 18-4.

**Listing 18-4: The WebAppSetup Servlet's doGet() Method**

```
public void doGet(HttpServletRequest request,
    HttpServletResponse response)
    throws IOException, ServletException {
    response.setContentType("text/html");
    PrintWriter out = response.getWriter();
    out.println("<html>");
    out.println("<head>");
    out.println("<title>Admin</title>");
    out.println("</head>");
```

*Continued*

**Listing 18-4** *(Continued)*

```
    out.println("<body>");
    String cmd = request.getParameter("cmd");
    if (cmd != null) {
        try {
            if (cmd.equals("refreshmenus")) {
                createMenus();
                out.println("Admin action: Refresh menus");
            }
        } catch (Exception e) {
            System.out.println("Error initializing "
                + "the web application " + e);
        }

    }
    out.println("</body>");
    out.println("</html>");
}
```

In a low-load environment, it would probably be adequate to synchronize the init() and getLinks() methods to delay menu requests until after the menus exist. In a higher load environment, you would probably want to make several changes.

First, re-creating all of the menu link JavaBeans when only one menu has changed is wasteful, so you'd probably want to set a flag on HttpLinksBean to indicate that the menu is no longer valid and should be rebuilt. Listing 18-5 shows a modified HttpLinksCacheBean.getLinks() method that recreates an invalid menu.

**Listing 18-5: The HttpLinksCacheBean.getLinks() Method Updated with Synchronized Links Creation Code**

```
public HttpLinksBean getLinks(String listName) {
    HttpLinksBean links =
        (HttpLinksBean) linksMap.get(listName);
    synchronized (this) {
        if ((links == null) || (links.invalid())) {
            createLinks(listName);
            links = (HttpLinksBean) linksMap.get(listName);
        }
    }
    return links;
}
```

A synchronized block still executes on each menu request, but it's as short as possible, since in almost all cases it terminates when menu.invalid() returns false.

When the menu is invalid, the call to the `createLinks()` method (also synchronized) rebuilds the list of links.

You still have room for at least one problem in this code, however. It's possible (if unlikely) that even as thread A calls `getLinks()` and finds an invalid menu, thread B has already called `getLinks()` and is now executing the synchronized `createLinks()` code. By the time thread A gets to `createLinks()` the menu again exists. It would be best for `createLinks()` to make sure the menu is still invalid before proceeding.

Developing multithreaded applications takes constant attention to "what-if" scenarios. Always assume another thread is out there just waiting to mess with your beautifully constructed code.

# JSP Threading Issues

Be aware of some scope issues when developing custom tags. The 1.1 JSP specification mandates that when you use a tag on a page, the JSP implementation should obtain an instance of that tag from a tag pool, initialize it, and then use it on the page. Tomcat 3.*x*, however, creates all custom tags from scratch. The code to create and initialize a `MenuTag` instance in the `jspService()` method looks something like this:

```
ch15.MenuTag _jspx_th_ch15_menu_0 = new ch15.MenuTag();
_jspx_th_ch15_menu_0.setPageContext(pageContext);
_jspx_th_ch15_menu_0.setParent(null);
_jspx_th_ch15_menu_0.setMenuName("leftsidemenu");
```

Having a new object created for each call to the `jspService()` method has its benefits. Since these objects are unique to this method call, you have no worries about sharing data within the tag, as you might have with servlets. You can treat custom tags the same way you would a servlet that implements `SingleThreadModel`.

Of course, the downside is similar to that of `SingleThreadModel`. The more objects the JSP creates, and the larger those objects are, the greater the performance penalty. Even once, or if the Tomcat developers address this situation, try to keep custom tags lightweight. Wherever possible, remove sharable code from the custom tags and place it in a bean stored in the application context. You can then retrieve the object using the `pageContext.getAttribute()` method, which is a lot less expensive than creating the object's functionality from scratch.

# Summary

Developing Web applications with Java requires some special attention to multi-threading issues. A Web server may have to support a large number of users, and it can by allowing multiple threads access to the same resources. Key points to remember include:

◆ Developing multithreaded applications requires a much different mindset than developing single-threaded applications.

◆ The Java virtual machine allocates method data per thread, and shares class data between threads.

◆ One servlet method can easily be running on multiple different threads at the same time.

◆ You can mediate access to blocks of code with a `synchronized` statement, or mark entire methods as synchronized.

◆ When you synchronize code blocks, the Java virtual machine serializes access to the code; only one thread can run through the synchronized code at a time.

◆ In general, you want to synchronize as little code as possible, because synchronized code also causes bottlenecks in your applications.

◆ Custom tags are generally free from synchronization issues because they're created as needed, but this makes them potentially expensive to use, so you should keep your custom tags as lightweight as possible.

# Part IV

## Database-Driven Site Strategies

# Chapter 19

# Authenticating Users

## IN THIS CHAPTER

- ◆ Using authentication to retrieve user credentials
- ◆ Creating security constraints, roles, and users in Tomcat
- ◆ Testing basic and form-based security with the Tomcat `examples` application
- ◆ Creating a customized security system in an MVC application framework

IF YOUR WEB SITE is wide open to the public, then this chapter doesn't concern you. But even if you think your Web site should be wide open, you may find advantages to restricting access to some areas. For instance, you may want to provide some administrative functions on your site, such as updating the Web site database or viewing access statistics.

User security usually happens in two steps: authentication and authorization. *Authentication* determines who is attempting access, and *authorization* decides if access is allowed. In this chapter, you'll learn how to use Tomcat's authentication features, and you'll discover that it's not that difficult to create a customized authentication system based on JDBC and MySQL.

# Authentication

Authentication usually involves a user submitting a user ID and password. You can authenticate users with just a user ID or password, or you can choose to identify users by IP address. The latter works only when users have a static IP, which isn't that common. Most Web sites that use authentication rely on HTTP authentication, which comes in two flavors: Basic and Digest.

## Basic authentication

Basic authentication is a cooperative effort between the Web browser and the Web server. Most Web servers allow you to mark certain pages or directories as protected. When a user requests a protected page, the Web server examines the request headers to see if they contain a user id and password. If the identifying information is not present, or if it is invalid, the Web server returns a result code of 401. The Web server may also return HTML to be displayed if a preset number of attempts fail or the user cancels the authentication. The browser then pops up a window asking the user for a user ID and password. The user enters the ID and password and clicks OK, and the browser submits the original request again, but this time with the ID and password. Most browsers allow three attempts at a page before displaying an "access denied" type of message. If the server sent HTML along with the 401 code, the browser will display this HTML instead of its own error message.

Basic authentication uses Base64 encoding (not encryption!) of the ID and password, and while this hides the password from the casual reader of a data stream (keeping in mind that anyone reading your data stream probably isn't doing so casually), it doesn't take a lot of effort to find and decode this information. In addition, once the user is authenticated on a site the browser sends the user ID and password with each and every request to that site. Still, where convenience is more important than absolute security, Basic authentication is still the method of choice. Tomcat versions 3.2 and greater include support for Basic authentication.

## Digest authentication

Digest authentication is a more secure approach to authentication than Basic. Like Basic authentication, the server responds with an error on a restricted page, but sends along a string called a "nonce," which has a unique value. The browser uses this information along with the password and additional information about the request to create an MD5 encrypted string. The browser sends this string along with the user ID (in clear text) back to the server. The server looks up the user's password and goes through the same encryption process as the browser, and compares the two strings. If they match, the server considers the user authentic.

This method has the advantage that the user's password is not directly sent over the network connection. Digest authentication is considerably less common than Basic authentication because browser support has only recently become widespread. Tomcat versions 4 and greater support Digest authentication.

## Form-based authentication

Besides Basic and Digest, you can authenticate with an HTML form. In form-based authentication, the server provides a Web page with prompts for the user ID and password instead of relying on the dialog box the browser displays. This enables you to present additional information and options to the user at logon time.

You should use a password text-entry field that displays asterisks as the user types the password, but the browser still sends the password itself as plain text: not encrypted, not Base64 encoded, but plain text! And if you unwisely use the GET method to submit the form data back to the server, the user's browser will display the password in the URL, in plain view. No doubt the browser will save that URL, complete with password and user ID, in its list of most recently viewed pages, as well. If you do implement form-based authentication, be sure you use the POST method to submit the authentication form data to the server so the password data is at least hidden from the user.

The Tomcat 3.2 examples Web application contains an early version of form-based authentication.

## Using SSL

None of the authentication options I've discussed so far offers any security for the content of the transmission. If you really need to secure your traffic, you need to look into Secure Sockets Layer (SSL) and certificates. When the server is running SSL, it communicates with the browser using some level of encryption. Most browsers can support at least 40- or 56-bit encryption, but for better security they should use 128 bits. Tomcat 3.*x* does not support SSL directly, but Tomcat 4.0 does.

# Security in Tomcat

The Tomcat `examples` Web application demonstrates Basic and form-based authentication. To configure either of these, you first need to set up a security constraint in the Web application's `web.xml` file.

## Security constraints

Listing 19-1 shows the security constraint settings from the `examples` Web application's `web.xml`. They contain two parts: the `web-resource-collection`, and the `auth-constraint`. The `web-resource-collection` defines a URL pattern to protect and the HTTP methods the server should protect. The `auth-constraint` defines which roles can access the restricted area.

**Listing 19-1: Security Constraint Settings for the Tomcat Examples Web Application**

```
<security-constraint>
    <web-resource-collection>
        <web-resource-name>Protected Area</web-resource-name>
        <!-- Define the context-relative URL(s) to be protected -->
        <url-pattern>/jsp/security/protected/*</url-pattern>
        <!-- If you list http methods, only those methods are
            protected -->
        <http-method>DELETE</http-method>
        <http-method>GET</http-method>
        <http-method>POST</http-method>
        <http-method>PUT</http-method>
    </web-resource-collection>
    <auth-constraint>
        <!-- Anyone with one of the listed roles may access this
            area -->
        <role-name>tomcat</role-name>
     <role-name>role1</role-name>
    </auth-constraint>
</security-constraint>
```

## UNDERSTANDING ROLES

Roles are simply groups of users. The relationship between users and restricted Web resources is potentially a many-to-many relationship, so rather than duplicate the user data, you assign the user to one or more roles and assign one or more roles to the restricted resource. The `<auth-constraint>` section in `web.xml` specifies which roles can access which Web resources.

## CREATING USERS

Users appear in `conf/tomcat-users.xml`. Note that this is a Tomcat-wide configuration file, not a per-Web-application file. The `tomcat-users.xml` file contains the following settings:

```
<tomcat-users>
  <user name="tomcat" password="tomcat" roles="tomcat" />
  <user name="role1"  password="tomcat" roles="role1"  />
  <user name="both"   password="tomcat" roles="tomcat,role1" />
</tomcat-users>
```

As the example of user `"both"` shows, you can list multiple roles for any user.

# Tomcat's form-based authentication

By default, the sample application uses form-based authentication. The `examples` Web application's `web.xml` defines the `login-conf` setting as follows:

```
<login-config>
    <auth-method>FORM</auth-method>
    <realm-name>Example Form-Based Authentication Area</realm-name>
    <form-login-config>
        <form-login-page>/jsp/security/login/login.jsp</form-login-
            page>
        <form-error-page>/jsp/security/login/error.jsp</form-error-
            page>
    </form-login-config>
</login-config>
```

Within the `<login-config>` section, you define the method, the name of the realm to use, and the login and error pages. Listing 19-2 shows the code for `login.jsp`.

**Listing 19-2: Source Code for login.jsp**

```
<html>
<body>
<h1>Login page for examples</h1>
```

```
<form method="POST" action="j_security_check" >
 Username: <input type="text" name="j_username"><br>
 Password: <input type="password" name="j_password"><br>
 <br>
 <input type="submit" value="login" name="j_security_check">
</form>

</body>
</html>
```

If you're using Tomcat's Form-based login, you have to stick with the predefined names for the form action, user ID, password, and submit button. Tomcat looks for j_security_check, j_username, and j_password when it extracts the security information from the form submission.

To try out Tomcat's form-based security, just go to a restricted page. If you're running Tomcat locally, you can use this URL:

```
http://localhost:8080/examples/jsp/security/protected/
```

Tomcat detects the access attempt and, if you aren't already logged in, presents the login page.

## Tomcat's Basic authentication

To try Tomcat's Basic authentication you need to comment out the form-based <login-config> section of web.xml and uncomment the following:

```
<login-config>
    <auth-method>BASIC</auth-method>
    <realm-name>Example Basic Authentication Area</realm-name>
</login-config>
```

Basic authentication is much simpler to set up than form-based authentication because it's up to the browser to ask the user for the ID and password. Otherwise, Basic authentication follows the same approach as form-based authentication.

## Authentication request interceptors

Tomcat tightly integrates support for users and roles, but special classes (called RequestInterceptor classes) handle specific security implementations. The server.xml file lists these classes. The following are two request interceptors that handle simple authentication and authorization:

```
<RequestInterceptor
    className="org.apache.tomcat.request.AccessInterceptor"
        debug="0" />
```

```
<RequestInterceptor
    className="org.apache.tomcat.request.SimpleRealm"
        debug="0" />
```

Tomcat loads the request interceptors when it starts. As their name suggests, RequestInterceptor classes intercept page requests. You can create your own request interceptors and optionally load some interceptors that come with Tomcat.

For an example of an interceptor that creates server logs, see Chapter 23.

The AccessInterceptor class determines if a particular request is part of a Web resource collection. If the request is part of such a Web resource, Access-Interceptor retrieves that resource's list of roles and stores the roles in the request object. The AccessInterceptor doesn't do any validation or authentication.

The servlet container calls the SimpleRealm request interceptor after it calls AccessInterceptor. The SimpleRealm request looks up the user's roles, compares these roles with the information AccessInterceptor attached to the request, and allows or denies access to the page. Both Basic and form-based authentication use SimpleRealm by default.

## USING JDBCREALM

Although you can use XML files to store roles and users, they don't offer the most efficient approach, since any change to the XML files requires you to reload Tomcat before the change takes effect.

In a production environment, you're better off using the optional JDBCRealm request interceptor. If you're using the tables described in the next section in a database called "test" installed on the local machine, you can use the following settings:

```
<RequestInterceptor
    className="org.apache.tomcat.request.JDBCRealm"
        debug="0"
    driverName="org.gjt.mm.mysql.Driver"
    connectionURL="jdbc:mysql://localhost/test"
    userTable="Users"
    userNameCol="UserName"
    userCredCol="Password"
    userRoleTable="UserRoles"
    roleNameCol="RoleName"
    connectionName="test"
    connectionPassword="test" />
```

## CREATING THE TABLES

You'll need only two tables: one to store the users, and another for the combination of users and roles. Roles themselves are still defined in the Web application's web.xml, but you may want to record them in the Roles table for completeness. Figure 19-1 shows the relationships between the Users, Roles, and UserRoles tables, and Listing 19-3 provides the code for creating these tables.

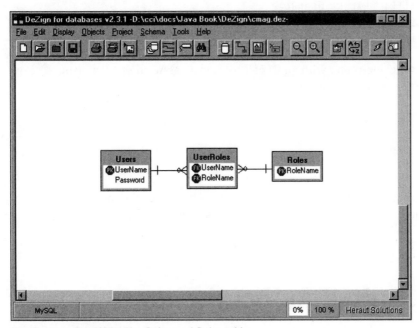

Figure 19-1: The Users, UserRoles, and Roles tables

Listing 19-3: Creating the Users, Roles, and UserRoles Tables

```
CREATE TABLE Roles(
RoleName VARCHAR(30) NOT NULL,
PRIMARY KEY (RoleName));

CREATE TABLE Users(
UserName VARCHAR(30) NOT NULL,
Password VARCHAR(30),
PRIMARY KEY (UserName));

CREATE TABLE UserRoles(
UserName VARCHAR(30) NOT NULL,
RoleName VARCHAR(30) NOT NULL,
PRIMARY KEY (UserName,RoleName));
```

## SETTING INTERCEPTOR PERMISSIONS

Since JDBCRealm will be accessing the Users and UserRoles tables, it needs SELECT rights. Execute the following statements to allow access using the ID 'test' and the password 'test'.

```
GRANT SELECT ON test.Users TO
test@localhost IDENTIFIED BY 'test';
GRANT SELECT ON test.UserRoles
TO test@localhost IDENTIFIED BY 'test';
FLUSH PRIVILEGES;
```

To test the interceptor with an ID of 'Me' and a password of 'mypassword' execute the following SQL statements:

```
INSERT INTO Users
VALUES('Me','mypassword');
INSERT INTO UserRoles
VALUES('Me','tomcat');
```

The examples/WEB-INF/web.xml file already defines the tomcat role, so you should now be able to log into the restricted page at:

```
http://localhost:8080/examples/jsp/security/protected/
```

# Customized Authentication

Sometimes you just need or want to roll your own authentication. Perhaps you don't have the option of installing request interceptors, or the standard authentication doesn't do what you need.

The deweb-example application (available at www.covecomm.com/java) uses a Basic authentication under the direction of ControllerServlet, which manages all requests for .html pages. Listing 19-4 shows the code for that servlet's doGet() method.

**Listing 19-4: The ControllerServlet doGet() Method That Handles User Authentication**

```
public void doGet(HttpServletRequest request, HttpServletResponse
response)
    throws ServletException, IOException {
    UserBean user=null;
    String forwardTo;
    int status = 0;
    String jsp = messageJsp;
    count++;
```

```
// get the user's session
HttpSession session = request.getSession();

// get the request URI
String uri = request.getServletPath();
String origUri = uri;
System.out.println("uri " + uri);

// try to get the user from the session -
// if not found, create a new user
user = (UserBean)session.getAttribute("user");
if (user == null) {
    user = new UserBean();
    session.setAttribute("user",user);
}
user.setHostname(request.getRemoteAddr());
String username = null;
String password = null;
String decoded;
String authHeader = (String) request.getHeader("Authorization");
if (authHeader != null) {
    authHeader = authHeader.substring(6).trim();
    synchronized (this) {
        decoded = new String(decoder.decodeBuffer(authHeader));
    }
    int colon = decoded.indexOf(":");
    if (colon > 0) {
        username = decoded.substring(0, colon);
        password = decoded.substring(colon + 1);
    }
    user.setPassword(password);
    user.setUsername(username);
}

// get a document object corresponding to the uri
WebDocBean webdoc = null;
SecurityBean security = new SecurityBean();
java.sql.Connection connection = null;

// check for various errors. Default jsp is messageJsp.
do {
    if (!findDbPool()) {
        uri = systemErrorHtml;
        status = security.NO_DBPOOL;
        break;
```

*Continued*

**Listing 19-4** *(Continued)*

```
        }
        connection = dbPool.getConnection();
        if (connection == null) {
            uri = systemErrorHtml;
            status = security.NO_CONN;
            break;
        }
        webdoc = security.getWebDocBean(connection, uri);
        if (!webdoc.isInDatabase()) {
            uri = notFoundHtml;
            status = security.NO_FILE;
            break;
        }

        // If public access then forward to its JSP
        if (!webdoc.isRequireRights()) {
            jsp = webdoc.getJspName();
            status = security.AUTHORIZED;
            break;
        }
        switch (status) {
            case security.INVALID_USER :
                response.setContentType("text/html");
                response.setStatus(response.SC_UNAUTHORIZED);
                response.setHeader("WWW-Authenticate",
                    "BASIC realm=\"Subscribers\"");
                uri = invalidUserHtml;
                break;
            case security.NOT_AUTHORIZED :
                uri = notAuthorizedHtml;
                break;
            case security.AUTHORIZED :
                jsp = webdoc.getJspName();
                break;
        }
    } while (false);

    if ((connection != null) && (dbPool != null))
        dbPool.freeConnection(connection);
    if (jsp == null)
        throw new ServletException("Cannot forward to this page");

    if (uri != null)
        request.setAttribute("includePage", uri);
```

```
    RequestDispatcher dispatcher =
getServletContext().getRequestDispatcher(jsp);
    if (dispatcher != null)
        dispatcher.forward(request, response);
    return;
}
```

The `ControllerServlet` class retrieves the authorization information with a call to the request's `getHeader` method. The authorization header contains the string "BASIC:" followed by the user ID and password Base64 encoded.

```
authHeader = authHeader.substring(6).trim();
synchronized (this) {
    decoded = new String(decoder.decodeBuffer(authHeader));
}
```

The servlet then strips the prefix string, revealing the user ID and password separated by a colon.

```
int colon = decoded.indexOf(":");
if (colon > 0) {
    username = decoded.substring(0, colon);
    password = decoded.substring(colon + 1);
}
```

The servlet stores the user ID and password in an instance of the `UserBean` class.

```
    user.setPassword(password);
    user.setUsername(username);
```

## The UserBean class

The UserBean class, shown in Listing 19-5, stores information about the user, such as the user's ID, password, and so forth. This bean can then be stored in the user's session, ready for the next access.

**Listing 19-5: The UserBean Class**

```
package com.covecomm.deweb.control;

public class UserBean {
    private String username;
    private String password;
    private String hostname;
```

*Continued*

**Listing 19-5** *(Continued)*

```java
    private String realname;
    private int ID;
    private boolean readAll = false;

    public UserBean() {
        super();
    }

    public UserBean(String newUsername, String newPassword,
        String newHostname) {
        super();
        setUsername(newUsername);
        setPassword(newPassword);
        setHostname(newHostname);
    }

    public java.lang.String getHostname() {
        return hostname;
    }

    public int getID() {
        return ID;
    }

    public java.lang.String getPassword() {
        return password;
    }

    public java.lang.String getRealname() {
        return realname;
    }

    public java.lang.String getUsername() {
        return username;
    }

    public boolean isReadAll() {
        return readAll;
    }

    public void setHostname(java.lang.String newHostname) {
        hostname = newHostname;
    }
```

```
    public void setID(int newID) {
        ID = newID;
    }

    public void setPassword(java.lang.String newPassword) {
        password = newPassword;
    }

    public void setReadAll(boolean newReadAll) {
        readAll = newReadAll;
    }

    public void setRealname(java.lang.String newRealname) {
        realname = newRealname;
    }

    public void setUsername(java.lang.String newUsername) {
        username = newUsername;
    }

    public String toString() {
        return (getUsername() + ","
            + getPassword() + ","
            + getHostname());
    }
}
```

The UserBean class doesn't have any means of setting its own values; another class called SecurityBean handles that task.

## The SecurityBean class

The SecurityBean class obtains all necessary security-related information from the database and determines if a specific user can access a specific Web page. Listing 19-6 shows the source code for SecurityBean.

**Listing 19-6: SecurityBean Determines Who Can Read Which Pages**

```
package com.covecomm.deweb.control;

import java.sql.*;
import com.covecomm.deweb.doc.*;

public class SecurityBean {
    public final static int NO_DBPOOL = 1002;
```

*Continued*

**Listing 19-6** *(Continued)*

```
public final static int NO_CONN = 1001;
public final static int NO_FILE = 404;
public static final int INVALID_USER = 4010;
public static final int NOT_AUTHORIZED = 401;
public static final int AUTHORIZED = 4000;

public SecurityBean() {
    super();
}

public int getAccess(Connection conn, UserBean user,
        WebDocBean webdoc) {
    Statement stmt = null;
    int rights = INVALID_USER;

    Object[] articleGroups = webdoc.getArticleGroups();
    try {
        stmt = conn.createStatement();
        ResultSet rs =
            stmt.executeQuery(
                "select NameID,FirstName,LastName, UserID,
                    Password"
                + ",ReadAllGroup from Names "
                + "where UserID = '"
                + user.getUsername()
                + "'");
        if (rs.next()) {
            user.setID(rs.getInt("NameID"));
            user.setRealname(rs.getString("FirstName")
                + rs.getString("LastName"));
            if (user.getPassword().equals(rs.getString
                ("Password"))) {
                if (rs.getString("ReadAllGroup").equals("Y")) {
                    user.setReadAll(true);
                    rights = AUTHORIZED;
                } else {
                    rights = NOT_AUTHORIZED;
                    for (int i = 0; i < articleGroups.length;
                        i++) {
                        rs =
                            stmt.executeQuery(
                                "select RightID "
                                + "from Rights "
                                + "where ArticleGroupID = "
```

```
                                            + articleGroups[i]
                                            + " "
                                            + "and NameID = "
                                            + user.getID());
                        if (rs.next()) {
                            rights = AUTHORIZED;
                            break;
                        }
                    }
                }
            }
        }
    } catch (SQLException e1) {
        System.out.println("SQL Error: " + e1);
    } finally {
        try {
            if (stmt != null) {
                stmt.close();
            }
        } catch (SQLException e2) {
        }

    }
    return rights;
}

public WebDocBean getWebDocBean(Connection conn, String URI) {
    WebDocBean webdoc = new WebDocBean();
    webdoc.setInDatabase(false);
    webdoc.setUri(URI);
    Statement stmt = null;
    try {
        stmt = conn.createStatement();
        int JspID = 0;
        ResultSet rs =
            stmt.executeQuery(
                "select a.Title,a.JspID,a.RequireRights,
                    a.FileName"
                + ",a.FilePath,a.ArticleID,a.PublicationDate "
                + ",a.IncludePage,a.ExtraInfo,a.HasForm "
                + "from Articles a left join "
                + "AuthorArticle l using (ArticleID) "
                + "left join Names n on l.AuthorID=n.NameID "
```

*Continued*

**Listing 19-6** *(Continued)*

```
                              + "where a.URI= '"
                              + URI
                              + "'");
              if (rs.next()) {
                  webdoc.setTitle(rs.getString("Title"));
                  webdoc.setID(rs.getInt("ArticleID"));
                  webdoc.setExtraInfo(rs.getString("ExtraInfo"));
                  webdoc.setIncludePage(rs.getString("IncludePage"));
                  JspID = rs.getInt("JspID");
                  webdoc.setInDatabase(true);
                  String access = rs.getString("RequireRights");
                  if ((access != null) && access.equals("N"))
                      webdoc.setRequireRights(false);
                  String hasForm = rs.getString("HasForm");
                  if ((hasForm != null) && hasForm.equals("Y"))
                      webdoc.setFormPage(true);
                  if (JspID > 0) {
                      rs = stmt.executeQuery("select j.Jsp from Jsps j "
                          + "where j.JspID= " + JspID);
                      if (rs.next())
                          webdoc.setJspName(rs.getString("Jsp"));
                      rs =
                          stmt.executeQuery(
                              "select g.Name,g.ArticleGroupID "
                                  + "from ArtGrpLink l,ArticleGroups g "
                                  + "where l.ArticleID = "
                                  + webdoc.getID()
                                  + " and l.ArticleGroupID =
                                      g.ArticleGroupID");
                      while (rs.next()) {
                          webdoc.addArticleGroup
                              (rs.getInt("ArticleGroupID"));
                      }

                  }
              }
          } catch (SQLException e1) {
              System.out.println("SQL Error: " + e1);
          } finally {
              try {
                  if (stmt != null) {
```

```
                    stmt.close();
                }
            } catch (SQLException e2) {
            }


        }
        return webdoc;
    }
}
```

Before `SecurityBean` can determine a user's access, it needs an instance of the `WebDocBean` class.

## The WebDocBean class

The `WebDocBean` class, which, like `HttpLinkBean`, is derived from the `Document` class, models the document the user is attempting to retrieve. The `WebDocBean` class is mostly setter and getter methods, but it does have a `HashSet`, which stores the `ArticleGroups` to which the document belongs. Listing 19-7 shows the source code for `WebDocBean`.

**Listing 19-7: The WebDocBean Class Models a Web Page and Its Associated ArticleGroup Records**

```
package com.covecomm.deweb.doc;

import java.util.*;

public final class WebDocBean extends Document {
    private String jspName;
    private String realPath;
    private boolean requireRights = true;
    private boolean onDisk = false;
    private boolean inDatabase = false;
    private Set articleGroups;
    private String extraInfo;
    private String includePage;
    private String forwardPage;
    private boolean formPage;

    public WebDocBean() {
        super();
        articleGroups = new HashSet();
    }
```

*Continued*

**Listing 19-7** *(Continued)*

```java
    public void addArticleGroup(int group) {
        articleGroups.add((new Integer(group)));
    }

    public Object[] getArticleGroups() {
        return articleGroups.toArray();
    }

    public java.lang.String getExtraInfo() {
        return extraInfo;
    }

    public java.lang.String getForwardPage() {
        return forwardPage;
    }

    public java.lang.String getIncludePage() {
        return includePage;
    }

    public java.lang.String getJspName() {
        return jspName;
    }

    public java.lang.String getRealPath() {
        return realPath;
    }

    public boolean isFormPage() {
        return formPage;
    }

    public boolean isInDatabase() {
        return inDatabase;
    }

    public boolean isOnDisk() {
        return onDisk;
    }

    public boolean isRequireRights() {
        return requireRights;
    }
```

```
    public void setExtraInfo(java.lang.String newExtraInfo) {
        extraInfo = newExtraInfo;
    }

    public void setFormPage(boolean newFormPage) {
        formPage = newFormPage;
    }

    public void setForwardPage(java.lang.String newForwardPage) {
        forwardPage = newForwardPage;
    }

    public void setIncludePage(java.lang.String newIncludePage) {
        includePage = newIncludePage;
    }

    public void setInDatabase(boolean newInDatabase) {
        inDatabase = newInDatabase;
    }

    public void setJspName(java.lang.String newJspName) {
        jspName = newJspName;
    }

    public void setOnDisk(boolean newOnDisk) {
        onDisk = newOnDisk;
    }

    public void setRealPath(java.lang.String newRealPath) {
        realPath = newRealPath;
    }

    public void setRealPath(
        java.lang.String newRealName,
        java.lang.String newRealPath) {
        realPath = newRealPath + newRealName;
    }

        public void setRequireRights(boolean newRequireRights) {
        requireRights = newRequireRights;
    }
}
```

As with UserBean, SecurityBean sets all of WebDocBean's properties. The SecurityBean.getWebDocBean method creates a new WebDocBean instance, and then looks for an Articles record that matches the URI passed to the method. The SELECT statement uses a left join to bring in a matching Names record if one is found.

```
stmt.executeQuery(
    "select a.Title,a.JspID,a.RequireRights,a.FileName"
        + ",a.FilePath,a.ArticleID,a.PublicationDate "
        + ",a.IncludePage,a.ExtraInfo,a.HasForm "
        + "from Articles a left join "
        + "AuthorArticle l using (ArticleID) "
        + "left join Names n on l.AuthorID=n.NameID "
        + "where a.URI= '"
        + URI
        + "'");
```

If the Article record exists, the next step is to find out which ArticleGroups correspond to the Article.

```
rs = stmt.executeQuery(
    "select g.Name,g.ArticleGroupID "
    + "from ArtGrpLink l,ArticleGroups g "
    + "where l.ArticleID = "
    + webdoc.getID()
    + " and l.ArticleGroupID = g.ArticleGroupID");
while (rs.next()) {
    webdoc.addArticleGroup(rs.getInt("ArticleGroupID"));
}
```

Once SecurityBean has a WebDocBean instance, the ControllerServlet.doGet() method calls SecurityBean.getAccess to find out if the user has a right to read the page. First, that method gets an array of ArticleGroupIDs:

```
Object[] articleGroups = webdoc.getArticleGroups();
```

Next, getAccess looks for a Names record matching the UserBean:

```
ResultSet rs = stmt.executeQuery(
    "select NameID,FirstName,LastName,UserID,Password"
    + ",ReadAllGroup from Names "
    + "where UserID = '"
    + user.getUsername()
    + "'");
```

If the passwords match, the method looks for the ReadAll flag, which is a shorthand way of providing superuser access to the site. If the code doesn't find this flag, it defaults the rights NOT_AUTHORIZED.

```
if (user.getPassword().equals(rs.getString("Password"))) {
    if (rs.getString("ReadAllGroup").equals("Y")) {
        user.setReadAll(true);
        rights = AUTHORIZED;
    } else {
        rights = NOT_AUTHORIZED;
```

All that remains now is for getAccess to check the list of articleGroups from the WebDocBean instance against the records in the database:

```
for (int i = 0; i < articleGroups.length; i++) {
    rs =
        stmt.executeQuery(
            "select RightID "
                + "from Rights "
                + "where ArticleGroupID = "
                + articleGroups[i]
                + " "
                + "and NameID = "
                + user.getID());
    if (rs.next()) {
        rights = AUTHORIZED;
        break;
    }
}
```

Aside from system errors, the possible authorization outcomes are the following static values from SecurityBean:

◆ SecurityBean.AUTHORIZED — the user has passed all security checks.

◆ SecurityBean.INVALID_USER — the user doesn't exist in the database, or did not have a correct password.

◆ SecurityBean.NOT_AUTHORIZED — the user does exist in the database and supplied the correct password, but is not authorized to view this page.

The distinction between SecurityBean.INVALID_USER and SecurityBean. NOT_AUTHORIZED can be an important one. Out-of-the-box Basic authentication doesn't differentiate between the two, so if you allow some users into one part of your site and other users into another part, a user going to the wrong part gets an authorization failure when she should get a message saying she's an accepted user, but not for that part of the site.

On an INVALID_USER result, doGet() sets the response status to SC_UNAUTHORIZED (401), and sets the header to the appropriate WWW-Authenticate value:

```
response.setContentType("text/html");
response.setStatus(response.SC_UNAUTHORIZED);
response.setHeader("WWW-Authenticate", "BASIC realm=\"Subscribers\"");
uri = invalidUserHtml;
```

If you fail to set the authenticate header correctly, including the authentication type and realm, the user's browser does not display the login window.

The rest of the `doGet()` method follows the MVC example spelled out in Chapter 15. Since each article requested has an associated view JSP, the method sets the `uri` string variable to the requested article's page, or to an appropriate error page.

# Summary

Tomcat provides some core support for Basic and form-based authentication using information stored in XML files. Where user information changes regularly, you can use the optional `JDBCRealm` request interceptor and a couple of SQL tables. Of course, you can always customize security by writing your own code. Key points to remember include:

◆ Basic authentication encodes, but does not encrypt, the user ID and password, and sends this information with each request.

◆ If you use form-based authentication with Tomcat's built-in support, you must use the specified form field names (`j_username`, `j_password`) and action/submit values (`j_securitycheck`).

◆ You set security restrictions in `web.xml`; for default security you must add users and realms to `/conf/tomcat-users.xml`; if you're using `JDBCRealm` you add users and realms to your SQL tables.

◆ For customized security, your options are wide open: a `RequestInterceptor` applies to all Web applications and is not necessarily portable to non-Tomcat servlet containers, while a controller servlet-based approach applies only to that particular Web application.

# Chapter 20

# Updating Databases with HTML Forms

THE TOMCAT WEB SERVER doesn't have any built-in support for database forms, and its support for HTML forms of any kind is rudimentary. Creating the form and retrieving the form results from the request object when a user submits that form is still up to you. You can write completely new HTML and Java code each time you need to create a form, or you can create a set of classes that model typical form behavior. Once you have these base classes, you create fairly small, derived classes for each specific form.

In this chapter, you'll learn how to model an HTML form using a JavaBean, and how to populate that form JavaBean with field JavaBeans. You'll use the form and field JavaBeans to validate the user's request and store validated form data in a MySQL database.

## Understanding HTML Forms

Chapter 4 mentions that HTML provides a simple form mechanism that enables users to submit values to the database. Listing 20-1 shows a very simple form with two text fields and a submit button. It also contains a hidden field that is not visible to the user, but submits a predetermined value to the server.

**Listing 20-1: A Simple HTML Form with Two Fields and a Submit Button**

```
<form method="GET" action="/servlet/forms">
<input type="hidden" name="FormID" value="true">
<p>Name: <input type="text" name="name" size="25"></p>
<p>Email: <input type="text" name="name" size="25"></p>
<p><input type="submit" value="Save" name="submit"></p>
</form>
```

When a user fills in the fields in the form from Listing 20-1 and presses the submit button, the Web browser submits the data to the Web server in a GET request or a POST request. A GET request (which is what the form in Listing 20-1 uses) sends this data as text appended to the URL, while a POST sends the data in the body of the request. With a POST request the user never sees the submitted data.

You tell the browser where to send the GET or POST data by setting the form's ACTION attribute. Traditionally the action is a CGI script, and CGI scripts are still common. In CGI the Web server places the form data in an INI file or environment variables, and the script processes the data and generates the appropriate HTML to send back to the user.

In a Java server-side environment, the routine is slightly different. You can set the form's action to a JSP or URL that maps to one of your servlets, and that JSP or servlet can read the form data using code such as this servlet example:

```
Enumeration e = request.getParameterNames();
while (e.hasMoreElements()) {
    String key = (String) e.nextElement();
    String[] values = request.getParameterValues(key);
}
```

Each field in the form generates a parameter name in the GET or POST, followed by one or more values (a multiselect list box could generate several values, for instance). The request.getParameterNames method essentially returns the list of fields, and getParameterValues returns the value(s) for each field as a string array. This process is the raw stuff of forms handling, and while you could work with this data directly, just as you would in a CGI program, there's a better way, particularly if you're using the Model-View-Controller, or Model 2, approach to designing your Web application.

# Forms in an MVC Application

Recall from Chapter 14 that the MVC or Model 2 application contains a controller (typically a servlet) that accepts all requests for pages. This servlet then updates the application's model (stored in JavaBeans) and forwards the request to a JSP, which displays data based on the current state of the model (as stored in those JavaBeans). Figure 20-1 diagrams the relationship of the different aspects of an MVC application.

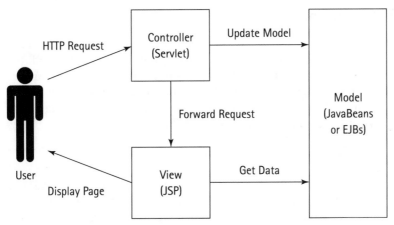

Figure 20-1: A Model-View-Controller pattern for Java-based, Web-site development

In an MVC application, you probably don't want one block of code, that is, the servlet, handling the request and creating the resulting HTML. Doing so would negate many of the benefits of the MVC model, such as separation of business logic and presentation logic. Rather, the controller servlet should handle all requests for forms and create appropriate beans, and then forward to a display JSP that can present data to the user based on those beans.

## Requesting a form

Form processing involves two actions. First, the browser retrieves the form from the server, and second, the browser submits the completed form to the server. The link you set up to take the user to the form in the first place determines the former, and the action attribute of the HTML form determines the latter. In a non-MVC Web application that uses static pages, the link to take the user to the form might look like this:

```
<a href="updateuser.html">Update user information</a>
```

In an MVC Web site, you will process all form requests through the controller servlet, just as you mapped all requests for HTML files through the controller (as in Chapter 15). To make it a bit easier to distinguish forms from other HTML pages, you could also use a special extension, which you map to the controller servlet:

```
<a href="updateuser.frm">Update user information</a>
```

Note that updateuser.frm (or updateuser.html) doesn't need to actually exist. Because the controller servlet is intercepting the page requests, you can forward to any page you like. The most important aspect of the form request is that it is a URI that uniquely identifies the form you wish to send to the user.

## Displaying a form

Recall from Chapter 16 that each `Articles` record can have a link to the `Jsps` table. This link tells the controller to which view JSP it should forward the requested page. I use a similar approach for forms – from an MVC application perspective, a form is just another page to be displayed using a view JSP. I create the forms themselves as JSPs, which allows them to use beans and custom tags. That means that the view JSP actually includes another JSP.

## Saving a form

When the user submits a form, the browser sends the data (using `GET` or `POST`) to the URL specified in the action attribute. In an MVC Web application this URL points to the controller servlet. The servlet (or code the servlet calls) has to decide what action to take based on the data.

## Validating a form

Users don't always read instructions, and sometimes they fill out forms incorrectly. You need a way of validating form data on the server before processing.

Validating data on a Web form is a bit more complex than validating data on a desktop application form, simply because you don't have complete control over the data the user is sending. You can use a scripting language like JavaScript to perform edit checks as the user is completing a form, but you should never, ever rely entirely on scripts. One problem is that you can't assume that the user has scripting enabled on her browser, or even that the browser supports scripting at all (although that's becoming less and less of a concern). But the real reason you can't rely on client-side validation is that you can't restrict your form handler to accepting data only from that form. A form's action attribute is just a URL. Anybody from anywhere your firewall permits connections can submit a `GET` or `POST` request to your server. A malicious user could wreak havoc on your application if you don't screen the incoming data.

You certainly can use client-side validation; it can be an important help to your users. It also makes your application seem more responsive since client-side scripts can catch errors immediately. But always back up client-side validation with server-side validation.

## An MVC forms strategy

You can handle forms in an MVC application in a number of ways; I use the following approach:

- ◆ Model each form with a JavaBean.

- ◆ Add an `Articles` table record for each form, and store the class name of the form's JavaBean in the record.

- ◆ When a request comes in for a form, or a form completion (with parameters), the controller servlet looks up that request URI in the database.

- ◆ If the request is valid, the controller creates a form JavaBean from the class name stored in the form's `Articles` record.

- ◆ The controller lets the JavaBean look at the request parameters to determine if the request is for a new instance of the form JavaBean, or if the user has submitted the form.

- ◆ If the user is requesting a new instance of the form, save the JavaBean with the request and forward it to the view JSP, telling the view JSP which form JSP to include; the view JSP receives the request and the accompanying JavaBean and uses that JavaBean to build the form.

- ◆ If the user is submitting a completed form, have the JavaBean verify the data; if the data is good, call the JavaBean's `save` method and forward to a specified completion page; if the data is not good, pass the JavaBean along as if it is a new form, but with any initial field values set to those values it has received.

Note that the form JavaBean is responsible for knowing how to validate itself, and to save itself. The `save` method takes a `Connection` instance as a parameter, and the JavaBean can use that connection to record any necessary changes to the database. All the form-specific logic is in the form JavaBean (and any beans it uses), and not in the controller. The controller simply creates the JavaBean, asks the JavaBean if it is a new form or one the user has filled out, and then tells the JavaBean to save itself, or passes the JavaBean back to the form JSP for another try.

Also the Web application uses the same request URI to return a new form as it does to save the form. If you're restricting access to the form, it's easier to set permissions for just one URI than for two.

On to the details!

# Using JavaBeans to Model a Form

An HTML form is really just a collection of form components, or fields, and those fields can be of different types, including single-line text entry, multiline text entry, check box, and so forth. Most HTML fields share a number of common properties, such as name and value, but they vary in their representation on the page, and in the kind of data they store.

HTML fields are ideal candidates for inheritance, since a base class can model all of the essential capabilities of the field, with the derived classes adding the specific functionality needed. Listing 20-2 shows the source code for the `FormFieldBean` class.

**Listing 20-2: The FormFieldBean Class**

```java
public abstract class FormFieldBean {
    private String type = "text";
    private String name = "text1";
    private String prompt = "prompt";
    private String ID = "";
    private String value = "";
    private int width = 25;
    private int height = 1;
    private String html;

    public FormFieldBean() {
        super();

    }

    public void clear() {
        value = "";
    }

    public int getHeight() {
        return height;
    }

    public abstract java.lang.String getHtml();

    public java.lang.String getID() {
        return ID;
    }

    public java.lang.String getName() {
        return name;
    }

    public java.lang.String getPrompt() {
        return prompt;
    }

    public java.lang.String getType() {
        return type;
    }

    public java.lang.String getValue() {
        return value;
    }
```

```java
    public int getWidth() {
        return width;
    }

    public void setHeight(int newHeight) {
        height = newHeight;
    }

    public void setID(java.lang.String newID) {
        ID = newID;
    }

    public void setName(java.lang.String newName) {
        name = newName;
    }

    public void setPrompt(java.lang.String newPrompt) {
        if (newPrompt != null)
            prompt = newPrompt;
    }

    public void setType(java.lang.String newType) {
        if (newType != null)
            type = newType;
    }

    public void setValue(java.lang.String newValue) {
        if (newValue != null) {
            value = newValue;

        }
    }

    public void setWidth(int newWidth) {
        width = newWidth;
    }
}
```

As Listing 20-2 shows, `FormFieldBean` is an abstract class, which means that it can never be directly instantiated. All it does is establish some standard behaviors, such as setting/getting some standard field properties such as name, value, height, and width. The `FormFieldBean` also lists one method as abstract, as well. The derived class must implement all abstract methods. The `FormFieldBean` class overrides the `getHtml()` method, which returns the HTML string used to create the field inside the form. Each field in the form has to generate its own HTML string, not just because the field type and name vary, but because fields may need initial values that the JavaBean can also store and set.

To use `FormFieldBean`, you need to create a derived class, such as `FormFieldTextBean`, shown in Listing 20-3. This particular JavaBean models a single-line entry field.

**Listing 20-3: The FormFieldTextBean Class**

```
public class FormFieldTextBean extends FormFieldBean {

    public FormFieldTextBean() {
        super();
    }

    public FormFieldTextBean(String newId,int newWidth) {
        this();
        setID(newId);
        setName(newId);
        setValue("");
        setWidth(newWidth);
    }

    public String getHtml() {
        return (
            "<input type=\"text\" name=\""
                + getName()
                + "\" size=\""
                + getWidth()
                + "\" value=\""
                + getValue()
                + "\">");
    }
}
```

The `FormFieldTextBean` class has two constructors, one default, and the other that provides a shorthand way of creating this particular kind of field with its most-used values. You can set additional values with the base class's setter methods, if desired.

The `FormFieldTextBean` class also implements the `getHtml()` method, which is an abstract `FormFieldBean` method. You cannot compile any class derived from `FormFieldBean` without first implementing `getHtml()`. All that method does is construct an HTML string for a one-line text field, which looks something like this:

```
<input type="text" name="name" size="25">
```

Another implementation of `FormFieldBean` is `FormFieldTextAreaBean`, which models a multiline text box. As you can see in Listing 20-4, this JavaBean implements a slightly different `getHtml()` method, appropriate to multiline text boxes. It also has a different shorthand constructor.

**Listing 20-4: The FormFieldTextArea Class**

```
public class FormFieldTextAreaBean extends FormFieldBean {

    public FormFieldTextAreaBean() {
        super();
    }

    public FormFieldTextAreaBean(String newId,
        int newWidth, int newHeight) {
        this();
        setID(newId);
        setName(newId);
        setValue("");
        setWidth(newWidth);
        setHeight(newHeight);
    }

    public String getHtml() {
        return (
            "<textarea name=\""
                + getName()
                + "\" rows=\""
                + getHeight()
                + "\" cols=\""
                + getWidth()
                + "\">"
                + getValue()
                + "</textarea>");
    }
}
```

# Collecting fields into a form

Now that I have some field beans, I can collect them into a form JavaBean. In object-oriented programming terms, storing references to one object inside another object is an example of composition. To arrange the field beans inside the form JavaBean, I use a `HashMap`, which is part of the Java2 Collections API. The `HashMap`, called `fieldsMap`, is a private property of `FormBean` and can't be accessed from outside the JavaBean, so `FormBean` provides an `addField()` method:

```
public void addField(FormFieldBean formField) {
    fieldsMap.put(formField.getID(), formField);
}
```

The addField() method stores the passed FormFieldBean using the field's ID as the key.

Notice that I'm passing in an object of type FormFieldBean, which is the abstract base class. I may have a number of different kinds of fields I want to use in a form, but I don't want to have to code for all these different varieties of fields. Instead, I just cast up the class hierarchy to the base class. All the methods that FormBean needs to use are in the base class, though the derived classes override some of these methods, which means that the derived code in those cases executes instead of the code in the base class.

Besides providing a way of storing field beans, FormBean also initializes any needed objects and values in its constructor:

```
public FormBean() {
    super();
    fieldsMap = new HashMap();
    FormFieldHiddenBean field = new FormFieldHiddenBean();
    field.init("formID","true");
    addField(field);
}
```

The FormBean constructor creates the fieldsMap instance to store the fields, and then automatically adds a FormFieldHiddenBean to its list of fields. A hidden field is a convenient way of storing some non-displaying information on a form; the browser sends hidden field data to the server along with the rest of the form data. In this case, the hidden field is a hard-coded identifier (formID) that tells the controller servlet when this is a form submission, not a form request. I explain this feature, along with the setParameters() method, shortly. Listing 20-5 shows the source for the base FormBean class.

### Listing 20-5: The FormBean Class

```
import java.util.*;
import java.sql.Connection;

public abstract class FormBean {
    private String method = "GET";
    private String action = "";
    private HashMap fieldsMap;
    private String uri = "";
    private HashMap params;
    private boolean newForm = true;
```

```java
public FormBean() {
    super();
    fieldsMap = new HashMap();
    FormFieldHiddenBean field = new FormFieldHiddenBean();
    field.init("FormID", "FormID", "true");
    addField(field);
}
public void addField(FormFieldBean formField) {
    fieldsMap.put(formField.getID(), formField);
}

public java.lang.String getAction() {
    return action;
}
public Object getField(String fieldID) {
    Object f = fieldsMap.get(fieldID);
    return f;
}

public java.lang.String getMethod() {
    return method;
}

public java.lang.String getUri() {
    return uri;
}

public boolean isNewForm() {
    return newForm;
}
public abstract void Save(Connection conn);

public void setAction(java.lang.String newAction) {
    action = newAction;
}

public void setMethod(java.lang.String newMethod) {
    method = newMethod;
}

public void setNewForm(boolean newNewForm) {
    newForm = newNewForm;
}
```

*Continued*

Listing 20-5 *(Continued)*

```java
    public void setParameters(HashMap requestParams) {
        System.out.println("setting form parameters");
        String[] paramValues;
        FormFieldBean field;
        // Look for the FormID hidden field in the form.
        // If found, this is a GET or POST of the form.
        if (requestParams.containsKey("FormID")) {
            paramValues = (String[]) requestParams.get("FormID");
            if (paramValues[0].equals("true"))
                setNewForm(false);
        }
        if (!isNewForm()) {
            Iterator iterator = fieldsMap.values().iterator();
            while (iterator.hasNext()) {
                // get the next form field
                field = (FormFieldBean) iterator.next();
                // look for a match in the request parameters
                if (requestParams.containsKey(field.getID())) {
                    // get the parameter values from the request
                    paramValues = (
                        String[]) requestParams.get(field.getID());
                    // only the first element of the
                    // array is used at present
                    field.setValue(paramValues[0]);
                } else {
                    field.clear();
                }
            }
        }

    }


    public void setUri(java.lang.String newUri) {
        uri = newUri;
    }


    public abstract boolean validate();
```

Since FormBean is an abstract class, you can't use it directly. Instead, you create a derived class (call it TestFormBean) and implement a new constructor to create the fields, and the save and validate methods, which in this case do nothing (yet). Listing 20-6 shows the code for TestFormBean.

**Listing 20-6: Creating a Form Bean with Fields**

```
public class TestFormBean extends FormBean {

    public TestFormBean() {
        super();

        FormFieldTextBean f4 =
            new FormFieldTextBean("firstName", 30);
        addField(f4);

        FormFieldTextBean f5 =
            new FormFieldTextBean("lastName", 30);
        addField(f5);

        FormFieldTextBean f6 =
            new FormFieldTextBean("email", 30);
        addField(f6);

        FormFieldTextAreaBean f7 =
            new FormFieldTextAreaBean("comments", 30, 10);
        addField(f7);

        FormFieldSubmitBean f8 =
            new FormFieldSubmitBean("submit");
        addField(f8);

    }
    public void save(Connection conn) {
        return;
    }
    public boolean validate() {
        return true;
    }
}
```

As Listing 20-6 shows, TestFormBean creates the individual fields with the necessary values, and then adds them to the form. You would normally create one form
JavaBean for each form.

## Processing the form JavaBean

When a request comes in for a form, the controller servlet creates an instance of the
appropriate form JavaBean and forwards it to the form page by storing the
JavaBean as an attribute of the request, and then forwarding to the form page using
a request dispatcher. I provide a detailed example in the next chapter; for now, you

can take it as a given that the JSP that contains the form has a form JavaBean attached to the request object.

To create a form, you use a set of tags that take a form JavaBean and extract the HTML needed to define the form header. The HTML for such a form looks similar to what you see in Listing 20-7.

**Listing 20-7: An HTML Form Created Using Form Bean Tags**

```
<deweb:form formName="form">
<deweb:formField formName="form" fieldName="formID"/>
<table border="0" cellpadding="8" cellspacing="0" width="79%"
height="198">
  <tr>
    <td width="34%" height="45" valign="top">Rating</td>
    <td width="66%" height="45" valign="top">
    <p><deweb:formField formName="form" fieldName="ratingGood"/>
Good</p>
    <p><deweb:formField formName="form" fieldName="ratingBad"/>
Bad</p>
    <p><deweb:formField formName="form" fieldName="ratingUgly"/>
Ugly</p>
    </td>
  </tr>
  <tr>
    <td width="34%" height="21" valign="top"></td>
    <td width="66%" height="21" valign="top"></td>
  </tr>
  <tr>
    <td width="34%" height="21" valign="top">First Name:</td>
    <td width="66%" height="21" valign="top">
      <deweb:formField formName="form" fieldName="firstName"/></td>
  </tr>
  <tr>
    <td width="34%" height="21" valign="top">Last Name</td>
    <td width="66%" height="21" valign="top">
      <deweb:formField formName="form" fieldName="lastName"/></td>
  </tr>
  <tr>
    <td width="34%" height="21" valign="top">Email</td>
    <td width="66%" height="21" valign="top">
      <deweb:formField formName="form" fieldName="email"/></td>
  </tr>
  <tr>
    <td width="34%" height="196" valign="top">Comments</td>
    <td width="66%" height="196" valign="top">
      <deweb:formField formName="form" fieldName="comments"/></td>
```

```
    </tr>
    <tr>
      <td width="100%" height="47" valign="top" colspan="2">
        <p align="center">
          <deweb:formField formName="form" fieldName="submit"/>
        </p></td>
    </tr>
</table>
<p></p>
</deweb:form>
```

The form in Listing 20-7 begins with the start of the form tag:

```
<deweb:form formName="form">
```

There is no terminator on the form tag because this tag has a body. The tag's
doStartTag() method, which is shown in Listing 20-8, looks for a form JavaBean
in the request, and then writes the form header line in the tag body using information from that JavaBean.

### Listing 20-8: The FormTag Class

```
package com.covecomm.deweb.taglib;



import javax.servlet.jsp.tagext.*;
import javax.servlet.jsp.*;
import javax.servlet.*;
import java.io.Writer;
import java.util.*;
import java.io.IOException;
import com.covecomm.deweb.forms.*;

public class FormTag extends TagSupport {
    private String formName;
    private FormBean form = null;

    public int doEndTag() throws JspException {
        JspWriter out = pageContext.getOut();
        try {
            if (form != null)
                out.print(form.getFooter());
            else
                out.print("</form>");
        } catch (IOException e) {
```

*Continued*

**Listing 20-8** *(Continued)*

```java
            throw new JspException(e.toString());
        }
        return EVAL_PAGE;
    }

    public int doStartTag() throws JspException {
        ServletRequest request = pageContext.getRequest();
        try {
            form = (FormBean) request.getAttribute(getFormName());
        } catch (ClassCastException e) {
            throw new JspException("FormTag class cast exception");
        }
        if (form == null) {
            System.out.println("formbean is null, skipping menu");
            return SKIP_BODY;
        }
        JspWriter out = pageContext.getOut();
        try {
            out.print(form.getHeader());
        } catch (IOException e) {
            throw new JspException(e.toString());
        }
        return EVAL_BODY_INCLUDE;
    }

    public java.lang.String getFormName() {
        return formName;
    }

    public void setFormName(java.lang.String newFormName) {
        formName = newFormName;
    }
}
```

Listing 20-9 shows FormTag's definition in deweb.tld.

**Listing 20-9: The FormTag Descriptor in deweb.tld**

```xml
<tag>
    <name>form</name>
    <tagclass>com.covecomm.deweb.taglib.FormTag</tagclass>
    <bodycontent>JSP</bodycontent>
    <attribute>
        <name>formName</name>
        <required>true</required>
```

```
      <rtexprvalue>false</rtexprvalue>
   </attribute>
</tag>
```

The only attribute to `FormTag` is `formName`. The `doStartTag()` method takes this form and attempts to locate a `FormBean` object in the request that corresponds to this name. If the `doStartTag()` method finds a `FormBean` object, it writes out the form's header, which the form constructs out of its method and action attributes.

Similarly, `doEndTag()` writes out the form's footer, which is really just `</form>`.

The first tag in the form JSP is the form tag that writes the form header. Next come the `formField` tags that write the HTML for each of the form's fields. For instance, the tag

```
<deweb:formField formName="form" fieldName="firstName"/>
```

generates this HTML:

```
<input type="text" name="firstName" size="30" value=" ">
```

Of course, the origin of the field is back in the form's constructor, in this code:

```
FormFieldTextBean f4 = new FormFieldTextBean("firstName", 30);
addField(f4);
```

The last field in the form is the submit button, which has this tag:

```
<deweb:formField formName="form" fieldName="submit"/>
```

The generated code for the submit button looks like this:

```
<input type="submit" value="Save Comments" name="submit">
```

Listing 20-10 shows the `FormFieldTag` class, which generates the named field's HTML into the JSP.

**Listing 20-10: The FormFieldTag Class for Placing Fields on a Form**

```
package com.covecomm.deweb.taglib;

import javax.servlet.jsp.tagext.*;
import javax.servlet.jsp.*;
import javax.servlet.*;
import java.io.Writer;
import java.util.*;
import java.io.IOException;
```

*Continued*

**Listing 20-10** *(Continued)*

```java
import java.sql.*;
import com.covecomm.deweb.forms.*;

public class FormFieldTag extends TagSupport {
    private String formName;
    private String fieldName;
    private String attribute = null;
    public int doStartTag() throws JspException {
        ServletRequest request = pageContext.getRequest();
        //System.out.println("FormFieldTag doStartTag");
        FormBean fb = null;
        try {
            fb = (FormBean) request.getAttribute(getFormName());
        } catch (ClassCastException e) {
            System.out.println(
                "FormTag class cast exception on "
                + getFormName());
            return SKIP_BODY;
        }
        if (fb == null) {
            System.out.println(
                "Unable to create FormBean "
                + getFormName());
            return SKIP_BODY;
        }
        FormFieldBean field = (
            FormFieldBean) fb.getField(getFieldName());
        if (field == null) {
            System.out.println(
                "Unable to get field "
                + getFieldName()
                + " in FormBean "
                + getFormName());
            return SKIP_BODY;
        }
        JspWriter out = pageContext.getOut();
        try {
            if ((attribute != null)
                && (attribute.equalsIgnoreCase("prompt"))) {
                out.print(field.getPrompt());
            } else {
                out.print(field.getHtml());
            }
        } catch (IOException e) {
```

```
            throw new JspException(e.toString());
        }

        return (EVAL_BODY_INCLUDE);
    }

    public java.lang.String getAttribute() {
        return attribute;
    }

    public java.lang.String getFieldName() {
        return fieldName;
    }

    public java.lang.String getFormName() {
        return formName;
    }

    public void setAttribute(java.lang.String newAttribute) {
        attribute = newAttribute;
    }

    public void setFieldName(java.lang.String newFieldName) {
        fieldName = newFieldName;
    }

    public void setFormName(java.lang.String newFormName) {
        formName = newFormName;
    }
}
```

As with a lot of classes, `FormFieldTag` contains a number of setter/getter methods. The main work of `doStartTag()`, like `FormTag`, is to locate a form object in the request, and then to find the requested field in the form, before obtaining the field's HTML representation. Listing 20-11 shows the `FormFieldTag` descriptor.

**Listing 20-11: The FormFieldTag Descriptor from deweb.dtd**

```
<tag>
    <name>formField</name>
    <tagclass>com.covecomm.deweb.taglib.FormFieldTag</tagclass>
    <bodycontent>JSP</bodycontent>
    <attribute>
        <name>formName</name>
        <required>true</required>
```

*Continued*

Listing 20-11 *(Continued)*

```
        <rtexprvalue>false</rtexprvalue>
    </attribute>
    <attribute>
        <name>fieldName</name>
        <required>true</required>
        <rtexprvalue>false</rtexprvalue>
    </attribute>
    <attribute>
        <name>attribute</name>
        <required>false</required>
        <rtexprvalue>false</rtexprvalue>
    </attribute>
</tag>
```

The only point of note in Listing 20-11 is the optional `attribute` property. If you set this property to "prompt," `FormFieldTag` returns any value set by a call to the field JavaBean's `setPrompt()` method.

# Processing the Form

When the user presses submit, the browser sends the form to the destination specified in the form's action attribute. Now you may wish to have separate URLs for the form request and the form processing, but there are some advantages to using a single URL.

By using a single URL for both the request and response, you make security issues easier, should you want to protect access to the form. You only have to validate one URL, perhaps using the approach I outlined in Chapter 19. In addition, the form JavaBean can "round-trip" the page. When a user requests a form, the controller servlet creates the form JavaBean, and then loads that JavaBean with default values. When the user submits the form, the controller again creates the form JavaBean but this time loads it with the values specified by the user. The controller can then call the form's `validate` method and if necessary, submit the form back to the user for correction. Listing 20-12 shows an extract of code the controller servlet uses to process a form request.

Listing 20-12: Controller Servlet Code to Process a Form Request

```
    try {
        Class c = Class.forName(webdoc.getExtraInfo());
        form = (FormBean) c.newInstance();

        Enumeration e = request.getParameterNames();
        HashMap params = new HashMap();
```

```
            while (e.hasMoreElements()) {
                String key = (String) e.nextElement();
                String[] values = request.getParameterValues(key);
                params.put(key,values);
            }
            form.setParameters(params);

        } catch (ClassNotFoundException e) {
            System.out.println(e);
        } catch (InstantiationException e) {
            System.out.println(e);
        } catch (IllegalAccessException e) {
            System.out.println(e);
        } catch (NullPointerException e) {
            System.out.println(e);
        }
        if (!form.isNewForm()){
            System.out.println("saving a form");
            if (form.validate()) {
                if (findDbPool()) {
                    Connection connection = dbPool.getConnection();
                    if (connection != null)
                        form.save(connection);
                }
            }
        }
    }
```

Listing 20-12 assumes that the controller servlet has created a WebDocument object called webdoc, of the kind described in Chapter 19. A form request is, after all, another page, and it makes sense to treat it like any other page and give it an entry in the Articles table. By this point, the controller servlet will have determined if the user has access to this particular form.

The name of the form JavaBean associated with this form is stored in the ExtraInfo field in the Articles table, and the controller servlet retrieves this value with the webdoc.getExtraInfo() method. The controller servlet then attempts to create an instance of the form JavaBean. If the controller is successful, it creates a HashMap of the request parameters and passes it to the form's setParameters() method.

## Setting the form values

When a user submits a form to the server and the controller servlet passes the request parameters to the form's setParameters() method, the form JavaBean examines the request parameters to learn what data accompanies the request. If the request contains the formID parameter, the form JavaBean assumes this is a form submission and not a new form request. Listing 20-13 shows the code for the form's setParameters() method.

**Listing 20–13: The FormBean setParameters() Method**

```
public void setParameters(HashMap requestParams) {
    String[] paramValues;
    FormFieldBean field;
    // Look for the FormID hidden field in the form.
    // If found, this is a GET or POST of the form.
    if (requestParams.containsKey("formID")) {
        System.out.println("found the formID hidden field");
        paramValues = (String[]) requestParams.get("formID");
        if (paramValues[0].equals("true"))
            setNewForm(false);
    }
    if (!isNewForm()) {
        Iterator iterator = fieldsMap.values().iterator();
        while (iterator.hasNext()) {
            // get the next form field
            field = (FormFieldBean) iterator.next();
            // look for a match in the request parameters
            if (requestParams.containsKey(field.getID())) {
                // get the parameter values from the request
                paramValues =
                    (String[]) requestParams.get(field.getID());
                // only the first element of the
                // array is used at present
                field.setValue(paramValues[0]);
            } else {
                field.clear();
            }

        }
    }

}
```

If the form is new, form JavaBean will load the default values (if any) as defined in the constructor method. If the form is a submission, then the form obtains an iterator of its own list of fields, and for each field looks for a matching field in the submission. If the form JavaBean doesn't find a matching parameter, it clears the field's value; otherwise, it sets the value.

The other approach would be to look through each of the request parameters and look for a corresponding field in the form. This approach will fail, however, when it comes to check boxes. An unchecked check box doesn't generate a request parameter. However, if you look for a request value for a check box field, and if you don't find it, you know that you can clear that check box field's value.

## Editing the form

Once `setParameter()` completes, the form JavaBean mirrors the data the user has submitted, and if for any reason some of that data is incorrect, or missing, it's a simple matter to forward again to the form page, and attach the form JavaBean to the request. The JSP will recreate the form for the user, with all of the previously entered data intact. I show an example of this behavior in the next chapter.

## Saving the form

If the user has filled out the form correctly, and all the edit checks have been completed, the controller servlet tells the form JavaBean to save the data to the database. Exactly how this happens is entirely up to the form JavaBean's `save` method, which takes only a `Connection` instance as a parameter. As with validating the form, I show an example in the next chapter.

# Summary

Forms are an important way of allowing users to contribute data to a Web site. In an MVC or Model 2 framework, you should control access to forms the same way you control access to other pages. Similarly, you can display forms using view JSPs just as you display other documents. Key points to remember include:

◆ Using the same URL to request and save a form simplifies access control.

◆ The controller servlet creates a form JavaBean from the class name stored with the `Articles` record.

◆ The form JavaBean's constructor creates all the needed field beans.

◆ The form JavaBean examines any request data to determine if it is a new or a submitted form.

◆ You create the form on the JSP using a form tag, and one or more form field tags.

◆ You must override the FormBean's `validate` and `save` methods in the derived class.

# Chapter 21

# Forms and Databases

## IN THIS CHAPTER

- ◆ Creating a form JavaBean to model the form

- ◆ Using form and form field tags to create a form in a JSP

- ◆ Creating a message tag to display form error messages

- ◆ Setting up form-related MySQL table data

- ◆ Handling the initial form request

- ◆ Validating a submitted form

- ◆ Saving the validated form to a MySQL table

NOW THAT YOU HAVE a handle on modeling HTML forms and form fields in Java, you're ready to set up an MVC Web application to handle form data. In this chapter, you learn how to derive a form JavaBean from the base `FormBean` class, and create an HTML form using a JSP, the form JavaBean, and some custom tags. You modify the controller servlet to handle form requests and create an instance of your derived FormBean, and you discover how to validate the user's form submission and write the results to the MySQL database.

## Modeling the Form

Chapter 20 outlines a strategy for working with forms in an MVC or Model 2 environment. A summary of this approach follows:

- ◆ Model each form with a JavaBean.

- ◆ Design a JSP that uses values from the JavaBean by way of some standard custom tags.

- ◆ Give each form an `Articles` record and store the JavaBean's class name in the `ExtraInfo` field.

- ◆ Handle the form request the same as any other article request, that is, verify and authenticate.

♦ If this form is a new one, create a form JavaBean instance with the default values and forward it to the appropriate JSP.

♦ If this form is a submitted form, create a form JavaBean instance, populate it with values from the request, and validate it.

♦ If the submitted form is valid, save it; otherwise, send it back to the user with an error message.

Before you begin to model the form, make sure you have a good idea of what the form looks like. You'll be creating an article feedback form so users can offer opinions on your site's content. Here's the data:

♦ First name

♦ Last name

♦ E-mail address

♦ Comments

♦ The user's quality rating of the article

You want to create the user's first name, last name, and e-mail address as HTML text input fields and Comments as a textarea field. You can find information on both those field types in Chapter 20. You want something standard for the user's quality rating, which usually allows the user to choose one of a predefined set of options. And that usually means radio buttons. A set of radio buttons in a form looks something like this:

```
<p><input type="radio" value="Good"  name="rating"> Good</p>
<p><input type="radio" value="Bad"  name="rating"> Bad</p>
<p><input type="radio" value="Ugly" checked name="rating"> Ugly</p>
```

The browser knows the three radio buttons belong together because they each have the same name attribute, but different values. The name of the radio buttons is set to the value of the chosen button when the user submits the form. (The radio button with the checked attribute is the default button.) If the user checks Ugly, and the form is using the GET method, the following appears in the URL:

```
http://localhost:8080/test.frm?rating=Ugly
```

A simple FormFieldBean derivative, such as FormFieldRadioBean, won't do the trick, because you'll need three beans (one for each radio button), but the form only returns a value from the checked radio button. And if the user doesn't check any radio button, the form won't submit any radio button value at all.

# A radio button handler class

To make radio buttons work with the `FormBean` class you need a way to group multiple radio button JavaBeans into one functional group. One solution is to use a slightly different derivative of `FormFieldBean` that manages the three `FormFieldRadioBean` instances. Listing 21-1 shows the source code for this JavaBean.

**Listing 21-1: The FormFieldRadioHandlerBean for Managing Groups of Radio Buttons**

```
package com.covecomm.deweb.forms;

import java.util.*;

public class FormFieldRadioHandlerBean extends FormFieldBean {
    private HashMap fieldsMap;

    public FormFieldRadioHandlerBean() {
        super();
        fieldsMap = new HashMap();
    }

    public FormFieldRadioHandlerBean(String newId) {
        this();
        setID(newId);
        setName(newId);
    }

    public void addField(FormFieldBean formField) {
        fieldsMap.put(formField.getID(), formField);
    }

    public String getHtml() {
        return null;
    }

    public void setValue(String newValue) {
        super.setValue(newValue);
        Iterator iterator = fieldsMap.values().iterator();
        FormFieldRadioBean field = null;
        while (iterator.hasNext()) {
            /*  loop through all the radio buttons that
                are part of this set. If their value
                matches the handler's value, then set
                the radio to checked. Clear all other
                buttons.
```

*Continued*

Listing 21-1 *(Continued)*

```
                */
                field = (FormFieldRadioBean) iterator.next();
                if (field.getValue().equals(getValue()))
                    field.setChecked(true);
                else
                    field.setChecked(false);
            }
        }
    }
```

When you create your radio button field JavaBeans, you add them to the radio button handler, as shown in Listing 21-2.

**Listing 21-2: Creating Radio Buttons and Adding Them to the Handler**

```
FormFieldRadioBean f0 =
    new FormFieldRadioBean("ratingGood","rating","Good");
addField(f0);

FormFieldRadioBean f1 =
    new FormFieldRadioBean("ratingBad","rating","Bad");
addField(f1);

FormFieldRadioBean f2 =
    new FormFieldRadioBean("ratingUgly","rating","Ugly");
f2.setChecked(true);
addField(f2);

FormFieldRadioHandlerBean f3 =
    new FormFieldRadioHandlerBean("rating");
f3.addField(f0);
f3.addField(f1);
f3.addField(f2);
addField(f3);
```

Listing 21-1 shows a form JavaBean constructor that creates three radio JavaBeans and a radio JavaBean handler. The constructor then passes each of these beans to the radio JavaBean handler with the addField() method. The form JavaBean still has all four of these field JavaBeans in its list of form fields.

The form JavaBean can still use the three radio JavaBeans the same way it would any other form field. Each radio JavaBean has a unique ID (the first constructor parameter) and value (the third constructor parameter), but all have the same name ("rating"). When the user submits the HTML form with the radio buttons, the form will pass the value of the selected radio button as the "rating" parameter. The controller servlet will create a form JavaBean instance to handle the request, and the radio JavaBean handler has an ID of "rating", that is where the form JavaBean will store the selected radio button's value.

## Setting radio buttons from form data

If your users always fill out the form correctly on the first try, then you don't need to add the radio beans to the JavaBean handler. The problem arises when the user submits an incorrect form, and the controller serlvet has to return the submitted values to the user for correction. The handler JavaBean's setValue() method compares its own value to the values stored in each of the radio beans:

```
while (iterator.hasNext()) {
    field = (FormFieldRadioBean) iterator.next();
    if (field.getValue().equals(getValue()))
        field.setChecked(true);
    else
        field.setChecked(false);
}
```

If the value of the handler matches the value of the JavaBean, the setValue() method sets the JavaBean's checked attribute to true. The radio button JavaBean then generates its JavaBean HTML this way:

```
<input type="radio" value="Ugly" checked name="rating">
```

The addition of the checked attribute tells the browser this radio button is the one to highlight. If, for instance, the newly created form has three radio buttons set us as

```
<p><input type="radio" value="Good" checked name="rating"> Good</p>
<p><input type="radio" value="Bad"  name="rating"> Bad</p>
<p><input type="radio" value="Ugly" name="rating"> Ugly</p>
```

with Good selected by default, and the user selects Ugly, the parameter returned to the controller servlet is:

```
rating=Ugly
```

When the form loads up its values from the request, it looks for a match with "rating," finds the handler JavaBean, and sets its value to Ugly. The handler JavaBean looks at its list of radio beans, finds the one with a value of Ugly, and sets its checked attribute to true.

## Creating TestFormBean

Listing 21-3 shows the complete source code for TestFormBean, a derived class of FormBean, that models the form for this chapter.

**Listing 21-3: The TestFormBean Class, Which Models the Chapter's Form Example**

```java
package com.covecomm.deweb.example;

import java.sql.*;
import com.covecomm.deweb.forms.*;

public class TestFormBean extends com.covecomm.deweb.forms.FormBean {

    public TestFormBean() {
        super();
        setFormPage("/test.jsp");
        setFormDonePage("/thanks.html");

        FormFieldRadioBean f0 =
            new FormFieldRadioBean("ratingGood", "rating", "Good");
        addField(f0);

        FormFieldRadioBean f1 =
            new FormFieldRadioBean("ratingBad", "rating", "Bad");
        addField(f1);

        FormFieldRadioBean f2 =
            new FormFieldRadioBean("ratingUgly", "rating", "Ugly");
        f2.setChecked(true);
        addField(f2);

        FormFieldRadioHandlerBean f3 = new ↵
FormFieldRadioHandlerBean("rating");
        f3.addField(f0);
        f3.addField(f1);
        f3.addField(f2);
        addField(f3);

        FormFieldTextBean f4 = new FormFieldTextBean("firstName", 30);
        f4.setRequired(true);
        addField(f4);

        FormFieldTextBean f5 = new FormFieldTextBean("lastName", 30);
        addField(f5);

        FormFieldTextBean f6 = new FormFieldTextBean("email", 30);
        addField(f6);

        FormFieldTextAreaBean f7 =
            new FormFieldTextAreaBean("comments", 30, 10);
        addField(f7);
```

```
        FormFieldSubmitBean f8 = new FormFieldSubmitBean("Save Comments");
        addField(f8);

    }
    public void save(Connection conn) {
        try {
            Statement stmt = conn.createStatement();
            stmt.executeQuery(
                "insert into Comments "
                    + "(FirstName,LastName,Email,Comments) values("
                    + "\""
                    + getFieldValue("firstName")
                    + "\",\""
                    + getFieldValue("lastName")
                    + "\",\""
                    + getFieldValue("email")
                    + "\",\""
                    + getFieldValue("comments")
                    + "\")");

        } catch (SQLException e) {
            System.out.println("Unable to add Messages record: "
                + e.toString());
        }
        return;
    }
}
```

At the beginning of TestFormBean's constructor are a couple of hard coded pages:

```
setFormPage("/test.jsp");
setFormDonePage("/thanks.html");
```

You call the setFormPage() method to tell the form JavaBean which JSP you will use to create the form. You call the setFormDonePage() method to set the page the user should see after successfully completing the form JavaBean (typically a "thank you for your submission" page). You can store these values in the database, but that may not be of great benefit. You generally create form beans for specific forms, and since you have form information in the Articles table, you'd probably need to add two more columns that wouldn't be used by most records. A one-to-one Forms table is another possibility.

# Creating the JSP

You've created all of the form and field JavaBeans the form requires; now you need to create a JSP to contain the form. Keep in mind that you also have a view JSP that contains all of the standard formatting appropriate to your site. For normal nonform page requests, you include the content page in the view JSP; for a form request, you include a form JSP inside the view JSP.

Listing 21-4 shows test.jsp, which contains all the tags required to create the form and fields at request time.

**Listing 21-4: The test.jsp File, Which Contains the Tags to Create the Form**

```
<html>
<head>
<meta http-equiv="Content-Type" content="text/html; charset=iso-8859-1">
<title>Clarion Magazine -</title>
<link rel="stylesheet" type="text/css" href="/cm_articles.css">
</head>

<body>
<%@ page language="java"%>
<%@ taglib uri="/WEB-INF/deweb.tld" prefix="deweb" %>

<deweb:form formName="form">
<deweb:formField formName="form" fieldName="formID"/>
<table border="0" cellpadding="8" cellspacing="0" width="79%" height="198">
  <tr>
    <td width="100%" height="45" valign="top" colspan="2"
      align="center"><deweb:message messenger="form"/></td>
  </tr>
  <tr>
    <td width="34%" height="45" valign="top">Rating</td>
    <td width="66%" height="45" valign="top">
    <p><deweb:formField formName="form" fieldName="ratingGood"/> Good</p>
    <p><deweb:formField formName="form" fieldName="ratingBad"/> Bad</p>
    <p><deweb:formField formName="form" fieldName="ratingUgly"/> Ugly</p>
    </td>
  </tr>
  <tr>
    <td width="34%" height="21" valign="top">First Name:</td>
    <td width="66%" height="21" valign="top">
      <deweb:formField formName="form" fieldName="firstName"/></td>
  </tr>
  <tr>
    <td width="34%" height="21" valign="top">Last Name</td>
    <td width="66%" height="21" valign="top">
```

```
        <deweb:formField formName="form" fieldName="lastName"/></td>
    </tr>
    <tr>
      <td width="34%" height="21" valign="top">Email</td>
      <td width="66%" height="21" valign="top">
        <deweb:formField formName="form" fieldName="email"/></td>
    </tr>
    <tr>
      <td width="34%" height="196" valign="top">Comments</td>
      <td width="66%" height="196" valign="top">
        <deweb:formField formName="form" fieldName="comments"/></td>
    </tr>
    <tr>
      <td width="100%" height="47" valign="top" colspan="2">
        <p align="center"><deweb:formField formName="form"
         fieldName="submit"/></p></td>
    </tr>
</table>
<p></p>
</deweb:form>

</body>
```

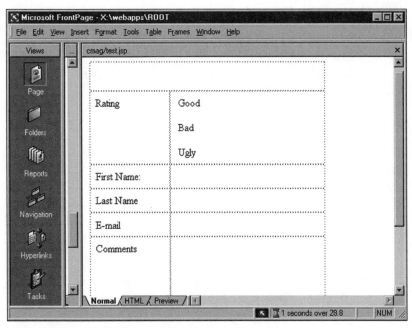

Figure 21-1: Displaying the test.jsp in the FrontPage editor

Figure 21-1 shows `test.jsp` in the FrontPage editor. The dashed lines show the table used to align the prompts and fields. The top two cells of the table have been merged, and the text inside the merged cell is centered to allow for the placement of an error message to the user should the form be filled out incorrectly.

The tag in the top cell shown in Figure 21-1 is as follows:

```
<deweb:message messenger="form"/>
```

If you look in `deweb.tld`, you see the message tag's descriptor, which is shown in the following example:

```
<tag>
    <name>message</name>
    <tagclass>com.covecomm.deweb.taglib.MessageTag</tagclass>
    <bodycontent>JSP</bodycontent>
    <attribute>
        <name>messenger</name>
        <required>true</required>
        <rtexprvalue>false</rtexprvalue>
    </attribute>
</tag>
```

The message tag uses the `com.covecomm.deweb.taglib.MessageTag` class, which is shown in Listing 21-5.

**Listing 21-5: Using the MessageTag Class to Display Messages to the User**

```
package com.covecomm.deweb.taglib;

import javax.servlet.jsp.tagext.*;
import javax.servlet.jsp.*;
import javax.servlet.*;
import java.io.Writer;
import java.util.*;
import java.io.IOException;
import java.sql.*;
import com.covecomm.deweb.util.*;

public class MessageTag extends TagSupport {
    private String messenger;
    public int doStartTag() throws JspException {
        ServletRequest request = pageContext.getRequest();
        Object object = request.getAttribute(getMessenger());
        Message message = null;
```

```
          try {
              if (object instanceof Message) {
                  message = (Message) object;
                  JspWriter out = pageContext.getOut();
                  String s = message.getMessage();
                  if (s != null) {
                      out.print(s);
                      return EVAL_BODY_INCLUDE;
                  }
              } else
                  System.out.println(
                      "MessageTag: object does not implement Message");↲
          } catch (IOException e) {
              System.out.println("MessageTag: IO error " + e.toString());
          }

          return SKIP_BODY;
      }

      public java.lang.String getMessenger() {
          return messenger;
      }

      public void setMessenger(java.lang.String newMessenger) {
          messenger = newMessenger;
      }
  }
```

As you can see in Listing 21-5, MessageTag is simple. It attempts to find an
object with the name given by the messenger attribute in the request. If it finds an
object, it checks to see if that object is an instance of com.covecomm.deweb.util.
Message. Actually, Message is an interface, not a class, and is defined as follows:

```
public interface Message {
    public String getMessage();
    public void setMessage(String newMessage);
}
```

The instanceof operator tests for interface implementation as well as class
type, and as long as the object being tested implements com.covecomm.dweb.
util.Message, the code can safely call the getMessage or setMessage methods
defined by the interface. You can use any object at all with the MessageTag class
provided that object implements the Message interface.

For information about the tags that create the form and the form fields, see Chapter 20.

# Setting Up the Table Data

Next, you need to set up the table data so that the controller servlet finds the appropriate information. You need one record in the Articles table, and one in Jsps. The key data from the Articles table is as follows:

| JspID | URL | ExtraInfo |
|-------|-----|-----------|
| 2 | /test.frm | com.covecomm.deweb.example.TestFormBean |

The corresponding record in the Jsps table, with the ID of 2, has this data:

| JspID | Jsp | Description |
|-------|-----|-------------|
| 2 | /article.jsp | Standard article page |

When the request arrives, the controller does the usual authentication, so if you're restricting rights you may also need to ensure the controller servlet allows the user to access the form page. Notice that the URI has the extension .frm. This extension is completely arbitrary — all you need to do is use an extension that you've mapped to your controller servlet, and which the servlet recognizes as a form and handles accordingly.

# Handling the Initial Request

It's the traffic servlet's responsibility to respond to form requests, create the form object, and call the form's validation code when necessary. The user retrieves the form by clicking on (or typing in) a URL that ends in .frm. The traffic servlet has to be able to recognize and respond to the request. To map all .frm requests to the controller servlet, you need a servlet mapping in web.xml, something like the following:

```
<servlet-mapping>
    <servlet-name>
        traffic
    </servlet-name>
    <url-pattern>
        *.frm
    </url-pattern>
</servlet-mapping>
```

You previously defined `traffic` servlet as the `ControllerServlet` class in `web.xml`, of course.

## The ControllerServlet doGet() method

When the servlet container receives a form request, it calls the `doGet()` or `doPost()` method (depending on the form's action) on `traffic`, which is an instance of `ControllerServlet`. As is common practice with servlets, `ControllerServlet` maps `doPost()` to `doGet()`. The `doPut()` method is mapped directly to the `doGet()` method. Accordingly, Listing 21-6, which shows the `ControllerServlet` `doGet()` method, contains the entire request processing logic.

**Listing 21-6: The ControllerServlet's doGet() Method**

```
public void doGet(HttpServletRequest request, HttpServletResponse ⏎
    response)
    throws ServletException, IOException {
    String uri = request.getServletPath();
    System.out.println("uri " + uri);
    String origUri = uri;
    String forwardTo;
    String jsp = messageJsp;
    int status = 0;
    count++;
    // *** get the user information ***
    // todo: get session info
    String username = null;
    String password = null;
    String decoded;
    String authHeader = (String) request.getHeader("Authorization");
    if (authHeader != null) {
        authHeader = authHeader.substring(6).trim();
        synchronized (this) {
            decoded = new String(decoder.decodeBuffer(authHeader));
        }
        int colon = decoded.indexOf(":");
```

*Continued*

**Listing 21-6** *(Continued)*

```
        if (colon > 0) {
            username = decoded.substring(0, colon);
            password = decoded.substring(colon + 1);
        }
    }
    UserBean user = new UserBean(username, password, ↵
        request.getRemoteAddr());
    if (findLogger())
        logger.write(request.getRemoteAddr(),
            username, uri, "", "uri requested");

    WebDocument webdoc = null;
    // get a document object corresponding to the uri
    SecurityBean security = new SecurityBean();
    java.sql.Connection connection = null;

    // check for various errors. Default jsp is messageJsp.
    do {
        if (uri.endsWith(".pdf")) {
            uri = notFoundHtml;
            status = security.NO_FILE;
            break;
        }
        if (!findDbPool()) {
            uri = systemErrorHtml;
            status = security.NO_DBPOOL;
            break;
        }
        connection = dbPool.getConnection();
        if (connection == null) {
            uri = systemErrorHtml;
            status = security.NO_CONN;
            break;
        }
        webdoc = security.getWebDocument(connection, uri);
        if (!webdoc.isInDatabase()) {
            uri = notFoundHtml;
            status = security.NO_FILE;
            break;
        }

        // If public access then forward to its JSP
        if (!webdoc.isRequireRights()) {
            jsp = webdoc.getJspName();
            status = security.AUTHORIZED;
```

```
            break;
        }
        // a hack to clear the login
        status = security.getAccess(connection, user, webdoc);
        if (uri.equals("/logoff.html")) {
            status = security.INVALID_USER;
            uri = "/index.html";
        }

        switch (status) {
            case security.INVALID_USER :
                response.setContentType("text/html");
                response.setStatus(response.SC_UNAUTHORIZED);
                response.setHeader("WWW-Authenticate",
                    "BASIC realm=\"Subscribers\"");
                uri = invalidUserHtml;
                break;
            case security.NOT_AUTHORIZED :
                uri = notAuthorizedHtml;
                break;
            case security.AUTHORIZED :
                jsp = webdoc.getJspName();
                break;
        }
} while (false);

if (findLogger())
    logger.write(
        request.getRemoteAddr(),
        user.getUsername(),
        origUri,
        Integer.toString(status),
        "forwarding " + uri + " to " + jsp);
System.out.println("*** status: " + status + ", uri " + uri);
do {
    if ((status == security.AUTHORIZED) && (uri.endsWith(".frm"))) {

        FormBean form = null;
        FormFieldBean b = null;
        try {
            Class c = Class.forName(webdoc.getExtraInfo());
            form = (FormBean) c.newInstance();

            Enumeration e = request.getParameterNames();
            java.util.HashMap params = new java.util.HashMap();
```

*Continued*

**Listing 21-6** *(Continued)*

```
                while (e.hasMoreElements()) {
                    String key = (String) e.nextElement();
                    String[] values = request.getParameterValues(key);
                    params.put(key, values);
                }
                form.setParameters(params);

            } catch (ClassNotFoundException e) {
                System.out.println(e);
                uri = systemErrorHtml;
                break;
            } catch (InstantiationException e) {
                System.out.println(e);
                uri = systemErrorHtml;
                break;
            } catch (IllegalAccessException e) {
                System.out.println(e);
                uri = systemErrorHtml;
                break;
            } catch (NullPointerException e) {
                System.out.println(e);
                uri = systemErrorHtml;
                break;
            }

            form.setAction(webdoc.getUri());
            request.setAttribute(form.getName(), form);
            if ((!form.isNewForm()) && (form.validate())) {
                form.save(connection);
                uri = form.getFormDonePage();
            } else
                uri = form.getFormPage();
        }

    }
    while (false);
    if ((connection != null) && (dbPool != null))
        dbPool.freeConnection(connection);
    if (jsp == null)
        throw new ServletException("Cannot forward to this page");
    if (uri != null)
        request.setAttribute("includePage", uri);
    RequestDispatcher dispatcher =
        getServletContext().getRequestDispatcher(jsp);
    System.out.println("got dispatcher " + dispatcher);
```

```
    if (dispatcher != null)
        dispatcher.forward(request, response);
    return;
}
```

Much of the code in Listing 21-6 revolves around ensuring the user has rights to the page requested, and Chapter 19 covers that code in detail. I've placed the form-handling code, which begins about halfway down the listing, in a do/while block. A do/while loop executes until the condition at the end of the loop evaluates as false; since the while condition in this loop is always false, I don't intend to ever loop, but I can use a break statement to exit this loop at any time. In this way, do/while functions a little like a try/catch block, but without the exception-handling overhead.

## Creating the form JavaBean

If the controller has authorized the page request and the user is requesting a form, the controller attempts to create an instance of the class name you've stored in that page's database record. In this case, the form JavaBean is com.covecomm.deweb.example.TestFormBean. The controller casts the page-specific form JavaBean to a FormBean, since all of the form-handling code only knows about FormBean.

```
try {
    Class c = Class.forName(webdoc.getExtraInfo());
    form = (FormBean) c.newInstance();
```

The FormBean class contains the methods the controller requires to handle any form; if you want to implement code that's specific to your particular form, you just override FormBean methods in your derived class.

Assuming the controller has successfully created the form JavaBean, the controller initializes the JavaBean with any values the user may have submitted with the form request. On a new form request there won't be any parameters, but on a saved form request there should be.

Next, the controller sets the form's action, which is the URI the form will post to.

```
form.setAction(webdoc.getUri());
```

As you recall from Chapter 19, webdoc is an object that the controller creates when it first receives a page request. The webdoc object models the document.

## Forwarding the form JavaBean

Next, the controller attaches the form JavaBean to the request so the form JSP can retrieve the form JavaBean.

```
request.setAttribute(form.getName(), form);
```

If the user submits a properly filled out form, the form JavaBean's validate() method will return true. The controller then saves the form to the database, or rather tells the form JavaBean to save itself to the database, using the save() method. The controller then prepares to send the user to the form's "Thank you" page.

```
if ((!form.isNewForm()) && (form.validate())) {
    form.save(connection);
    uri = form.getFormDonePage();
} else
    uri = form.getFormPage();
```

## Forwarding to the form page

The controller forwards the form request to a view JSP exactly as Chapter 19 describes. Recall that the controller servlet receives requests, typically for .html pages, and forwards these requests to a JSP that uses the IncludePage tag to display the HTML document. This way one JSP with all the fancy formatting, menus, and whatnot can display any number of documents.

As you recall, IncludePageTag rewrites the .html extension to an extension (and potentially a directory) not known to the user, so users are unlikely to guess the name of the file and bypass the ControllerServlet. Keep in mind that IncludePage only rewrites the .html extension; it leaves extensions like .jsp unchanged. The controller servlet sets the includePage attribute expected by IncludePageTag like this:

```
request.setAttribute("includePage", uri);
```

If the controller sets uri to a value like /test.jsp, then the display JSP includes /test.jsp in its output.

But where did /test.jsp come from? Recall that in the TestFormBean constructor two lines of code set the form page and the completion page:

```
setFormPage("/test.jsp");
setFormDonePage("/thanks.html");
```

The controller servlet really doesn't have to do much with the form. It simply creates the JavaBean, sets any request parameters that may have come with the request, and lets the form JavaBean say where the controller should send it next.

# Validating the Request

Chapter 19 mentions client side validations can be an important tool in making your applications more user friendly. However, you should never rely on validation code that executes on the browser simply because it's always possible for someone to submit form data directly to your server.

The form classes in the deweb package provide a very simple kind of NOT NULL validation. If you call the setRequired method on a field JavaBean with a true value, the JavaBean's validate fails if the JavaBean has no value. The TestFormBean class does this with the firstName field:

```
FormFieldTextBean f4 = new FormFieldTextBean("firstName", 30);
f4.setRequired(true);
addField(f4);
```

If you require a field and don't populate it on your form, and the field does not have an initial value, your users can't complete the form.

# Validating Form Fields

When the form's validate method is called, and the base class's validate has not been overridden, the following code executes:

```
Iterator iterator = fieldsMap.values().iterator();
FormFieldBean field;
while (iterator.hasNext()) {
    // get the next form field
    field = (FormFieldBean) iterator.next();
    if (!field.validate()) {
        setMessage(field.getMessage());
        return false;
    }
}
return true;
```

If any one field's validate() method fails, the field's error message is stored in the form's message property, and the validation terminates.

The form's validate method, in the base FormFieldBean, makes sure that a required field contains a value of some sort:

```
if ( (isRequired())  && (value.equals("")) ) {
    setMessage("The field \"" + getPrompt()
        + "\" is required");
    return false;
}
else return true;
```

Next, `MessageTag` retrieves the field error message, now stored in the form:

```
<deweb:message messenger="form"/>
```

The `MessageTag` class retrieves the form object from the request and calls its `getMessage` method, displaying the result on the form.

You can easily extend this simple validation by overriding the `FormFieldBean`'s `validate` method.

# Saving the Data

If controller servlet is able to validate the form, it calls the form JavaBean's `save()` method. The `save()` method is an abstract method in the base `FormBean` class, so you have to override it, even if your `save()` method does nothing. Listing 21-7 shows the `TestFormBean`'s `save()` method.

**Listing 21-7: The TestFormBean save() Method to Add a Record to the Comments Table**

```
public void save(Connection conn) {
      try {
          Statement stmt = conn.createStatement();
          stmt.executeQuery(
              "insert into Comments "
                  + "(FirstName,LastName,Email,Comments) values("
                  + "\""
                  + getFieldValue("firstName")
                  + "\",\""
                  + getFieldValue("lastName")
                  + "\",\""
                  + getFieldValue("email")
                  + "\",\""
                  + getFieldValue("comments")
                  + "\")");

      } catch (SQLException e) {
          System.out.println("Unable to add Messages record: "
              + e.toString());
      }
      return;
  }
```

The `save()` method simply creates a SQL `INSERT` statement and executes it with the passed connection. The following shows the statement used to create the Comments table in MySQL:

```
CREATE TABLE Comments(
ID INT AUTO_INCREMENT NOT NULL,
FirstName VARCHAR(30),
LastName VARCHAR(30),
Email VARCHAR(60),
DateTime TIMESTAMP,
comments TEXT,
PRIMARY KEY (ID));
```

# Summary

In this chapter, you learned how to take form and field beans, a set of form and field tags, a form JSP, and a controller servlet and turn them into an HTML form-handling system capable of validating user input and storing form data in a MySQL database. Key points to remember include:

◆ You should check form requests for access rights by the controller servlet, just as you would any other page request.

◆ Specifying the form JavaBean to create in the `Articles` record enables you to modify the form's `validation` and `save` code at any time without recompiling the JSP.

◆ The controller servlet passes the form JavaBean to the form JSP in the request; the form JSP populates the form and field using custom tags.

◆ The `TestFormBean` class's `validation()` method validates each of its fields in turn, and if any field is in error, the field JavaBean stores an error message that the form JSP can display to the user when the controller returns the form for another edit.

◆ The `TestFormBean` class's `save()` method uses a SQL `INSERT` statement to store the form values in the MySQL database.

# Chapter 22

# User Surveys

WEB SITES WITH EVER-CHANGING content generate a lot more traffic than static Web sites. Brief user surveys with immediate graphic feedback are an excellent way to collect and provide information of interest to you and your users. In this chapter you learn how to apply form-handling techniques to a specialized survey form. You store the survey results in a MySQL table, create a graph of the current survey results, and return this graph to the user.

## Creating a User Survey

User surveys are a handy way to get feedback from your users. I like single-question, multiple choice surveys because they only take a user a few seconds to fill out. You've already learned how to create a form to store user input in a MySQL database. It's not that difficult to tabulate the survey results and show the user the current survey results in a bar graph. The form-handling system Chapters 20 and 21 describe already knows how to display a "thank you" page to the user who completes a form. To show the user a graph instead of a thank you note, you don't have to do more than create an appropriate HTML file with an IMG tag that points to the graph.

### A survey example

Figure 22-1 shows an example of a survey that asks users to indicate which version of a particular product they use, in this case the Windows development tool Clarion.

385

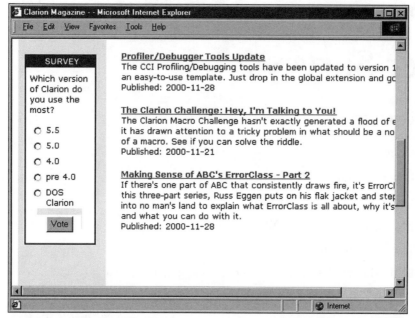

Figure 22–1: A user survey example

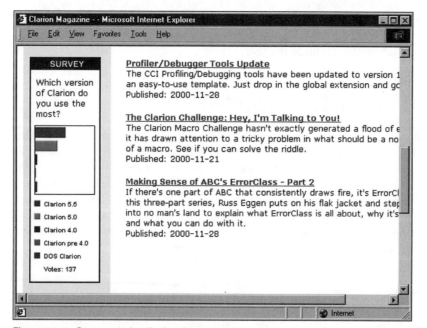

Figure 22–2: Survey results displayed as a graph

When the user selects one of the radio buttons and clicks the Vote button, the user's browser submits the survey to the server, which responds by redisplaying the same page with a graph of the results to date, as shown in Figure 22-2.

You'll typically run a survey like the one shown in Figures 22-1 and 22-2 for a short time, perhaps several days or weeks, and then replace it with another survey. You only need to change two items to create a different survey. One is an entry in the appropriate Articles table, where the ExtraInfo field records the JavaBean class to instantiate for the survey form, and the other is the survey JavaBean. Listing 22-1 shows an example of a survey JavaBean.

**Listing 22-1: The SurveyBean1 Class**

```java
package com.covecomm.deweb.cmag;

/**
 * Insert the type's description here.
 * Creation date: (12/15/00 11:55:06 AM)
 * @author:
 */

import com.covecomm.deweb.forms.*;
import com.covecomm.deweb.graph.GraphBean;
import com.covecomm.deweb.graph.FormSurveyBean;

public class SurveyBean1
    extends com.covecomm.deweb.graph.FormSurveyBean {

    public SurveyBean1() {
        super();
        setFormPage("/cmag/survey.jsp");
        setFormDonePage("");
        setSurveyNumber(1);
        setName("survey");
        setMessage("Which version of Clarion do you use the most?");

            addRadioButton("a","Clarion 5.5","5.5");
            addRadioButton("b","Clarion 5.0","5.0");
            addRadioButton("c","Clarion 4.0","4.0");
            addRadioButton("d","Clarion pre 4.0","pre 4.0");
            addRadioButton("e","DOS Clarion","DOS Clarion");

        // create the radio button handler object
        // and submit JavaBean
        finishSetup();

    }
```

*Continued*

Listing 22-1 *(Continued)*

```
public void prepareGraph(GraphBean graph) {
    graph.setWidth(108);
    graph.setLegendHeight(15);


    }
}
```

Listing 22-1 doesn't contain a lot of code; all it really does is set a few parameters and create some radio buttons. A few JavaBeans and a servlet do the real survey handling work, as follows:

- ◆ `ControllerServlet` — handles the survey form request just as it would any other form request.
- ◆ `FormBean` — provides the underlying form handling capabilities.
- ◆ `FormSurveyBean` — layers survey-specific code onto FormBean.
- ◆ `GraphBean` — models the graph and creates a JPEG image for display.

## Creating the survey data tables

You store the survey data in two tables: `Surveys` and `SurveyData`. Listing 22-2 shows the `CREATE TABLE` statements for these two tables. None of the JavaBeans described in this chapter actually use the `Surveys` table, but it is useful as a place to store the individual surveys used. The `SurveyData` table stores the survey results.

**Listing 22-2: The Surveys and SurveyData Tables**

```
CREATE TABLE Surveys(
ID INT AUTO_INCREMENT NOT NULL,
Name VARCHAR(30),
Description VARCHAR(255),
PubDate DATE,
LastModified TIMESTAMP,
PRIMARY KEY (ID));

CREATE TABLE SurveyData(
ID INT AUTO_INCREMENT NOT NULL,
SurveyID INT NOT NULL,
Value VARCHAR(20) NOT NULL,
Source VARCHAR(255),
DateTime TIMESTAMP,
FOREIGN KEY (SurveyID) REFERENCES Surveys (ID),
PRIMARY KEY (ID),
INDEX IDX_SurveyData_Survey (SurveyID,Value));
```

# Designing the Survey Beans

Since a survey is just another form, you can use the `FormBean` from Chapter 20 to handle basic form requests. As you may recall from that chapter, you can create forms using a set of form-related tags in a JSP. When `ControllerServlet` gets a request for a page, it determines if that page has an associated form. If this is the case, `ControllerServlet` creates an appropriate form JavaBean and passes it to the view JSP.

The view JSP includes the form JSP, which provides access to the form JavaBean. The form JSP uses the form JavaBean to create the HTML form via the form tags. That sounds a bit complicated, but once it's all in place you don't think about it at all. You just create your forms using the tags, and create the appropriate form JavaBean to go with them, linking the two in the database.

Since form handling is in place, collecting survey data per se isn't a problem. The trick is that survey handling and form creation should be as automated as possible. You don't want to have to create a new JSP each time you start a new survey. The form JSP needs to handle only a single question, but that question should be able to handle any number of options. Ideally the form JSP should generate the question options, as radio buttons, automatically. You can do this with the `iterate` tag, as shown in the survey form JSP in Listing 22-3.

**Listing 22-3: A Survey Form JSP That Uses an iterate Tag to Display Repeating Fields**

```
<html>

<head>
<title>A Survey</title>
</head>

<body>
<%@ page language="java"%>
<%@ taglib uri="/WEB-INF/deweb.tld" prefix="deweb" %>
<deweb:form formName="survey">
<deweb:formField formName="survey" fieldName="formID"/>
<table border="0" cellpadding="8" cellspacing="0">
  <tr>
    <td width="100%" valign="top" colspan="2" align="center">
    </td>
  </tr>
<deweb:iterate collection="survey" iteratedItemName="formField"
    iteratedItemClass="com.covecomm.deweb.forms.FormFieldBean"
    scope="request">
  <tr>
    <td valign="top">
    <jsp:getProperty name="formField" property="html"/>
```

*Continued*

**Listing 22-3** *(Continued)*

```
      </td>
      <td valign="top">
      <jsp:getProperty name="formField" property="prompt"/>
      </td>
   </tr>
</deweb:iterate>
   <tr>
     <td width="100%" valign="top" colspan="2">
       <p align="center">
       <deweb:formField formName="survey" fieldName="sid"/>
       <deweb:formField formName="survey" fieldName="submit"/>
       </p></td>
   </tr>
</table>
<p></p>
</deweb:form>
</body>
```

The JSP in Listing 22-3 assumes that the FormBean delivered to this page has the ability to deliver an iterator of survey radio buttons, which it uses as instances of FormFieldBean. You'll need to add a getIterator method to FormBean.

First, FormBean needs a way of storing a list of form fields. It already has this in the form of a HashMap:

```
private HashMap fieldsMap;
```

You could create a getIterator() method in FormBean that returns an iterator of fieldsMap, but this solution has several problems. For one thing, fieldsMap contains all of the fields in the form, including any hidden fields and the submit field. If IterateTag has to try to differentiate between these different kinds of fields, it's going to require some special-purpose code, and ideally, IterateTag should be as generic as possible.

A second problem with using fieldsMap is that it's an instance of HashMap, and HashMaps do not guarantee the ordering of the objects they contain, which means you can add fields to your survey form JavaBean and have them display in an unexpected order.

## A sorted collection

The Java Collections API has several implementations of sorted collections, one of which is TreeSet. You can add a TreeSet to FormBean like this:

```
private TreeSet repeatFields=null;
```

The FormBean constructor needs to intialize TreeSet:

```
repeatFields = new TreeSet();
```

You also need a method to add a field to repeatFields:

```
public void addRepeatField(FormFieldBean formField){
    repeatFields.add(formField);
}
```

Finally, you should add a getIterator() method with the signature expected by IterateTag:

```
public java.util.Iterator getIterator() {
    if (repeatFields == null)
        repeatFields = new TreeSet();
    return repeatFields.iterator();
}
```

## Implementing the comparator

One other vital element to working with a sorted collection is something called a *comparator*. When you add an object to a sorted collection, it needs a way to sort those objects, and it does this by calling a method defined in the Comparable interface:

```
public interface Comparable {
    public int compareTo(Object o);
}
```

Before you add any fields to the repeatFields TreeSet, you need to implement Comparable in any of those fields. This implementation is easiest in the base FormFieldBean class:

```
public abstract class FormFieldBean
    implements com.covecomm.deweb.util.Message,
    Comparable {
```

The TreeSet collection calls the compareTo() method every time it executes its add() method. Since you're implementing compareTo(), you can decide what part of FormFieldBean the tree will sort. I've used the form field's ID:

```
public int compareTo(java.lang.Object o){
    FormFieldBean otherField = (FormFieldBean)o;
    return(getID().compareTo(otherField.getID()));
}
```

Listing 22-4 shows the complete source for the updated `FormFieldBean` class.

**Listing 22-4: The FormFieldBean Class with Support for a TreeSet of Repeating Fields**

```
package com.covecomm.deweb.forms;

public abstract class FormFieldBean
    implements com.covecomm.deweb.util.Message, Comparable {
    private String type = null;
    private String name = null;
    private String prompt = null;
    private String ID = "";
    private String value = "";
    private int width = 25;
    private int height = 1;
    private String html;
    private boolean required = false;
    private String message;

    public FormFieldBean() {
        super();
    }

    public void clear() {
        value = "";
    }

    public int compareTo(java.lang.Object o) {
        FormFieldBean otherField = (FormFieldBean) o;
        return (getID().compareTo(otherField.getID()));
    }

    public int getHeight() {
        return height;
    }

    public abstract java.lang.String getHtml();

    public java.lang.String getID() {
        return ID;
    }

    public java.lang.String getMessage() {
        return message;
    }
```

```java
public java.lang.String getName() {
    return name;
}

public java.lang.String getPrompt() {
    if (prompt != null)
        return prompt;
    if (name != null)
        return name;
    if (ID != null)
        return ID;
    return ("unknown field");
}

public java.lang.String getType() {
    return type;
}

public java.lang.String getValue() {
    return value;
}

public int getWidth() {
    return width;
}

public boolean isRequired() {
    return required;
}

public void setHeight(int newHeight) {
    height = newHeight;
}

public void setID(java.lang.String newID) {
    ID = newID;
}

public void setMessage(java.lang.String newMessage) {
    message = newMessage;
}

public void setName(java.lang.String newName) {
    name = newName;
}
```

*Continued*

Listing 22-4 *(Continued)*

```
    public void setPrompt(java.lang.String newPrompt) {
        if (newPrompt != null)
            prompt = newPrompt;
    }

    public void setRequired(boolean newRequired) {
        required = newRequired;
    }

    public void setType(java.lang.String newType) {
        if (newType != null)
            type = newType;
    }

    public void setValue(java.lang.String newValue) {
        if (newValue != null) {
            value = newValue;
        }
    }

    public void setWidth(int newWidth) {
        width = newWidth;
    }
    public boolean validate() {
        if ((isRequired()) && (value.equals(""))) {
            setMessage("The field \"" + getPrompt() + "\" is
required");
            return false;
        } else
            return true;
    }
}
```

## Creating the radio buttons

The sample survey JavaBean in Listing 22-1 creates radio buttons with a call to the
`addRadioButton()` method. This method takes an ID, name, and prompt as parameters, and uses them to create a `FormFieldRadioBean` instance. It then transfers the
ID, name, and prompt. A slight translation is involved, as is the case with radio buttons: the method passes the ID straight across, but assigns the name to the radio
button's value and the ID to `handlerName`, a hard coded value.

```
public void addRadioButton(String id, String name, String prompt) {
    FormFieldRadioBean rb =
```

```
        new FormFieldRadioBean(id, handlerName, name);
    rb.setPrompt(prompt);
    addField(rb);
    addRepeatField(rb);
}
```

The addRadioButton() method also adds the radio button to the field list *and* to the repeating fields list. The former is so the radio button will function normally in a form context, and the latter is so it can be populated automatically on the survey form via IterateTag.

After creating the radio buttons, SurveyBean1 calls the finishSetup() method. This method creates an instance of FormFieldRadioHandlerBean with the hard-coded ID "question." The radio button handler iterates through the list of radio buttons and stores a reference to each:

```
while (iterator.hasNext()) {
    FormFieldBean f = (FormFieldBean)iterator.next();
    frh.addField(f);
}
addField(frh);
```

The finishSetup method also creates a hidden form with the survey number, and a form submit button:

```
FormFieldHiddenBean surveyID =
    new FormFieldHiddenBean("sid",
    Integer.toString(getSurveyNumber()));
addField(surveyID);
FormFieldSubmitBean fsb = new FormFieldSubmitBean("Vote");
addField(fsb);
```

## Requesting the survey

Users don't specifically request the survey; instead, the user requests a page, the controller servlet looks up that page's corresponding view JSP, and if the view JSP has an associated survey JavaBean, the controller creates an instance of that class. To make this happen you create a record in the Articles table with the HasForm field set to 'Y'; put the name of the survey JavaBean in the ExtraInfo field.

| Title | ExtraInfo | URI | HasForm |
|-------|-----------|-----|---------|
| Home | com.covecomm.deweb.cmag.SurveyBean1 | /index.html | Y |

When `ControllerServlet` receives a request for `/index.html`, it creates a `WebDocument` instance. Among other things, a `WebDocument` instance contains a `boolean` called `formPage` — accessed via the `isFormPage()` method — which corresponds to the `HasForm` field in the `Articles table`. Listing 22-5 shows the code from `ControllerServlet's doGet()` method that creates the form JavaBean.

**Listing 22-5: Creating the form JavaBean in ControllerServlet.doGet**

```
do {
    if ((status == security.AUTHORIZED) && (webdoc.isFormPage())) {
        FormBean form = null;
        FormFieldBean b = null;
        try {
            Class c = Class.forName(webdoc.getExtraInfo());
            form = (FormBean) c.newInstance();
        } catch (ClassNotFoundException e) {
            System.out.println(e);
            uri = systemErrorHtml;
            break;
        } catch (InstantiationException e) {
            System.out.println(e);
            uri = systemErrorHtml;
            break;
        } catch (IllegalAccessException e) {
            System.out.println(e);
            uri = systemErrorHtml;
            break;
        } catch (NullPointerException e) {
            System.out.println(e);
            uri = systemErrorHtml;
            break;
        }
        form.setServletInfo(request,response,getServletContext());
        form.setAction(webdoc.getUri());
        request.setAttribute(form.getName(), form);
        if ((!form.isNewForm()) && (form.validate())) {
            form.save(connection);
            uri = form.getFormDonePage();
        } else
            uri = form.getFormPage();
        System.out.println("form URI is " + uri);
    }
}
```

Form creation follows the pattern Chapter 20 describes. The controller servlet creates a form JavaBean and passes this in the request to the view JSP. The JSP creates the form using the form and `formField` tags. The only difference is that the controller servlet never needs to respond to an explicit "new form" request, since the user never asks for the survey directly.

# Duplicate survey entries

One of the problems you face when surveying Web site users is weeding out duplicate entries. For a public access site you can't do this completely, of course, and for this reason you should always take Web survey results with an appropriately sized grain of salt.

The FormSurveyBean class attempts to handle duplicate entries using a two-cookie system. It sends one cookie to the user on the first request for a form, and then looks for the cookie during form submission. If the cookie is not present, the controller servlet redisplays the page, and the form's message tells the user that the survey requires cookies.

If the first cookie is present and the user has submitted the form, FormSurveyBean assumes that this is a valid, first submission. It does take one additional precaution against duplicates, which is to delete any existing entry for this combination of survey ID and user IP address. (You may want to disable this option since users behind a proxy server will all have the same address. Dialup users also reuse IP addresses, though it's less likely this will cause a problem.) You can still place duplicate entries in the database, but you need to delete the cookies and change IP addresses, which is a lot of bother. If you suspect someone of stuffing the ballot box, a look through the survey data, comparing IP addresses and timestamps should give you some idea. Again, public Internet polls are by their nature a little unreliable and subject to fiddling.

Listing 22-6 shows the source code for FormSurveyBean, which is the superclass of SurveyBean1 from Listing 22-1.

**Listing 22-6: The FormSurveyBean Class Provides Core Survey Form-Handling Functionality**

```
package com.covecomm.deweb.graph;

import java.sql.*;
import com.covecomm.deweb.forms.*;
import java.io.*;
import java.util.Iterator;
import javax.servlet.http.*;
import javax.servlet.ServletContext;
import com.covecomm.deweb.graph.GraphBean;
import java.awt.*;
import java.awt.image.BufferedImage;
import com.sun.image.codec.jpeg.*;
import java.awt.font.*;
import java.util.HashMap;
```

*Continued*

**Listing 22-6** *(Continued)*

```java
public abstract class FormSurveyBean
    extends com.covecomm.deweb.forms.FormBean {
    private boolean saveSurvey = false;
    private int surveyNumber = 99999;
    private Color[] colors =
        {
            new Color(164, 0, 0),
            new Color(0, 164, 0),
            new Color(0, 0, 164),
            new Color(0, 128, 128),
            new Color(128, 0, 128),
            new Color(128, 128, 0)
        };
    private int colorIndex = 0;
    private String handlerName = "question";

    public FormSurveyBean() {
        super();
    }

    public void addRadioButton(String id,
        String name, String prompt) {

        FormFieldRadioBean rb =
            new FormFieldRadioBean(id, handlerName, name);
        rb.setPrompt(prompt);
        addField(rb);
        addRepeatField(rb);
    }

    public boolean allowedValue(String value) {
        Iterator iterator = getIterator();
        while (iterator.hasNext()) {
            FormFieldBean field = (FormFieldBean) iterator.next();
            if (value.equals(field.getValue()))
                return true;
        }
        return false;
    }

    public void finishSetup() {

        FormFieldRadioHandlerBean frh =
            new FormFieldRadioHandlerBean(handlerName);
        Iterator iterator = getIterator();
```

```
        while (iterator.hasNext()) {
            FormFieldBean f = (FormFieldBean) iterator.next();
            frh.addField(f);
        }
        addField(frh);

        FormFieldHiddenBean surveyID =
            new FormFieldHiddenBean("sid",
                Integer.toString(getSurveyNumber()));
        addField(surveyID);

        FormFieldSubmitBean fsb = new FormFieldSubmitBean("Vote");
        fsb.setRequired(true);
        addField(fsb);
    }

    public Color getNextBarColor() {
        if (colorIndex >= colors.length)
            colorIndex = 0;
        return (colors[colorIndex++]);
    }

    public int getSurveyNumber() {
        return surveyNumber;
    }

    public void prepareGraph(GraphBean graph) {
    }

    public void save(Connection conn) {
        if (!saveSurvey)
            return;
        String notes = request.getRemoteAddr();
        String value = getFieldValue(handlerName);
        String sid = getFieldValue("sid");
        colorIndex = 0;
        // dump all invalid survey IDs to 99999
        if ((sid == null) || (sid.equals("")))
            sid = "99999";
        System.out.println("sid: " + sid);
        int surveyId;
        try {
            surveyId = Integer.parseInt(sid);
        } catch (NumberFormatException e) {
            surveyId = 99999;
```

*Continued*

**Listing 22-6** *(Continued)*

```
            notes = "invalid sid: " + sid + " " + e.toString();
            System.out.println(notes);
        }
        int responses = 0;
        GraphBean graph = new GraphBean();

        // prepareGraph can be overridden in the derived
        // class to set up graph properties such as the font
        prepareGraph(graph);

        Iterator iterator = getRepeatFields().iterator();
        Statement stmt = null;
        ResultSet rs = null;

        // make sure this is an allowed value
        if (allowedValue(value)) {
            try {
                stmt = conn.createStatement();
                // first delete any record previosly
                // inserted for this host name and survey ID

                stmt.executeQuery(
                    "DELETE FROM SurveyData WHERE SurveyID="
                        + surveyId
                        + " AND Source='"
                        + notes
                        + "'");
                stmt.executeQuery(
                    "INSERT INTO SurveyData "
                        + "(SurveyID,Value,Source) VALUES("
                        + surveyId
                        + ",'"
                        + value
                        + "','"
                        + notes
                        + "')");

                // iterate through the survey fields
                int count;
                int idx = -1;
                while (iterator.hasNext()) {
                    FormFieldBean field =
                        (FormFieldBean) iterator.next();
                    count = 0;
                    rs =
```

```
                        stmt.executeQuery(
                            "SELECT COUNT(*) FROM SurveyData "
                                + "WHERE SurveyID="
                                + surveyId
                                + " AND Value='"
                                + field.getValue()
                                + "'");
                    if (rs.next())
                        count = rs.getInt("COUNT(*)");
                    graph.addBar(idx, field.getValue(),
                        count, getNextBarColor());
                    responses += count;
                    idx--;
                }
                graph.setMaxValue(responses);

            } catch (SQLException e1) {
                System.out.println("SQL Error: " + e1);
            } finally {
                try {
                    if (stmt != null) {
                        stmt.close();
                    }
                } catch (SQLException e2) {
                };
            }
        }

        // get the survey results
        Frame frame = null;
        Graphics g = null;
        try {
            File tempHtm = null;
            FileWriter out = null;
            String path = context.getRealPath("/");

            // create the graph
            String jpgName = graph.createJpg(path);
            File tempDir = new File(path);
            tempHtm = File.createTempFile(
                "survey-", ".htm", tempDir);
            out = new FileWriter(tempHtm);
            out.write("<html><body>");
            out.write("<img border=\"0\" src=\"/");
            out.write(jpgName);
```

*Continued*

**Listing 22-6** *(Continued)*

```java
            out.write(
                "\" width=\"" + graph.getWidth() + "\" height=\""
                + graph.getHeight() + "\">");
            out.close();
            setFormDonePage("/" + tempHtm.getName());
            setFormPage(getFormDonePage());
            System.out.println("FormDonePage " + getFormDonePage());
            context.setAttribute(getName()
                + "-lastgraph", getFormDonePage());
        } catch (Exception e) {
            System.out.println("exception " + e.toString());
        } finally {
            if (g != null)
                g.dispose();
            if (frame != null)
                frame.removeNotify();
        }

        return;
    }
    public void setServletInfo(
        javax.servlet.http.HttpServletRequest newRequest,
        javax.servlet.http.HttpServletResponse newResponse,
        javax.servlet.ServletContext newContext) {

        super.setServletInfo(newRequest,
            newResponse, newContext);

        String newSurvey =
            String.valueOf(getSurveyNumber()) + "-abc";
        String filledSurvey =
            String.valueOf(getSurveyNumber()) + "-def";
        String surveyNum =
            String.valueOf(getSurveyNumber());

        // look for an existing survey cookie in the request
        boolean newSurveyCookie = false;
        boolean filledSurveyCookie = false;
        Cookie[] cookies = request.getCookies();
        for (int i = 0; i < cookies.length; i++) {
            if (cookies[i].getName().equals(getName() + newSurvey))
                newSurveyCookie = true;
            else
                if (cookies[i].getName().equals(getName()
                    + filledSurvey)) {
```

```
                    filledSurveyCookie = true;
            }
    }


    /* if this is the first time around
        (say after restarting tomcat) then
        there will be no lastGraph to display
        for users who have already voted. So
        let the first person in this situation vote
        again. Vote early, vote often!
        */

    String lastGraph = (String) context.getAttribute(getName()
        + "-lastgraph");
    if ((filledSurveyCookie) && (lastGraph == null)) {
        filledSurveyCookie = false;
    }


    if (filledSurveyCookie) {
        if (lastGraph != null) {
            setNewForm(false);
            setFormDonePage(lastGraph);
            setFormPage(lastGraph);
        }
    } else {
        if (isNewForm()) {
            // create the new form cookie
            Cookie cookie = new Cookie(getName()
                + newSurvey, surveyNum);
            cookie.setMaxAge(60 * 60 * 24 * 30);
            response.addCookie(cookie);
        } else {
            // this request is a form submission
            if (newSurveyCookie) {
                // create the saved form cookie
                // create the new form cookie
                Cookie cookie = new Cookie(getName()
                    + filledSurvey, surveyNum);
                cookie.setMaxAge(60 * 60 * 24 * 30);
                response.addCookie(cookie);
                saveSurvey = true;
            } else {
                setMessage("You must have cookies"
                    + " enabled to fill out this survey");
                setNewForm(true);
```

*Continued*

**Listing 22-6** *(Continued)*

```
                }
            }
        }

    }

    public void setSurveyNumber(int newSurveyNumber) {
        surveyNumber = newSurveyNumber;
    }

    public boolean validate() {
        String value = getFieldValue(handlerName);
        if ((value != null) && (allowedValue(value)))
            return true;
        else
            return false;
    }
}
```

# Getting the Survey Results

The FormSurveyBean class assembles the survey results in its save() method by iterating through the radio buttons stored in the form and counting the number of matching records in the SurveyData table:

```
"SELECT COUNT(*) FROM SurveyData "
    + "WHERE SurveyID="
    + surveyId
    + " AND Value='"
    + field.getValue()
    + "'");
if (rs.next())
    count = rs.getInt("COUNT(*)");
```

The save() method stores the record counts so it can create a graph of this data to display to the user. For that, FormSurveyBean uses an instance of GraphBean.

## Graphing the survey results

The FormSurveyBean class obtains a JPG of the survey results from GraphBean, in Listing 22-7.

**Listing 22-7: The GraphBean Instance Models Bar Graphs and Can Render
a JPG Image to a File**

```
package com.covecomm.deweb.graph;

import java.awt.*;

import java.util.*;
import java.awt.image.BufferedImage;
import java.awt.font.*;
import com.sun.image.codec.jpeg.*;
import java.io.*;
public class GraphBean {

    class Bar {
        private float value;
        private String name;
        private int height;
        private int width;
        private int maxWidth;
        private Color barColor;
        private String barName;
        private float barvalue;
        private float barValue;

        public java.awt.Color getBarColor() {
            return barColor;
        }

        public java.lang.String getBarName() {
            return barName;
        }

        public float getBarValue() {
            return barValue;
        }

        public void setBarColor(java.awt.Color newBarColor) {
            barColor = newBarColor;
        }

        public void setBarName(java.lang.String newBarName) {
            barName = newBarName;
        }

        public void setBarValue(float newBarValue) {
```

*Continued*

**Listing 22-7** *(Continued)*

```
            barValue = newBarValue;
        }
    };
    private HashMap bars;
    private Font font;
    private int inset = 5;
    private int width;
    private int height;
    private float maxValue = 100;

    public GraphBean() {
        super();
        font = new Font("sansserif", Font.BOLD, 10);
        bars = new HashMap();
    }

    public void addBar(int newID, String newName,
        float newValue, Color newColor) {
        Integer ID = new Integer(newID);
        Bar bar = (Bar) bars.get(ID);
        if (bar == null) {
            bar = new Bar();
            bars.put(ID, bar);
            System.out.println("created new bar");
        }
        bar.setBarName(newName);
        bar.setBarValue(newValue);
        System.out.println("set bar value to " + bar.getBarValue());
        bar.setBarColor(newColor);
    }

    public void draw(Graphics g) {
        if (bars.isEmpty()) return;

        g.setFont(font);

        // getHeight actually calculates the appropriate height
        setHeight(getHeight());

        // create a new graphics object of the correct size
        g = g.create(0, 0, width, height);

        // draw the graph foreground
        g.setColor(fgColor);
```

```
g.fillRect(0, 0, width, height);

// set the start Y position
int yPos = inset;

// draw the bars
Bar bar;
int barWidth = width - (inset * 2) - 2;
int xPos = inset;
Iterator iterator = bars.values().iterator();
while (iterator.hasNext()) {
    bar = (Bar) iterator.next();
    g.setColor(bar.getBarColor());

    // calcuate the bar width
    if (bar.getBarValue() != 0) {
        int thisBarWidth = (int)
            (barWidth * (bar.getBarValue() / maxValue));
        g.fill3DRect(xPos, yPos, thisBarWidth, barHeight,↵
            true);
    }
    yPos += (barHeight + inset);

}

// draw a box around the bars
g.setColor(Color.black);
g.drawRect(
    inset,
    inset - 3,
    barWidth,
    (bars.size() * (barHeight + inset)) - inset + 6);

// draw the legend
yPos += inset;
iterator = bars.values().iterator();
while (iterator.hasNext()) {
    bar = (Bar) iterator.next();
    g.setColor(bar.getBarColor());
    g.fill3DRect(xPos, yPos + 3, legendHeight - 6,
        legendHeight - 6, true);
    g.setColor(Color.black);
    g.drawString(bar.getBarName(), xPos + legendHeight,
        yPos + legendHeight - 3);
    yPos += (legendHeight + inset);
```

*Continued*

**Listing 22-7** *(Continued)*

```java
        }

    }

    public float getMaxValue() {
        return maxValue;
    }

    public void setMaxValue(float newMaxValue) {
        maxValue = newMaxValue;
    }

    private int barHeight = 16;
    private java.awt.Color bgColor = Color.gray;
    private java.awt.Color fgColor = Color.white;
    private HashMap fontHeights;
    private int legendHeight = 12;
    private int tics;

    public String createJpg(String dirName) {
        File tempJpg = null;
        FileOutputStream outJpg = null;
        Frame frame = null;
        Graphics g = null;
        try {
            // create the jpg file
            File tempDir = new File(dirName);
            tempJpg =
                File.createTempFile("survey-", ".htm", tempDir);

            // prepare to draw the jpg
            frame = new Frame();
            frame.addNotify();

            // Get a graphics region, using the Frame
            Image image =
                frame.createImage(getWidth(), getHeight());
            g = image.getGraphics();

            // draw the graph
            draw(g);

            // create an output stream
            outJpg = new FileOutputStream(tempJpg);
```

```
            JPEGImageEncoder jpg =
                JPEGCodec.createJPEGEncoder(outJpg);

            // set the image quality to max
            JPEGEncodeParam param =
                jpg.getDefaultJPEGEncodeParam((BufferedImage)↲
                    image);
            param.setQuality(0.95f, false);
            jpg.setJPEGEncodeParam(param);

            // encode the image
            jpg.encode((BufferedImage) image);
            outJpg.close();

        } catch (IOException e) {
            System.out.print("IO Exception creating jpg "
                + e.toString());
        } catch (Exception e) {
            System.out.println("exception " + e.toString());
        } finally {
            if (g != null)
                g.dispose();
            if (frame != null)
                frame.removeNotify();
        }
        if (tempJpg != null)
            return (tempJpg.getName());
        else
            return "";
    }

public int getBarHeight() {
    return barHeight;
}

public java.util.HashMap getBars() {
    return bars;
}

public java.awt.Color getBgColor() {
    return bgColor;
}

public java.awt.Color getFgColor() {
    return fgColor;
```

*Continued*

**Listing 22-7** *(Continued)*

```java
    }

    public java.awt.Font getFont() {
        return font;
    }

    public int getHeight() {
        height = (bars.size()
            * (barHeight + (inset * 2) + legendHeight))
        + (inset * 3);
        return height;
    }

    public int getInset() {
        return inset;
    }

    public int getLegendHeight() {
        return legendHeight;
    }

    public int getTics() {
        return tics;
    }

    public int getWidth() {
        return width;
    }

    public void setBarHeight(int newBarHeight) {
        barHeight = newBarHeight;
    }

    public void setBars(java.util.HashMap newBars) {
        bars = newBars;
    }

    public void setBgColor(java.awt.Color newBgColor) {
        bgColor = newBgColor;
    }

    public void setFgColor(java.awt.Color newFgColor) {
        fgColor = newFgColor;
    }
```

## Using Inner Classes

As of the 1.1 release of Java, you can create a class inside another class. These classes are called *inner classes*, and you can declare them inside a class, or even inside a block of code. Inner classes are not visible outside the class in which you declare them, but they can see all of the class's instance variables, and when declared inside a code block they can see all of the variables that are in scope in that code block.

Inner classes are useful in many situations, particularly when you have a large class that you'd like to break into smaller, more maintainable classes. If you use all top-level classes, then each of these classes is public. If you create inner classes instead of top-level classes, you can still hide your multiclass implementation.

```
    public void setFont(java.awt.Font newFont) {
        font = newFont;
    }


    public void setHeight(int newHeight) {
        height = newHeight;
    }


    public void setInset(int newInset) {
        inset = newInset;
    }


    public void setLegendHeight(int newLegendHeight) {
        legendHeight = newLegendHeight;
    }


    public void setTics(int newTics) {
        tics = newTics;
    }


    public void setWidth(int newWidth) {
        width = newWidth;
    }
}
```

The GraphBean instance uses an inner class called Bars to model the individual graph bars. For the most part GraphBean uses a typical approach to drawing images; you can follow the code in the draw method. The createJpg() method calls draw:

```
draw(g);
```

After `createJpg()` calls draw, it creates a `FileOutputStream` using a randomly named temporary file.

```
outJpg = new FileOutputStream(tempJpg);
```

The `createJpg()` method then passes this output stream to an encoder, which takes the image created by draw and writes it to disk in the appropriate format.

 While `GraphBean` works just fine on a Windows machine, it may or may not be able to create an image on a Unix/Linux machine because the graphics subsystem requires the operating system's GUI to create a drawing surface, even though it never displays the image. You have two options: either run X-Windows (which may not be ideal), or get your hands on Xvfb, which is a virtual frame buffer for Unix and Unix-like operating systems.

## Image encoders

When Web sites create images, they typically do so in GIF format, using either a licensed GIF encoder or one of the freely available encoders. The GIF format is subject to licensing restrictions, but happily, Java2 includes a JPG encoder, which serves the purpose just as well.

### CREATING A JPG IMAGE

The `createJpg()` method creates the graph JPG by using an instance of `JPEGImageEncoder`, which it obtains from the static `JPEGCodec` object.

```
JPEGImageEncoder jpg =
    JPEGCodec.createJPEGEncoder(outJpg);
```

### CREATING A QUALITY JPG IMAGE

If you encode a JPG image with the default settings, chances are you'll get a graph that looks a bit fuzzy around the edges, and which may have some unpleasant dithering or other lossy compression features. The solution is to obtain the `JPEGEncodeParam` object from the image encoder, using a `BufferedImage` downcast of the image as a parameter. If you set the quality to 1.0, the encoder uses lossless compression. Use values less than 1.0 for better compression. A value of 0.95 reduces image size by approximately ⅓ without significantly degrading quality. The sample five-element graph comes in at about 10K at high-color resolution, although that's still about twice the size of a comparable 256 color GIF.

```
// set the image quality to max
JPEGEncodeParam param =
    jpg.getDefaultJPEGEncodeParam((BufferedImage) image);
```

```
param.setQuality(0.95f, false);
jpg.setJPEGEncodeParam(param);
```

Finally, let the encoder do its thing, and write the image out to the file.

```
// encode the image
jpg.encode((BufferedImage) image);
outJpg.close();
```

## DISPLAYING THE IMAGE TO THE USER

In normal form operations, on successful completion `ControllerServlet` sets the `includePage` attribute to the value returned by the form JavaBean's `getFormDonePage()` method. The `FormGraphBean` class uses this approach to display the form results instead of the form itself. Listing 22-8 shows an excerpt from the `createJpg()` method, demonstrating how `FormGraphBean` creates a small HTML file with some message text and a link to the JPG.

**Listing 22-8: The createJpg() Method Creates an HTML File with a Link to the Graph Image**

```
String jpgName = graph.createJpg(path);
File tempDir = new File(path);
tempHtm = File.createTempFile("survey-", ".htm", tempDir);
StringBuffer message = new StringBuffer("<p>"
                    + getMessage());
message.append(" (");
message.append(responses);
message.append(" response");
if (responses > 1)
    message.append("s");
message.append(")</p>");
out = new FileWriter(tempHtm);
out.write("<html><body>");
out.write(message.toString());
out.write("<img border=\"0\" src=\"/");
out.write(jpgName);
out.write("\" width=\"" + graph.getWidth()
    + "\" height=\"" + graph.getHeight()
    + "\">");
out.close();
setFormDonePage("/" + tempHtm.getName());
setFormPage(getFormDonePage());
context.setAttribute(getName()
                    + "-lastgraph", getFormDonePage());
```

## Keeping the user informed

When a user submits the survey, FormSurveyBean shows the results immediately. If the user returns later and requests the same page, FormSurveyBean detects the return visit via the cookie placed on the user's machine when the user completes the survey form. Since this visit is a return one, displaying the current state of the survey would be a courtesy. It's quite easy to show the current survey results; simply store the URI of the last survey image in the application's context and retrieve and send it back to the user via the getFormDonePage() method as needed:

```
String lastGraph = (String) context.getAttribute(getName()
    + "-lastgraph");
if ((filledSurveyCookie) && (lastGraph == null)) {
    filledSurveyCookie = false;
}
if (filledSurveyCookie) {
    if (lastGraph != null) {
        setNewForm(false);
        setFormDonePage(lastGraph);
        setFormPage(lastGraph);
    }
}
```

# Summary

One-question surveys are a quick and easy way to collect information from your users and provide immediate, graphical feedback, which can help generate interest in your Web site. Key points to remember include:

◆ Surveys are forms, and they can be handled just like any other form.

◆ The FormSurveyBean class's save() method stores survey results in a MySQL table, and creates a JPG on the fly to graph the results.

◆ The JPG encoder uses lossy compression by default, which can degrade image quality; for a good quality graph you'll want to set compression loss to a minimum, or use an encoder that can create an image in a loss-less format such as GIF.

◆ It's almost impossible to prevent duplicate votes, but you can come close by using cookies, and you may also want to allow only one vote per IP address.

# Chapter 23

# Collecting Server Statistics

## IN THIS CHAPTER

◆ Deciding which way to log requests

◆ Logging requests mapped to a servlet

◆ Using a request interceptor to log requests

◆ Interpreting logs

ONE OF THE VERY ENJOYABLE aspects of running a Web site is seeing people visit it! Most Web servers provide standard ways of logging HTTP requests to a file, which can then be read by a Web statistics package that summarizes site activity. Log files are also important for checking for broken links and attempts to break into restricted parts of a Web site.

Tomcat, at least in release 3.*x*, doesn't include a logging facility — most likely because the developers originally expected most Tomcat users would run behind a Web server like Apache, which can create the necessary logs. Increasingly, however, Tomcat users are finding that Tomcat is quite capable as a standalone Web server, if you can live without logging. Happily, it isn't that difficult to add this feature. In this chapter you'll learn how to create a `RequestInterceptor` that logs all server requests to a MySQL database.

# Deciding Which Way to Log Requests

You can approach request logging in Tomcat 3.*x* in two ways. One way is to map requests to a controller servlet, and log all of those requests. The other way is to use a special class called a `RequestInterceptor`, which, as the name suggests, intercepts Web server requests.

## Logging from the controller servlet

Mapping requests to a controller servlet seems like an ideal solution, since it can be easily implemented at a Web-application level, without necessitating any changes to Tomcat's own configuration. But mapping requests is highly limiting as well.

Typically, you map only certain kinds of requests to a servlet. In the `deweb-example` Web application, all requests for `.html` files and all requests for `.frm` files are redirected to the controller. Tomcat's static file interceptor handles all other requests. Consider the case where a user requests a `.html` document that is handled by the controller servlet. The servlet passes the URI to a suitable JSP, which includes the requested page. Suppose that page (articles.jsp) contains some GIF files. Table 23-1 shows the requests that ensue.

**TABLE 23-1  FILE REQUESTS IN A DEWEB-EXAMPLE PAGE RETRIEVAL**

| Request | Action Taken | Controller Intercepts |
|---|---|---|
| `/somearticle.html` | Forward to articles.jsp | Yes |
| `articles.jsp` | Include `/somearticle.newextension` | No |
| `/somearticle.newextension` | Includes image links | No |
| `/image1.gif` | No special action | No |
| `/image2.gif` | No special action | No |

As you can see in Table 23-1, the only file the controller servlet logs is the initial page request. Your logging system won't pick up attempts to download files that aren't mapped to your controller servlet, such as included article pages or image files.

You could set up a servlet mapping for GIF files, but then you'd need to do something like the `IncludePageTag`'s extension mapping trick or you'd have to create an image server servlet. On the other hand, you could write the servlet to log the request and then serve up the file directly, but then you're duplicating code that already exists inside Tomcat.

This is starting to sound like a lot of work.

There is a place for logging in a controller servlet, but for logging all requests, you really need to consider writing a `RequestInterceptor`. I'll cover the `RequestInterceptor` approach a little later.

In Tomcat 4, you can use valves to intercept requests. Valves take a slightly different and theoretically more efficient approach to request handling than `RequestInterceptors`, and you can use them at the Web-application level. For more information on valves, download a Tomcat 4 build from `jakarta.apache.org`.

# Where to keep the log

In addition to deciding where to place your logging code, you have a choice of where to keep the log data. Traditionally, logs are flat text files. Text files are always an option, but you should also consider storing the log in a MySQL (or another database) table. A SQL log offers the following advantages:

♦ The Web server can create log entry timestamps, which, if the database server is on a separate machine, removes one additional bit of processing from the Web server.

♦ SQL's query capabilities are a great improvement over piping a text file through a search utility like `grep`.

♦ You can prune unwanted data from a SQL table far more easily than from a text file.

♦ You can still generate a text file from the SQL data if that's what the Web statistics program requires.

♦ SQL logs make locating errors associated with particular users much easier.

I provide a few tips and tricks for extracting log data from a SQL table later on in this chapter.

# Log formats

You may want to be aware of certain standard log formats as you design your logging code. If you go with a SQL log table, you have the option of creating whatever log format you like later, but of course you won't be able to supply any data you haven't already collected.

The Common Log Format supplies the following information, with fields separated by spaces:

```
host ident user date "request" status bytes
```

Web servers don't necessarily provide data for each of these fields, and if a field has no value, the server inserts a hyphen. The log data can include the following:

♦ `host` – either the IP address or the fully qualified domain name. Normally when the server creates the log it only stores the IP address, since reverse DNS lookups take time. A utility program or the statistics package translates the IP address to a host name before running the statistics.

♦ `ident` – identifying information returned by the client. Collecting `ident` data can introduce lengthy delays while the server makes a request of `identd` on the client machine, and is not commonly used by servers or supported by clients.

◆ `user` – the username, if the user has logged in.

◆ `date` – the date/time of the request, in [day/month/year:hour:minute: second timezone] format. Timezone is +/- a four digit hour, relative to GMT.

◆ `request` – the URL requested, which is enclosed in double quotes.

◆ `status` – the status code of the request.

◆ `bytes` – the number of bytes sent.

A variant on the Common Log Format adds host information before the `host` field. A typical line in a log (not storing virtual host information) looks like this:

```
206.27.161.176 - - [04/Dec/2000:12:50:46 -0600]
    "GET /images/cm_cdr.gif HTTP/1.0" 200 1615
```

This example doesn't have any `ident` or user information, so the log contains hyphens in place of these fields. The HTTP request is a `GET` using the HTTP 1.0 protocol, and the status code is 200, meaning the request was successful. The file size is 1615 bytes.

Log files also frequently store the referrer, and the browser or agent. An entry in Common Log Format would have something like the following appended to each line:

```
"http://www.clarionmag.com/common/links_bycategory.html"
    "Mozilla/4.0 (compatible; MSIE 5.0; Windows NT; DigExt)"
```

Agent information can be most useful. Once you know which browsers your users have, you can determine which browser-specific features you can safely use in your site. Or at least you'll have an idea of how many users you can potentially annoy.

# Logging Mapped Requests

As mentioned earlier, when logging a mapped request you're really only logging a fraction of the actual requests made to the server, so you can afford to get a fair amount of detail. Listing 23-1 shows a logging bean that records the IP address, user name (which the controller servlet determines – see Chapter 19), request, status code, referrer, browser, and any text notes.

**Listing 23-1: The LoggerBean Class**

```
package com.covecomm.deweb.util;

import java.util.*;
import java.sql.*;
```

```
import javax.servlet.*;
import javax.servlet.http.*;

public class LoggerBean {
    private ConnectionPoolAdapter dbPool;

    public LoggerBean() {
        super();
    }

    public void setDbPool(ConnectionPoolAdapter newDbPool) {
        dbPool = newDbPool;
    }

    public void write(String IP, String user, String request) {
        write(IP, user, request, "");
    }

    public void write(String IP, String user, String request, int ↵
status) {
        write(IP, user, request, status, "", "", "");
    }

    public void write(
        String IP,h
        String user,
        String request,
        Int status,
        String referrer,
        String userAgent,
        String info) {
        if (dbPool == null)
            System.out.println(
                "No dbpool, can't record log events");
        else {
            Connection conn = null;
            Statement stmt = null;
            try {
                conn = dbPool.getConnection();
                stmt = conn.createStatement();
                if (IP == null)
                    IP = "";
                if (user == null)
                    user = "";
```

*Continued*

**Listing 23-1** *(Continued)*

```
                if (request == null)
                    request = "";
                if (info == null)
                    info = "";
                if (referrer == null)
                    referrer = "";
                if (userAgent == null)
                    userAgent = "";
                stmt.executeQuery(
                    "insert into AccessLog "
                        + "(IP,User,Request,"
                        + "Status,Referrer,UserAgent,Info) "
                        | "VALUES('"
                        + IP
                        + "','"
                        + user
                        + "','\""
                        + request
                        + "\","
                        + status
                        + ",'"
                        + referrer
                        + "','\""
                        + userAgent
                        + "\",'\""
                        + info
                        + "\"')");

            } catch (SQLException e1) {
                System.out.println("SQL Error: " + e1);
            } finally {
                try {
                    if (stmt != null) {
                        stmt.close();
                    }
                } catch (SQLException e2) {
                };

                // Return the connection to the Broker
                if (dbPool != null)
                    dbPool.freeConnection(conn);
```

```
            }

        }
    }
    public void write(
        String user,
        HttpServletRequest request,
        String info,
        int status) {
        StringBuffer uri =
            new StringBuffer(request.getServletPath());
        String s = request.getQueryString();
        String ref = request.getHeader("Referrer");
        if (ref == null)
            ref = "";
        String agent = request.getHeader("User-Agent");
        if (agent == null)
            agent = "";
        if (s != null)
            uri.append(" " + s);
        if (user == null)
            user = "";
        if (info == null)
            info = "";
        uri.append(" " + request.getProtocol());
        write(
            request.getRemoteAddr(),
            user,
            uri.toString().trim(),
            Integer.toString(status),
            info,
            ref.trim(),
            agent.trim());
    }

}
```

Normally, a bean would be as implementation-independent as possible and would not import any servlet-related packages, but as this bean's only purpose is to log HTTP requests I'm prepared to bend the rules just a little. This lets me create a write() method that takes a servlet request as a parameter, which means that the logging bean can extract a lot of the information needed for the log from the request.

All calls to the LoggerBean write() method ultimately result in a call to the write() method with seven parameters, which does the actual insert in the SQL database. This method hard codes the table and field names; the class would be more flexible if you set these values using initialization parameters.

The `LoggerBean` class uses a connection pool object called `dbPool`. The `WebAppSetup` servlet creates this object, which places the pool in the Web application context. It then creates the logger object and gives it a reference to the pool:

```
LoggerBean logger = new LoggerBean();
logger.setDbPool(dbPool);
```

The `ControllerServlet` has a `findLogger()` method that verifies the servlet has a reference to the logger, and then calls the logger's `write()` method:

```
if (findLogger())
    logger.write(username, request,status,"uri requested");
```

The `LoggerBean` class uses a table created with the script shown in Listing 23-2.

**Listing 23-2: SQL Code to Create the AccessLog Table**

```
CREATE TABLE AccessLog(
LogID INT NOT NULL AUTO_INCREMENT,
IP VARCHAR(16),
DateTime TIMESTAMP,
User VARCHAR(30),
Request VARCHAR(255),
Status INT,
Referrer VARCHAR(255),
UserAgent VARCHAR(255),
Info TEXT,
PRIMARY KEY (LogID));
```

As with any SQL table, `AccessLog` has a primary key, but that's the only index currently used on this table. If the table becomes particularly large, and you're doing many queries, you'll probably want to add some additional indexes. Do keep in mind that the more indexes you add to a table, the longer it takes to insert a record, since all the indexes have to be updated as well. Make your indexes as few and as short as possible.

# Using Request Interceptors

Logging mapped requests is great, but it doesn't tell you about all the traffic really going on at your Web site. To get that information with Tomcat 3.*x*, you have to write a request interceptor. Request interceptors handle core Tomcat functions such as displaying directory listings (where allowed), mapping requests to servlets, and

returning static files to the user. You can find these classes in the `org.apache.`
`tomcat.request` package. You configure request interceptors via the `conf/`
`server.xml` global configuration file; Listing 23-3 shows the stock interceptor
settings.

**Listing 23-3: Configuration Settings for Request Interceptors, from server.xml**

```
<!-- ===================== Interceptors ===================== -->


        <!--
        ContextInterceptor className="org.apache.tomcat.↵
context.LogEvents"
        -->


        <ContextInterceptor className="org.apache.tomcat. ↵
context.AutoSetup" />


        <ContextInterceptor
            className="org.apache.tomcat.context.WebXmlReader" />


        <!-- Uncomment out if you have JDK1.2 and want to use policy
        <ContextInterceptor
            className="org.apache.tomcat.context.PolicyInterceptor" />
        -->


        <ContextInterceptor
            className="org.apache.tomcat.context.LoaderInterceptor" />
        <ContextInterceptor
            className="org.apache.tomcat.context.DefaultCMSetter" />
        <ContextInterceptor
            className="org.apache.tomcat.context.WorkDirInterceptor" />


        <!-- Request processing -->
        <!-- Session interceptor will extract the session id↵
from cookies and
            deal with URL rewriting ( by fixing the URL )
          -->
        <RequestInterceptor
            className="org.apache.tomcat.request.SessionInterceptor" />


        <!-- Find the container ( context and prefix/extension map )
            for a request.
          -->
        <RequestInterceptor
            className="org.apache.tomcat.request.SimpleMapper1"
            debug="0" />
```

*Continued*

**Listing 23-3** *(Continued)*

```
        <!-- Non-standard invoker, for backward compat. ( /servlet/* )
             You can modify the prefix that is matched by adjusting the
             "prefix" parameter below.  Be sure your modified pattern
             starts and ends with a slash.

             NOTE:  This prefix applies to *all* web applications that
             are running in this instance of Tomcat.
        -->
        <RequestInterceptor
            className="org.apache.tomcat.request.InvokerInterceptor"
            debug="0" prefix="/servlet/" />

        <!-- "default" handler - static files and dirs.  Set the
             "suppress" property to "true" to suppress directory↵
listings
             when no welcome file is present.

             NOTE:  This setting applies to *all* web applications that
             are running in this instance of Tomcat.
        -->
        <RequestInterceptor
            className="org.apache.tomcat.request.StaticInterceptor"
            debug="0" suppress="false" />
```

Creating your own interceptors is not that difficult; you just create a class derived from `org.apache.tomcat.core.BaseInterceptor` and follow the example of the existing classes regarding initialization.

## Creating a logging request interceptor

To create a logging interceptor, derive a class from `BaseInterceptor`. You're mainly concerned with two methods: `engineInit()` and `requestMap()`. The servlet container calls the `engineInit()` method when the container starts up; use this method to prepare the logging interceptor for use. The servlet container also calls the `requestMap()` method on each and every file request, so that's where you'll do the logging. Listing 23-4 shows a request interceptor, which logs all requests to a SQL table.

**Listing 23-4: A RequestInterceptor for Logging Page Requests to a SQL Table**

```
package com.covecomm.deweb.util;

import org.apache.tomcat.core.*;
import java.io.*;
import java.sql.*;
```

```
public class LoggingInterceptor extends BaseInterceptor {

    public LoggingInterceptor() {
    }

    public void engineInit(ContextManager cm) throws TomcatException {
        super.engineInit(cm);
        try {
            Class.forName(driverName);
            connection =
                DriverManager.getConnection(connectionURL,
                    connectionName, connectionPassword);
            System.out.println("created connection " + connection);
        } catch (ClassNotFoundException ex) {
            throw new RuntimeException("Logger can't find database
driver");
        } catch (SQLException ex) {
            throw new RuntimeException("Logger: SQL Exception " + ex);
        }
    }

    public int requestMap(Request request) {
        Context context = request.getContext();
        String pathInfo = request.getServletPath();
        if (pathInfo == null)
            pathInfo = "";
        String absPath = null;
        long size = 0;
        int status = 0;
        absPath = context.getRealPath(pathInfo);
        if (absPath != null) {
            File file = new File(absPath);
            if (file.exists())
                size = file.length();
            else
                status = 404;
        }
        logRequest(request, status, size);
        return 0;
    }

    private Connection connection = null;
    private String connectionName = null;
```

*Continued*

**Listing 23-4** *(Continued)*

```java
    private String connectionPassword = null;
    private String connectionURL = null;
    private boolean dbInitialized = false;
    private sun.misc.BASE64Decoder decoder; /**
    private String driverName = null;
    private String logColFileSize = null;
    private String logColIP = null; /**
    private String logColRequest = null;
    private String logColStatus = null;
    private String logColUserName = null;
    private String logTable = null;
    private PreparedStatement preparedStmt = null;

    public synchronized void logRequest(
        Request request, int status, long bytes) {

        try {
            if ((connection == null) || connection.isClosed()) {
                System.out.println("Connection is closed");
                connection = DriverManager.getConnection(connectionURL);
                if ((connection == null) || connection.isClosed()) {
                    System.out.println("Unable to reopen the ⏎
connection");
                    return;
                }
            }

            if (preparedStmt == null) {
                String sql =
                    "INSERT INTO "
                        + logTable
                        + " ("
                        + logColIP
                        + ","
                        + logColUserName
                        + ","
                        + logColRequest
                        + ","
                        + logColStatus
                        + ","
                        + logColFileSize
                        + ") VALUES (?,?,?,?,?)";
                System.out.println("Prepared statement: " + sql);
                preparedStmt = connection.prepareStatement(sql);
```

```
            }
        preparedStmt.setString(1, request.getRemoteAddr());
        preparedStmt.setString(2, ""); //request.getRemoteUser());
        preparedStmt.setString(3, request.getRequestURI());
        preparedStmt.setInt(4, status);
        preparedStmt.setLong(5, bytes);
        preparedStmt.executeQuery();
        return;
    } catch (SQLException ex) {

        System.out.println("Error adding log record: " + ex);

        if (preparedStmt != null) {
            try {
                preparedStmt.close();
            } catch (Exception e) {
            }
            preparedStmt = null;
        }
        if (connection != null) {
            try {
                connection.close();
            } catch (Exception e) {
            }
            connection = null;
        }

    }
    return;

}

public void setConnectionName(String connectionName) {
    this.connectionName = connectionName;
}

public void setConnectionPassword(String connectionPassword) {
    this.connectionPassword = connectionPassword;
}

public void setConnectionURL(String connectionURL) {
    this.connectionURL = connectionURL;
}

public void setDriverName(String driverName) {
```

*Continued*

Listing 23-4 *(Continued)*

```
        this.driverName = driverName;
    }

    public void setLogColFileSize(java.lang.String ↵
newLogColFileSize) {
        logColFileSize = newLogColFileSize;
    }

    public void setLogColIP(java.lang.String newLogColIP) {
        logColIP = newLogColIP;
    }

    public void setLogColRequest(java.lang.String newLogColRequest) {
        logColRequest = newLogColRequest;
    }

    public void setLogColStatus(java.lang.String newLogColStatus) {
        logColStatus = newLogColStatus;
    }

    public void setLogColUserName(java.lang.String newLogColUserName) {
        logColUserName = newLogColUserName;
    }

    public void setLogTable(java.lang.String newLogTable) {
        logTable = newLogTable;
    }
}
```

 Because all of Tomcat uses the request interceptor, you need to place the class files in a JAR file and place that JAR in Tomcat's path, or put it under the Tomcat `classes` directory.

# Initializing the interceptor

The `LoggingInterceptor` class takes a somewhat different approach to writing records to the database. Since this interceptor is one that works for all Web applications, it probably isn't a good idea to obtain the database connection from a connection pool that belongs to one Web application. That Web application may not be running. Instead, the interceptor creates its own connection object, based on parameters set in `server.xml`, as shown in Listing 23-5.

Listing 23-5: Initialization Parameters for LoggingInterceptor

```
<RequestInterceptor
          className="org.apache.tomcat.request.LoggingInterceptor"
          driverName="org.gjt.mm.mysql.Driver"
          connectionURL="jdbc:mysql://localhost:3306/↵
deweb-example"
          connectionName="username"
          connectionPassword="password"
          logTable="DetailLog"
          logColIP="IP"
          logColRequest="Request"
          logColStatus="Status"
          logColUserName="User"
          logColFileSize="FileSize"/>
```

You may be surprised to see that at no point does `LoggingInterceptor` actually read any of these values itself. When Tomcat starts up, its XML parsing code reads `server.xml` and deduces the appropriate setter method names. Tomcat then calls those setter methods in each request interceptor.

# Connection handling

The `LoggingInterceptor` class creates the connection from the URL, name, and password specified in server.xml. It then keeps this connection open. To avoid problems with multiple method calls, the interceptor uses a synchronized method to store the actual request information.

You should always use synchronized methods with caution since they remove Tomcat's ability to run multiple copies of those methods simultaneously. Under heavy load situations, with a slow database server, serialized database writes could become a bottleneck. For small to medium volume sites with reasonably fast hardware, however, this approach will probably suffice. MySQL inserts are unlikely to be a limiting factor in site performance, but if you want to guard against delays you can use `INSERT DELAYED` instead of `INSERT`. The `DELAYED` keyword returns control to the logging interceptor immediately, even if MySQL is not immediately ready to write the record to the table.

Also, note that `LoggingInterceptor` isn't storing all of the information that `LoggerBean` stores. The interceptor just tracks the request and the response code, and checks to see if the file actually exists on the server.

The "file exists" check can be a little misleading if you're using servlet mapping to redirect requests to a JSP. The originally requested file may not need to exist at all, and the log report of a missing file will be spurious.

Tomcat treats `LoggingInterceptor` like any other interceptor: it keeps a list of interceptors, and as it receives a request, depending on the nature of the request and the current status, it calls specified methods in each interceptor. The servlet container doesn't call all methods for each request. The container only calls the authorize and authenticate methods, for instance, if it also has a list of roles and Web resources (you can define these in `web.xml`).

One method that Tomcat calls consistently is `requestMap()`, and this place is a convenient one to hook in the request interceptor. All this method does is make that one check for an existing file before calling `logRequest()`.

```
absPath = context.getRealPath(pathInfo);
if (absPath != null) {
    File file = new File(absPath);
    if (file.exists())
        size = file.length();
    else
        status = 404;
}
```

I use `LoggingInterceptor` as a bare-bones logger. I really want it to tell me how many bytes (or a reasonable estimate thereof) I'm serving, how many hits I've taken, and when my peak periods are. You just don't need to retrieve detailed information here. Why track referrer information for the 17 GIF files contained in an HTML document? That's only important in reference to the request for a Web page, which I can trap in the controller servlet.

The following example shows the create script for `DetailLog`, which is what I use with `LoggingInterceptor`. As you can see, this script has fewer fields, and I'm even less likely to use indexes on this table unless absolutely essential, and the script doesn't even declare a primary key.

```
CREATE TABLE DetailLog(
IP VARCHAR(20),
User VARCHAR(30),
DateTime TIMESTAMP,
Request VARCHAR(255),
Status INT,
FileSize INT);
```

# Interpreting the Logs

The best logs won't do you any good if you don't spend any time reading them. And they contain a wealth of useful information. You can use logs to uncover broken links, determine how many bytes your site serves in a given period of time and what your peak times are, and much more. You can even learn a lot about your users, whether or not they're logging in to your server.

# Tracking referrers

The referrer is the page the user visited before the current page, and often, though not always, indicates that a link exists on the referring page. You can learn all sorts of interesting things from the referrer. Consider the following three referrals to one of my Web sites:

```
"http://www.google.com/search?q=excel+chart+hdc"
"http://www.google.com/search?q=Microsoft+word+access+mail+merge+⏎
automate"
"http://www.google.com/search?q=picture+of+a+airplane+flying"
```

All three of these referrals were from the Google search engine, and I can take some satisfaction in knowing Google indexes my site. The first two searches pointed to relevant pages on my site, and the third I am pretty sure came as a surprise to the searcher.

You can extract referral information from the AccessLog table in several ways. One is with the following SELECT DISTINCT statement:

```
select DISTINCT Referrer FROM AccessLog limit 5;
```

which returns

```
+----------------------------------------------------------------+
| Referrer                                                       |
+----------------------------------------------------------------+
| "http://localhost:8080/anything.html"                          |
| "http://localhost:8080/col/index.html"                         |
| "http://localhost:8080/index.html"                             |
| "http://www.clarionmag.com/index.shtml"                        |
| "http://www2.clarionmag.com/cmag/login.html"                   |
+----------------------------------------------------------------+
```

Note the use of SELECT DISTINCT to remove duplicates, so that you see only a list of referrers, not each time the referrer shows up in the table.

If you want to know how many times a referrer sent a user to your site, you can employ the COUNT function and the GROUP BY statement, as follows:

```
SELECT Referrer,COUNT(*) FROM AccessLog GROUP BY Referrer LIMIT 5;
```

The COUNT(*) function sums all the rows that match each unique field (or combination of fields) specified in GROUP BY:

```
+-------------------------------------------------+-----------+
| Referrer                                        | count(*)  |
+-------------------------------------------------+-----------+
| "http://localhost:8080/anything.html"           |         3 |
| "http://localhost:8080/col/index.html"           |         6 |
| "http://localhost:8080/index.html"               |         7 |
| "http://www.clarionmag.com/index.shtml"          |         4 |
| "http://www2.clarionmag.com/cmag/login.html"     |         2 |
+-------------------------------------------------+-----------+
```

This SELECT statement produces a better result, but the referral count is in record order, and seeing referrals sorted by count would be more helpful. That's not a problem; this statement:

```
SELECT Referrer,COUNT(*) AS Total
FROM AccessLog GROUP BY Referrer
ORDER BY Total DESC LIMIT 5;
```

returns:

```
+------------------------------------------------+-------+
| Referrer                                       | Total |
+------------------------------------------------+-------+
| "http://www2.clarionmag.com/col/index.jsp"      |    52 |
| "http://www2.clarionmag.com/index.html"         |    24 |
| "http://www2.clarionmag.com/col/index.html"     |    13 |
| "http://localhost:8080/index.html"              |     7 |
| "http://localhost:8080/col/index.html"          |     6 |
+------------------------------------------------+-------+
```

This last SQL statement declares a temporary field called Total. The Total field contains the value of COUNT(*) and because it's a field, you can use it in an ORDER BY clause. If you sort on Total in descending order, you can see which are the most common sources for referrals. To remove internal links, just use a WHERE clause to filter out the unwanted records:

```
SELECT Referrer,count(*) AS Total FROM AccessLog
WHERE Referrer NOT LIKE '%localhost%'
GROUP BY Referrer ORDER BY Total DESC LIMIT 5;
```

which returns:

```
+----------------------------------------------------+-------+
| Referrer                                           | Total |
+----------------------------------------------------+-------+
| "http://www2.clarionmag.com/col/index.jsp"         |    52 |
| "http://www2.clarionmag.com/index.html"            |    24 |
| "http://www2.clarionmag.com/col/index.html"        |    13 |
| "http://www.clarionmag.com/index.shtml"            |     4 |
| "http://www2.clarionmag.com/col/99-06-virtuallawyer.html" |  4 |
+----------------------------------------------------+-------+
```

## Counting page requests

You can use a similar approach to that taken for referrers to count the number of times pages have been requested. The following statement:

```
SELECT Request,COUNT(*) AS Total FROM AccessLog
GROUP BY Referrer ORDER BY Total DESC LIMIT 5;
```

returns:

```
+-------------------------------------------+-------+
| Request                                   | Total |
+-------------------------------------------+-------+
| "/col/99-03-fomin.html HTTP/1.0"          |  1352 |
| "/cmag/v2/v2n11cciprof.html HTTP/1.1"     |  1224 |
| "/col/99-06-virtuallawyer.html HTTP/1.1"  |  1213 |
| "/anything.html HTTP/1.1"                 |  1210 |
| "/col/index.html HTTP/1.1"                |   697 |
+-------------------------------------------+-------+
```

You can further refine the results with this statement:

```
SELECT Request,COUNT(*) AS Total FROM AccessLog
WHERE TO_DAYS(DateTime) > (TO_DAYS(NOW()) - 7)
GROUP BY Referrer ORDER BY Total DESC LIMIT 7;
```

to specify that you want to see only records from the past seven days:

```
+-------------------------------------------+-------+
| Request                                   | Total |
+-------------------------------------------+-------+
| "/col/99-03-fomin.html HTTP/1.0"          |   311 |
| "/cmag/v2/v2n11cciprof.html HTTP/1.1"     |   221 |
| "/col/99-06-virtuallawyer.html HTTP/1.1"  |   193 |
| "/anything.html HTTP/1.1"                 |   170 |
```

```
| "/col/index.html HTTP/1.1"                      |   137 |
+-------------------------------------------------+-------+
```

## Checking user access

If part of your Web site requires a logon, and you're using the authentication scheme from Chapter 19, then failed login attempts are recorded in the log as a 4010 status (this number is a variation on a 401, which means authorization required — I use 4010 to indicate that the authorization was attempted and failed). This statement:

```
SELECT DateTime,User,Request,COUNT(*) as Total
FROM AccessLog
WHERE Status=4010
GROUP BY User
ORDER BY Total DESC;
```

   returns:

```
+----------------+----------+----------------------------------------+-------+
| DateTime       | User     | Request                                | Total |
+----------------+----------+----------------------------------------+-------+
| 20001221161203 |          | "/cmag/v2/v2n11cciprof.html HTTP/1.1"  |    12 |
| 20001222014936 | password | "/cmag/v2/v2n11cciprof.html HTTP/1.1"  |     8 |
| 20001222014839 | lemmein! | "/cmag/v2/v2n11cciprof.html HTTP/1.1"  |     7 |
| 20001222014827 | thisisme | "/cmag/v2/v2n11cciprof.html HTTP/1.1"  |     4 |
| 20001222014958 | nobody   | "/cmag/v2/v2n11cciprof.html HTTP/1.1"  |     3 |
+----------------+----------+----------------------------------------+-------+
```

   You may also want to query for the IP addresses with failed logins, if you suspect someone is trying to guess passwords.

## Finding missing files

The above examples all use AccessLog, which has the most detail on requests mapped to the controller servlet. To find missing files, however, you may want to use DetailLog, which is created by LoggingInterceptor. This statement:

```
SELECT Request,COUNT(*) AS Total
FROM DetailLog
WHERE Status=404
GROUP BY Request
ORDER BY Total DESC limit 5;
```

   returns:

```
+-------------------------------------+-------+
| Request                             | Total |
+-------------------------------------+-------+
| /cmag/images/blank.gif              |  1034 |
| /cmag/images/headerlineleftbg_2.jpg |   489 |
| /col/index.html                     |    35 |
| /cmag/cm_articles.css               |    33 |
| /anything.html                      |    23 |
+-------------------------------------+-------+
```

In this example, you clearly have some commonly used files not where they ought to be!

## Server stats

It's easy to generate reports from `DetailLog` on how many files you've served, and how many bytes you've served. First the file count can be generated with this statement:

```
SELECT COUNT(*) FROM DetailLog;
```

to return:

```
+----------+
| COUNT(*) |
+----------+
|     9444 |
+----------+
```

This example gives you a simple count of all the log records. You can use date ranges to get a more focused tally.

Files served is also easy, using the `SUM()` method this way:

```
SELECT SUM(FileSize) FROM DetailLog;
```

to get this result:

```
+---------------+
| SUM(FileSize) |
+---------------+
|      67100115 |
+---------------+
```

How about the number of times individual files where served, and the total bytes served per file? It's easy to do with this statement:

```
SELECT Request,COUNT(*) AS Total,
SUM(FileSize) AS Bytes
FROM DetailLog
GROUP BY Request
ORDER BY Bytes DESC
limit 5;
```

to get this result:

```
+--------------------------------+-------+---------+
| Request                        | Total | Bytes   |
+--------------------------------+-------+---------+
| /col/articles/files/06046751.exe |   2 | 2815522 |
| /images/cm_logo3.gif           |   249 | 1572186 |
| /col/articles/files/13202272.exe |   3 | 1337691 |
| /col/article.jsp               |   525 | 1302378 |
| /cmag/betanotice.htm           |   903 | 1013166 |
+--------------------------------+-------+---------+
```

To sort by the number of times a file was served, just change the ORDER BY clause.

It should be no surprise that SQL is ideally suited to reporting on server logs. After all, SQL does stand for Structured Query Language. Just imagine the hoops you'd have to go through to create some of these simple queries with a text file, using piping and filtering. SQL is there for a reason. Make the most of it.

# Summary

Tomcat 3.*x* doesn't include a server logging function, but it isn't that difficult to add your own. You can log requests using a controller servlet, or you can employ a logging RequestInterceptor. Both approaches have their merits and drawbacks. Key points to remember include:

♦ Logging by way of a controller servlet does not trap all requests to the server.

♦ You can log by way of a controller servlet on a per-Web-application basis.

♦ Logging by way of a request interceptor traps all requests to the server.

♦ Logging by way of a request interceptor is Tomcat-specific and applies to all Web applications.

◆ You can use server logs for many purposes, such as locating missing links, tracking logins, monitoring server traffic, determining the browsers your users employ, and much more.

◆ SQL is a powerful tool for examining server logs – you can often retrieve information with a single statement that would be difficult to obtain from a text log.

# Chapter 24

# The Struts Application Framework

## IN THIS CHAPTER

♦ Understanding the concepts behind the Struts application framework

♦ Modeling a user action with an `Action` class

♦ Modeling an HTML form with a `FormBean` class

♦ Understanding the `ActionServlet`'s role in creating and validating forms and actions

♦ Following the sequence of events in a typical Struts application

IF YOU'RE PLANNING on developing a Java-based Web application using the Model-View-Controller, or Model 2 design pattern, you can follow the examples in this book, you can roll your own code, or you can use any of a number of other Model 2 implementations, such as Struts.

Struts is the brainchild of Craig McClanahan, a Sun engineer and one of the Tomcat developers. Craig donated Struts to the Apache Jakarta project, and although a number of other committers are on the project, Craig is still the driving force. In this chapter you'll learn how a Struts application works, how to install the Struts package, and how to run the sample application.

## The Struts Package

You can find Struts and the other Jakarta subprojects at `http://jakarta.apache.org`. As of this writing, the Jakarta subprojects include those listed in Table 24-1.

TABLE 24-1 THE JAKARTA SUBPROJECTS

| Project | Description |
| --- | --- |
| Ant | A Java-based build tool similar to make but uses XML configuration files |
| ECS | The Element Construction Set, used for generating HTML, XML, and other markup languages at runtime |
| ORO | Text processing classes that provide Perl5 regular expressions |
| Regexp | A regular expressions package, but more lightweight than ORO |
| Slide | An implementation of Web-based Distributed Authoring and Versioning (WebDAV), including a content management system, a servlet implementing the WebDAV protocol, a Java WebDAV/HTTP client library, and a command-line client |
| Struts | A Model 2 application framework, and the subject of this chapter |
| Taglibs | An open source tag library repository, including tags for querying application and page contexts, requests, responses and sessions, handling scripts, creating HTML form elements, handling dates/times, JNDI, JSP specification examples, performing regular expressions, using SQL, and processing XML documents with XSL style sheets |
| Tomcat | The JSP and Servlet reference implementation |
| Velocity | An MVC templating system that does not use JSPs |
| Watchdog | Validation tests for the Servlet and JSP specifications |

# Getting Struts

You can download the Struts package from the Struts home page at http://jakarta.apache.org/struts/index.html. As with most Jakarta projects, you have numerous builds to choose from: milestone releases are generally your best bet for the latest stable code. If you want to participate in development, get the nightly builds.

You need the following components to run a Struts application:

◆ A Java2 or later Java Development Kit

◆ A servlet container, such as Tomcat, that is compatible with the Servlet API Specification version 2.2 or later, and with the JavaServer Pages Specification version 1.1 or later

◆ A servlet.jar file with the Servlet and JSP API classes

- An XML parser such as Xerces

If you wish to build Struts from the source distribution, you also need the following:

- The Jakarta Ant build system
- The Xalan XSLT processor version 1_2_D01 or later (Xalan includes Xerces)

# Installing a binary Struts build

To install a binary version of Struts, first download and install the required components. I'll assume you're already running Tomcat, in which case you have the first three requirements (Java2, Tomcat, and `servlet.jar`) in hand. Download the JAXP parser from `http://java.sun.com/xml/` and place `jaxp.jar` in Tomcat's `lib` directory to make it available the next time Tomcat is started. You also need to copy `struts.jar` into Tomcat's `lib` directory.

Struts installation varies slightly depending on whether you're installing the Struts Example Applications, or installing just the Struts package so you can use it with your own applications. I recommend you start with the Example Applications.

### INSTALLING THE EXAMPLE APPLICATIONS

To install the Struts Example Applications, copy `struts-documentation.war`, `struts-example.war`, and `struts-test.war` to Tomcat's `webapps` directory. When you next start or restart Tomcat, these WAR files will be expanded into their own directories.

You don't need to copy any additional files or change any settings since all the files needed by the Struts Example Applications, other than `struts.jar` and the XML parser, are contained in the Example Applications.

### INSTALLING STRUTS IN YOUR OWN APPLICATIONS

To install Struts for use with your own applications you also need `struts.jar` and the XML parser in the Tomcat `lib` directory, but in addition you must copy the Struts tag library descriptor files into your application's `WEB-INF` directory.

### THE STRUTS TAG LIBRARY DESCRIPTORS

As of release 1.0, the Struts package includes the following tag library descriptors:

- `struts-bean.tld` — tags used to define and use JavaBeans
- `struts-logic.tld` — tags useful for various script-like operations such as comparisons, string matching, and looping through arrays and collections
- `struts-html` — tags for creating HTML components, largely for forms (but also for links)

◆ `struts-template.tld` — tags for creating JSP templates (where one page is made up of several included pages)

For more information on the contents of these tag libraries, see Appendix A.

# Struts Concepts

As an MVC Web application framework, Struts uses the same controller servlet concept discussed in this book. The Struts controller contains no application-specific logic, however. Instead, you configure your Struts application by creating XML data in the `WEB-INF/struts-config.xml` file.

You can create several different kinds of XML entries in `struts-config.xml`. One of these is the action mapping represented by an XML `<action/>` tag:

```
<action      path="/logon"
              type="org.apache.struts.example.LogonAction"
              name="logonForm"
              scope="request"
              input="/logon.jsp">
</action>
```

This action mapping means that when the user requests the /logon URL, the controller servlet (called `ActionServlet`) should load (if necessary) and call the `org.apache.struts.example.LogonAction` class, which is derived from the Struts `Action` class. An `Action` class can either direct a response back to the user (normally by way of a view JSP), or it can forward to another `Action` class. You control much of this behavior by settings in `struts-config.xml`.

Besides actions, you can define forwards in `struts-config.xml`. A forward is a shorthand name for a resource such as a JSP. Once you've defined a forward, you can use the forward in links and as an initialization parameter to an action. The `struts-config.xml` file also lets you store information about JavaBeans that model HTML forms.

To create a Struts application, you need to define at least one `Action` class that knows how to respond to a particular request or kind of request, and you need to set up a mapping in `struts-config.xml` so that the controller servlet knows which requests to forward to that `Action` class. I'll explain action mapping in more detail when I discuss the struts-example Web application.

In a simple Struts application, you might have a single `Action` class that contains all the logic for the Web application. It's more likely, however, that you'll create a number of `Action` classes, each listed in `struts-config.xml`. If you use forms, you'll also list your form JavaBeans in `struts-config.xml` so the controller servlet knows when to associate a form JavaBean with a request.

# The struts-example Application

The `struts-example` application demonstrates many Struts features, including action and form handling. The standard Struts configuration files largely determine the behavior of this application, and include the following:

- ◆ `WEB-INF/web.xml` — is the standard Web application configuration file, which is used to set up the `ActionServlet` mapping and the tag library descriptors.

- ◆ `WEB-INF/struts-config.xml` — contains all of the Struts-specific configuration information.

- ◆ `WEB-INF/database.xml` — is an XML file that substitutes for a proper database.

## The web.xml file

In the `struts-example` application, `web.xml` contains a servlet mapping that forwards all requests ending in `.do` to `ActionServlet`, which is the controller in any Struts application:

```
<servlet-mapping>
    <servlet-name>action</servlet-name>
    <url-pattern>*.do</url-pattern>
</servlet-mapping>
```

In the struts-example application, on the main page you see a link that looks like this:

```
<a href="editRegistration.do;jsessionid=eilcc3acd1?action=Create">
Register with the MailReader Demonstration Application</a>
```

The link has some parameters, but the part that matters to the servlet mapping is just this:

```
editRegistration.do
```

When `ActionServlet` receives a request for `editRegistration.do`, it strips off the `.do` extension and looks up the `editRegistration` value in a list of action mappings, which are defined in `WEB-INF/struts-config.xml`. It finds an action (which is represented by an instance of the Struts `Action` class) that corresponds to `editRegistration`, and then passes the request to the `Action`. It's up to the `Action` class to decide what to do with the request, and then dispatch control to an appropriate view mechanism (usually a JSP) via an `ActionForward` object.

The `web.xml` file, shown in Listing 24-1, holds few surprises. The `DatabaseServlet`, which I discuss in the next section, reads/writes `WEB-INF/database.xml`, and `ActionServlet` handles all requests that end in `.do`. Finally, `web.xml` lists the Struts tag library definitions.

**Listing 24-1: The struts-example web.xml File**

```
<?xml version="1.0" encoding="ISO-8859-1"?>

<!DOCTYPE web-app
   PUBLIC "-//Sun Microsystems, Inc.//DTD Web Application 2.2//EN"
   "http://java.sun.com/j2ee/dtds/web-app_2_2.dtd">

<web-app>


  <!-- Database Initialization Servlet Configuration -->
  <servlet>
    <servlet-name>database</servlet-name>
    <servlet-
class>org.apache.struts.example.DatabaseServlet</servlet-class>
    <init-param>
      <param-name>debug</param-name>
      <param-value>2</param-value>
    </init-param>
    <load-on-startup>1</load-on-startup>
  </servlet>


  <!-- Action Servlet Configuration -->
  <servlet>
    <servlet-name>action</servlet-name>
    <servlet-class>org.apache.struts.action.ActionServlet</servlet-class>
    <init-param>
      <param-name>application</param-name>
      <param-value>org.apache.struts.example.ApplicationResources ↵
</param-value>
    </init-param>
    <init-param>
      <param-name>config</param-name>
      <param-value>/WEB-INF/struts-config.xml</param-value>
    </init-param>
```

```
    <init-param>
      <param-name>debug</param-name>
      <param-value>2</param-value>
    </init-param>
    <init-param>
      <param-name>detail</param-name>
      <param-value>2</param-value>
    </init-param>
    <init-param>
      <param-name>validate</param-name>
      <param-value>true</param-value>
    </init-param>
    <load-on-startup>2</load-on-startup>
</servlet>


<!-- Action Servlet Mapping -->
<servlet-mapping>
  <servlet-name>action</servlet-name>
  <url-pattern>*.do</url-pattern>
</servlet-mapping>


<!-- The Welcome File List -->
<welcome-file-list>
  <welcome-file>index.jsp</welcome-file>
</welcome-file-list>

<!-- Application Tag Library Descriptor -->
<taglib>
  <taglib-uri>/WEB-INF/app.tld</taglib-uri>
  <taglib-location>/WEB-INF/app.tld</taglib-location>
</taglib>

<!-- Struts Tag Library Descriptors -->
<taglib>
  <taglib-uri>/WEB-INF/struts-bean.tld</taglib-uri>
  <taglib-location>/WEB-INF/struts-bean.tld</taglib-location>
</taglib>

<taglib>
  <taglib-uri>/WEB-INF/struts-html.tld</taglib-uri>
  <taglib-location>/WEB-INF/struts-html.tld</taglib-location>
</taglib>
```

*Continued*

Listing 24-1 *(Continued)*

```
<taglib>
  <taglib-uri>/WEB-INF/struts-logic.tld</taglib-uri>
  <taglib-location>/WEB-INF/struts-logic.tld</taglib-location>
</taglib>

</web-app>
```

## The struts-example database

The first servlet defined in web.xml is DatabaseServlet. In the struts-example application, this servlet doesn't connect to a JDBC database, but simply reads (using the load method) and writes (using the unload method) the database.xml file in the WEB-INF directory. In a real-world application, you'd want to replace DatabaseServlet with a servlet that reads/writes an actual database (probably one using SQL). However, DatabaseServlet does make for a more portable demonstration. Listing 24-2 shows the contents of database.xml.

**Listing 24-2: The Demonstration "Database" Stored in database.xml**

```
<database>
    <user username="user"
        password="pass"
        fullName="John Q. User"
        fromAddress="John.User@somewhere.com">
        <subscription host="mail.yahoo.com"
            type="imap"
            username="jquser"
            password="foo"/>
        <subscription host="mail.hotmail.com"
            type="pop3"
            username="user1234"
            password="bar"/>
    </user>
</database>
```

The DatabaseServlet servlet translates the database in Listing 24-2 into a hash table of objects by an instance of Digester, which is a Struts XML parser implementation:

```
digester.addObjectCreate("database/user",
  "org.apache.struts.example.User");
digester.addSetProperties("database/user");
digester.addSetNext("database/user", "addUser");
```

```
digester.addObjectCreate("database/user/subscription",
    "org.apache.struts.example.Subscription");
digester.addSetProperties("database/user/subscription");
digester.addSetTop("database/user/subscription", "setUser");
```

The resulting database object resides in the application context so it can be later retrieved and used by Struts tags:

```
getServletContext().setAttribute(Constants.DATABASE_KEY,
    database);
```

## The struts-example struts-config.xml file

The second servlet defined in web.xml (see Listing 24-1) is ActionServlet. The ActionServlet servlet decides what to do with any requests it receives by comparing the request with a list of path mappings, each of which corresponds to an Action. These actions are defined in WEB-INF/struts-config.xml, shown later in this chapter. An action entry may look like this:

```
<action     path="/editRegistration"
              type="org.apache.struts.example.EditRegistrationAction"
              name="registrationForm"
              scope="request"
              validate="false">
```

The attributes of an action mapping include, but are not limited to:

- ◆ path — the context-relative URL path that the controller servlet will map

- ◆ type — the fully qualified name of the class that will handle this action

- ◆ name — the name of the form bean, if any, associated with this action

- ◆ scope — the action's scope, which can be request or session

- ◆ validate — a flag that determines whether the action object's form should be validated

In this action example, a URL of /editRegistration (relative to the application's context) tells ActionServlet to pass the request to an instance of EditRegistrationAction. The action defines the associated form as registrationForm, and to see what that form actually is, you have to look near the beginning of struts-config.xml in the <form-beans> section:

```
<form-bean     name="registrationForm"
                type="org.apache.struts.example.RegistrationForm"/>
```

For definitions of all of the `struts-config.xml` elements and attributes see the `<strutsdir>/lib/struts-config_1_0.dtd` file.

Listing 24-3 shows the `struts-config.xml` used by the Struts Example Application.

**Listing 24-3: The struts-example Web Application's struts-config.xml File**

```xml
<?xml version="1.0" encoding="ISO-8859-1" ?>

<!DOCTYPE struts-config PUBLIC
          "-//Apache Software Foundation//DTD Struts Configuration ↵
1.0//EN"
          "http://jakarta.apache.org/struts/dtds/struts-config_1_0.dtd">

<struts-config>

<!-- ========== Data Source Configuration ============================= -->
<!--
  <data-sources>
    <data-source
       autoCommit="false"
      description="Example Data Source Configuration"
      driverClass="org.postgresql.Driver"
        maxCount="4"
        minCount="2"
        password="mypassword"
            url="jdbc:postgresql://localhost/mydatabase"
            user="myusername"
    />
  </data-sources>
-->

  <!-- ========== Form Bean Definitions =================================== -->
  <form-beans>

    <!-- Logon form bean -->
    <form-bean        name="logonForm"
```

```
                                    type="org.apache.struts.example.LogonForm"/>

    <!-- Registration form bean -->
    <form-bean      name="registrationForm"

type="org.apache.struts.example.RegistrationForm"/>

    <!-- Subscription form bean -->
    <form-bean      name="subscriptionForm"

type="org.apache.struts.example.SubscriptionForm"/>

  </form-beans>


  <!-- ========== Global Forward Definitions ↵
============================== -->
  <global-forwards>
    <forward    name="logon"                path="/logon.jsp"/>
    <forward    name="success"              path="/mainMenu.jsp"/>
  </global-forwards>


  <!-- ========== Action Mapping Definitions ↵
============================== -->
  <action-mappings>

    <!-- Edit user registration -->
    <action     path="/editRegistration"

type="org.apache.struts.example.EditRegistrationAction"
                name="registrationForm"
                scope="request"
                validate="false">
      <forward name="success"
path="/registration.jsp"/>
    </action>

    <!-- Edit mail subscription -->
    <action     path="/editSubscription"
                type="org.apache.struts.example.EditSubscriptionAction"
                name="subscriptionForm"
                scope="request"
                validate="false">
```

*Continued*

**Listing 24-3** *(Continued)*

```
        <forward name="failure"                    path="/mainMenu.jsp"/>
        <forward name="success"
path="/subscription.jsp"/>
    </action>

    <!-- Process a user logoff -->
    <action    path="/logoff"
               type="org.apache.struts.example.LogoffAction">
        <forward name="success"                    path="/index.jsp"/>
    </action>

    <!-- Process a user logon -->
    <action    path="/logon"
               type="org.apache.struts.example.LogonAction"
               name="logonForm"
               scope="request"
               input="/logon.jsp">
    </action>

    <!-- Save user registration -->
    <action    path="/saveRegistration"

type="org.apache.struts.example.SaveRegistrationAction"
               name="registrationForm"
               scope="request"
               input="/registration.jsp"/>

    <!-- Save mail subscription -->
    <action    path="/saveSubscription"

type="org.apache.struts.example.SaveSubscriptionAction"
               name="subscriptionForm"
               scope="request"
               input="/subscription.jsp">
        <forward name="success"
path="/editRegistration.do?action=Edit"/>
    </action>


    <!-- The standard administrative actions available with Struts -->
```

```
<!-- These would be either omitted or protected by security -->
<!-- in a real application deployment -->
<action      path="/admin/addFormBean"
             type="org.apache.struts.actions.AddFormBeanAction"/>
<action      path="/admin/addForward"
             type="org.apache.struts.actions.AddForwardAction"/>
<action      path="/admin/addMapping"
             type="org.apache.struts.actions.AddMappingAction"/>
<action      path="/admin/reload"
             type="org.apache.struts.actions.ReloadAction"/>
<action      path="/admin/removeFormBean"
            type="org.apache.struts.actions.RemoveFormBeanAction"/>
<action      path="/admin/removeForward"
             type="org.apache.struts.actions.RemoveForwardAction"/>
<action      path="/admin/removeMapping"
             type="org.apache.struts.actions.RemoveMappingAction"/>

</action-mappings>

</struts-config>
```

# Forwards

Along with forms and `actions`, `struts-config.xml` defines `forward` elements. At application load time, `ActionServlet` and the Struts XML parser translates these elements to instances of `ActionForward`. Forwards have the following attributes:

◆ `name` – is a name by which the `Action` can obtain the `ActionForward`.

◆ `path` – is the path of the resource to forward to, relative to the application's context.

◆ `redirect` – is an optional attribute, which, if set to true, will cause `ActionForward` to use a `sendRedirect` instead of `RequestDispatcher`.forward.

# The welcome page

The `struts-example` `web.xml` file defines the welcome page as `/index.jsp`, so if you simply specify `http://localhost/struts-example` as the URL, the `struts-example` Web application displays `index.jsp`, as shown in Figure 24-1.

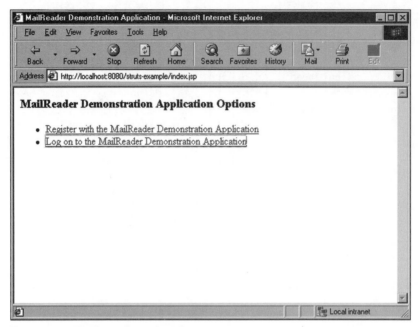

Figure 24-1: The Struts Example welcome page

Don't let the name of the application fool you — struts-example won't read any mail. This application simply demonstrates how you can use Struts to control access to forms, and use forms to update a database (in this case the WEB-INF/database.xml file).

The "Log on to the MailReader Demonstration Application" link points to a URL that is something like this (the session ID will be different on your machine):

```
http://localhost:8080/struts-example/logon.jsp;jsessionid=eilcc3acd1
```

The source for logon.jsp is in Listing 24-4. As you can see from the code, the only part of the link that is hard coded is /logon.jsp. The link tag automatically appends the session ID to the URL.

**Listing 24-4: The Source Code for index.jsp**

```
<%@ page language="java" %>
<%@ taglib uri="/WEB-INF/struts-bean.tld" prefix="bean" %>
<%@ taglib uri="/WEB-INF/struts-html.tld" prefix="html" %>
<%@ taglib uri="/WEB-INF/struts-logic.tld" prefix="logic" %>

<html:html locale="true">
<head>
<title><bean:message key="index.title"/></title>
```

```
<html:base/>
</head>
<body bgcolor="white">

<logic:notPresent name="database" scope="application">
  <font color="red">
    ERROR:  User database not loaded -- check servlet container logs
    for error messages.
  </font>
  <hr>
</logic:notPresent>

<logic:notPresent name="org.apache.struts.action.MESSAGE" scope="application">
  <font color="red">
    ERROR:  Application resources not loaded -- check servlet container
    logs for error messages.
  </font>
</logic:notPresent>

<h3><bean:message key="index.heading"/></h3>
<ul>
<li><html:link page="/editRegistration.do?action=Create"><bean:message ↵
key="index.registration"/></html:link></li>
<li><html:link page="/logon.jsp"><bean:message key="index.logon"/> ↵
</html:link></li>
</ul>


</body>
</html:html>
```

Notice several points of interest in `logon.jsp`. A `message` tag creates the title of the page, obtaining it from the `WEB-INF/classes/org/apache/jakarta/struts/example/ApplicationResources.properties` file using the key `index.title`. The `ApplicationResources.properties` file contains the default locale strings used in the application. You can support additional locales by creating copies of this file with the name `ApplicationResources_xx.properties` where `xx` is the standard locale code.

The `notPresent` tag looks for a particular object in a given context, and if it doesn't find that object, displays an error message. This page checks for the `database` object, and the `MESSAGE` object, both of which are essential to the operation of this application.

Click on the "Log on to the MailReader Demonstration Application" link to go to `/logon.jsp`. Although many links in a Struts application are mapped through `ActionServlet` by way of the `.do` extension, this isn't one of them; it isn't necessary for `logon.jsp` to have any preprocessing.

# The logon form

Figure 24-2 shows the logon page, which simply asks for a user ID and a password.

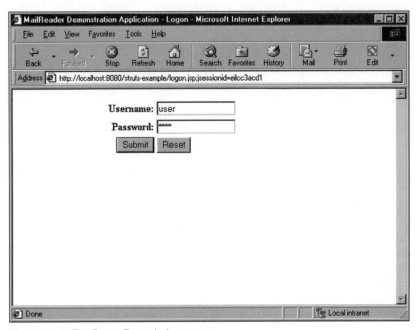

Figure 24-2: The Struts Example logon page

The source for `logon.jsp` is shown in Listing 24-5. As in `index.jsp`, `logon.jsp` uses a `message` tag to obtain the page title, this time with the `logon.title` key. To send the ID and password back to the server, you need a form, and `logon.jsp` uses a set of tags to create and manage that form. The `text` tag creates a text field, the `password` tag a password field, the `submit` tag a Submit button, and so forth.

### Listing 24-5: The Source Code for logon.jsp

```
<%@ page language="java" %>
<%@ taglib uri="/WEB-INF/struts.tld" prefix="struts" %>
<%@ taglib uri="/WEB-INF/struts-bean.tld" prefix="bean" %>
<%@ taglib uri="/WEB-INF/struts-html.tld" prefix="html" %>

<html:html locale="true">
<head>
<title><bean:message key="logon.title"/></title>
<html:base/>
</head>
```

```
<body bgcolor="white">

<struts:errors/>

<html:form action="logon.do" focus="username">
<table border="0" width="100%">

  <tr>
    <th align="right">
      <bean:message key="prompt.username"/>
    </th>
    <td align="left">
      <html:text property="username" size="16" maxlength="16"/>
    </td>
  </tr>

  <tr>
    <th align="right">
      <bean:message key="prompt.password"/>
    </th>
    <td align="left">
      <html:password property="password" size="16" maxlength="16"/>
    </td>
  </tr>

  <tr>
    <td align="right">
      <html:submit property="submit" value="Submit"/>
    </td>
    <td align="left">
      <html:reset/>
    </td>
  </tr>

</table>

</html:form>

</body>
</html:html>
```

When you click on the Submit button, the browser submits the form to the form's action, which is logon.do. The application's web.xml file maps all .do extensions to ActionServlet.

## Processing requests with ActionServlet

When `ActionServlet` receives a `logon.do` request, it strips off the `.do` extension and looks for a match for the remaining string in its list of actions. The `struts-config.xml` file defines the logon action this way:

```
<action    path="/logon"
           type="org.apache.struts.example.LogonAction"
           name="logonForm"
         scope="request"
         input="/logon.jsp">
</action>
```

The logon action's name attribute points to `logonForm`, which `struts-config.xml` defines as follows:

```
<form-bean    name="logonForm"
              type="org.apache.struts.example.LogonForm"/>
```

You can find the source for both these classes in `WEB-INF/classes/org/apache/struts/example`.

When you click on the Submit button, Struts first validates the form, and if that validation is successful, calls `LogonAction`'s `perform()` method, passing the `ActionMapping` object (which contains information about all action mappings for the application), the form, and the request and response. You can find the core code that manages validation in `ActionServlet`'s `process(HttpServletRequest, HttpServletResponse)` method.

You might think that `LogonForm` verifies the user's ID and password, but that's not the case. All `LogonForm` does is make sure that any tag-specific validation rules are met, that is, that any required fields are filled in, and the like. It's `LogonAction` that checks the form data against the authorization database. If the user ID and password are valid, `LogonAction` passes control to the "success" forward, using this code:

```
return (mapping.findForward("success"));
```

Remember that the `LogonForm.process()` method receives an `ActionMapping` as a parameter. The process method uses the `ActionMapping` to look up "success" and sees a `forward` by that name, as defined in `struts-config.xml`:

```
<forward    name="success"    path="/mainMenu.jsp"/>
```

## The main menu

The application's main menu has only two options: "Edit your user registration profile," and "Log off." The following code creates these links:

```
<li><html:link page="/editRegistration.do?action=Edit">
<bean:message key="mainMenu.registration"/>
</html:link></li>
<li><html:link page="/logoff.do">
<bean:message key="mainMenu.logoff"/>
</html:link></li>
```

The text for the link comes from the bean:message tag, and the link from the link tag. Both are .do links, and have corresponding entries in struts-config.xml. The entry for logoff looks like this:

```
<action    path="/logoff"
              type="org.apache.struts.example.LogoffAction">
    <forward name="success"                 path="/index.jsp"/>
    </action>
```

The logoff action is quite simple. LogoffAction's perform method removes the login information from the session object, and forwards to "success", which maps to the index page.

The editRegistration entry in struts-config.xml is similar to the entry for logonForm:

```
<action    path="/editRegistration"

type="org.apache.struts.example.EditRegistrationAction"
              name="registrationForm"
              scope="request"
           validate="false">
    <forward name="success"                 path="/registration.jsp"/>
    </action>
```

The editRegistration action has a form, declared in the form-beans section:

```
<form-bean  name="registrationForm"
              type="org.apache.struts.example.RegistrationForm"/>
```

When ActionServlet receives the editRegistration request, it creates a RegistrationForm and passes this to EditRegistrationAction, which among other things checks to see if the user is logged in, an important consideration since the user may have just bookmarked this page from a previous, logged-in session. If the user is not logged in, EditRegistrationAction forwards to the logon page:

```
return (servlet.findForward("logon"));
```

If the user is logged in, EditRegistrationAction forwards to registration. jsp. This page has a security check which uses the equal tag:

```
<logic:equal name="registrationForm" property="action"
           scope="request" value="Edit">
  <app:checkLogon/>
</logic:equal>
```

The `equal` tag verifies that the `registrationForm` object in the request scope has an action equal to `"Edit"`, and if so, uses the `app:checkLogon` tag to verify that the user is logged on. The app tag library is not part of Struts per se, but is unique to the `struts-example` application.

Figure 24-3 shows the registration update form, which includes a table of existing mail subscriptions and the option to add more.

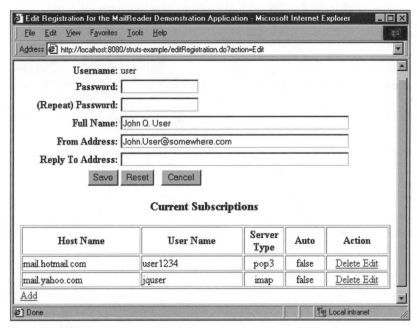

Figure 24-3: The registration update form

An `iterate` tag handles the table of existing registrations as shown in Listing 24-6.

Listing 24-6: Using the iterate Tag to Create Rows of Data

```
<logic:iterate id="subscription" name="user" property="subscriptions">
  <tr>
    <td align="left">
      <bean:write name="subscription" property="host" filter="true"/>
    </td>
    <td align="left">
```

```
        <bean:write name="subscription" property="username" filter= ⏎
"true"/>
    </td>
    <td align="center">
      <bean:write name="subscription" property="type" filter="true"/>
    </td>
    <td align="center">
      <bean:write name="subscription" property="autoConnect"/>
    </td>
    <td align="center">
      <app:linkSubscription
page="/editSubscription.do?action=Delete">
        <bean:message key="registration.deleteSubsjcription"/>
      </app:linkSubscription>
      <app:linkSubscription page="/editSubscription.do?action=Edit">
        <bean:message key="registration.editSubscription"/>
      </app:linkSubscription>
    </td>
  </tr>
</logic:iterate>
```

This `iterate` tag is similar in concept to the `iterate` tag Chapter 17 describes but is considerably more flexible. In Listing 24-6 the `iterate` tag exposes an object called `subscription`, and the `write` tag obtains data from the object and places it in the table.

The `iterate` tag is a powerful tool for displaying table data, but it still requires that you create a suitable bean from which you can extract that data. The Struts mailing list has included discussion about creating a tag that can read data directly from a result set. This would simplify data retrieval considerably.

# The Struts Tag Libraries

You can loosely divide Struts functionality into three areas, corresponding to the three parts of the MVC/Model 2 design pattern. The Controller portion includes the `Action`, `ActionServlet`, `ActionMapping` and related classes. The Model portion, most of which you write yourself, includes the `ActionForm` and related classes. The View portion of Struts includes various custom tag libraries.

The Struts tag libraries are extensive, and most are not dependent on the rest of the Struts framework; I find it hard to imagine a Web application that can't benefit from using at least some of these tags. The Struts tag libraries include the following:

◆ JavaBean tags that extend the basic bean-handling capabilities of the standard JSP bean tags

◆ Logic tags that manage the conditional generation of text into a JSP

◆ HTML tags that create HTML components like forms, form fields, and land links

◆ Template tags that build JSPs by including output from other JSPs

Each of these tag libraries has features useful to almost any Java Web developer. Happily, you can use the Struts custom tags whether or not you implement the application framework. See Appendix A for more information on Struts tags.

# Summary

The Struts package is an open source Model 2 Web application framework that provides core controlling logic and form management. Key points to remember include:

◆ Application behavior is largely determined by the settings in `struts-config.xml`, which defines actions, forms, and forwards.

◆ URLs with a specific extension (or path) are mapped to actions.

◆ Actions can have an associated form.

◆ If an action has a form, the controller servlet validates the form before it validates the action.

◆ After the controller servlet validates an action, it passes the action to a named forward, which is usually a JSP.

◆ The view component (usually a JSP, reached via a forward) displays data back to the user.

# Appendix A

# The Struts Tag Libraries

THIS APPENDIX LISTS the Struts tags along with notes about their implementation and common usage. For a complete explanation of each tag's syntax, please refer to the Struts documentation.

## Using Beans in Struts

The JSP specification provides three standard ways to interact with beans: the `jsp:useBean` tag locates or creates a bean; the `jsp:setProperty` tag sets a bean property; and the `jsp:getProperty` tag retrieves a bean's property. You will still often use these tags in Struts applications, but there are some important differences in how the standard tags behave and how most Struts tags behave.

- Bean scope – in a Model 2 application, the controller servlet passes beans to the view JSP by storing the beans in one of three scopes: request, session, and application.

- Request Scope – to store a bean in a request, the controller servlet calls the request object's `setAttribute()` method:
  `request.setAttribute("objectname",object);` Once the servlet has placed the object in the request, any other code that has access to the request can obtain the object with `request.getAttribute`.

- Session Scope – the controller servlet can call `request.getSession` to obtain the session object associated with the user, and then store the object in the session: `session.setAttribute("objectname",object);`. Any code that has access to the session can call `session.getAttribute` to retrieve the object.

- Application Scope – the servlet can store an object in application scope with this code: `getServletContext().setAttribute("objectname",object);`. You won't normally place objects in the application scope except when initializing a servlet, since such objects are globally visible.

- Page Scope – One additional scope that the controller servlet doesn't have access to is page scope. Objects with page scope are visible only to the current JSP; therefore, the JSP must create any beans with page scope.

# Common Struts tag attributes

By convention, most Struts tags have the following attributes:

- ◆ id – the name of the object the tag will create. A tag often declares an object, whether that object is a simple string or something more complex. When a tag has an id attribute, the value of that attribute is the name given the object in the JSP. This is also the name by which the tag stores the object in a page, request, session, or application context.

- ◆ name – the value the tag uses to look up an existing object; this is not the same as id, which is the value of a newly created object.

- ◆ property – a property of a JavaBean identified by the name attribute; the servlet container will translate the property into an accessor method using the JavaBeans naming conventions.

- ◆ scope – the scope in which the tag should look for, and create if necessary, the required objects; if not specified, the tag will normally search all contexts in this order: page, request, session, and application.

# Setting Struts properties

Struts tags let you use an expanded syntax for setting bean properties. With the standard jsp:setProperty and jsp:getProperty tags you indicate the name of the property on the bean, and the JSP engine calls a corresponding accessor method. If the property is color, the setter method is, by convention, setColor() and the getter method getColor(). In Struts, you can use this same syntax. You can also specify nested and indexed properties.

## NESTED PROPERTIES
If you have objects that contain references to other objects, you can set these in Struts using nested properties. Suppose you're currently working with a Purchase object that has a User object reference. If you want to set the user's credit status, you could do it this way:

```
property= "user.creditStatus" value="OK"
```

If you're setting the value, the Struts tag translates the property into getUser().setCreditStatus("OK"). You can have more than one level of nesting. Similarly, on a getter the Struts tag will translate the property to getUser().getCreditStatus(). Note that only the last method in the hierarchy is either a setter or getter – all the rest are always getter methods. You can use multiple levels of nesting.

### INDEXED PROPERTIES

Along with nested properties, you can also employ indexed properties. Struts translates a property of `color[3]` into `getColor(3)` or, for a setter, `setColor(3,value)`. You can combine indexed and nested properties freely in the same property attribute.

# The Bean Tags

The Struts bean tags are primarily concerned with creating or locating beans, and with setting and getting bean properties. The driving concept is that in a Model 2 application the controller initiates changes to the application's model, which resides in JavaBeans or EJBs, and then passes control to the view JSP, which retrieves the necessary data from the application's model (JavaBeans or EJBs).

## The cookie tag

The `cookie` tag looks for a specified cookie, and if successful, it stores that cookie as the named object:

```
<bean:cookie id="sess" name="JSESSIONID"/>
```

The cookie tag can also look for multiple cookies:

```
<bean:cookie id="sess" name="JSESSIONID" multiple="true"/>
```

If `multiple` is set to any value at all, the tag stores a `Cookie[]` array rather than just a `Cookie`.

## The define tag

The `define` tag examines a bean for a property and then stores this property in the page context. The tag converts simple data types to their class equivalents. The `define` tag can retrieve any data type, including arrays. In the `struts-test` application, the `define` tag retrieves various data types from a `TestBean` class:

```
<jsp:useBean id="test1" scope="page" class="org.apache.struts.test.TestBean"/>
<bean:define id="test1_boolean" name="test1" property="booleanProperty"/>
<bean:define id="test1_double" name="test1" property="doubleProperty"/>
<bean:define id="test1_float" name="test1" property="floatProperty"/>
<bean:define id="test1_value" value="ABCDE"/>
```

The `TestBean` class has the usual getter methods, such as `getBooleanProperty` and `getDoubleProperty`. The `define` tag can also convert a `String` literal to a page scope attribute, as the last line of the example shows.

## The header tag

The `header` tag retrieves the specified attribute from the request header. To display the name of the user's machine, you can use the following code:

```
<bean:header id="header" name="Host"/>
<p>Host: <%=header%></p>
```

If you use the `multiple="somevalue"` attribute, the `header` tag retrieves a `String[]` of the header attributes.

## The include tag

The `include` tag works a bit like `jsp:include`, except that it takes the output from whatever resource you wish to include and stores that output in page context as a string object:

```
<bean:include id="index" name="/index.jsp"/>
```

You can then decide what you want to do with the string object, whether to place its content in the page one or more times, or perform some other operation.

The `include` tag uses a `URLConnection` object to establish a connection with the resource (appending the session ID to the URL), and then retrieves the resource's output in an `InputStream`. The tag returns the saved data to the page as a string.

## The message tag

The `message` tag looks up a specified key in a properties file and outputs that message to the JSP. To use the message tag, you have to create a properties file with your messages in it. The `message` tag looks in the application context for a `MessageResources` object with the name defined in the `Action.MESSAGES_KEY` static `String`:

```
public static final String MESSAGES_KEY =
    "org.apache.struts.action.MESSAGE";
```

In the `struts-example` Web application you can find the Struts messages in the `WEB-INF/classes/org/apache/struts/example/ApplicationResources.properties` file. You can override the name of the `MessageResources` object with a parameter to the `message` tag. However, in most cases, if you want to change the message resource, you do so in the `ActionServlet` configuration in `web.xml`, by way of the application parameter:

```
<init-param>
    <param-name>application</param-name>
```

```
     <param-value>org.apache.struts.example.ApplicationResources ↵
</param-value>
</init-param>
```

The application properties file contains key/value pairs:

```
button.cancel=Cancel
button.confirm=Confirm
button.reset=Reset
button.save=Save
```

When using the tag, you specify the key to display a particular message:

```
<bean:message key="logon.title"/>
```

The message tag fully supports the Java platform's internationalization features, and automatically displays messages for different locales, provided the application has detected the locale and you have provided a suitable variant of the properties file.

## The page tag

The page tag retrieves one of the following objects, as specified in the property attribute:

- application — the ServletContext object
- config — the ServletConfig object
- request — the current request
- response — the current response
- session — the current session To place the request into the page context under the name "req", use the following code:

  ```
  <bean:page id="req" property="request"/>
  ```

## The parameter tag

The parameter tag extracts the named parameter from the request and makes it available to the page as a String or an array of String:

```
<bean:parameter id="param1" name="param1"/>
```

## The resource tag

The resource tag makes a resource, such as a file, available to the JSP either as a string or as an InputStream. Unlike the include tag, the resource tag retrieves data from a local resource (that is, a disk file). The following code retrieves the contents of the application's `web.xml` file as a String:

```
<bean:resource id="webxml" name="/WEB-INF/web.xml"/>
```

## The struts tag

The `struts` tag retrieves a Struts object, which can be a form bean, a forward, or a mapping. The code

```
<bean:struts id="tb" formBean="testbean"/>
```

retrieves the `formBean`, which `struts-config.xml` identifies by the name `testbean`.

## The write tag

The `write` tag writes a bean's text to the JSP. If the bean implements the `PropertyEditor` interface, the `write` tag calls the `getAsText` method; if not, the `write` tag calls the `toString` method.

You can use two optional tags with `write`. If `filter` is set to true, the tag filters the bean's output for HTML characters including <>& and " and replaces them with their HTML equivalents. To do this, `write` uses the `BeanUtils.filter` method.

If the `ignore` attribute is set to true, the `write` tag ignores any problems and returns an empty string.

# The HTML Tags

The HTML tags deal mainly with creating HTML forms. You can also use them to create links, images, and a few other elements.

## The base tag

The `base` tag creates an HTML `<base>` element. In the `struts-example` application, the `<html:base/>` tag in `logon.jsp` creates this base element:

```
<base href="http://localhost:8080/struts-example/index.jsp">
```

It's common to use relative references to other pages or images in an HTML document, and the `base` reference tells the server to what document those references are relative.

# The errors tag

The errors tag displays a list of errors from an ActionErrors object, a String, or a String array stored in the request. The ActionForm typically adds these errors during form validation. The errors tag also assumes that you've created two entries for your MessageResources bean with the following keys:

◆ errors.header — the text to display before the errors list

◆ errors.footer — the text to display after the errors list

The struts-example application defines these keys this way (in WEB-INF/classes/org/apache/struts/example/ApplicationResources.properties):

```
errors.header=<h3><font color="red">Validation Error</font>
</h3>You must correct the following error(s) before proceeding:<ul>
errors.footer=</ul><hr>
```

# The form tag

The form tag creates an HTML form on the JSP. Listing A-1 shows the form from logon.jsp in the struts-example application.

**Listing A-1: The form Tag as Used in logon.jsp**

```
<html:form action="logon.do" focus="username">
<table border="0" width="100%">
  <tr>
    <th align="right">
      <bean:message key="prompt.username"/>
    </th>
    <td align="left">
      <html:text property="username" size="16" maxlength="16"/>
    </td>
  </tr>
  <tr>
    <th align="right">
      <bean:message key="prompt.password"/>
    </th>
    <td align="left">
      <html:password property="password" size="16" maxlength="16"/>
    </td>
  </tr>
  <tr>
```

*Continued*

**Listing A-1** *(Continued)*

```
    <td align="right">
      <html:submit property="submit" value="Submit"/>
    </td>
    <td align="left">
      <html:reset/>
    </td>
  </tr>
</table>
</html:form>
```

As Listing A-1 shows, you define the form's action and the field that is to receive the initial focus in the form tag, which has a body. You then create the form fields inside the form tag body in the JSP. The form tag collects all of the form fields and associates them with the ActionForm bean associated with this form. You can set numerous attributes for the form. For example, you can set the style sheet and class. You can even add various JavaScript event handlers.

## The form field tags

The Struts form field tags support the following HTML field types: checkboxes, hidden fields, password input fields, radio buttons, reset buttons, select lists with embedded options, submit buttons, text fields, and multiline text area fields. These correspond to the basic HTML elements you use to create a form (button, cancel, checkbox, file, hidden, option, options, password, radio, reset, select, submit, text, and textarea).

## The html tag

The html tag creates an <html> element in the JSP, with an optional locale or xhtml attribute. The following tag:

```
<html:html locale="true">
```

generates this HTML:

```
<html lang="en">
```

## The link tag

The link tag creates an HTML link. This tag has a body, which means you need to specify the text of the link by entering the text directly, or preferably by obtaining the text from the message:bean tag:

```
<html:link page="/editRegistration.do?action=Create">
<bean:message key="index.registration"/>
</html:link>
```

# The Logic Tags

The Struts logic tags allow you to code value comparisons, perform substring matching, and iterate through a collection. In essence, these turn custom tags into a minimal, but highly customizable, scripting language.

## Comparison tags

Struts has a number of tags that test for equality between objects. For instance, the equal tag compares a variable obtained from the named object and property with the value attribute. If the two values are equal, the tag evaluates its body. This check from the struts-example registration.jsp determines if the registrationForm object's action value is "Edit" and if so, checks for a user logon:

```
<logic:equal name="registrationForm" property="action"
             scope="request" value="Edit">
  <app:checkLogon/>
</logic:equal>
```

Struts comparison tags include equal, greaterEqual, greaterThan, lessEqual, lessThan, and notEqual.

## The forward tag

Not a logic test per se, the forward tag redirects a request to the specified destination, using either pageContext.forward or HttpServletResponse.sendRedirect. If you've defined an ActionForward for the name attribute, the forward tag calls pageContextForward; if the tag doesn't find an ActionForward by that name, then it assumes you mean a real URL and calls sendRedirect, which adds session data to the URL (if you've enabled URL rewriting).

```
<logic:forward name= "newLocation"/>
```

## The iterate tag

The iterate tag repeats the contents of its body for as many elements as exist in the specified collection, subject to the optional length and offset attributes. This tag does not work with primitive data types – it only supports objects and it requires Java2.

For instance, `iterate.jsp` in the `struts-text` Web application creates an instance of `TestBean` using `jsp:useBean`:

```
<jsp:useBean id="bean" scope="page" class="org.apache.struts.test. ↵
TestBean"/>
```

The `iterate` tag receives bean as its name attribute and `stringArray` as its property attribute. The `iterate` tag then calls the `getStringArray()` method on the bean object, which returns an arrayed `String`. All `iterate` tag has to do then is expose each `String` in the array as an object named `element`:

```
<logic:iterate id="element" name="bean" property="stringArray">
  <li><em><bean:write name="element"/></em></li>
</logic:iterate>
```

The `iterate` tag is one of the most powerful and useful tags in Struts; `iterate` can work with object arrays as well as `Collection`, `Iterator`, and `Map` objects.

## The match tag

The `match` tag matches a substring with the requested variable and evaluates the tag body if the `value` it finds is the substring within the requested variable. This tag has several attributes that allow you to search for matches in cookies, headers, and request parameters conveniently.

```
<logic:match cookie="JSESSIONID" value="0">
      match
    </logic:match>
```

## The notMatch tag

The `notMatch` tag is similar to the `match` tag except that it evaluates its body if the specified `value` cannot be found in the requested variable.

```
<logic:notMatch cookie="JSESSIONID" value="0">
      notMatch
    </logic:notMatch>
```

## The notPresent tag

The `notPresent` tag evaluates its body if it is unable to find the specified `value` in the current request. Tag attributes let you conveniently check for values in cookies, headers, request parameters, user roles, and user principles.

```
<logic:notPresent name="bean">
      notPresent
    </logic:notPresent>
```

## The present tag

The present tag evaluates its body if it finds the specified value in the current request. Tag attributes let you conveniently check for values in cookies, headers, request parameters, user roles, and user principles.

```
<logic:present name="bean">
      present
    </logic:present>
```

## The redirect tag

The redirect tag does a HttpServlet.sendRedirect to the specified URL. If the application is using URL rewriting, the redirect tag adds the session data to the URL. Redirects happen without user intervention, provided the browser supports this feature.

```
<logic:redirect href="http://jakarta.apache.org/struts"/>
```

# The Template Tags

Most Java-based Web applications have more than one JSP, but it's also common for pages on a Web site to share a common look and feel. At some point, you'll probably be faced with duplicating some of these pages, which makes maintenance more difficult and consistency less likely.

In a traditional HTML Web site you'd probably address the problem with server-side includes. Web pages on any given site usually have a consistent structure, perhaps a common header and footer, and a common left-side menu. You may have other elements that repeat on some but not all pages.

You can do something similar in JSPs using the jsp:include tag and the include directive. In each actual JSP you have an overall page framework (typically created using HTML tables) with strategically placed includes.

The problem with this approach is that if you decide to make a design change to your site that affects the page framework, you have to go to all of your JSPs and apply the changes. It's better to create (preferably) just one template that breaks the page up into regions, again, most likely using HTML tables. You can design this page visually, and then in each region of the page where you want a particular component to appear you place a tag saying which component you want.

Listing A-2 shows a simple template page with four template components, placed in the top, left, bottom, and center cells of the page's HTML table. Each get tag marks a placeholder for a subsequent put tag.

**Listing A-2: Creating a Template Page**

```
<%@ taglib uri='/WEB-INF/struts-template.tld' prefix='template' %>
<html>
```

*Continued*

Listing A-2 *(Continued)*

```
<head>
</head>
<body bgcolor="white">

<table border="0" cellpadding="8" cellspacing="0" width="500">
  <tr>
    <td width="464" colspan="2"><template:get name="header"/></td>
  </tr>
  <tr>
    <td width="120"><template:get name="leftsidemenu"/></td>
    <td width="344"><template:get name="content"/></td>
  </tr>
  <tr>
    <td width="464" colspan="2"><template:get name="footer"/></td>
  </tr>
</table>
</body>
</html>
```

The next step is to create a JSP that makes use of this template, and to do that you use the `insert` and `put` template tags. The JSP you create to use the template can be very simple and maintainable. The following example uses the `insert` tag to read in the template page from Listing A-2, and then stocks that page with named pages, using the `put` tag:

```
<%@ taglib uri='/WEB-INF/struts-template.tld' prefix='template' %>
<template:insert template="/template.jsp">
    <template:put name="header" content="/header.jsp"/>
    <template:put name="footer" content="/footer.jsp"/>
    <template:put name="content" content="/content.jsp"/>
    <template:put name="menu" content="/menu.jsp"/>
</template:insert>
```

You can, of course, use all of the other Struts tags along with the template tags, which makes it relatively easy to conditionally include different templates depending on the nature of the request, the user's access rights, and so forth. You can also include text directly in a template by using the direct attribute:

```
<template:put name="content" content="Some text..." direct="true"/>
```

The template system is a bit deceptive in its simplicity; templates are a powerful addition to any Web developer's toolset.

# Appendix B

# Java Web-Development Resources

YOU CAN FIND the source code for the book's examples, as well as corrections and errata, at `http://www.covecomm.com/java`. You can also contact the author through this page. The balance of this appendix lists recommend Java Web-developer resources.

## Servlet and JSP Specifications

Your starting point for server-side Java Web development should be Sun Microsystems, specifically the Servlet and JSP specifications. Both specifications are in constant revision, and are the guiding documents for the Tomcat server, which is the reference implementation for the official specifications.

◆ The Servlet specification

`http://java.sun.com/products/servlet/download.html`

◆ The JavaServer Pages specification

`http://java.sun.com/products/jsp/download.html`

## Java Development Kits

While you're at the Sun Java site, you may also want to download the latest JDK.

◆ The JDK 1.2 Standard Edition

`http://java.sun.com/products/jdk/1.2/index.html`

◆ The JDK 1.3 Standard Edition

`http://java.sun.com/j2se/1.3/`

◆ The Java2 Platform, Enterprise Edition

`http://java.sun.com/j2ee/index.html`

♦ If you can't find the JDK edition you're looking for, visit the Java products page at:

`http://java.sun.com/products/`

This page has a drop list of all of the Java products available from Sun Microsystems.

♦ For JDK ports to platforms other than those supported by Sun Microsystems, see:

`http://java.sun.com/cgi-bin/java-ports.cgi`

# Other Sun Resources

You will probably want to look at Sun Microsystems' Java2 Enterprise Edition Blueprints. These documents and examples describe approaches to developing a variety of J2EE applications, including those with Web front ends.

`http://java.sun.com/j2ee/blueprints/`

# The Jakarta Home Page

The Jakarta home page at `http://jakarta.apache.org/` is home to a number of web-related Java projects, including Tomcat.

# Getting Tomcat

To download the latest release of Tomcat, go to: `http://jakarta.apache.org/tomcat/index.html`

Also available at the Tomcat page is Tomcat documentation on the following subjects:

♦ Installing and using Tomcat

`http://jakarta.apache.org/tomcat/jakarta-tomcat/src/doc/uguide/tomcat_ug.html`

♦ Database authentication using JDBC

`http://jakarta.apache.org/tomcat/jakarta-tomcat/src/doc/JDBCRealm.howto`

◆ Using a security manager to protect a running Tomcat server from mis-behaving JavaBeans, servlets, JSPs, and tag libraries

http://jakarta.apache.org/tomcat/jakarta-tomcat/src/doc/
uguide/tomcat-security.html

◆ Configuring one or more instances of Tomcat to serve requests for a Web server, using the workers.properties file

http://jakarta.apache.org/tomcat/jakarta-tomcat/src/doc/
Tomcat-Workers-HowTo.html

◆ Using Tomcat with SSL, either standalone or with Apache

http://jakarta.apache.org/tomcat/jakarta-tomcat/src/doc/
tomcat-ssl-howto.html

◆ Running Tomcat as a service under Windows NT

http://jakarta.apache.org/tomcat/jakarta-tomcat/src/doc/
NT-Service-howto.html

◆ Running Tomcat as an in-process servlet container with Netscape or IIS

http://jakarta.apache.org/tomcat/jakarta-tomcat/src/doc/
in-process-howto.html

◆ Running Tomcat as a servlet container behind Apache

http://jakarta.apache.org/tomcat/jakarta-tomcat/src/doc/
tomcat-apache-howto.html

◆ Running Tomcat as a servlet container behind IIS

http://jakarta.apache.org/tomcat/jakarta-tomcat/src/doc/
tomcat-iis-howto.html

◆ Running Tomcat as a servlet container behind Netscape Web servers

http://jakarta.apache.org/tomcat/jakarta-tomcat/src/doc/
tomcat-netscape-howto.html

◆ An overview of Tomcat Web-application development

http://jakarta.apache.org/tomcat/jakarta-tomcat/src/doc/
appdev/index.html

# Mailing Lists

The Jakarta project maintains mailing lists for most of its subprojects, including Tomcat and Struts. For most of the subprojects there are developer and user mailing lists; the developer lists are for those participating in the product's development. I highly recommend you subscribe to the Tomcat user list if you use Tomcat at all, or if you use another server based on Tomcat. If you have an interest in MVC/Model 2 development, you should also subscribe to the Struts user list.

```
http://jakarta.apache.org/site/mail.html
```

# MySQL-Related Resources

◆ To download the MySQL database, or to find further information on MySQL, visit:

```
http://www.mysql.com/
```

◆ I recommend the mm.MySQL driver if you're going to use MySQL. You can find this driver at:

```
http://mmmysql.sourceforge.net/
```

◆ For performance benchmarks on various Java Virtual Machines, read the Volano (not "Volcano") Report:

```
http://www.volano.com/benchmarks.html
```

◆ You can find a FAQ, MySQL development news, and other information at:

```
http://www.mysqldeveloper.com/
```

# Index

## Symbols & Numerics

! (exclamation mark)
   servlet variable declaration operator, 89
   SQL comparison operator, 209

!= (exclamation mark, equal sign) SQL
   comparison operator, 209

% (percent sign) MySQL wildcard
   character, 161

%> (percent sign, arrow)
   directive delimiter, 81
   scriptlet delimiter, 84

&& (ampersands) SQL comparison
   operator, 209

* (asterisk) JavaServer Page (JSP) wildcard
   operator, 96

*/ (asterisk, slash) Java comment
   delimiter, 45

--> (dash, dash, arrow) XML comment
   delimiter, 45

/* (slash, asterisk) Java comment
   delimiter, 45

; (semicolon) SQL statement suffix,
   152, 153

< (arrow) SQL comparison operator, 209

<!-- (arrow, exclamation mark, dash, dash)
   XML comment delimiter, 45

<% (arrow, percent sign) scriptlet
   delimiter, 84

<%@ (arrow, percent sign, at sign)
   directive delimiter, 81

<= (arrow, equal sign) SQL comparison
   operator, 209

<=> (arrow, equal sign, arrow) SQL
   comparison operator, 209

<> (arrows) SQL comparison operator, 209

<P> </P>JavaServer Page (JSP) paragraph
   delimiters, 78

= (equal sign) SQL comparison
   operator, 209

> (arrow) SQL comparison operator, 209

>= (arrow, equal sign) SQL comparison
   operator, 209

? (question mark) form data delimiter, 65

_ (underscore) MySQL wildcard character,
   161, 210

|| (pipes) SQL comparison operator, 209

3NF. *See* third normal form (3NF)

## A

access control. *See also* authentication;
   permissions; security
   databases, 155–156, 162, 222–223
   design, 188–190
   host domain, restricting, 161
   MySQL, 140, 155–163
   page deletion/update, 68
   speed, effect on, 191
   user interface design, 188
   user rights records, 190–191, 194

AccessInterceptor class, 322

ActionErrors objects, 467

Active Scripting Organization, 23

active server pages (ASPs), 23

ActiveX, 4

adapter design pattern, 235

add() method, 391

addField() methods, 347–348, 366

addRadioButton() method, 394

ALL PRIVILEGES privilege, 162

ALTER COLUMN statements, 177

ALTER privilege, 162, 163

ALTER TABLE DROP statements, 178

ALTER TABLE statements, 176, 177

Alter_priv field, 156

American National Standards Institute
   (ANSI), 122

AND SQL comparison operator, 209

Animals class, 284–285, 287–289

**477**

*continued*

*continued*

# Professional Mindware™

## Master today's cutting-edge technologies with M&T Books™

As an IT professional, you know you can count on M&T Books for authoritative coverage of today's hottest topics. From ASP+ to XML, just turn to M&T Books for the answers you need.

Written by top IT professionals, M&T Books delivers the tools you need to get the job done, whether you're a programmer, a Web developer, or a network administrator.

---

Open Source: The Unauthorized White Papers
408 pp • 0-7645-4660-0 • $19.99 U.S. • $29.99 Can.

XHTML™: Moving Toward XML
456 pp • 0-7645-4709-7 • $29.99 U.S. • 44.99 Can.

Cisco® IP Routing Handbook
552 pp • 0-7645-4695-3 • 29.99 U.S. • $44.99 Can.

Cross-Platform Perl, 2nd Edition
648 pp • 0-7645-4729-1 • 39.99 U.S. • $59.99 Can.

Linux® Rapid Application Development
648 pp • 0-7645-4740-2 • $39.99 U.S. • $59.99 Can.

XHTML In Plain English
750 pp • 0-7645-4743-7 • $19.99 U.S. • $29.99 Can.

XML In Plain English, 2nd Edition
750 pp • 0-7645-4744-5 • $19.99 U.S. • $29.99 Can.

The SuSE™ Linux® Server
600 pp • 0-7645-4765-8 • $39.99 U.S. • $59.99 Can.

Red Hat® Linux® Server, 2nd Edition
816 pp • 0-7645-4786-0 • $39.99 U.S. • $59.99 Can.

Java™ In Plain English, 3rd Edition
750 pp • 0-7645-3539-0 • $19.99 U.S. • $29.99 Can.

The Samba Book (Available Spring '01)
550 pp • 0-7645-4773-9 • $39.99 U.S. • $59.99 Can.

Managing Linux® Clusters (Available Spring '01)
xx pp • 0-7645-4763-1 • $24.99 U.S. • $37.99 Can

MySQL™/PHP Database Applications
(Available Spring '01)
504 pp • 0-7645-3537-4 • $39.99 U.S. • $59.99 Can.

---

## Available wherever the very best technology books are sold.
## For more information, visit us at www.mandtbooks.com